🐍 Narration, Identity, and Historical Consciousness 🐍

MAKING SENSE OF HISTORY
Studies in Historical Cultures
General Editors: Jörn Rüsen, Alon Confino, Alan D. Megill

Volume 1
Western Historical Thinking: An Intercultural Debate
   Edited by Jörn Rüsen

Volume 2
Identities: Time, Difference, and Boundaries
   Edited by Heidrun Friese

Volume 3
Narration, Identity, and Historical Consciousness
   Edited by Jürgen Straub

Volume 4
Thinking Utopia: Steps into Other Worlds
   Edited by Jörn Rüsen, Michael Fehr, and Thomas W. Rieger

Volume 5
History: Narration–Interpretation–Orientation
   Jörn Rüsen

NARRATION, IDENTITY, AND HISTORICAL CONSCIOUSNESS

Edited by
Jürgen Straub

Berghahn Books
New York • Oxford

Published in 2005 by
Berghahn Books
www.berghahnbooks.com

Copyright © 2005 Jürgen Straub
First paperback edition published in 2006

All rights reserved. Except for the quotation of short passages for the purpose of criticism and review, no part of this book may be reproduced in any form or by any means, electronic or mechanical, including photocopying, recording, or any information storage and retrieval system now known or to be invented, without written permission of the publisher.

Library of Congress Cataloguing-in-Publication Data

Narration, identity, and historical consciousness / edited by Jürgen Straub.
   p. cm. — (Making sense of history)
Includes bibliographical references and index.
ISBN 1-57181-777-8
   1. History—Philosophy. 2. Consciousness. 3. Historiography. I. Straub, Jürgen, 1958– II. Series.

D16.9.N36 2005
907'.2—dc22

2005047349

British Library Cataloguing in Publication Data

A catalogue record for this book is available from the British Library.

Printed in the United States on acid-free paper.

ISBN 1-57181-777-8 hardback
ISBN 1-84545-039-6 paperback

Contents

Preface to the Series   vii

Foreword   xiii

Part I: Theoretical Positions and Reflections

Chapter 1: Narrative Psychology and Historical Consciousness: Relationships and Perspectives   3
Donald E. Polkinghorne

Chapter 2: Past and Present as Narrative Constructions   23
Jerome S. Bruner

Chapter 3: Telling Stories, Making History: Toward a Narrative Psychology of the Historical Construction of Meaning   44
Jürgen Straub

Chapter 4: Narrative, Moral Identity, and Historical Consciousness: A Social Constructionist Account   99
Kenneth J. Gergen

Chapter 5: Narrative Truth and Identity Formation: Abduction and Abuse Stories as Metaphors   120
Donald P. Spence

Part II: On the Development of Narrative Competence and Historical Consciousness

Chapter 6: The Concept of Time and the Faculty of Judgment in the Ontogenesis of Historical Consciousness   135
Micha Brumlik

Chapter 7: Historical Consciousness: The Progress of Knowledge
    in a Postprogressive Age   141
    Peter Seixas

Part III: Empirical Research / Case Studies

Chapter 8: Empirical Psychological Approaches
    to the Historical Consciousness of Children   163
    Elfriede Billmann-Mahecha and Monika Hausen

Chapter 9: The Psychological Study of Historical Consciousness   187
    Samuel S. Wineburg

Chapter 10: Biography—A Dream? Self-Chronicling
    in the Age Psychoanalysis   211
    Brigitte Boothe

Chapter 11: Authenticity and Authority:
    On Understanding the Shoah   228
    Alexandre Métraux

Chapter 12: Albert Speer's Memories of the Future: On the Historical
    Consciousness of a Leading Figure in the Third Reich   245
    Harald Welzer

Bibliography   257

Notes on Contributors   273

Index of Names   277

Preface to the Series

At the turn of the twenty-first century, the very term "history" brings extremely ambivalent associations to mind. On the one hand, the last ten to fifteen years have witnessed numerous declarations of history's end. In referring to the fundamental change of the global political situation around 1989/1990, or to postmodernism, or to the challenge of Western dominance by decolonization and multiculturalism, "history," as we know it in Western tradition, has been declared to be dead, outdated, overcome, and at its end. On the other hand, there has been a global wave of intellectual explorations into fields that are "historical" in their very nature: the building of personal and collective identity through "memory"; the cultural, social, and political use and function of "narrating the past"; and the psychological structures of remembering, repressing, and recalling. Even the subjects that seemed to call for an "end to history" (globalization, postmodernism, multiculturalism) quickly turned out to be intrinsically "historical" phenomena. Moreover, "history" and "historical memory" have also entered the sphere of popular culture (from history channels on television to Hollywood movies). They have also become an ever-important ingredient of public debates and political negotiations (e.g., in discussions about the aftermath of the wars in former Yugoslavia, as well as in discussions about European unification or the various heritages of totalitarian systems). In other words, ever since "history" has been declared to be at its end, "historical matters" seem to have come back with a vengeance.

This paradox calls for a new orientation, or at least a new theoretical reflection. Indeed, it calls for a new theory of history. Such a theory should serve neither as a subdiscipline reserved for historians, nor as a systematic collection of definitions, "laws," and rules claiming universal validity. What is needed is an interdisciplinary and intercultural field of study. For in the very moment when history was declared to be "over," what, in fact, did abruptly come to an end was historical theory. Hayden White's deconstruction of the narrative strategies of the nineteenth-century historicist paradigm somehow became regarded as historical theory's final word—as if the critique of the discipline's claim for rationality could set an end to the rational self-reflection of that discipline; as if this very critique were not a rational self-reflection in itself. Nevertheless, since the late 1980s, the "critical study of historical memory" began to multiply within historical theory. What has been overlooked in this substitution, however, is the fact that any exploration into the ways of historical memory in different cultural contexts is not only a field of critical studies, but also contains the keystones of a more general theory of history. Any analysis of even a simple instance of historical memory touches on questions of the theory and philosophy of history. And vice versa: the most abstract thoughts of philosophers of history have an intrinsic counterpart in the most profane procedures of memory (for example, when parents narrate past experiences to their children, or when an African community remembers its own colonial subordination and its liberation from it). As long as we fail to acknowledge this intrinsic connection between the most sophisticated historical theory and the procedures of historical memory most deeply imbedded in the culture and the everyday lives of people, we will remain caught in an ideology of linear progress, which considers cultural forms of memory simply as interesting objects of study rather than recognizing them as examples of "how to make sense of history."

The book series Making Sense of History aims at bridging this gap between historical theory and the study of historical memory. It contains contributions from virtually all fields of cultural and social studies, which explore a wide range of phenomena falling within the domain of what can be labeled "making historical sense" *(Historische Sinnbildung)*. Not only does the series cross the boundaries between academic disciplines, but also those between cultural, social, political, and historical contexts. Rather than reducing historical memory to just another form of the social or cultural "construction of reality," its contributions deal with concrete phenomena of historical memory: it seeks to interpret them as case studies in the emerging empirical and theoretical field of "making historical sense." Along the same lines, the rather theoretical essays intend not only to establish new methods and theories for historical research, but also to provide perspectives for a comparative, interdisciplinary, and intercultural understanding of what could be called the "global work of historical memory." This does not entail the exclusion of critical evaluations of the ideological functions of historical memory, but it is not the major aim of the series to find an ideal, politically correct, and ideology-free mode or method of how to "make sense of history." Rather, it intends to explore the cultural practices involved in generating historical sense as an extremely important realm of human thought and action, the study of which may contribute to new forms of mutual understanding. In an age of rapid globalization, which primarily manifests itself on an economic and political level (and much less so on a cultural level), finding such forms is an urgent task.

Historians, anthropologists, philosophers, sociologists, psychologists, literary theorists, as well as specialists in fields such as media and cultural studies, explore questions such as the following: What constitutes a specifically historical "sense" and meaning? What are the concepts of "time" underlying different historical cultures? Which specific forms of "perception" inform these concepts and which general problems are connected with them? What are the dominating strategies used to represent historical meaning? Ranging from general overviews and theoretical reflections to case studies, the essays will cover a wide range of contexts related to the question of "historical sense," including topics such as collective identity, the psychology and psychoanalysis of historical memory, or the intercultural dimension of historical thinking. In general, they will indicate that historical memory is not an arbitrary function of the cultural practices used by human beings to orient themselves in the world in which they are born, but that such memory covers special domains in the temporal orientation of human life. These domains demand precisely those mental procedures of connecting past, present, and future that became generalized and institutionalized in the West as that specific field of culture we call "history." Among those special areas of human thought, action, and suffering that call for a specifically "historical thinking" are (1) the construction and perpetuation of collective identity, (2) the reconstruction of patterns of orientation after catastrophes and events of massive destruction, (3) the challenge of given patterns of orientation presented by and through the confrontation with radical otherness, and (4) the general experience of change and contingency.

In accordance with the general aim of the book series Making Sense of History to outline a new field of interdisciplinary research (rather than offering a single theory), the volumes are not designed to establish those general domains and functions of historical remembrance as keystones for a new historiographical approach; instead, they explore them further as subfields of the study of "historical cultures." One focus, for instance, is on the notion of collective identity. General theoretical aspects and problems of this field are considered, with special emphasis on the interrelationship between identity, otherness, and representation. At the same time, case studies on the construction of gender identities (especially of women), on ethnic identities, and on different forms and politics of national identity are also be included. The essays on this subject will aim to point out that any concept of "identity" as being disconnected from historical change not only leads to theoretical problems, but also eclipses the fact that most modern forms of collective identity take into account the possibility of their own historical transformation. Thus, the essays will suggest considering identity not as a function of difference, but rather as the concrete cultural and ongoing "practice" of difference. They will therefore aim to prove the production of "sense" to be an epistemological starting point as well as a theoretical and empirical research field in and of itself.

Other volumes will focus on the psychological construction of "time" and "history," analyzing the interrelation between memory, morality, and authenticity in different forms of historical or biographical narrations. The findings of empirical psychological studies (on the development of temporal and historical consciousness in children, or on the psychological mechanisms of reconstructing past experiences) will be discussed in the light of attempts to outline a psychological concept of historical consciousness around the notions of "narration" and the "narrative structure of historical time." A special volume is dedicated to specifically psychoanalytical approaches to the study of historical memory, reconsidering older debates on the relation between psychoanalysis and history, as well as introducing more recent research projects. Instead of simply pointing out some psychoanalytical insights that can be adopted and applied in certain areas of historical studies, this volume will strive to combine psychoanalytical and historical perspectives, thus exploring the history of psychoanalysis itself, as well as the "unconscious" dimensions underlying and informing academic and nonacademic forms of historical memory. Moreover, it will put special emphasis on transgenerational forms of remembrance, on the notion of trauma as a key concept in this field, and on case studies that may indicate directions for further research.

There will be a collection of essays dealing explicitly with the intercultural dimension of historical thinking, offering an overview of historical cultures ranging from ancient Egypt to modern Japan. With a view to encouraging comparative research, it will consist of general essays and case studies written with the intention of providing comparative interpretations of concrete material, as well as possible paradigmatic research questions for further comparisons. In light of the ongoing success of ethnocentric worldviews, the volume will focus on the question of how cultural and social studies could react to this challenge. It will aim at counteracting ethnocentrism by bridging the current gap between a rapid globalization, manifesting itself in ever-increasing economic and political interdependencies of states and continents, and the almost similarly increasing lack of mutual understanding in the realm of culture. The essays will strive to point out the necessity of intercultural communication about the common ground of various historical cultures, as well as about the differences between them. Such communication seems not only possible; it seems to be a necessary presupposition for any attempt to negotiate cultural differences on a political level, whether between states or within the increasingly multicultural societies in which we live.

The special emphasis the series puts on the problem of cultural differences and intercultural communication reveals the editors' intentions to aim beyond the realm of academic interest. For the question of intercultural communication represents a great challenge, as well as a great hope, of a project committed to the general theoretical reflection on the universal phenomenon of "remembering the past." Despite the fact that "cultural difference" became something of a master phrase during the 1990s, this topic is characterized by a paradox quite similar to that underlying the current fate of the notion of "history."

The industrialized states have intensified their political intervention and economic interest in the affairs of the rest of the world. For their part, developing countries and the formerly or still officially communist states have undertaken increased (if a sometimes peculiar) appropriation of modern economic and political structures. Yet this process of mutual rapprochement on the political and economic level is characterized by a remarkable lack of knowledge of, or even interest in, the cultural and historical backgrounds of the respective nations. Thus, the existing official forms of intercultural communication, so often demanded in public discourse, lack precisely what is "cultural" about them, leaving the themes and problems analyzed in this series (identity, memory, cultural practices, history, religion, philosophy, literature) outside of what is explicitly communicated—as if such matters would not strongly affect political as well as economic agendas.

On the other hand, however, the currently dominant approaches of cultural theorists and critical thinkers in the West either claim the general impossibility of an intercultural communication about the common ground of "cultural identities"—based on the assumption that there is no common ground (the hypostatization of "difference")–or they politicize cultural differences in such a way that they are relegated to mere material for the construction of cultural subject positions. Despite their self-understanding as "critique," these intellectual approaches appear to correspond to the exclusion of "culture" on the level of state politics and economic exchange alike. Thus, cultural theory seems to react to the marginalization of culture by way of its own self-marginalization.

The series Making Sense of History intends to challenge this marginalization by introducing a form of cultural studies that takes the very term "culture" seriously again without dissolving it into either identity politics or a hypostasized concept of unbridgeable "difference." At the same time, it aims to reintroduce a notion of "historical theory" that no longer disconnects itself from historical memory and remembrance as concrete cultural practices, but seeks to explore those practices, interpreting them as different articulations of the universal (if heterogeneous) effort to "make sense of history." Thus, the series Making Sense of History relies on the idea that an academic contribution to the problem of intercultural communication should assume the form of a new opening of the academic discourse to its own historicity and cultural background, as well as a new acknowledgment of other cultural, but nonacademic, practices of "sense formation" as being equally important forms of human orientation and self-understanding (practices that in their general function are not much different from the efforts of academic thought itself). Such a reinscription of the universal claims of modern academic discourses into various cultural contexts, with the intention of providing new starting points for intercultural communication, is an enterprise that cannot be entirely fulfilled, or even outlined, in a series of a few books. Therefore, the series Making Sense of History should be regarded as something like a first attempt to circumscribe one possible research field that might prove to suit those general intentions: the field of "historical cultures."

The idea for this book series was born when a research project on "Making Sense of History: Interdisciplinary Studies in the Structure, Logic, and Function of Historical Consciousness—an Intercultural Comparison" was successfully completed. This project took place at the Center for Interdisciplinary Studies (Zentrum für interdisziplinäre Forschung; ZiF) at the University of Bielefeld, Germany, in 1994/1995. It was supported in part by the Kulturwissenschaftliches Institut Essen (KWI) im Wissenschaftszentrum Nordrhein-Westfalen (Institute for Advanced Study in the Humanities at Essen, at the Scientific Center of Northrhine Westfalia). The project included a series of conferences and workshops. A selection of contributions to them is the core of the various books of this series. The constellating, editing, and completion of these texts took a good deal of time, with the first volume appering in 2002. The ongoing debate in the humanities about its foundation and especially about the character and function of history has not changed but confirmed the focus in which the books of this series thematize basic issues of making sense by historical thinking.

I would like to express my gratitude to the staff of the Center for Interdisciplinary Study at the University of Bielefeld, as well as the staff of the Institute for Advanced Studies in the Humanities at Essen. I also want to thank the editors and co-editors of the individual volumes of this series and, of course, all the contributors for their efforts and patience in making these books possible. Finally, my thanks go to Angelika Wulff for her engaged management of this series, and to my wife, Inge, for her intensive support in editing my texts.

Jörn Rüsen

Foreword

Until now, psychology has barely dealt with the topics of historical consciousness and historical thought. Although the discipline has given thorough attention to other forms of thought—to other forms of the construction of reality—there is no distinctive tradition with the theoretical or clinical objective of establishing a psychology of specifically historical acts of meaning-construction. Seen properly, this is astonishing. Psychology is commonly considered one of the key modern sciences that aspire to investigate as well as to shape our relationships to others and to the world from a genetic, structural, and functional perspective. However, a generally acknowledged characteristic precisely of modern life, namely, the temporalization of experience, inextricable from our intensified experience of contingency and difference, has, until now, remained largely outside the discipline's purview. With a few exceptions, neither the biographization nor the historicization of reality have attracted its particular attention. The construction, representation, and reflection of *time*, of *narrative*, and of *history* have always possessed marginal significance at most in psychological discourses. Wherever questions about the development, structure, and function of the concept of time have been posed—by Piaget, for example, and other founders of genetic structuralism—they have been concerned predominantly with concepts of "physical," chronometrical time, and related concepts (e.g., "velocity").

Well over a decade ago, Jerome Bruner described the investigation of autobiographical consciousness, in subjects as well as in cultures, as an urgent task for contemporary psychology.[1] In fact, Bruner wrote that he could imagine no more important project. Even if autobiographical self-conceptions and related phenomena such as autobiographical memory are no longer so sadly neglected, Bruner's diagnosis applies now as it did then: psychology is far from possessing any adequate research into (auto)biographical thought. One might add that *historical* thought, as well as any other mode of historical meaning-construction, also still await psychological investigation.

All the contributions to the present volume attempt to close this gap. A majority are especially interested in the narration of stories, and can thus be included with the narrative psychology so much the focus of discussion in the United States. Overviews of the relevant literature, as well as empirical case studies, appear alongside theoretical and methodological reflections. Most contributions refer to specifically historical phenomena and meaning-constructions. Some touch on the subjects of biographical memory and biographical constructions of reality. Of all the various affinities between the contributions collected here, the most important is their consistent attention to issues of the constitution and representation of temporal experience.

The important question—whether or how the constitution and representation of time and history necessarily depend on *narrative* acts of meaning-construction—is not answered in the same way throughout the present volume. There is also disagreement about whether a narratively structured consciousness of time and history fulfills indispensable orientative functions in the rational formation of human praxis, as well as in processes of identity formation, or if such functions are beneficial. The advocates of this conception will encounter criticism that they are overlooking the illusionary and repressive character of narrative cognitive and verbal forms, or even that they are justifying them ideologically.

The still outstanding debate over a psychology of historical-narrative conceptions of self and world would not only have to clarify, with empirical means, how subjects historicize their world and themselves, and how they ontogenetically acquire the necessary *historical competence;* a narrative psychology of historical meaning-construction is unavoidably caught up in normative questions. Whoever is concerned with historical acts of meaning-construction must in one way or another explain whether (and on what ground) such "acts" should be considered beneficial. Naturally, this presupposes that "historical meaning" indeed represents a *potential* for symbolizing reality in a particular way, but not a necessity.

The research program envisioned in the present volume will soon have to examine, through comparative historiographical and ethnological studies, *which* persons actually think historically, and which acts are or were once guided by such thought. It is hardly incontestable, after all, that historical thought and historical consciousness represent *universal* anthropological constants, about whose general structure, function, and ontogenesis an empirically based psychology will finally be able to inform us. Quite the contrary: the evidence indicates the cultural specificity of at least that kind of historical thought with which "we" (inhabitants of the modern West) have long been familiar, and which has become second nature, though perhaps even a questionable "sociocultural compulsion" to some.

Be that as it may, the continuing vigorous discussion about the universality claims of Piaget's theories of theoretical and practical-moral thought makes imperative a certain skepticism about *any* universality claims for psychology's theoretical constructs. This admonition can hardly be taken seriously enough if we are to maintain our goal: an investigation, leading beyond the tradition of Piaget, of the *possible forms of human reason*—and thus of the very concept of reason. It should certainly be possible to extend the research begun by Piaget into the structural and formal investigation of specific rational abilities and expand them into areas that psychology has until now shamefully neglected. Indeed, the empirical investigation of theoretical-scientific reason and practical-moral judgment should be accompanied not only by a developmental psychology concerned with aesthetic judgment, but precisely also by a psychology of historical (and biographical) thought, neglected by both Piaget *and* Kant.

There are, in my view, numerous justifications for the proposal that such a psychology of historical (and biographical) thought be conceived as narrative psychology. The issue for the present volume, the *thought of human time,* and the acts of reality construction, argumentation, and rational justification connected with it, are, from a structuralist or formalist perspective, probably explicable only through an analysis of the structure or form of *narrated stories,* even if our task will hardly be completed by such analysis alone. An empirically based "epistemology" that can categorize human thought into different, mutually irreducible domains or "rational faculties," in order to then investigate them in their elementary and complex forms, could thus be conceptualized not least as a psychology of historical-*narrative* acts of meaning-construction. How far such research will lead is not immediately apparent. We hope, however, that the present volume can provide abundant points of orientation and suggestions for the clarification of this question.

This volume is one of the publications resulting from the work of a research group at the Center for Interdisciplinary Research (Zentrum für interdisziplinäre Forschung) at the University of Bielefeld. This research group took up the topic of "Historical Meaning-Construction: Interdisciplinary Research into the Structure, Logic, and Function of Historical Consciousness—an Intercultural Comparison." In this context, members of the research group, along with invited speakers, met in a symposium on questions about a narrative psychology of historical consciousness. The present volume originates from that symposium. However, not all the papers discussed at the symposium found their way into this volume, and it does include additional invited contributions.

As organizer of the symposium as well as editor of this volume, I would like to thank all the participants for their contributions, but especially the speakers, as well as the writers subsequently added to this collection. They all encouraged my belief that interdisciplinarity and internationalism are among the factors that can, from time to time, transform scholarship into vital praxis.

How much the present volume owes to the preliminary work, unflagging commitment, and encouragement of a passionate scholar—of course, I can only mean Jörn Rüsen, who brought this research group into existence—is obvious. I would like to thank him, along with all the group's participants, especially

Heidrun Friese, whose "counterpart" taught me even more than she intended, as so often happens. The people who are undoubtedly the most important to the emergence of this volume, however, will all have their say in the following pages.

Jürgen Straub

Erlangen, May 1997/Pisa and Chemnitz, May 2003

Note

1. Jerome S. Bruner, "Life as Narrative," *Social Research* 54 (1987): 15.

Part I

THEORETICAL POSITIONS AND REFLECTIONS

CHAPTER 1

Narrative Psychology and Historical Consciousness
Relationships and Perspectives

DONALD E. POLKINGHORNE

Postmodern theory has severely undercut the notion that historians can produce objective and accurate descriptions of past episodes. Instead, it proposes that discovering the factual truth about historical events is extremely problematic because knowledge production is relative to the values and agenda of the inquirer. The question of the validity of historical knowledge has informed the general topic "Making Sense of History," the theme of the book series of which the present volume is a part. The postmodern critique of the modernist epistemology of the humanities and social sciences has produced considerable consternation and disturbance in most of these disciplines. Of the social science disciplines, psychology is perhaps the least affected in this regard thus far. In general, psychology has continued its research programs with the modernist assumptions that proper adherence to methodological algorithms will produce statements that accurately correspond to independent psychological phenomena.[1] Within psychology, however, a growing number of scholars have taken the postmodern critique seriously and are working to advance positions in the field that are responsive to the challenges of postmodernism. These scholars can be grouped together as advocates of a narrative psychology.

The purpose of this essay is to put forward the outlines of narrative psychology as a contribution to the Making Sense of History series. In the struggle to produce a psychology informed by the postmodern critique, narrative psychology has been confronted with the problems of objective versus relative knowledge, universal versus culturally diverse cognitive processes, empirical ver-

---

Notes for this section begin on page 20.

sus hermeneutic understanding, and the synchronic versus diachronic nature of human being. The expectation is that the attempts of narrative to overcome these dichotomies might be useful adjuncts to the work of historians as they, too, endeavor to confront and integrate postmodern theory into their discipline.

Narrative Psychology and Postmodernism

Narrative psychology is a renewal of a theme in psychology that emphasizes the importance of story-making for human understanding and action. Earlier interest in the storied description of human lives (for example, Freud's case studies[2] and Murray's[3] and Allport's[4] studies of individual lives) had been subdued by psychology's turn to the objective and positivistic search for behavioral laws. The recent turn to narrative by a number of psychologists is, in part, one of the responses in psychology to the limits inherent in positivism for the understanding of human experience and action. The impetus for the focus on narrative can be traced to developments in four areas of psychology: (1) psychoanalytic therapy,[5] (2) personality theorists,[6] (3) cognitive psychology,[7] and (4) psychological theory and philosophy.[8] These developments have been merged into what is now called *narrative psychology*. The beginning of this general movement can be marked by Theodore R. Sarbin's 1986 publication of a collection of essays in which authors employed narrative principles in their examination of a range of psychological topics.[9] In the nine years since the appearance of Sarbin's collection, an extensive literature using narrative principles has emerged.

The turn by some psychologists to narrative as an explanatory framework for understanding human beings has occurred within the historical context in which other academic disciplines have begun attending to the importance of the narrative principle, disciplines such as anthropology,[10] literary criticism,[11] history,[12] ethics,[13] and philosophy.[14] The interaction between narrative psychology and these other sources gives narrative psychology a more interdisciplinary tone compared with many other approaches in psychology. The appearance of the interest in narrative across the human disciplines has occurred within the context of postmodernism. Postmodernism is a general cultural movement in which the belief in the efficacy of the scientific method to solve the social and personal problems of people has been called into question. This postmodern loss of faith in traditional science has been conditioned by Western experiences of world wars and nuclear threat, and by critiques of the epistemological assumptions of traditional science.[15] Poststructural writers have challenged the Western tradition, which held that truths about an independent reality can, through applying appropriate methodological procedures, be accurately grasped by thought.[16] In its place, postmodern theorists have proposed that understandings are constructions of the mental realm and, thus, subject to the distortions of historically varied conceptual schemes, human biology, and personal needs and agendas.[17] Mostly, narrative psychologists position themselves within a constructivist understanding and hold that narrative is the primary structuring scheme through which people organize and make meaning of their interaction with self, others, and the physical environment.

The next part of this essay is divided into two major divisions: narrative structure and narrative function. In various parts of the discussions about the structure and function of narrative, two tensions, which are inherent in narrativity, appear: the tension between cosmological time and phenomenological time,[18] and the tension between the landscape of action and the landscape of consciousness.[19] Although narrative is an experiential construction, it concurrently addresses time as both (1) a universal phenomenon of movement from past to present to future that conditions and limits all human experience, and (2) a unique phenomenon that appears as a personally appropriated interpretation for each person.[20] Narrative also simultaneously recounts events and actions as real occurrences and the participants' intentional beliefs, hopes, and evaluations of those occurrences. It is one of the powers of narrative thinking to reconcile these tensions, that is, to overcome the subject–object or science–art split in comprehending self, others, and the physical environment.

Narrative Structuring

In general, narrative is a kind of cognitive structuring that uses the configural properties of emplotment to organize actions and happenings into temporal wholes. This process gives meaning to events by identifying their role in and contribution to an outcome. Narrative structuring is an operation that occurs retrospectively to fulfill the potential narrative meaning of actions and happenings that originally appeared as meaningful at a prenarrative level. Narrative structuring results in narrative products that make use of cultural plots and characterizations in their compositions.

Narrative is, first of all, a cognitive process that serves understanding by organizing events and happenings into frames of meaning. Jerome S. Bruner notes that "People do not deal with the world event by event or with text sentence by sentence. They frame events and sentences in larger structures."[21] Bruner holds that humans employ two primary structuring processes: a paradigmatic process and a narrative or narrative-like process. Through paradigmatic processing, cognition frames encounter particular events and objects as members of conceptual categories. The paradigmatic process presents an object as an instance of a particular category (for example, the category *desk*). The narrative process frames events as contributing parts of an unfolding story. These cognitive operations serve to constitute experience as a composition of namable objects and linked happenings. Thus, the world does not show up in experience as a meaningless flux, but as already meaningfully organized as named or namable things and as purposeful temporally unfolding processes.

In everyday experience, the activity of cognitive processing occurs primarily outside of awareness, that is, it occurs within what Seymour Epstein[22] refers to as the *experiential system* as differentiated from the *rational system*. These cognitive processes do not simply process passively received information; rather, they are directed by the focus of attention on those aspects of the world that are of interest to the person's needs and desires.[23] When encountered events cannot be assimilated by a person's repertoire of frames, or the frames accommodated to include them,[24] the rational system is engaged to assist in the framing activity.

Narrative structuring operates by configuring actions and events into a temporal whole. As concepts serve to give meaning to particular objects and actions by giving them a categorical identity, plots serve to give meaning to particular happenings and actions by identifying them as contributors to the outcome of an episode. Plots accomplish this function by weaving together individual elements into the whole cloth of an entire episode, and thereby display the parts as contributors to an episode's outcome.[25] Plots compose events into a story by (1) delimiting a temporal range that marks the beginning and end of the story, (2) providing criteria for the selection of events to be included in the story, (3) temporally ordering events into an unfolding movement culminating in a conclusion, and (4) clarifying or making explicit the meaning that events have as contributors to the story as a unified whole.[26]

The Source of the Capacity for Narrative Structuring

Within narrative psychology, there are different positions on whether the capacity for narrative operations is innate (and universal) or whether it is a learned skill acquired from one's culture. The difference in positions is roughly correlated with whether the writer approaches the issue from a cognitive psychologist view or from a social constructionist or social learning view. Jerome S. Bruner can be used as a representative of the innate position. He differentiates his position from Noam Chomsky's postulation of a deep language structure. Although Bruner holds that the capacity for narrative structuring is innate, he emphasizes that narrative acquisition requires much more assistance from and interaction with others than Chomsky's postulations about language acquisition recognized. Bruner writes, "We have an 'innate' and primitive predisposition to narrative organization that allows us quickly and easily to comprehend and use it." There is a prelinguistic readiness for narrative that is triggered and cued by the acts and expressions of others, and "narrative structure is even inherent in the praxis of social interaction before it achieves linguistic expression." In recognition of the important effect of social interaction on the development of narrative competence, Bruner holds that while children come equipped with a readiness for narrative understanding, "the culture soon equips us with new powers of narration through its tool kit and through the traditions of telling and interpreting in which we soon come to participate."[27] Alyssa McCabe can serve as a representative of the social learning view. She argues that narrative structuring is a property of linguistic representations and not of innate structures of consciousness.[28] She holds that the capacity for narrative structuring is acquired through internalizing the structure of cultural stories one has heard and read.

Although differing on whether the capacity to use and understand narratives is innate or learned, both positions acknowledge the role of culture in providing the concepts and plots used by cognitive processing in making experience meaningful. The particular conceptual network used by people in identifying what items are linked together as members of a category and the dominative plots and subplots used to order events into a narrative are, in the main, socially provided. Yet people still have a capacity for innovation and creation of new concepts and plots. Thus, narrative production is not only the reproduction of cultural plots, but also the production of new plots.[29]

Narrative Structuring as Lived-through-Experience or Reflection

Whether one holds that narrative structuring is a consequence of social triggering of an innate capacity or the learned internalization of cultural styles of storytelling,[30] there is agreement that people attain the capacity to tell and understand stories and that they engage in structuring their actions and happenings narratively. However, there is disagreement as to whether people construct experience narratively as it occurs, or whether narrative construction is a reflective processing that occurs after a series of actions have occurred. Before addressing this question, a distinction needs to be drawn between a fully formed narrative and a proto- or prenarrative.[31]

Jean M. Mandler describes a fully developed narrative accounting as beginning with a setting in which the narrator introduces the characters, the location, and the time in which the story takes place.[32] After the setting has been established, the story proceeds with one or more episodes, each of which has a beginning and a development. In the episode, the character, reacting to the beginning events, sets a direction and outlines a path to achieve an outcome. Each episode includes the outcome of the attempts to reach the goal and assumes that the attempts are understood as the reasons that bring about the outcome. When the outcome has been given, the episode ends, and the ending links the episode to the whole story. After the whole series of episodes has been presented, the narrative includes ending portions that show that the episodes coalesce into one story.

Such fully developed narrative coherence doesn't seem to present itself in our ordinary, unreflective, everyday lived-through experience. And although we do not experience events at the time of their occurrence as fully integrated parts of a plot, neither are they experienced as mere disconnected fragments following one after another. Lived-through experience is primordially structured as temporally ordered events; actions already appear as contoured and linked sequences in which what has happened earlier can affect the present.[33] Lived-through experience also draws on an inherent understanding that human actions differ from physical movements.[34] Human actions appear in lived-through experience as purposeful consequences of human actors. Our unreflective, everyday experience of human conduct does not appear as disconnected and meaningless, but as already having the characteristics of temporal occurrences and directed actions. These characteristics give our primordial experience a "prenarrative quality," that is, a prefiguredness that "constitutes a demand for narrative."[35]

The notion that everyday lived-through experience has a prenarrative quality is a middle position regarding the narrative character of unreflective experience.[36] On the one side are those who hold that primordial experience manifests a fully developed narrative structure;[37] on the other side are those who maintain that experience presents itself originally as disconnected and fragmentary, and that narrative ordering is an imposition on this primordial chaos.[38] For those who hold the middle position and such as Ricoeur,[39] the knowledge presented by our prenarrative understanding of human conduct, on reflection, appears as unfinished. It calls for a reflective review that can consider the unintended (as well as the intended) effects of past actions—effects that, at the time of the act, one could not be aware of. The reflective review produces a fully articulated narrative by integrating the remembered prenarrative understandings people had at the time of the happenings with understandings that they have after the outcome of the episodes.

Narrative knowing, then, is a reflective explication of the prenarrative quality of unreflective experience; it is a drawing out of the story that experience embodied. The presence of unarticulated prenarrative experiences serves as a corrective or guide to the reflectively produced story. Not just any telling can authentically integrate the prenarrative into a legitimate account. People's "felt meanings" of their prenarrative experiences serve to produce phrases and plots that more closely conform to their "pre-thematic" understanding.[40] Narrative constructions must be continually adjusted until one is satisfied that they are adequate symbolic transformations of lived experience as known from one's present standpoint.

The retrospective nature of narrative knowing and human understanding has been described by Gadamer: "All beginnings lie in darkness, and what is more, they can be illuminated only in the light of what came later and from the perspective of what followed."[41] And Merleau-Ponty, whose work preceded Gadamer's hermeneutic theory, said, "[I understand my past] by following it up with a future which will be seen after the event as foreshadowed by it, thus introducing historicity into my life."[42] As a retrospective process of attributing meaning to a person's life events and actions, reflective narratives are more than a simple recounting of a person's life activities as they were experienced; rather, narratives present the meaning of these experiences from the present perspective of the person. Several features of narratives differentiate them from simply accurate reproductions of life as it was lived: (1) memory as reconstruction of past events, (2) the smoothing processes of Gestalt-type configuration, and (3) the use of culturally available plots.

Memory as Reconstruction

In personal stories, narrative structuring draws experiential traces from memory. Memory is not a container of taped replays of life events. Recollection is a partial reconstruction of the past that attends to and connects memory traces according to the press of present needs and interpretations. Artifacts such as photos and letters serve as guides for recollecting traces, but the recollections they bring into awareness still undergo interpretation.[43] Narrative structuring operates dialectically with memory to re-create past occurrences in light of the emplotting task to produce coherence and closure. Thus, the recollected images that make up the retrospective story are not simple replications of the actual events as they originally occurred.

Narrative Smoothing

Life as lived is more diverse and disjointed than the stories we tell about it. Our daily lives consist in eating and sleeping, going to and from our work, and running errands. Narratives are not simply a running description or videotape that includes descriptions of every moment of the time covered by a storied episode. Narrative structuring highlights and marks off from the flow of one's mundane daily tasks the happenings, thoughts, and actions that are needed to comprehend the way in which the storied episode unfolded. In life, we are engaged in many projects at once, not all of which interlock into significant episodes. An event may be extraneous and irrelevant to one episode, but important for understanding another. A narrative production, in contrast to life as lived, usually concerns a single major plot, incorporating only the subplots and events that contribute to that plot and selecting out all irrelevant happenings.[44] In configuring a story of a life episode, narratives often omit details and condense parts ("flattening"), elaborate and exaggerate other parts ("sharpening"), and make parts more compact and consistent ("rationalization") to produce a coherent and understandable explanation.[45] Narrative, like the visual Gestalt process, draws out from a background those elements that compose the patterned figure or plot that is the focus of attention. In addition, narrative operates according to a principle of closure in which incomplete figures are perceived as whole by the process of "smoothing."[46]

Culturally Available Plots

Meaning-giving interpretative plots are adapted from the repertoire of stories made available in a person's culture. While chosen plots need to resonate with the prenarrative experiences that they configure into meaningful stories, they also function dialectically to select for the told story only those remembered events and actions that are significant contributors to the story's resolution.[47] People may simply accept the role assigned to them by the plot the dominant culture has prepared for people with their particular gender, social standing, and background, or they may revise or refashion the assigned plot and author an innovative personal identity.

To summarize, narrative knowledge is not a simple recall of the past. Narrative comprehension is a retrospective, interpretive composition that displays past events in the light of current understanding and evaluation of their significance. While referring to the original past life events, narrative transforms them by ordering them into a coherent part–whole plot structure. Narrated descriptions of life episodes are not mirrored reflections of what occurred. Narrative structuring is an interpretation of life in which past events and happenings are understood as meaningful from a current perspective of their emplotted contribution to an outcome.

The creative and constructive character of narrative knowing allows for different stories about the same past events. The interpretive point of view that informed the first narrative retrospection can change over time and in different settings. The outcome of a previous episode may be evaluated differently as new experiences are accumulated, and the significance of an element's contribution to the completion of an episode may be differently understood as its effects are reconsidered. What is known narratively about a life episode from the perspective of the accumulated experience of old age may differ from the narrative understanding of the episode developed in midlife.[48]

Although the discussion has so far emphasized the use of prenarratively structured meanings of remembered actions as the elements used in the construction of a narrative, it is important to note that these remembered action meanings are only some of the elements gathered together by a plot. Previous reflective narrativations of life episodes are also part of our past experience. Life, as remembered, consists of the previous narratively interpreted understandings of the events that are renarrativized in a new story.[49] Because narratives about life episodes are not created from scratch, narrative processing most always recounts events that already carry sedimented narratively reflected meanings.

Products of the Structuring Process

The reflective process of *narrativizing* (a verb) produces a product, a *narrative* or story (a noun). Narrative cognitive processing may operate out of awareness, but whether it is a consciously or unconsciously directed process, it moves dialectically to and from parts to possible wholes until a whole is generated that fits and gives sense to the parts. Prior to the resolution of the narrative process, potential integrating story lines are continually adjusted until they produce a gestalt that brings the parts into focus and displays them as meaningfully integrated. The result of narrative cognitive processing is a story that can function to give an integrating identity to the self and meaning to one's actions and life experiences. The products of self-narrativizing are often retained out of explicit awareness,[50] yet circumstances can provide occasions for them to be expressed through the signifiers of one's language. Several dimensions within which narrative products can appear will now be discussed.

Public and Private Stories

The storied understanding may be retained as private knowledge, or it may be made public. Some stories remain in the possession of the person who conceived them; these are stories we tell ourselves. Some private stories end up becoming public and available to investigation, such as the private self-talk of baby Emily, whose storytelling soliloquies were tape recorded,[51] or stories recorded in private diaries that later become public. Other stories are made public when they are told to others or when they are written down. Private stories become public when they reach the threshold of public communication. Investigations of the structure of narrative accounts are necessarily limited to stories that become public.

Short- and Long-Lived Stories

Storied productions vary in their "staying power." Some narratively constructed understandings are short lived. They are lost to memory or discarded as not worth preserving. Other stories are preserved. A few of a person's private stories may be retained by him or her as memorable for understanding the self or others. These stories may be recalled at various times because they serve as significant interpretations of past life episodes. Stories that are made public, either in oral or written form, become available to be retold or reread by others beyond the lifetime of their producers. A very few are granted such importance that they become part of a culture's or civilization's collection and are passed on from generation to generation. Biblical stories are an example of lasting stories.

Impromptu and Crafted Stories

Storied productions can vary according to the extent of the crafting used in their production. Some stories are told "off the top of the head," as when friends tell stories about their day's experiences. Other stories are carefully crafted productions designed for publication and dissemination; for example, the autobiographical accounts of skilled writers. Hans Blumenberg[52] gave an interesting account of the evolutionary development of classical myths. He posits that storytellers traveled from town to town and entertained the audiences that came to hear them. The amount of payment the storytellers received depended on how well the audience responded to the stories. On the basis of this response, storytellers dropped certain stories from their repertoire and refined the plots and characters of others. Over generations, the stories that were retained were the ones that audiences had found most meaningful and entertaining. Blumenberg suggests that this is the scenario that produced the classical myths, which have retained the interest of audiences and readers over centuries.

Structural Variation

While some theorists hold that there is a common structure to the storied productions of the narrativizing process, others hold that there is no common structure. The structure of narrative productions has been analyzed primarily by scholars of narratology, but narrative psychologists have made use of their work. Representative of those who have proposed a universal structure underlying the diverse surface differences in stories are Claude Lévi-Strauss and Jean M. Mandler.[53] Lévi-Strauss proposed that narratives from all cultures could be could be characterized in terms of the opposition between nature and culture. Mandler argued that all well-formed stories include a protagonist's goals and their formation, the protagonist's attempts to achieve these goals, and the outcomes of the efforts. However, the attempts to specify the general ingredients of the storied products of narrative formation has turned out to be more difficult and controversial than first supposed.[54] Scholars have recently "documented ways in which native Americans, African-Americans, Africans, Hawaiians, and other groups, tell narratives with structures rather different from those of our white middle-class American culture."[55] C. Jan Swearingen's examination of the stories of classical Greece led him to conclude that the present structure of narrative expressions is of recent origin and differs in structure from the Greek tales.[56] The position of cultural diversity in the structures of narrative products is consistent with Vygotsky's view that cultural products, like language and other symbolic systems, mediate thought and place their stamp on people's representations of reality.[57] A middle position is that the capacity for narrative configuration is universal, while the products that result from this innate process are articulated through the plot forms and conceptual network of the culture in which they are produced.

The Media of Narrative Productions

The essential form of narratives is mental and is different from any particular expression of them. Narrative production is equipotential in that the same story can be expressed through various media. For example, a story may be set forth as a dramatization or a motion picture. The words of a story can be set to music and presented as a song. Ballet and modern dance can also serve as vehicles for communicating stories. The same story can be told over and over in different words, yet the essential meaning of the story is the same. Thus, a story is not the same as its expression. Although it is possible to express the same story through various communicative modes, narrative productions are most often expressed in natural languages, in either their spoken or written forms. Stories that are committed to writing lose the fluidity of oral presentations and the capacity for ongoing revision. Also, the oral presentation of a story can be enriched through the use of gestures, intonations, and facial expressions.

Narrative Functions

The primary function served by narrative structuring is to give meaning to actions, events, and happenings. Bruner wrote, "our capacity to render experience in terms of narrative is not just child's play, but an instrument for making meaning that dominates much of life in culture—from soliloquies at bedtime to the weighing of testimony in our legal system."[58] Scripts for ritualized episodes—going to a restaurant, for example—serve as adequate means for understanding events that conform to expectations, but when the unexpected occurs, its meaning is unclear. One of the chief functions of narrative is to "deal with events that are contrary to expectations."[59] Narrative processing is triggered when cultural canons are violated or routines are breached.[60] Narrative structuring reflectively reviews the unusual event and makes sense of it by "appeal to a subjective state of the protagonist";[61] that is, narrative structuring situates the event as a part of a story contributing to a desired outcome.

Personal Identity

Narrative psychology has been especially concerned with how narrative operations function with regard to personal identity. People differentiate themselves from others and define themselves through their identity. Roy F. Baumeister[62] points out that it wasn't until after about 1800 that a significant number of Westerners wrote of doubts about their experience of self as a uniquely self-same person over time and in different situations. Personal identity, as a problematic, may be of recent origin, and historically linked to the industrial revolution. This does not mean that people in other cultures do not have identities, or that people in other historical periods did not have identities. Rather, it means that identity was scripted by cultural norms and beliefs and did not reach the threshold of concern. In contrast to other times, contemporary Western culture does not provide its members with a coherent and stable definition of self. Instead, it views the self as an accomplishment to be constructed within everyday social life.[63] Building the self takes time and is a developmental process.[64]

In place of a single integrating model of identity, contemporary culture besieges people with many conflicting models, and leaves the task of building a unifying identity to the person. Narrative psychologists[65] hold that identity is a storied construction that is displayed as a person's self-narrative. Self-narratives function to integrate people's lives by binding together their disparate memories of past happenings, their current beliefs and experiences, and their imagined and anticipated future actions. Because of the temporal dimension of human existence,[66] however, life stories are eroded as people are confronted with physiological and cognitive changes and challenged by modifications in social demands made on them as they pass through different developmental markers. The passage of time erodes a person's narratively constructed identity, making it necessary to reconstruct it time after time.

Dan P. McAdams traces the course of construction, erosion, and reconstruction throughout life's developmental stages.[67] McAdams divides the development of identity into three eras: the prenarrative, the narrative, and the postnarrative.[68] The prenarrative era, which is the period of infancy through early adolescence, is a time in which materials are gathered for the self-stories individuals will construct during the narrative period. Although children in the prenarrative era are not yet engaged in the construction of unifying self-identity stories, their experiences will have an effect on the production of their later identity stories. For example, experiences of the first two years of life leave one with "a set of unconscious and nonverbal 'attitudes' about self, other, and world" regarding the trustworthiness of one's human and physical environment and its responsiveness to one's needs.[69] The attitudes developed during these years can show up in later self-stories as a tone of hopelessness and mistrust or as a tone of hopefulness and trust. The narrative era extends from the time in adolescence when a young adult begins to construct self-stories and continues through adulthood, during which the self-stories are refined and reconstructed. McAdams's third era, the postnarrative era, does not occur in all lives. It corresponds to Erikson's mature age stage in which the developmental task is to obtain integrity in one's life. In this third era, one's life can be looked at as something that is approaching culmination, and the life story is a nearly completed tale. During this era, one's life story can be accepted (integrity) or rejected (despair), but can no longer be substantially altered.

McAdams's notion of the necessity for people to revise their narrativized self-identity in response to changing life circumstances is consistent with Paul Ricoeur's view of time as disruptive of identity.[70] Western culture has conceived of time in two conflicting ways: (1) cosmological time, which has the characteristics of unity (that is, the quality of sameness), unidirectionality, and unidimensionality; and (2) phenomenological time, which has the characteristics of uniqueness to the experiencer and the quality of endurance. Narrative reconciles these two views of time and makes their difference productive;

it configures these notions of time into a single story. Narratives include both the cosmological dimension of time as a series of discrete events happening one after another in linear succession and the phenomenological dimension in which the temporal aspect is characterized by integration, culmination, and closure. Because of the need to confront cosmological time in establishing identity, knowledge of the self cannot be fulfilled simply through unmediated phenomenological reflection, nor can it be fulfilled when viewed only as a series of movements. Ricoeur posits that knowledge of the self's identity has to be indirect and interpretative. Narrative configuration provides this indirect approach to self-identity. Thus, self-identity is configured rather than discovered.

In support of this understanding of the figural construction of self-identity, new understandings of the therapeutic process and new approaches to therapy have emerged. Donald P. Spence and Roy Schafer have proposed that psychoanalytic interpretations are less recoveries of real events of early childhood and the operation of real psychic structures than they are narratively organized creations that serve to give unity and wholeness to the patient's life.[71] Michael White and David Epston have led the development of an approach to therapy whose rubric is *narrative therapy*.[72] In narrative therapy, clients are viewed as understanding themselves as the protagonist of a narrative. The narratives people employ for this purpose are those proposed for them by their cultures. The dominant cultural stories assign them roles in which they are the scapegoat for problems they encounter. Narrative therapy assists clients in separating the problematic aspects of their concerns from their self-definition. For example, when clients report that they are responsible for not controlling their eating behavior, narrative therapists ask them to externalize the problem by viewing it as not being a part of themselves but as another character in their life story. The therapy focuses on how clients might do battle with this character. Narrative therapy also helps clients become aware of past actions and beliefs that have been deselected as parts of themselves (unique outcomes) in order that they might fit the self-image imposed by the culturally dominant story. In the process of reintegrating these previously deselected self parts, clients *re-vision* their self-story and establish a more agentic self-identity.[73]

Narrativization functions not only to construct an identity of who I have been, but also of who I plan to be. People construct imagined hypothetical stories as a means to plan their future actions or to anticipate possible future actions of others. They can play out various stories in their imagination to produce *what if* scenarios. These imagined stories draw analogically on their prior collection of storied understandings of the connections among actions and outcomes to assist in planning future action episodes.[74] The collection of stories is searched to find one whose outcome is similar to the one that the person wants to achieve or avoid.

Other Psychological Functions

Narrative's primary function—meaning-making—has been extended to other traditional areas of psychological interest. It is not within the purpose of this chapter to address how narrative theory has affected these areas, but several of these areas will be mentioned along with references to scholars who are employing narrative thinking as a means for understanding these psychological phenomena. Theodore R. Sarbin has provided a narratively informed theory of emotions;[75] Roger C. Schank proposes that intelligence is primarily the capacity to tell and understand stories;[76] and Donald E. Polkinghorne has analyzed narrative as means for psychological understanding with respect to research design and methodological issues.[77]

Narrative Psychology and History

Narrative psychology is part of the struggle within psychology to come to grips with postmodern theory with its constructivist and social constructionist epistemological principles.[78] Narrative psychology and the discipline of history share a commitment to the idea that human activity is best understood through narrative explanations rather than covering-law explanations.[79] The meaning-making operations of narrative structuring that serve to order and interpret personal experiences are also employed to construct historical explanations of past events. The focus of interest of narrative psychology is the operation of narrative understanding as it functions within individuals. Its concern is with first-person narration, that is, how individuals employ narrative in comprehending their own selves, actions, and happenings, and in making sense of the actions of others with whom they interact. The focus of historical studies is primarily on understanding the actions of others with whom historians and readers have usually not interacted. Historians usually work with documents and other evidence to construct an explanatory account of past episodes. They produce third-person narratives about others' lives. Narrative psychology investigates an individual's autobiographical understanding, whereas history composes biographies about others.

Although historical productions differ from narrative psychology's interest in first-person narrative productions, both rely on the innate human capacity to construct and understand narrative explanation. As described above, narrative explains human actions and happenings by configuring them as links in a temporal unfolding that culminates in a particular outcome. Historical narrative explanations serve to understand events of the historic past; they also serve to understand events of the more recent past. For example, narrative is often used to construct a story that provides an account of how a disastrous outcome came about. Investigators might interview participants and examine documents with the purpose of constructing the "true" story of how a train wreck happened. The results of these findings can be used to inform what changes are necessary to avoid the same kind of disaster in the future. Historical narrative explanation also serves to construct an account of what happened and who was involved in the commission of a crime. The purpose of many legal proceedings is to uncover the story that fully accounts for the diverse happenings and actions of the episode in question.

The world in which humans live consists not merely of physical objects, but perhaps, more significantly, of the actions, thoughts, and experiences of people. Narrative psychology and history share an interest in knowing the ways human beings make sense of this human world and choose to act in it. Narrative psychology tends to focus on the general characteristics of people's processes of understanding and action.[80] Historians' concerns are twofold: (1) reporting and comprehending the specific understandings and actions of people that have been undertaken in the past,[81] and (2) knowing the manner in which people produce this comprehension of past actions and events. Narrative psychologists and many historians hold that the narrativation is a basic process by which people of the past comprehended and acted in the world and people of the present comprehend and act. Because of this mutual interest in narrativation, the scholarship and insights of narrative psychologists and historians are of reciprocal interest to each.

Postmodern theory includes a reaction to the modernist assumption that scientific method can produce factual truths about how things really were or are. Postmodernists extended the Duhem-Quine thesis that falsifying observations are not unambiguous evidence that theories are wrong and Norwood Russell Hanson's notion that observations are commingled with theory and cannot serve as the foundation of certain knowledge as the logical positivists had contended.[82] Postmodern theorists responded to the idea that there is no foundation on which to base certain knowledge with skepticism about all knowledge.[83] They proposed that no knowledge is trustworthy and, thus, all knowledge claims are relative to the metanarrative of the claimant.[84] Postmodern theorists set up a dichotomy between historical truth and narrative "truth," and were skeptical about the possibility of establishing historical truths. This led them to the position that narrative explanations were more like imaginative fictional novels than explanatory interpretations of why established factual events occurred.

Traditional psychology has held its mission to be to produce knowledge that correctly pictures the structures of human mentality and the laws of human behavior. Postmodern theory challenges the possibility of achieving this mission, posing that all knowledge is interpretation and is more a projection of the knower's needs and values than an accurate representation of reality. The traditional notion that historians develop correct accounts of past episodes has also been challenged by postmodern theory. Contemporary historians have been engaged in a struggle within the discipline of history that is similar to that of narrative psychologists in the discipline of psychology. The issue is whether history is a creative and interpretive discipline with kinship to the literary disciplines, or whether it is a discipline that describes the past as it actually was, with kinship to the social sciences.[85] If historians are engaged in an interpretive enterprise, then through the use of contemporary narrative plots, their reports distort or add to what actually happened in the past by imposing their own cultural perspectives and agendas. Postmodern theory suggests that our consciousness of history is enveloped in present narrative constructions.

The acceptance of narrative as the discourse mode appropriate for displaying the motivations and reasons of actors need not be extended, as postmodern theory does, to exclude factual content from its interpretative explanations. Individuals who deny or exclude factual events, such as the death of their parents, from their personal narratives are considered delusional. The notion that historical narrative explanations are selective and interpretative does not lead to the conclusion that any actual occurrences referred to in the narrative are projections of the narrator. A response to the rejection of a foundation for certain knowledge need not be the postmodernist utter skepticism. Indeed, a more useful and pragmatic response is to accept knowledge claims about events that pass the muster of critical review. Although one can no longer be certain of the truth of the claim, evidence and argument can be convincing enough to allow acceptance of the claim as possibly being true.[86]

John Lukacs points out that historical consciousness has a history, that is, the sense of what the past consists of changes.[87] People's historical consciousness is contextually sensitive to the values and worldviews of their cultures. Although our present cultural tradition assigns a privileged status to science and its search for covering laws, there is a skeptical reaction to the Enlightenment belief in the capacity of science to produce the heavenly kingdom of peace and happiness on earth. Scholars have questioned the epistemological assumptions on which traditional science was based and have proposed that our knowledge is not referential to an independent reality but a reflection of language structures, including narrative structures. This bifurcation produces an unstable tension between people who privilege one approach over the other. This tension sometimes manifests itself within the same individual as he or she seeks to understand his or her own past and the past of his or her community, country, culture, and species.

Some modernist scholars had proposed that, if history were to be a science, narrative explanation would be inappropriate.[88] They submitted that history should aspire to scientific descriptions of events by subsuming them under covering laws. Others emphasized the narrative character of the historian's endeavor.[89] Ricoeur offers a mixed model for history in which both the nomic and purposive aspects are included.[90] Ricoeur writes that he "is no longer in agreement with the narrativists, for whom history is only an expansion of narration," nor does he agree that history should be a nomic science.[91] For him, historical explanations require a mixed explanatory mode; this mixed mode, however, gives history an unstable character. Ricoeur proposes that historians make use of singular causal explanations (rather than subsuming laws) in their accounts of human actors.

Historical explanations of a mixed mode, while not producing with certainty reports of what actually happened and why it happened, can employ evidence and argument to support their claims. Although not accepting the notion of general laws of history,[92] mixed-mode historical reports incorporate causal explanations of sequences of events that include, along with economic and political conditions, the purposes and aims of human actors. Bruner refers to these two factors as the landscape of action and the landscape of consciousness.[93] As a retrospective view of a past episode, narrative processing allows the historian to include in the explanation the unintended consequences of protagonists' actions, as well as descriptions of the protagonists' intended outcomes. Historical explanation emplots events and actions into a narrative that gives a plausible explanation constrained by the pragmatically accepted views of what occurred and by the general ideas about how people respond to various kinds of events and about factors that motivate human behavior. Thus, narrative interpretation is not free to simply create a past that meets the needs of a present constituency. Narrative accounts are constrained by past events (as they are presently pragmatically agreed on).

Narrative explanation need not be equated with a fictive projection of the narrator's values and agenda. Narrative thinking can serve as a vehicle for reconciling the split between the desire to know what happened in the past and the desire to know the meaning these events have for the present. Narrative structuring can function to repair the rupture between history as representing certain knowledge of what happened in the past and history as an interpretation of past episodes. Narrative thinking does not overcome these differences through a synthesis such as Hegel's dialectic resolution. Rather, the overcoming resembles Merleau-Ponty's notion of the hyperdialectic.[94] Merleau-Ponty proposed that the interrogation of the deepest levels of human existence requires the use of a hyperdialectic method. Unlike Hegel's dialectic, hyperdialectic is a dialectic without synthesis, one that remains aware that every thesis is but an abstraction from the lived world of experience. Thus, there is no final knowledge, no ultimate synthesis that integrates all into one concept. In this understanding, Merleau-Ponty opposes lessening the tension in understanding by opting for either the objectivist or subjectivist reduction. For him, there is no privileged road to understanding. Instead, we are to traverse the lived world, opening up concepts and reality without claim to knowing them absolutely. Thus, historical work is appropriately ambiguous, employing both the pragmatic scientific quest for accurate description of past actions as they occurred and the interpretative literary quest for narrative explanations that display these actions in a meaningful manner for the reader.

Notes

1. Donald E. Polkinghorne, "Postmodern Epistemology of Practice," in *Psychology and Postmodernism,* ed. Steinar Kvale (London, 1992), 146–165.
2. Peter Brooks, *Reading for the Plot: Design and Intention in Narrative* (New York, 1984).
3. Henry A. Murray, *Explorations in Personality: A Clinical and Experimental Study of Fifty Men of College Age* (New York, 1938).
4. Gordon W. Allport, *Letters from Jenny* (New York, 1965).
5. Roy Schafer, *The Analytic Attitude* (New York, 1983); Donald P. Spence, *Narrative Truth and Historical Truth* (New York, 1982).
6. Dan P. McAdams, *Power, Intimacy, and the Life Story* (Homewood, Ill., 1985).
7. Jerome S. Bruner, *Actual Minds, Possible Worlds* (Cambridge, Mass., 1986).
8. Kenneth J. Gergen and Mary M. Gergen, "Narrative Form and the Construction of Psychological Science," in *Narrative Psychology: The Storied Nature of Human Conduct,* ed. Theodore R. Sarbin (New York, 1986), 22–44; Donald E. Polkinghorne, *Narrative Knowing and the Human Sciences* (Albany, N.Y., 1988).
9. Theodore R. Sarbin, ed., *Narrative Psychology: The Storied Nature of Human Conduct* (New York, 1986).
10. Edward M. Bruner, "Ethnography as Narrative," in *The Anthropology of Experience,* ed. Victor W. Turner and Edward M. Bruner (Urbana, 1986), 139–155.
11. Wallace Martin, *Recent Theories of Narrative* (Ithaca, N.Y., 1986); W.J. Thomas Mitchell, ed., *On Narrative* (Chicago, 1981).
12. Frederick A. Olafson, *The Dialectic of Action* (Chicago, 1979).
13. Alasdair MacIntyre, *After Virtue: A Study in Moral Theory* (Notre Dame, Ind., 1981).
14. Paul Ricoeur, *Time and Narrative,* 3 vols. (Chicago, 1984–1988).
15. Richard Rorty, *Philosophy and the Mirror of Nature* (Princeton, 1979).
16. Jacques Derrida, *Of Grammatology* (Baltimore, 1976).
17. Robert A. Neimeyer and Michael J. Mahoney, *Constructivism in Psychotherapy* (Washington, D.C., 1995).
18. Ricoeur, *Time.*
19. Bruner, *Actual Minds.*
20. Edmund Husserl, *The Phenomenology of Internal Time Consciousness,* trans. James S. Churchill (Bloomington, Ind., 1964) (first published in German, 1893–1917).
21. Jerome S. Bruner, *Acts of Meaning* (Cambridge, Mass., 1990), 64.
22. Seymour Epstein, "Implications of Cognitive-Experiential Self-Theory for Personality and Development," in *Studying Lives through Time: Personality and Development,* ed. David C. Funder et al. (Washington, D.C., 1993), 399–434.
23. Edmund Blair Bolles, *A Second Way of Knowing* (New York, 1991).
24. Jean Piaget, *Genetic Epistemology* (New York, 1971).
25. Ricoeur, *Time.*
26. Donald E. Polkinghorne, "Narrative Configuration in Qualitative Analysis," *International Journal of Qualitative Studies in Education* 8 (1995): 8–25.
27. Bruner, *Acts of Meaning,* 77, 80.
28. Alyssa McCabe, preface to *Developing Narrative Structure,* ed. Alyssa McCabe and Carole Peterson (Hillsdale, N.J., 1991), ix–xvii.
29. Anthony Giddens, *Modernity and Self-Identity* (Stanford, 1991).
30. C. Jan Swearingen, "The Narrative Dialogue and Narration within Dialogue: The Transition from Story to Logic," in *Narrative Thought and Narrative Language,* ed. Bruce K. Britton and A.D. Pellegrini (Hillsdale, N.J., 1990), 173–197.
31. David Carr, Charles Taylor and Paul Ricoeur, "Discussion: Ricoeur on Narrative," in *On Paul Ricoeur: Narrative and Interpretation,* ed. David Wood (London, 1991), 160–187.
32. Jean Matter Mandler, *Stories, Scripts and Scenes: Aspects of Scheme Theory* (Hillsdale, N.J., 1984).

33. Bruner, *Acts of Meaning*.
34. Paul Ricoeur, "Narrative Identity," in Wood, *On Paul Ricoeur*, 188–199.
35. Ricoeur, *Time*.
36. Albert T. Fell, "Epistemological and Ontological Queries Concerning David Carr's *Time, Narrative, and History*," *Philosophy of the Social Sciences* 22 (1992): 370–380.
37. George S. Howard, "Culture Tales: A Narrative Approach to Thinking, Cross-Cultural Psychology, and Psychotherapy," *American Psychologist* 46 (1991): 187–197.
38. Hayden White, *Metahistory: The Historical Imagination in Nineteenth-Century Europe* (Baltimore, 1973).
39. Anthony Paul Kerby, *Narrative and the Self* (Bloomington, Ind., 1991); Carr, Taylor, and Ricoeur, "Discussion."
40. Eugene T. Gendlin, "Thinking beyond Patterns: Body, Language, and Situations," in *The Presence of Feeling in Thought*, ed. Bernard den Ouden and Marcia Moen (New York, 1991), 22–151.
41. Hans-Georg Gadamer, *Reason in the Age of Science* (Cambridge, Mass., 1981), 140.
42. Maurice Merleau-Ponty, *Phenomenology of Perception* (New York, 1962), 346 (first published in French. 1945).
43. Edward S. Casey, *Remembering: A Phenomenological Study* (Bloomington, Ind., 1987).
44. David Carr, *Time, Narrative, and History* (Bloomington, Ind., 1986).
45. Martin Cortazzi, *Narrative Analysis* (London, 1993).
46. Arnold Lewis Glass, Keith James Holyoak, and John Lester Santa, *Cognition* (Reading, Mass., 1979).
47. Donald E. Polkinghorne, "Narrative and Self-Concept," *Journal of Narrative and Life History* 1 (1991): 135–153.
48. Donald E. Polkinghorne, "Narrative Knowing and the Study of Lives," in *Aging and Biography: Exploration in Adult Development*, ed. James Birren et al. (New York, 1996).
49. Joseph Margolis, *Interpretation Radical but Not Unruly: The New Puzzle of the Arts and History* (Berkeley, 1995).
50. Donald E. Polkinghorne, "Explorations of Narrative Identity," *Psychological Inquiry* 7.4 (1996): 363–367.
51. Ruth Weir, *Language in the Crib* (The Hague, 1962).
52. Hans Blumenberg, *Work on Myth* (Cambridge, Mass., 1985).
53. Claude Lévi-Strauss, *Structural Anthropology* (New York, 1963); Jean Matter Mandler, *Stories, Scripts, and Scenes*.
54. John A. Robinson, "Narrative Thinking as a Heuristic Process," in *Narrative Psychology: The Storied Nature of Human Conduct*, ed. Theodore R. Sarbin (New York, 1986), 111–125.
55. McCabe, preface to McCabe and Peterson, *Developing Narrative Structure*, xii.
56. Swearingen, "The Narrative Dialogue."
57. Lev S. Vygotsky, *Mind in Society: The Development of Higher Psychological Processes* (Cambridge, Mass., 1978).
58. Bruner, *Acts of Meaning*, 97.
59. Wallace Chafe, "Some Things That Narratives Tell Us about the Mind," in Britton and Pellegrini, *Narrative Thought and Narrative Language*, 79–98.
60. Joan Lucariello, "Canonicality and Consciousness in Child Narrative," in Britton and Pellegrini, *Narrative Thought and Narrative Language*, 131–149.
61. Bruner, *Acts of Meaning*, 82.
62. Roy F. Baumeister, *Identity: Cultural Change and the Struggle for Self* (New York, 1986).
63. Charles Taylor, *Sources of the Self: The Making of the Modern Identity* (Cambridge, Mass., 1989).
64. Dan P. McAdams, "Personality, Modernity, and the Storied Self: A Contemporary Framework for Studying Persons," *Psychological Inquiry* 7 (1996): 295.
65. Hubert J.M. Hermans and Els Hermans-Jansen, *Self-Narratives: The Construction of Meaning in Psychotherapy* (New York, 1995); William Lowell Randall, *The Stories We Are: An Essay on Self-Creation* (Toronto, 1995); Polkinghorne, "Narrative."

66. Martin Heidegger, *Being and Time* (New York, 1962).

67. Dan P. McAdams, *The Stories We Live By: Personal Myths and the Making of the Self* (New York, 1993); Erik H. Erikson, *Identity and the Life Cycle,* vol. 1 (New York, 1959).

68. McAdams, "Personality."

69. McAdams, *The Stories,* 47.

70. Paul Ricoeur, "Life in Quest of Narrative," in Wood, *On Paul Ricoeur,* 20–33.

71. Roy Schafer, *Retelling a Life: Narration and Dialogue in Psychoanalysis* (New York, 1992); Spence, *Narrative Truth.*

72. Michael White and David Epston, *Narrative Means to Therapeutic Ends* (New York, 1990).

73. Alan Parry and Robert E. Doan, *Story Re-visions: Narrative Therapy in the Postmodern World* (New York, 1994).

74. Michael McGuire, "The Rhetoric of Narrative: A Hermeneutic, Critical Theory," in Britton and Pellegrini, *Narrative Thought and Narrative Language,* 219–236.

75. Theodore R. Sarbin, "Emotions as Narrative Emplotments," in *Entering the Circle: Hermeneutic Investigation in Psychology,* ed. Martin J. Packer and Richard B. Addison (Albany, N.Y., 1989), 185–201.

76. Roger C. Schank, *Tell Me a Story: A New Look at Real and Artifical Memory* (New York, 1990).

77. Polkinghorne, "Narrative Configuration."

78. Sheila McNamee and Kenneth J. Gergen, eds., *Therapy as Social Construction* (Newbury Park, Calif., 1992).

79. Polkinghorne, *Narrative Knowing.*

80. William M. Runyan, "A Historical and Conceptual Background to Psychohistory," in *Psychology and Historical Interpretation,* ed. William M. Runyan (New York, 1988), 3–60.

81. Fernand Braudel, *The Mediterranean and the Mediterranean World in the Age of Philip II,* 2 vols. (New York, 1972–1974).

82. Scott Gordon, *The History and Philosophy of Social Science: An Introduction* (New York, 1991); Norwood Russell Hanson, *Patterns of Discovery* (Cambridge, U.K., 1958).

83. Donald E. Polkinghorne, "Psychology after Philosophy," in *Reconsidering Psychology: Perspectives from Continental Philosophy,* ed. Richard N. Williams and James E. Faulconer (Pittsburgh, 1990), 92–115.

84. Rorty, *Philosophy.*

85. Joseph Margolis, *The Flux of History and the Flux of Science* (Berkeley, 1993).

86. Chaim Perelman, *The Realm of Rhetoric* (Notre Dame, Ind., 1982).

87. John Lukacs, *Historical Consciousness: The Remembered Past* (New Brunswick, 1994).

88. Carl G. Hempel, "The Function of General Laws in History," *Journal of Philosophy* 39 (1942): 35–48.

89. Louis O. Mink, "History and Fiction as Modes of Comprehension," *New Literary History* 1 (1970): 541–558.

90. Maria Villela Petit, "Thinking History: Methodology and Epistemology in Paul Ricoeur's Reflection of History from *History and Truth* to *Time and Narrative,*" in *The Narrative Path: The Later Works of Paul Ricoeur,* ed. T. Peter Demp and David Rasmussen (Cambridge, Mass., 1989), 33–46.

91. Quoted in Carr, *Time,* 183.

92. Karl R. Popper, *The Poverty of Historicism,* 3rd ed. (New York, 1961).

93. Bruner, "Ethnography."

94. Maurice Merleau-Ponty, "Everywhere and Nowhere," in *Signs,* ed. Maurice Merleau-Ponty (Evanston, Ill., 1964), 126–158.

CHAPTER 2

Past and Present as Narrative Constructions

JEROME S. BRUNER

What is gained and what lost when human beings have recourse to the narrative mode of construing meanings?

The usual answer to this question is a kind of doxology delivered in the name of "the scientific method": Thou shalt not indulge self-delusion, nor utter unverifiable propositions, nor commit contradiction, nor treat mere history as cause, and so on. Story is not the accepted stuff of science and "logic." If meaning-making were always dedicated to achieving a "scientific" understanding of the world, that would be one thing. But neither the empiricist's knowledge through the senses, nor the rationalist's route through necessary truths suffice: neither alone nor both together capture how ordinary people go about assigning meanings to their experiences—say, what a "cool" greeting from a friend meant, or what the Irish Republican Army meant by not using the word "permanent" in its 1994 ceasefire declaration.

Such meanings are neither sternly category bound nor even governed by base-level categories or prototypes. Rather, they grow in the dynamics of encounter—in response to assumptions about intersubjectivity, out of the requirements of praxis, by reference to normative standards—all of which are "nonstandard" criteria by which we assess whether we have got successfully from what is said to what is meant, from what seems the case to what "really" is. Although the scientific method is hardly irrelevant to all this, we all know that it is not the "all and only" of how we understand the world, for meaning attribution is drenched in folk psychology and practicalities of action, in the norms of one's culture.[1] And we know that the "nonstandard" criteria for

---

Notes for this section begin on page 40.

weighing meanings are particularly powerful when we construe meanings by recourse to their place in some fitting narrative (which we can call accordingly "narrative meanings"). Are narrative meanings, then, all just particular, idiosyncratic, and fitted to the occasion? Or are there also some universals in the realities we construct through narrative construal? I think there are indeed universals, and I think that universals are essential to living cooperatively in a culture. Indeed, cultures typically forefront these universals to keep the system on the road—through the procedures of law, through covert and overt coercion, and especially through education. To make my point, I want now to sample ten such universals of narrative construal. I choose ten not to propose a narrative doxology, but to clarify what follows from the narrative construal of meaning for our conception of "reality."

A few preliminaries are in order first, however, mostly having to do with what impels the present exercise. Why are so many people now so concerned with the nature and uses of narrative? Let me answer only for psychology. We already know from discussions of the "interpretive turn"[2] that there is widespread malaise in psychology with both the rationalist's and the empiricist's account of how "reality" is constructed—of how we achieve an understanding of our worlds. Old-fashioned empiricist "learning theory" died of a self-denying behaviorist ordinance: you cannot begin to deal with meaning if you start by banning mental life from your purview altogether, even if you only pretend to do so, which is what it mostly amounted to. But pretense can be fatal. Piaget's constructivist rationalism seemed, for a while, to fall the breach: at least he dealt with how the world seemed at different ages, and what children made of it. But now Piaget's muted rationalism has also come under sharp attack as too abstract, too founded on a notion of a generalized logical rationalism. Piagetian rational competence is supposed to be nourished and matured by the nutriment of experience. But the growth of the child's knowledge of "reality," critics argue, seems not to be even or smooth enough to justify attributing it to the orderly unfolding of rational principles. A leap ahead in one domain does not necessarily presage a comparable leap "across the whole board." Indeed, understanding a concept or principle in one domain does not assure it will be understood when instantiated in other domains. Understanding seems to be far more domain-specific than had been suspected: it does not automatically transfer like credit in an international banking system.

Piaget, a masterful observer, had, of course, encountered this unevenness often enough. He had even given it a name, *décalage,* a noun derived from the verb *décaler,* which simply denotes displacement in space or time. In fact, Piaget waved the problem aside as though it were a slight squeak in the otherwise smooth turning of the rational wheels. But other investigators continued to find large and stubborn discontinuities in the "transfer" of understanding from one domain to other formally isomorphic ones. How, where, and when original understanding had been achieved often mattered greatly. All this was more serious than a mere failure to replicate.[3] For if understanding and meaning-making are indeed domain specific, then this must imply that domains, so called, are worlds of their own, ones in which there are local heuristics and implicit procedures that enable or resist rational principles being brought locally to bear. The construal of meanings develops an integrity appropriate to the domain in which it occurs, each domain a self-sealed little "reality" of its own—rather like a little culture with its own toolkit of heuristics, its own criteria for governing what meanings make sense for action, intersubjective negotiation, and for meeting the canonical norms.

Not everybody was surprised by this turn of events in psychology, especially not anthropologists, who have long observed the self-contained nature of domains of knowledge and practice.[4] There is even a word in French for it: *déformation professionelle*. So now the shoe is on the other foot: psychologists always thought that parochialism was what needed explaining. Now it turns out that a universalizing rational intellect needs as much explaining as a localizing one. All cognition is "situated" cognition, and one aspect of situatedness is the meaning locally assigned to what we are doing and where we are doing it.[5] In response to this new view, and following the lead of Seely-Brown and Collins, the expression "distributed intelligence" has come into use to highlight the intimate relation between understanding (or meaning construal) and the nature of the situation in which it is achieved.[6] Distributed intelligence is always captive of its domain; it reflects a microculture of praxis—the reference books one uses, the notes one habitually takes, the computer programs and databases one relies upon, and perhaps most important of all, the network of friends, colleagues, or mentors on whom one leans for feedback, help, advice, and even just for company. Your chance of winning a Nobel Prize increases immeasurably if you work in a laboratory where somebody has already won one, not just because of "stimulation" or "visibility," but because you share access to a richer distribution network.[7]

So it is probably as true of the sciences as it is of messy daily life that the construal of meaning is not from some Appolonian "view from nowhere."[8] The young child, engaged in understanding the world of nature, really ought not to be characterized as a "little scientist."[9] That leaves out all the quirkiness and parochial specialization that "being a scientist" generates—the worlds of James Watson's Double Helix or of Richard Feynman's memoirs, or of Abram Pais's Einsteinian world.[10] The subcultures of science are neither like classroom cultures nor like the ordered microcosm of a psychologist's experiment. Indeed, when you make science classrooms more like the quirky habitats of working scientists—full of the humor of wild hypotheses, of the exhilaration of unconventional procedures, and the rest—the dividends in better performance are quickly evident.[11] Learning to be a scientist is not the same as "learning science": it is learning a culture, with all the attendant "nonrational" meaning-making that goes with it.

In sketching out ten ways in which narrative construals give shape to the realities they create, I have found it impossible to distinguish sharply what is a narrative mode of thought and what is a narrative text or discourse; each gives form to the other, just as thought eventually becomes inextricable from the language that expresses it and eventually shapes it—W.B. Yeats's old dilemma of how to tell the dancer from the dance. As our experience of the natural world tends to imitate the categories of familiar science, so our experience of human affairs comes to take the form of the narratives we use, for we use them not only to tell, but also, and first of all, to form them.[12]

And now to the announced ten features of narrative:

1. A Structure of Committed Time

A narrative accounts for events occurring over time, and it segments time not by clock time, but by the unfolding of events—at least into beginnings, middles, and ends. Even when we try to excise or "sociologize" the temporality from narrative, by referring, say, to the "the inevitable plight of the poor" or "the class struggle," the effort fails, for such terms implicate the unfolding of events over time. The time involved, as Ricoeur has noted,[13] is "humanly relevant time," whose significance is given by the meaning assigned to events within its compass, assigned by both the protagonists in the narrative and by the narrator in the telling. Some close students of narrative, such as William Labov, locate this inherent temporality of narrative in the meaning-preserving sequence of clauses that make up narrative discourse itself.[14] But while this is a useful linguistic point, it may obscure something deeper in the nature of narrative as a mode of thought. The temporal sequence of clauses certainly preserves meaning in a sequence such as "The king died. The queen mourned." But there are other conventionalized ways of expressing personal/durative meanings besides strict clausal sequencing (for example, flashbacks and flashforwards, temporal synechdoche, and so on). As Nelson Goodman quite rightly insists, there is an ensemble of ways of representing the human events of a narrative.[15] Narrative painting is a good example, in which the beholder imposes sequential structure without the aid of sequenced clauses, as would also be the case in the films of Robbe-Grillet, such as *Last Year at Marienbad,* in which prolepsis and analepsis are so cunningly used. What underlies our grasp of narrative is a "mental model" of its aspectual durativity—time that is bounded not simply by clocks, but by the humanly relevant action that occurs within its limits.

For all this, narratives seem to generate gists or morals (as in Aesop, for example) that suggest they have a push toward atemporal generality—even time-linked gists "a stitch in time saves nine." This may be why stories fall into genres, a matter to which we turn next.

2. Generic Particularity

Narratives deal with (or are "realized" in) particulars. But particularity seems only to be the vehicle of narrative "realization," for particular stories are construed as falling into genres or types: bad-boy-woos-nice-girl, bully-gets-his-comeuppance—even just-the-sort-of-thing-that-happens-in-our-family. From Aristotle to today, thoughtful students of narrative and drama have puzzled over the chicken–egg question about whether genres "generate" particular stories, in the sense of leading us to construe sequences of events according to their generic prescription, or whether genres are mere afterthoughts that occur to tidy academic minds? Two arguments predispose me to take genres as generative of their particulars. The first is the commonsensical one that certain stories just seem alike—versions of something more general, however particular they may be. Stories beget stories; they "remind" people effortlessly of "like" stories. This suggests that particular versions of the bad-boy-nice-girl tale are instances of a natural kind, much as Golden Delicious, Granny Smiths, and Cox's Pippins are versions of the natural kind, apple. But the phenomenological argument is not altogether convincing: one man's natural kind may be another's artificial kind.

The second argument is more powerful. To put it very briefly (for we shall be returning to it later), the characters and episodes of stories take their meanings from—are "functions" of—more encompassing narrative structures. Stories as wholes and their constituent "functions" are, in this sense, tokens of more inclusive types. The bad-boy-woos-nice-girl script requires filler episodes, and a range of them will serve appropriately. The "tempting of the nice girl" can be accomplished by presenting her a lavish gift, telling her of your Rolls Royce, referring to your famous friends, and on down the list. The lavish gift itself can be exotic orchids, a box at the opera, or even an endless golden thread. The particular of a narrative is achieved by its fulfilling a generic function. And it is by this "function filling" that narrative particulars can be varied or be "filled in" when omitted.

3. The Reasons for Action

Narratives are about what people do and what befalls them. What they do narratively is neither by chance nor is it strictly determined by cause-and-effect; it is motivated by beliefs, desires, theories, values, or other "intentional states." "Narrative actions," as you could call them, imply intentional states. Experimental (literary) narrative sometimes depicts action in a way that ruptures this connection between action and the intentional states that are its background—a literary trick sometimes used, for example, by Michel Leiris.[16] But even "antinarrative" fiction counts on the reader recognizing it as a departure from the expected, as off the track. When physical events play a role in story, they do so as "setting," interesting for the effects they have on the acts of protagonists and their intentional states and moral circumstances (as when a storm at sea creates the cowardice of Lord Jim deserting his pilgrim ship). As Baudelaire put it, "The first business of an artist is to substitute man for nature."

Yet intentional states in narrative never fully determine the course of action or the flow of events. Some element of freedom is always implied in narrative—some agency that can intrude on a presumed causal chain. Agency presupposes choice. Even when agency is reduced to near zero—as in Beckett's novels and plays, or in the "anonymist" novel of Jules Romain, *The Death of a Nobody*—its effect is achieved by contrast to narrative expectancy. Perhaps it is the ever-present intrusive possibility of human choice that pits narrative against the notion of causality in the human domain. Intentional states do not "cause" things. For what causes something cannot be morally responsible for it: responsibility implies choice. The search in narrative is for the intentional states "behind" actions: narrative seeks reasons, not causes. Reasons can be judged—evaluated in the normative scheme of things. And high on the agenda of narrative is exploring the reasons for action, reasons that can then be judged.

4. Hermeneutic Composition

What do we mean when we say that the comprehension of narrative is hermeneutic? For one thing it implies that no story has a single, unique construal. Its putative meanings are, in principle, multiple. There is neither a rational (formal) procedure to determine whether any particular "reading" is necessary as logical truths are necessary, nor an empirical method for verifying any particular reading. The object of hermeneutic analysis is to provide a convincing and noncontradictory account of what a story means, a reading in keeping with the particulars that constitute it. This creates the famous "hermeneutic circle": trying to justify the "rightness" of one reading of a text not by reference to the observable world or the laws of necessary reason, but by reference to other alternative readings. As Charles Taylor puts it, "we are trying to establish a reading for the whole text, and for this we appeal to readings of its partial expressions; and yet because we are dealing with meaning, with making sense, where expressions only make sense or not in relation to others, the readings of partial expressions depend on those of others, and ultimately of the whole."[17]

Since the meanings of the parts of a story are "functions" of the story as a whole, and, at the same time, the story as a whole depends for its formation upon appropriate constituent parts, story interpretation seems irretrievably hermeneutic. A story's parts and its whole must, as it were, be made to live together, and when a story captures our interest, we cannot resist the temptation to make them do so. That is what creates narratives' hermeneutic compulsion.[18] Some literary theorists and philosophers of mind argue that we resort to hermeneutic procedures only when a text or the world it depicts is "confused, incomplete, cloudy."[19] We are certainly more aware of falling into the interpretive mode under these circumstances. But is it really the case that interpretive thinking is forced upon us by poor illumination? Is this not confusing a process with our self-consciousness about it? A certain kind of facile narrative seduces us into thinking that it is simply about "the world as it is," with no thought needed. The famous Martian invasion "created" by Orson Welles's *War of the Worlds* did not stop interprative thinking; it simply channeled it by a brilliant exploitation of ready-made hermeneutics.[20] "Readings" of the broadcast were rife with narrative interpretation—"readerly ones," as Roland Barthes calls them. Barthes distinguishes between "readerly" texts and "writerly" ones, the former relying on routinized, well-rehearsed interpretive reactions, the latter provoking the hearer into reconsidering the speaker's task of creation.[21] Both are hermeneutic. Automatized interpretations of narratives are like "default settings" of a computer.

One feature of the hermeneutic compulsion is the push to know "why" a story is told under "these" circumstances by "this" narrator. Narratives are not taken as "unsponsored texts" cast by fate upon a printed page.[22] Even when the reader takes them in the most "readerly" way, he rarely renounces his right to question the narrator's motive for telling, or his own privilege of interpreting what has been told in the light of it. There is always a countervailing force to create an impression of "voices" or "sources" that are objective, authoritative, omniscient—the famous omniscient narrator. But this condition is itself not to be overlooked as uninteresting. In consequence, the issue of interpretation—or at least, "readerly" versus "writerly" interpretation—is inevitably at the fulcrum of struggles for power. So while narrative carries with it what I've called a "hermeneutic compulsion," the right to exercise it is everywhere and always a sport of struggles for power.

The philosopher Hilary Putnam proposes two principles that bear on this point. The first is a principle of benefit of doubt, the second a principle of reasonable ignorance. The first "forbids us to assume that ... experts are factually omniscient," the second that "any speakers are philosophically omniscient (even unconsciously)."[23] We judge their accounts accordingly. At the other extreme, we are charitable toward ignorance and forgive children and neophytes their incomplete knowledge, "filling in" for them as necessary. Although Putnam is not speaking directly about narrative hermeneutics—our "readings" of how stories should be construed—the principles are relevant to it. There must be many more like it—for example: "every narrator has a point of view and we have an inalienable right to question it."

5. Canonicity and Its Vicissitudes

To be worth telling, a narrative must run counter to expectancy, breaching canonical script or deviating from what Hayden White calls "legitimacy."[24] This feature of a narrative is usually called its reportability. Breaches of the canonical are often as conventional as the scripts that they violate—tales of the betrayed wife, the cuckolded husband, the fleeced innocent, and so forth. They are the stuff of "readerly" narratives. The "narrative reality" of the world, in consequence, tends, on the whole, to seem banal: life imitating readerly texts.

But there is another side to this story. For convention is a prodigious source of boredom. And boredom, like "necessity" in the proverb, is also the mother of invention. I will not be the first person to have commented on the role of boredom in creating the "literary impulse."[25] Indeed, referring back to the ideas of Šklovskij and Jakobson on *literaturnost*, some literary theorists even take the function of literature to be an attack on banality—using language in a way to make the all too familiar strange again. So conventional scenarios provide a rich opportunity not only for "reducing uncertainty," as is often argued, but also for exciting innovations that dispel the boredom that an excess of certainty produces.

We avail ourselves of this opportunity not only in the public spheres of literature, journalism, and history, but also in the privacy of construing meanings. But given the safeguards of verification built into the logical-propositional mode of construing meanings, it is the narrative mode that serves best in this pursuit of freshness and excitement. The innovative storyteller becomes a powerful cultural figure so long as his or her stories can be taken as "interesting" variations on conventional narrative scripts, guides to seeing what had never before been "noticed," yet guides that do not quite trespass on the forbidden. The shift from Hesiod to Homer, the advent of "inner adventures" in Laurence Sterne's *Tristram Shandy*, the advent of Flaubert's perspectivalism, of Joyce's epiphanies of the ordinary, or of Beckett's psychic reductivism—any of these can serve as examples. Each in their way tempts a new genre into being: Flaubert begets Italo Calvino or Roger Garnes or Malcolm Bradbury or David Lodge; Joyce begets Beckett; and one can even see reflections of long-gone Sterne in the contemporary novels of Don DeLillo or John Updike and in the plays of John Guare.

Eventually, new genres become old banalities. And so goes the construal of history: ideologically motivated revisionisms are often tempting out of their sheer freshness. Whatever covert populist ideology may have motivated the *Annales* historians in France, their volumes on the history of everyday life are refreshing for their contrast to the "kings-cabinets-and-treaties" histories from which they diverge. Without our being complicit, none of this would happen. Nor would we, without this hunger for freshness, be such robust defenders of the right to free thought and speech. Nor would we be so tolerant of scurrilous journalists, so intrigued by "gossip," or so uncertain of the limits of libel law. So while it is perfectly evident that we consume Barthesian "readerly" stories by the bushel, our fascination with innovative "writerly" stories leaves us strikingly ready to construe the world in fresh registers.

The power of fresh language adds to this susceptibility. The Russian Formalists used to distinguish between the plot of a narrative, its fabula, and its mode of telling—what they called its *sujet*.[26] Tzvetvan Todorov, who follows in that tradition, argues that inventive narrative language not only "fabulates" new plots, but renders previously familiar ones problematical by compelling fresh interpretive activity, which brings to mind Roman Jakobson's famous dictum about literature "making the ordinary strange again."[27]

6. Ambiguity of Reference

What a narrative is "about" is always open to some question, however much we may "check" its facts. For its facts, after all, are "functions" of the story. Narrative realism, whether "factual," as in journalism, or "fictional," is a matter of literary convention. Narrative creates or constitutes its reference, the "reality" to which it points, making it ambiguous in a way that the philosopher's reference does not. The atomic "single definite referring expression" is thwarted by the necessarily "functional" Proppian way that narrative manages reference. Even proper names in narrative are subject to this "whole–part" ambiguity. The Bloomsbury of a Virginia Woolf novel or story may, in some decontextualized sense, be "located" on a London A–Z Map, but it is not the Bloomsbury of the story. Nor can it even be said to be a "token" of the "type" Bloomsbury. Its role in the story—its function—is what defines it. The St. Stephen's Green along which Leopold Bloom strolls in Joyce's Ulysses can no more be checked for its singularity of reference as a "real place" in Dublin than can Leopold Bloom. Neither "Bloomsbury" nor "The Green" are in any strict sense "instances of the category" that one might think they are members of—certainly not in the sense that the term "a London neighborhood" can be imbedded in the broader category of "London neighborhoods."

This anomalous state of things led the linguist Roman Jakobson to distinguish two "axes" of language: a horizontal one and a vertical one. The vertical axis is the one illustrated by hyperonomy–hyponomy: country-city-neighborhood-block-address, England-London-Bloomsbury-Such Street-27b. The horizontal Jakobson axis, at least in his account, is given by the place of a word in an utterance, and by the role it plays in that sentence. So, knife-fork-plate-glass-claret-conversation form a horizontal axis constructed around an utterance dealing with a dinner party. One could say, then, that the horizontal axis is a somewhat meandering line through a conventional scenario, in the way that "board" becomes an element in one scenario that fits with "carpenter" and, in another, with "corporation."

Yet one might say that every time one refers to something in context, its reference becomes "horizontally" ambiguous—and this is so. This is probably why a dictionary is not of much help in deciding whether "board" is a piece of timber or a level of corporate authority. Conventional linguists sometimes deal with this aspect of meaning by invoking a distinction between denotative and connotative meanings, but that helps very little: Is "board" connotatively or denotatively one or the other of its construals? Perhaps this anomaly is what makes some of us uneasy at Frege's distinction between "reference" and "sense" as the two aspects of meaning,[28] not that such a distinction is insupportable in utterances such as "The cat is on the mat." In that example, any surplus meaning that relates to the requisite softness of mats upon which cats typically come to rest is plainly the "sense" and not the "reference" of the utterances.

Narrative construal (and interpretation) marinate "reference" in "sense" to the point where the former becomes only a way through which the latter expresses itself: Moby Dick is a whale and the book by that name is a tale about hunting for him. So why is he a white whale? Melville confided to Hawthorne that the book's "secret" was that Moby Dick stood for stifling "white" Christianity, the hunter-whaler *Pequod* was manned by a heathen crew, and so on.[29]

Is this only the case for "fiction"? Surely not. This is evident in the handling of news stories, particularly so when they are complex, as most business "scandals" are, for example. They very quickly get converted into polarized "excuse stories." Why did a once minister of trade and industry in the Irish Cabinet, later the prime minister, change his mind so "suddenly" about providing insurance coverage for beef shipments to Iraq by one Mr. Larry Goodman, a very rich and very suspect business operator. How could he have done so when "everybody in the know" knew that much of the beef was not of Irish origin but "intervention" beef from other countries in the European Union? The story (and its two contrastive versions) is of too familiar a genre to need retelling. And like many such, it will go unresolved. But I must add one detail.

There was a special Beef Tribunal appointed, chaired by a highly respected justice of the Irish Supreme Court. Shortly before the tribunal's report was released publicly, the prime minister, to whom it had been sent first out of courtesy, announced to the press that he had been "completely exonerated." In legal fact, the report was ambiguous, as such documents usually are. A few days after it was released, the leading Dublin newspaper, *The Irish Times,* ran a feature article listing fees paid to solicitors retained by the Beef Tribunal during its investigation. They were enormous, even as lawyers' fees go. The impression created was that all parties, even the impartial investigators, were "out for their own." By the time the issue reached the floor of the Dail (the Irish Parliament), virtually everything said or done by anybody was so subject to second thoughts, reconstruals, and arrières-pensées that a truly "postmodern" condition prevailed. Nothing happened in the Dail, except that it was noticed in the month following that all the major parties in Irish politics had lost badly in the opinion polls. In the end, it was not so much the facts that bothered the public, for the facts had rather disappeared in the marinade of narrative functions that they had come to serve. The facts, the sheer "referential" stuff of the Beef Tribunal's report, had finally been cooked out of recognition by the senses they had been made to serve. I offer this example not so much as a "typical" story, but as an emblematic one.

7. The Imperative of Genre

It may be all well and good for Alastair Fowler to say that a "genre is much less a pigeonhole than a pigeon,"[30] much less a drawer than what comes to lie in it. That may be the reaction of a literary theorist faced with carping critics in a typical boundary dispute. For the rest of us, genre have an astonishing, almost supernatural imperative. They embody something "real." So what might it be?

We can think of a genre as characterizing either a text or how a text is construed. Mary McCarthy wrote magazine short stories in several genres, mostly in what Northrop Frye called the genre of "irony."[31] She then organized the stories into a book, sequencing them by the age of the female protagonist. Between the stories she added commentary about her own life, and published the lot as an autobiography entitled *Memories of a Catholic Girlhood*. Thereafter (and doubtless to her dismay), readers almost invariably greeted each new story she published as a fresh installment of her autobiography. Both McCarthy and her readers were playing a risky game. For reading a text in the light of self-revelation is almost incommensurate with reading it in the light of story.[32]

So what, then, are genres, and where are they? How do we reconcile these two kinds of genres, the mental and the textual? One familiar way of resolving this puzzle is to say that both are, as it were, "representations" of universal human plights, one contained in memory, the other "in the text." But surely genres must be something more than just conventionalized representations of universal human plights. Conflicts of loyalty, the self-defeating spiral of greed, the vagaries of romance—for all that they may be universal, they can still serve as the stuff of very different genres: comedy, tragedy, romance, or irony. Plight, after all, is only fabula.

McCarthy's "The Man with the Brooks Brothers Shirt" is not just a story about meeting an interesting stranger. It is a way of thinking about strangers in anonymous urban society, about intimacy, and about convention. It depends more on its way of telling—its *sujet*—than on its plot. A *sujet*, then, is a way of telling that embodies a way of thinking about or imagining the world.[33] Perhaps that's why translating narrative from one language to another is so difficult.[34]

It is not surprising either that what writers write and how they are read do not always go in parallel. Edna O'Brien shocked her Irish readers with her early novels: she wrote them in protest against a woman's plight; readers took them as salacious explorations of infidelity. Today O'Brien's stories are hailed even in the respectable Dublin daily press as echoing a new and pioneering sensibility toward the male-dominated plight of women caught in the grip of passionate love, and her public readings are packed appreciatively in these times with the daughters of mothers who were shocked in theirs.[35] For narrative construal is deeply affected by cultural historical circumstances. In that respect, Alistair Fowler is right about genre being more a pigeon than a pigeonhole. Or, as Clifford Geertz puts it, genres get blurred.[36] But there are, nonetheless, imperatives for a genre, because we cannot begin to construe meaning without some sense of the way of thought and the way of reading that is required.

Which is hardly to say that particular genres are written into the human genome, or even that they are culturally "universal." But genres qua genres are universal. Indeed, no natural language that has been studied is without genres (for example, ways of conducting discourse, ways of construing the topics involved in the discourse, speech registers, and even idiolects characteristic of the discourse—often a specialized lexicon as well).[37] We would not know how to begin construing a narrative were we not able to make an informed guess about the genre to which it belonged. Genres, I would conclude, are culturally specialized ways of envisaging and communicating about the human condition.

8. The Vehicle of Changing Norms

Stories pivot on breached norms. Yet, save in Aesop and in homiletic tales, it is not usually clear how a particular breach exemplifies a larger "moral," or whether something new has been added of something old subverted. Nor does this slightly subversive aspect of narrative have to be "intentional," that is, planned by teller or narrator. There are cultural conventions everywhere that guide storytelling in this "indirection," whether it is a mythic tale being told by a shaman,[38] a real one of an ocean passage by a Pulawat navigator,[39] or *Death in Venice*, written by the master storyteller/moralist of his generation. Stories "worth telling" are ones that lend themselves to such anomalous framing. Biblical stories are particularly bright examples. What is breached in the Christian version of a Deity born to an ordinary woman: Mary as Mother of God and Queen of Heaven, news of which is brought to her in the Annunciation by an archangel messenger? Of course it is a sharp break with the Hellenic tradition of a "blooded" pantheon, so to speak, with power always descending but always transcendant. But is it really that alone? It seems to be metaphorically in keeping with such other "populist" stories in the christological genre as Jesus driving the money changers from the temple, the loaves and the fishes, and so on. Yet, when one studies pictorial representation of the Annunciation, it is soon evident that "populism" is an oversimplification of what had been set in moral motion. What did Piero della Francesco have in mind portraying the Virgin as a haughty young noblewoman receiving the Archangel's announcement with an expression of accepting the inevitable responsibility that went with her station? And how intriguing that Lutheran Virgins in Annunciations after the Reformation become less worldly, less well born, less haughty.[40]

To move to our own times, consider the narrative depictions in the coverage of the funeral of Richard Nixon, or of Jacqueline Kennedy Onassis, or of the draft riots at the time of the Vietnam War. Narrative carries echoes of changing norms in a manner that other forms of construing meanings cannot.

Return, for example, to Kenneth Burke's celebrated account of the dramatic "pentad." It consisted, recall, of an Agent, Action, Scene, Goal, and Instrument, with an imbalance in the conventional "ratio" between any of them being the Trouble that was the "engine" of the narrative. Nora in *A Doll's House,* for example, is a rebellious Agent in an inappropriately bourgeois Scene, and so forth. But Burke's pentad now seems epistemically thin in this age of skepticism. He emphasizes plight—fabula—as if it were given. His "dramatism" is morally and ontologically concerned with a cultural world whose arrangements are settled: they "exist." His Grammar of Motives is a product of the 1920s.

In the last quarter of the twentieth century, dramatism became epistemic, gripped not just by "what happens," but by the puzzle of how, in a turbulent world, we come to know or construct our realities. "Troubles" now inhere not only in a mismatch between a protagonist and her setting, but also in a protagonist's internal struggle in construing that setting at all. Flaubert's early and "revolutionary" perspectivalism gradually becomes more explicit in Julian Barnes's *Flaubert's Parrot;* Italo Calvino makes interpretation itself the "trouble" in his *If on a Winter's Night a Traveler.* In another genre, Michel Foucault writes of the construction of history and of "the archeology of ideas," and Eric Hobsbawm of the "invention" of traditions. In the early 1990s, a play of the season on Broadway was about a young black person who exploits the "correctness" of a well-placed and sophisticated New York couple by impersonating a college friend of their son's and builds a "scam" around it. Whereupon the playwright, John Guare, is sued by a young black person who alleges that the play was slanderously based on a "real-life" episode reported in the press in which he was involved. "Cover-up" becomes an emblematic concept, "smoke and mirrors" a popular metaphor. The "inward turn" of the novel becomes an inward turn on life itself.

The shape of breached norms and of the stances they evoke are not historically or culturally "once and for all"; they express a time and circumstance. Hence, the "same" stories change, and their construals change in sympathy, but always with a residue of what prevailed before. One "consolation of narrative" may be its very sensitivity to changing norms. If its archetypal "sameness" consoles, then the other side of the coin may be its chimerical quality.

One sees the same normative sensitivities in the law as in the novel, in historical writing, in journalism, even in gossip—though it alters more slowly and with more explicit justification. I had occasion recently to review the rather long, involved, and troubled history of zoning ordinances in force in American states and municipalities. The power to zone private property in America is under law an extension of police power exercised "to ensure public health and welfare." The original controlling image was a community's right to keep a "gunpowder magazine" from being placed right next to the village green. But zoning law since colonial days has reflected virtually every social change, every breach in expectancy, every violated legitimacy through which America has lived. After Emancipation, for example, it argued from the norm of "natural" segregation of the races. The growth of cities introduced the narrative of progress through commerce and industry; waves of immigration from abroad hardened neighborhood lines and doomed the "tenement" to commercial districts; the flight to the suburbs after the rise of suburban rail service reintroduced the utopian ideal of model homes in model communities on lots of a size and price to be out of reach of the "undesirable." Then the civil rights movement, along with the decay of inner cities, opened a new perspective on exclusionist suburban zoning. Even changing norms of sexuality have had their impact, relating first to "cohabitation" in single-family dwellings and then, inevitably to what constituted the "single family" of a single-family dwelling. There has not been a decade in the last century and a half of American legal history when a major zoning case was not either before or pending in the United States Supreme Court.[41] "Where-we-live" is, after all, the Scene in Kenneth Burke's dramatistic pentad, and each word in the expression has been subject to reinterpretation in the light of the prevailing norms. "Place" as a creator of narrative Troubles is as sensitive to norms in the docket of Supreme Court litigation as it is in Joyce's Dubliners stories or in Ibsen's plays.[42]

9. Inherent Negotiability

Coleridge's dictum that we suspend disbelief in listening to a story was intended for fiction, but it carries over into "real life" as well. We accept a certain essential contestability of stories; this is what makes narrative so viable in cultural negotiation. You tell your version, I tell mine, and only rarely do we need litigation to settle the difference. We easily take competing story versions with a perspectival grain of salt, much more so than arguments or proofs. Judy Dunn's remarkable book on the growth of social understanding in children makes plain that narrative negotiation starts early and is ubiquitous.[43] It may be this readiness to consider multiple narrative construals that provides the flexibility needed for coherence of cultural life.

10. The Accrual of History

Life is not just one story after another, each narratively sufficient unto itself. Plot, characters, setting—all recur again and again as cast, as "There you go again," as "Here we are again." We stabilize our worlds with an enduring pantheon of gods, with metanarratives of continuing fortunes or misfortunes, with our own circle of friends given to their particular foibles, and above all, with an identity-conserving Self who wakes up the next day still mostly the same. The sense of constancy we feel about our setting is also remarkable: "that's how it goes here in Carbery" (or New York or Perpignon). Ronald Dworkin proposes that precedents in law are like "continued stories."[44] Whatever history is, it is certainly not "one damned thing after another."[45] So too culture, so too our memory of things past. We impose coherence on it, make it into history.

That "history making" has not been studied more as a psychological phenomenon is probably less an oversight than a blind spot created by the archaic conviction that history is just "there" and in no need of being constructed. Obviously, historiographers have always been an exception to this rule, but they have usually stayed inside the walls of the academy.[46] So how do we cobble our narratives together to assure that the "reality" we construe by their use has the continuity over time that we require? And how much continuity do we require? Doesn't memory itself provide the continuity and time binding necessary?

Well, "memory" hardly begins to account for how one puts together the "story" of one's own life, let alone why we Americans include a potted Monroe Doctrine in our "continuing national story" while "forgetting" the equally stunning and symbolic Civil Service Act of 1883. Historical continuity is no problem for the hard sciences. They substitute "universal principles" for it: the law of gravity is forever, so long as there is mass and space. But "history" is full of quirky particulars that follow each other, and maybe even "follow" from each other. We create a continuity and then locate ourselves in its invented stream. Jews everywhere have always used as a scaffold of continuity a diaspora from a homeland. Now one hears of a diaspora in the forced emigration of blacks from Africa under slavery, even of an Irish diaspora in the Great Famine and the impoverished century that followed it. We even begin to appreciate that there are "procedures" by which families construct a collective family continuity through "dinner-table talk."[47]

Why do we find historical causality so irresistible? Take a classic example. Pope Leo III crowns Charlemagne Holy Roman Emperor at the Vatican on Christmas Day in 800 in the presence of the great and powerful of the then Europe. Irresistibly, some think of this event as a first step on the way toward the European Union a millennium later. It is so easy to move forward or backward in time from that long-ago Christmas day—backward to Pope Leo's concern with the steady Muslim advance and with the Vatican's need to cultivate allies to stem it; forward to the Thirty Years' War and the Treaty of Westphalia that ended it. Never mind the vast literature on the dangers of historicism. Even the well versed can't resist the temptation.

But something else needs explaining, too. We cultivate our "continuing story," to be sure.[48] But we also create "turning points" on those continuing stories, pivots in time when the "new" replaces the "old." We even do this in the microhistory of autobiography. The moralizing Tennyson even proposed a rule of divine intervention to account for this odd quirk.[49] It is not as odd as it seems, however. Hayden White helps us here.[50] Following the French *Annales* historians, White distinguishes between historical *annales, chroniques,* and *histoires.* An *annale* is made up of selected events roughly fixed in date, as, for example, in the Annals of St. Gall:[51]

> 709. Hard winter. Duke Gottfried died.
> 710. Hard year, deficient in crops.
> 711.
> 712. Floods everywhere.
> 713.
> 714. Pippin, Mayor of the Palace dies.
> 715.
> 716.
> 717.
> 718. Charles devastated the Saxons.
> 719.
> 720. Charles fought against the Saxons.
> 721. Theudo drove Saracens from Aquitaine.
> 722. Rich in crops.
> 723.
> 724.
> 725. Saracens came for the first time.
> 726.
> 727.
> 728.
> 729.
> 730.
> 731. Blessed Bede, the presbyter, died.
> 732. Charles fought the Saracens at Poitiers on Saturday.
> 733.
> 734.

The list is constructed of "happenings," the rest of time being when "nothing happened." So the annalist's selected events are themselves little turning points in history—candidate turning points in an implicit history. Pippin's death earns a place in the St. Gall annal: strong men matter in palace politics. The St. Gall annalist, like his colleagues since, is a trouble collector, always sensitive to Labov's "precipitating events"; they may upset the narrative apple cart, create the conditions for the overthrow of a legitimate state of things.

Hence, the *chronique,* whose function is to explore such possibilities. *Chroniques* accrue event-sized narratives into life-sized ones. A *chronique* would make it clearer why Pippin mattered, perhaps by dealing with the narrative of a reign. A good example is the deligitimizing of European power by Napoleon, with the Congress of Vienna as a restoration of legitimacy. In the telling of that *chronique,* the "restoration of legitimacy" theme is even helped by such details as Count Rosomovsky being the Russian ambassador to the Congress—the patron of Beethoven's "deathless" middle quartets!

The trouble with "great" *histoires* is that it is hard to fit them into the shape of narrative. In the classic view, they are supposed to give coherence and continuity to chronicles. That involves many difficulties, however. For one thing, *histoires* go beyond lifetimes, beyond the reach of the usual protagonists struggling their way out of trouble. What to do with Marx's transition from feudalism to capitalism to socialism, or with Hegel's "spirit of history"? History in the large, consequently, moves toward large-scale sociology. It is not surprising that philosophers of history regularly propose that history be treated as a science governed by "covering laws," rather like a sequence-rationalizing sociology,[52] only to have this proposal rejected by fellow historians who insist that the leap from *chronique* to *histoire* is not to be confused with getting over the chiasm between the humanities and the sciences, between interpretation and explanation.[53] But this is not a matter to be settled here.

Clio, the Muse of Poetry, remains the Muse of History, though her reign may be threatened. The point I would make, rather, is that we seem inevitably to convert impersonal, non-narrative *histoires* into more narrative guises. That is why I began the discussion with Pope Leo III crowning Charlemagne Holy Roman Emperor in the Great Hall of the Vatican on Christmas Day in the year 800 in the presence of a company of nobles as was rarely seen in the Europe of that day, a "Europe" that surely did not exist in the minds of any in attendance at that glittering event. Having then recounted that Pope Leo's act might have been motivated by the "Saracens" advance into Europe (the annalist of St. Gall also makes mention of them being "turned back" at Poitiers), and having thus evoked the idea of "alliance," it becomes almost impossible to resist a search for some narrative protagonist who "carries" that "idea" forward—perhaps Napoleon, caught in the romantic notion that the best allies are those you have conquered, or the fine gentlemen of the Congress of Vienna promulgating a gentlemanly notion of "balance of power."

The accrual of history is an extraordinary narrative enterprise, shot through with alien elements not easily tamed into Proppian "functions." It seems to be dedicated to finding some intermediate ground where large-scale, almost incomprehensible forces can be made to act through the medium of human beings playing out a continued story over time beyond mind.

The philosopher W.T. Stace proposed two philosophical generations ago that the only recourse we have against solipsism (the unassailable view that we cannot prove the existence of a real world, since all we can know is our own expecience) is that human minds are alike and, more important, that they "work in common."[54] One of the principal ways in which we work "mentally" in common, I would want to argue, is by the joint narrative accrual of history. For history, in some modest and domesticated way, is the canonical setting for individual autobiography. It is our sense of belonging to this canonical past that allows us to frame our self-accounts as somehow impelled by deviation from what was expected of us, while still maintaining complicity with the canon. Stace's concern with solipsism seems terribly old-fashioned two generations on. We would more likely be concerned today with whether the accrual of narrative into history leaves us connected or alienated.

What I have tried to do in this chapter is to describe some of the properties of a world of "reality" constructed according to narrative principles. In doing so, I have gone back and forth between describing narrative mental "powers" and the symbolic systems of narrative discourse that make the expression of these powers possible. It is only a beginning. My objective has been merely to lay out the ground plan of narrative realities. The daunting task that remains now is to show in detail how, in particular instances, narrative organizes the structure of human experience—how, in a word, "life" comes to imitate "art," and vice versa.

Notes

1. See Jerome S. Bruner, *Acts of Meaning* (Cambridge, Mass., 1990), in particular 33ff.

2. For the interpretive turn see, for example, Paul Rabinov and William M. Sullivan, eds., *Interpretative Social Science: A Reader* (Berkeley, 1979); the relevance of interpretative operations for psychology is also made clear by Bruner, *Acts of Meaning*.

3. See Judith Segal, Susan Chipuran, and Robert Glaser, *Thinking and Learning Skills* (Hillsdale, N.J., 1985).

4. Gladwin's study of Puluwat navigators who cross large bodies of open water by the use of a system of navigation part magical, part dead reckoning, and part celestial, is a case in point. When Gladwin finally convinced one navigator to take along a compass on one of his journeys, having first "explained" the idea of a polar coordinate system to him, the navigator, when he returned, explained to Gladwin that the compass was fine, that on the whole it had checked out well against the local way of doing things. See Thomas Gladwin, *East Is a Big Bird* (Cambridge, Mass., 1970).

5. A striking example of this new emphasis is provided by Carol F. Feldman's study, *The Development of Adaptive Intelligence* (San Fransisco, 1974). Feldman's study examines the way in which a highly concrete second language spoken only at home by Hawaiian-Japanese children discourages the very "transfer of training" that the children are expected to develop in English at school. The children need to be given special "transfer" practice to overcome this tendency.

6. John S. Brown, Allan Collins, and P. Duguid, "Situated Cognition and the Culture of Learning," *Educational Researcher* 18 (1988): 32–42.

7. Harriet Zuckermann, personal communication (Department of Sociology, Columbia University, New York).

8. See Bruner, *Acts of Meaning;* Clifford Geertz, *Local Knowledge* (New York, 1983); Gladwin, *East Is a Big Bird;* Renato Rosaldo, *Culture and Truth: The Remaking of Social Analysis* (Boston, 1989).

9. Sue Carey, *Conceptual Change in Childhood* (Cambridge, Mass., 1985).

10. James D. Watson, *The Double Helix: A Personal Account of the Structure of DNA* (New York, 1969); Richard Feynman, *Surely You're Joking, Mr. Feynman: Adventures of a Curious Character* (New York, 1985); Abraham Pais, *Subtle Is the Lord: The Science and the Life of Albert Einstein* (Oxford, 1982).

11. Ann L. Brown and Joseph C. Campione, "Communities of Learning and Thinking, Or a Context by Any Other Name," in *Developmental Perspectives on Teaching and Learning Thinking Skills: Contributions in Human Development*, ed. Denna Kuhn (Basel, 1990) vol. 21, 108–126.

12. Much of what I have to say will be familiar to some from the discussion on the "interpretive turn" in the human sciences. Indeed, that turn itself reflects the debates in literary theory of the last decade or two. I think one can even date it from the appearance of the collection of essays found in W.J. Thomas Mitchell, ed., *On Narrative* (Chicago, 1981). If some of what I have to say about "narrative" and "reality" seems old hat, it may be that the argument here is an annex to that collection.

13. Paul Ricoeur, *Time and Narrative*, vol. 1 (Chicago, 1984).

14. William Labov and Joshua Waletzky, "Narrative Analysis," in *Essays on the Verbal and Visual Arts* (Seattle, 1967); William Labov, "Speech Actions and Reactions in Personal Narrative," *Georgetown University Roundtable on Languages and Linguistics* (1981): 219–247.

15. Nelson Goodman, "Twisted Tales: or Story, Study, or Symphony," in Mitchell, *On Narrative*, 99–115.

16. See Michael Leiris, *L'Age d'homme: Précédé de la littérature considérée comme une tauromachie* (Paris, 1964).

17. Charles Taylor, "Interpretation and the Sciences of Man," in Rabinow and Sullivan, *Interpretive Social Science*, 25–72, here p. 28.

18. How little we know about how human beings go about the hermeneutics of narrative. Its neglect by students of mind can probably be traced to its remoteness from both the rationalist and the empiricst traditions. There is much new interest in the nature and use of narrative, as in psychoanalysis, in life history writing, and in clinical practice. See, for example, Donald P. Spence, *Narrative Truth: Meaning and Interpretation in Psychoanalysis* (New York, 1982); Roy Schafer, *Retelling a Life: Narration and Dialogue in Psychoanalysis* (New York, 1992); William Lowell Randall, *The Stories We Are: An Essay on Self-Creation* (Toronto, 1995); Donald E. Polkinghorne, *Narrative Knowing and the Human Sciences* (Albany, N.Y., 1988). Examples for the impetus of narrative psychology can, of course, also be found in the present anthology. It is to be remarked that this new interest is only lightly engaged with studying the psychological processes that constitute hermeneutic analysis.

19. Charles Taylor, "Interpretation and the Sciences of Man," in *Philosophy and the Human Sciences* (Cambridge, U.K., 1985), 15–57, here p. 15.

20. Hadley Cantril, *The Invasion from Mars* (Princeton, 1940).

21. Roland Barthes, *The Responsibility of Forms: Criticial Essay on Music, Art, and Representation* (New York, 1985).

22. Roy Harris, "How Does Writing Restructure Thought," *Language and Communication* 9 (1989): 99–106.

23. Hilary Putnam, *Mind, Language, and Reality* (Cambridge, U.K., 1975), 278.

24. Hayden White, "The Value of Narrativity in the Representation of Reality," in Mitchell, *On Narrative*, 5–27.

25. See Patricia M. Spacks, *Boredom: The Literary History of a State of Mind* (Chicago, 1995).

26. For a discussion of uses of this distinction by the Russian Formalists, see Jerome S. Bruner, *Actual Minds, Possible Worlds* (Cambridge, Mass., 1986).

27. Tzvetvan Todorov, *The Poetics of Prose* (Ithaca, N.Y., 1977). For a good statement of Roman Jakobson's view, see his "Linguistics and Poetics," in *Style in Language*, ed. T. Sebeok (Cambridge, Mass., 1960), 350–377.

28. Gottlob Frege, "Über Sinn und Bedeutung," *Zeitschrift für Philosophie und Kritik* 100 (1892): 25–50.

29. See Henry A. Murray, "In Nomine Diaboli," *New England Quarterly* 24 (1951): 435–452.

30. Alastair Fowler, *Kinds of Literature* (Cambridge, Mass., 1982), 37.

31. Northrop Frye, *Anatomy of Criticism* (Princeton, 1957); idem, "Fictional Modes and Forms," in *Approaches to the Novel,* ed. Richard Scholes (San Francisco, 1966), 23–42.

32. In a study by Feldman, Kalmar, and myself, for example, a Primo Levi semiautobiographical story about an episode at a riverboat stop in rural Russia was read to some subjects as "autobiography," and to another group of subjects as an adventure story. The former group, to take only one finding, found the characters in the story rather "thin"; the others found them "rich" and "suggestive." Such is the influence of genre even on the details of a textually identical account. See Carol F. Feldman and David Kalmar, "Autobiography and Fiction as Modes of Thought," in *Modes of Thought: Explorations in Culture and Cognition,* ed. David Olson and Nancy Torrance (Cambridge, U.K., 1996), 106–122.

33. See Feldman's interesting discussion, "Genres as Mental Models," in *Psychoanalysis and Development: Representations and Narratives,* ed. Massimo Ammaniti and Daniel N. Stern (New York, 1994), 111–121.

34. See Reuben Brower, ed., *On Translation* (Cambridge, Mass., 1959). This book contains critical essays on the task of translating fiction and nonfiction into English by some of the great practitioners of the craft.

35. Distinguished columnist of *The Irish Times* Nuala O'Faolai reported on the packed audiences of middle-class women to whom O'Brien was giving readings of her new published novel (*The Irish Times*, September 10, 1994).

36. See Clifford Geertz, "Blurred Genres: The Refiguration of Social Thought," in *Local Knowledge: Further Essays in Interpretive Anthropology* (New York, 1983), 19–35.

37. See Feldman, "Genres as Mental Models."

38. Stanley Diamond, "Introductory Essay: Job and the Trickster," in *The Trickster: A Study in American Indian Mythology,* ed. Paul Radin (New York, 1972), xi–xxii.

39. Gladwin, *East Is a Big Bird.*

40. See Jaroslav J. Pelikan, *Mary through the Centuries: Her Place in the History of Culture* (New Haven, 1996).

41. The legal and sociological literature on the settlement of quarters of living and business is, of course, immense and sometimes written in an extraordinary technical legal language. Only some texts and contributions on which my remarks are based shall be quoted: *Village of Euclid v. Ambler Realty Co.,* 272 U.S. 365 (1926); *So. Burlington County NAACP v. Township of Mt. Laurel,* 67 N.J. 151 (1975); *Village of Belle Terre v. Boraas,* 446 U.S. 1 (1974); Lawrence G. Sager, "Tight Little Islands: Exclusionary Zoning, Equal Protection, and the Indigent," *Stanford Law Review 21* (1969): 767–800; Richard Briffault, "Our Localism, Part 1: The Structure of Local Government Law," *Columbia Law Review* 90 (1991): 1–115; Thomas Ross, "The Rhetoric of Poverty: Their Immorality, Our Helplessness," *Georgetown Law Review* 79 (1991): 1499–1547. An excellent discussion of the question of how the law concerning zoning contributed to the realization of the ideal of the American suburb divided by classes can be found in Robert Fishman's, *The Rise and Fall of the Suburb* (New York, 1987).

42. See Frank Kermode, "Secrets and Narrative Sequence," in Mitchell, *On Narrative,* 79–97.

43. Judy Dunn, *Beginnings of Social Understanding* (Cambridge, Mass., 1988).

44. Ronald M. Dworkin, *Law's Empire* (Cambridge, Mass., 1986).

45. I have not been able to trace the origin of this well-known antihistorical chestnut, though I believe that whoever may have invented it, it was Henry Ford, in a moment of modernist enthusiasm, who put it back into circulation in America.

46. There have been notable exceptions to this rule; indeed, interest in historiography seems to erupt out of the academy almost rhythmically. See Leopold von Ranke, *The Theory and Practice of History* (Indianapolis, 1973); Friedrich Nietzsche, *Untimely Meditations* (Cambridge, U.K., 1983, first published in German, 1873); Robert G. Collingwood, *The Idea of History* (Oxford,

1961); Herbert Müller, *The Uses of the Past: Profiles of Former Societies* (New York, 1952); Karl R. Popper, *The Poverty of Historicism* (London, 1957); and most recently, and perhaps most vividly, Michel Foucault, *The Archeology of Knowledge* (London, 1972). All, in turn, have emerged from the privacy of professional history to capture the public imagination.

47. I am greatly indebted to Professor Elinor Ochs for sharing her still unpublished work of "dinner-table talk" at an informal seminar at UCLA during the winter term of 1990.

48. As to the distinction between *annales, chronique,* and *histoire,* see also Jerome S. Bruner, "Autobiography and Its Genres" (paper presented at the symposium "The Construction of the Self," University of Toronto, 1994).

49. "The old order changeth yielding place to new / And God fulfills himself in many ways / Lest one good order should corrupt the world" (Alfred Tennyson, "The Passing of Arthur," in *The Norton Anthology of English Literature,* 4th ed., ed. Meyer H. Abrams (New York, 1979) vol. 2, 1206.

50. See White, "The Value of Narrativity."

51. The following register of events of the years 709 to 734 [which is from the first volume of the scriptores series *Monumenta Germaniae Historica*—Ed.] is quoted by White, "The Value of Narrativity," 11.

52. See the classic essay by Carl G. Hempel, "The Function of General Laws in History," *The Journal of Philosophy* 39 (1942), 35–48.

53. Lawrence Stone, *The Causes of the English Revolution, 1529–1642* (London, 1972); Louis O. Mink, "Narrative Form as a Cognitive Instrument," in *The Writing of History: Literary Form and Historical Understanding,* ed. Robert H. Canary and Henry Kozicki (Madison, 1978), 129–149; Dale H. Porter, *The Emergence of the Past: A Theory of Historical Explanation* (Chicago, 1981).

54. See the s.v. "Stace, Walter T.," *Encyclopedia of Philosophy* (New York, 1967).

CHAPTER 3

Telling Stories, Making History
Toward a Narrative Psychology of the Historical Construction of Meaning

JÜRGEN STRAUB

It is a superstition, however, that our internal image of a thing represents its empirical being. Do things somehow, at such moments, by their own power, so to speak, copy themselves, write themselves, photograph themselves onto a pure passivum?

—Friedrich Nietzsche

The contemporary discussion of *Geschichte* and *Historie,* of historical consciousness and historical thought, seems infinite.[1] We especially encounter these terms when our collective practice is beset by difficulties, crises, or conflicts over psychosocial or political orientation. In Germany, more than fifty years after the end of the National Socialist dictatorship, there are still very "immediate" reasons for the importance of historical reflection. Whatever may occasion this reflection, historical communication is never simply a "medium" through which *groups* understand themselves—their past, present, and future. *Individuals,* too, understand themselves, that is, their lives, against the horizon of the history in which they find themselves involved. Theoretical and empirical interdisciplinary work on biographies, for example, has long considered history as the context of individual life histories, illustrating how closely autobiographical self-thematization can be interwoven with historical consciousness.[2] Our historical consciousness often shapes our autobiographical accounts and self-understanding quite directly. We understand both what happens to us and the attitude we assume toward it *historically;* we understand our present situation, our present activity or inactivity, and finally our plans for the future, in

---

Notes for this section begin on page 85.

part *historically*. The same holds for how we understand others. But what does it actually mean to understand oneself, one's world, and the world of others *historically?* What is the *historical construction of meaning?* What is *historical thought?* What does it even mean to regard the world, oneself, and others—as yet prior to any particular intellectual claims—as *historical reality?*

The present study attempts to answer these questions. The answer is not only provisional, as in any other scholarly study; it is also, and all too obviously, incomplete. The following reflections can only provide certain points of departure and signposts for a research program for the psychological analysis of the historical construction of meaning. They should at least state clearly the driving questions; they are not intended to answer them.

Like the other contributions to this volume, the following is intended to incrementally advance the *psychology of the historical construction of meaning*, which is presently still in its infancy. As in most of the other contributions, the focus will be on the *narration of stories*. On the one hand, I will understand narrative here from the perspective of the psychology of language, knowledge, and communication—as a *specific form of speech and a specific communicative practice* distinct from description, reportage, argument, and so on. On the other hand, I will consider narrative from the perspective of the psychology of cognition or of thought—as a mode of *thought*, in accordance with Jerome S. Bruner's influential distinction between the paradigmatic (or logical-scientific) and the narrative mode of thought.[3] The primary goal of this discussion is to justify the thesis that narration is central to the psychology of the historical construction of meaning—that the latter must, in other words, be devised as a *narrative* psychology. To justify this thesis, of course, we will have to reflect on its implications and consequences.

History as Meaning-Structured World

The historical construction of meaning can be understood as the most general and comprehensive term for the object of the present investigation. The term should indicate that my basic concern is with a *practice*, with a particular way of acting. The historical construction of meaning is a practice that operates with symbolic means. We have already stressed the role of language, and especially the narration of stories. A narrative psychology of the historical construction of meaning should also be interested in any symbolic form or practice that leads to the *active construction of historical realities*. Such historical construction is a particular mode for creating, negotiating, and inspecting reality as a symbolically represented world. It shares an important, fundamental feature with every other such mode: it represents reality as a *world structured to have meaning, to make sense*. It is based on previous interpretation, and is accessible only to someone who can perform an act of interpretation. Without interpretation, scholarly or not, there could be no history. Accordingly, the narrative psychology of the historical construction of meaning will here be understood as an interpretative psychology of action and of culture. Here, too, we should recall Bruner's formulation: narrative psychology is concerned with *acts of meaning*, and at the same time, performs such acts.[4]

Along with acts that create or communicate historical realities as symbolic constructs, we will examine these constructs themselves. In theory, historical realities *are* constructs. In many cases, such realities do not survive the moment of their construction. They then have the same transitory character as acts of human imagination and communication, and are just as ephemeral as other mental images, thoughts, and words. Such constructions are occasionally "recorded" or "objectivated"; however, whether by recording technology (as of verbal communication), or by the materiality they assume as they are being produced, without additional labor, as with writing. Documents, monuments, memorials, museums, and other meaningful objects or places are such objectivations of the historical construction of meaning, or, in other words, records of actions that represent historical reality with symbolic means, that is, records that create and shape this reality through creative acts.

The historical construction of meaning thus includes every act that somehow leads to the construction and representation of realities that we consider specifically historical. A "historical reality" should be understood, roughly and provisionally, as the representation of a *temporal succession* and *temporal coherence* comprised of events, happenings, and actions that are successive, but at any rate, coherent, by experiences and expectations that are significant to a *group*—to at least *one* group. History is basically made up of stories in which several, and in theory, arbitrarily many, people are involved—stories that concern, affect, or move many people. In contrast to biography, history represents a collective destiny; it represents the experiences, expectations, and orientations of more than one person. History thus acknowledges no temporal limits: everything that has been, is, or could be, might be its material. These two features—at least one group as a reference subject and no limit on temporal extent—will here be regarded as the defining features of history, and, hence, of historical consciousness.[5] It is thus always a historical reality that concerns conditions and circumstances, relationships and events thematized in their process of becoming—thematized as having become. We need hardly go as far as the defenders of the historical-hermeneutic maxim that Being can *basically* only be understood as that which has become. We need not embrace an ontology that conceives Being as Motion, nor an epistemology that equates "the understanding of 'what' with 'where from,' the understanding of a thing's essence and of its becoming, or, to use a different terminology, an actual with a genetic understanding."[6]

That conceptions of historical reality and acts of historical understanding are so prevalent in our culture is precisely what the psychology proposed here has to consider. Indeed, it is precisely this mode, this form of understanding, that it has to investigate. As a symbolic construct, history or historical reality is here basically a representation, and as such, it is analytically distinct from history as event. This terminological resolution takes up a familiar distinction generally made to take into account the ambiguity of the word *history*. We conventionally delineate two meanings. *History* thus designates that which happens as well as its subsequent representation, the *res gestae* as well as the *historia rerum gestarum*.[7] Karlheinz Stierle, from a literary-critical and action-theoretical perspective, which of course is not interested merely in the transformation of the first kind of history into the second, divides representation again into "history" on the one hand and "the text of history" on the other, in order to be able to separate the act of representation from the resulting objectivation. Not only is each term then defined relationally—what happens is the basis for history, which in turn is the basis for the text of history—but each expresses the fact that all three are realities sui generis.[8]

Here it should suffice to distinguish what happens in history from its representation through historical consciousness. The two basic meanings are already distinguished in everyday usage, albeit neither systematically nor consistently: "Thus history [*Geschichte*] in the expressions 'experiencing history,' 'making history,' or 'a part of history' means something different than in the expressions 'studying history,' Herodotus as 'the father of history.'"[9] Gerhard Bauer notes that the term *Historie* was long ago proposed as a designation for the latter concept, but it failed to catch on. We will follow this terminological distinction without being able to strictly maintain it. For one thing, the scholarly literature would be inconceivable without the term *Geschichtsbewußtsein* (consciousness of history); indeed, it would be completely artificial to avoid it and speak only of *historisches Bewußtsein* (historical consciousness). These terms will here mean one and the same thing. If a definition has to presuppose a certain "content," then either term can serve as a predicate with at least three moments: *a subject* possesses historical consciousness, and this consciousness is the consciousness *of something*. This "something" is thus strictly distinguished from the historical events themselves, which are to be made present to historical consciousness. Historical consciousness might possibly *represent* this past in a sense introduced by Karl Heussi, and stated more precisely by Paul Ricoeur, but it can never coincide with it: a representation *stands for* something by *taking its place*.[10]

This substitution can never be analyzed as a mental reproduction, however impartial or correct it claims to be. Representation, as Ricoeur describes in more detail, keeps to *traces* of what was, either given or still to be located. We appropriate the past by means of the *indirect reference* "proper to knowledge through traces."[11] A representation in this sense is neither identical with what is represented, nor does the latter remain completely alien and incomprehensible, as an other: historical representation operates neither "under the sign of the Same," nor "under the sign of the Other," but rather, according to Ricoeur, "under the sign of the Analogous," in order to demonstrate and make plausible a kind of *similarity* or inner correlation between itself and what it represents, thus producing understanding. The point is that historical representations basically are or comprise transformations, mediations. The hermeneutics established in the various disciplines, as well as a poetics or aesthetics attending especially to the formal definition of historical representations, could clarify essential aspects of this transformational and mediational process. A rhetoric with an interest in pragmatic aspects could also contribute to the analysis of historical depictions.[12]

Historical representations make the past present, basically under the condition that the representative is different from what is represented. This difference includes that between signifier and signified. "Representation" can additionally mean *(a)* below, as well as, more specifically, *(b)*:

> *(a)* This definition is more inclusive because the aforementioned interpretation, according to which representation is a *substitution*, always has a practical significance: *A* represents *B*; a particular subject represents something else in its act and in the result of its representation, and that generally means: it takes the place of other subjects, speaks in their place—about them, for or against them, in their name. The standpoint and the perspective, the worldview and vocabulary, the "rhetoric" of the representing subject inevitably determine its presentation of the past. Thus, historical representation is clearly a *practice* (as well as the objectivation of an act), and as such, it is implicated in issues of power.[13]
>
> *(b)* The significance of the relational concept of representation results not least from its specific function in the context that interests us here. *A represents B*: this relational definition, in the case of historical representation, always marks a *temporal difference*. A representation is a presentation of something that, although it must be represented within a present and from a present perspective, is precisely *not present*. Historical representations distance what they represent first, and in a particular way, *temporally,* in order then of course to create temporal relations and contexts. How precisely this happens, and in particular, what role individuals play are the central issues here. I will return to this point.

Historical representations are meaning-structured constructions and constructs. *Acts of meaning* lead to structures of meaning. Of course, historical events themselves are not simply part of an undifferentiated natural history without sense or meaning; they are, after all, shaped by human activity. History is not symbolically mediated after the fact, but is itself a world created entirely by means of verbal and representative symbolism, and necessitating, one way or another, the hermeneutics, the poetics, and the rhetoric of historical representation.[14]

Historical Consciousness: A Competence-Theoretical Approach

The term *historical construction of meaning* is, as we said, the most inclusive term for the object of the psychology we are proposing; in other words, it can include completely opposed historical constructions and representations of reality. This term does not distinguish whether such constructions and representations derive from unconscious, preconscious, or conscious subjective processes, whether they are cognitively complex or simple, rational or irrational, or emotionally, morally, or objectively motivated. In contrast, the concept of *historical consciousness* offers a *theoretical construct* with which we can then discuss a particular kind of historical construction of meaning—in other words, acts of *thought*, especially, historical-narrative thought as a specific "mode" of human *intelligence*. Insofar as historical constructions can be shown to be cognitive, intellectual acts, they should be understood as products of historical consciousness, that is, of a particular competence that individuals possess. The theoretical psychology of the historical-narrative construction of meaning is not least concerned with this cognitive competence.

If we keep in mind the previous definition of "historical consciousness," then this is quite evident: the psychology of the historical-narrative construction of meaning is clearly interested in more than the particular contents of the historical consciousness of certain individuals. From a theoretical view, historical consciousness is not only some person's consciousness, and this person's consciousness "of something," but is, at the same time, a general *psychological competence* as well. The proposed psychological theory of historical-narrative competence would deal with a specific *form* of thought (and therefore of speech and nonverbal action). This theory, accordingly, has to demonstrate its object by defining this *form* or *structure*. In this respect, our theory follows the model established by Piaget and Kohlberg. This reference is, of course, very provisional, and should be regarded with caution. The tenability of defining historical-narrative competence on the analogy of ethical consciousness, for example, is impossible to determine at this stage of the research, especially since the various criticisms of Piaget's and Kohlberg's theories would then have to be met. In my opinion, however, we can approach historical-narrative thought in terms of a cognitive structure constitutive for particular intellectual acts. Here, too, we are concerned with the reconstructive clarification of a competence, still formally to be defined, that we consider the precondition for performing certain acts.

In both cases, the theme is human rationality, where this faculty is regarded as internally differentiated. The "classic" fundamental distinction adopted by Piaget also separates theoretical from practical rationality; to these two forms we can add not only the faculty of aesthetic judgment thematized by Kant in his third critique, but historical rationality. It is precisely the latter, however, that remains rather unclearly defined, particularly as until recently psychologists made practically no attempt to clarify its structural preconditions (assuming that we are justified in speaking of a discrete mode of thought here). Of course, such attempts would now look much different from what they did even a few decades ago. We particularly have to guard against prematurely universalizing historical thought as a feature of the species and enthusiastically identifying it as the norm. An examination of the cultural specificity of historical thought by the contemporary psychology of historical-narrative meaning-construction can hardly avoid Nietzsche's question about "the advantages *and* disadvantages of history for life." Nevertheless, the undeniable fact that the modern West thinks historically, and the great practical consequences of this fact, are sufficient reason to investigate the general features of at least *this* type of rationally oriented speech and action. We can temporarily disregard the issues that were so important for genetic structuralism as a developmental theory, although they suggest a particularly important task for a future didactics of history.

The crucial point is that historical consciousness, a theoretical construct, is a faculty to which specific acts of cognition can be attributed. For reasons detailed below, a psychology of historical-narrative thought has to be concerned with the rationally oriented ability to construct history as well as to justify action historically. Historical consciousness, as historical-narrative competence, is conceived as the formalistically definable faculty of *thinking and arguing historically*. If the reader will permit the metaphor, we can interpret it as an orientative faculty: when we think historically, we move mentally in a particular construction or representation of historical reality, and can justify the direction of our movements.

We can hardly discuss the theoretical aspects of a psychology of the historical construction and accept the restrictions customary in this discipline. A theory of the historical construction of meaning will necessarily be interdisciplinary, as will become clearer in the following sections. In the next section, I return again to the concept of "historical consciousness." The significance of the narrative to the construction of history will be explained in the section on "Narratological and Temporal-Theoretical Assumptions." The section on "Historical Narrative, Contingency, and Narrative Intelligence" will justify the conception of historical consciousness as thought (and hence as a specific form of intelligence), after remarks on the different functions of historical-narrative constructions. Finally, the section "Narrative Competence and Other Aspects of the Historical Construction of Meaning" will demonstrate why any psychology of historical consciousness requires far more than just narratological conjecture, since historical competence itself requires far more than simply the ability to narrate and to understand stories. In this connection, I will return to the point that a psychology of "historical consciousness" basically concerned only with historical-narrative thought can only be a part of a broader psychology of the historical construction of meaning.

Historical Consciousness: Fundamental Concepts

There is no generally accepted definition of "historical consciousness." Karl-Ernst Jeismann notes its generally unspecific usage within various discourses, and complains about the lack of an accepted definition.[15] Hans-Jürgen Pandel also points out that the rampant usage of the term "historical consciousness" in the political media as well as in historical pedagogy contrasts with the small number of attempts at its conceptual and theoretical clarification.[16]

I want to understand history, and historical consciousness along with it, as a specific mode for organizing our experiences and expectations—as a "reflexive," distantiating mode of dealing with change.[17] When we think and speak historically, we are operating with *temporal distinctions.* The conventional, and in its basic form, still relatively simple model comprises the triad of past, present, and future. This model's complexity can easily be increased. We might initially subdivide both past and future: for example, the thematized past could be understood as a former present, to which various interpretations of the past and expectations for the future could, in turn, be ascribed. If we thus attempted to understand the actions of people in the past, we could not only differentiate our present from the past's present, and bring this difference into play as part of our attempt, but consider interested action as a temporally complex construct: this action, too, was carried out by human beings who shaped their practice in light of *their* (possibly contradictory or ambiguous) interpretations of the past and expectations of the future.

A further increase in complexity results as soon as we discard the conventional idea that the temporal system of past, present, and future should be thought of as strictly linear. As soon as we understand past, present, and future as *reciprocally dependent* symbolic constructs, we have already abandoned such simple linearity. Every past, as, for example, George Herbert Mead presented in his theory of time and history in *Philosophy of the Present,* thus becomes a conception determined completely by the moment in which it was created.[18] Arthur C. Danto has stated this theorem more precisely in his *Analytical Philosophy of History.*[19] For Danto, too, the past can never be conclusively defined. The past is necessarily subsequent, and hence dependent on retrospection. It is variable and, in fact, subject to variation, as suggested, and sometimes almost required, by discoveries that throw a new light on the old. "Openness" is not only characteristic of the future, but of the past as well, though of course in a particular way. What happened certainly did happen, and yet what happens does not thereby become the past. What holds for history holds for historical consciousness, and for every past with which this consciousness operates: we are always dealing with constructs. Of course, such constructs are not invented of whole cloth; they elude arbitrariness, or at least individual arbitrariness. Historical constructions have causes and motivations that exceed the desires and motivations merely of individuals: we all understand what Aleida Assmann has aptly called "the stabilizing factors in memory"; there are also—and not only in scholarship—criteria for the social acceptance of particular constructs.[20] If one were to connect this acceptance to the rational grounds formulated in the context of historiography generally, one could speak of the reasonableness of historical constructs. All these bases and institutions for regulating constructions of historical reality do not alter the fact that historical constructions, including images of the past, belong to that present and to that present practice which they serve. A past is different, as we said, from what happened in the past: a past is a reality sui generis, and only as such can it fulfill an orientative function for individuals and groups acting in the present.

Historical constructions have only limited room for play. When we comprehend "reality against the horizon of its alterability," we create a historical difference, and operate with this difference.[21] Of course, this hardly means that such differences could not be related to one another, or that history could not be thought as a continuous unit. In fact, just the opposite is true. We think of history as a context, as a unity that relates and integrates heterogeneity. This immediately becomes clear from current definitions of "historical consciousness." So, for example, Karl-Ernst Jeismann and Jörn Rüsen emphasize that acts of the historical construction of meaning operate with temporal differentiations *and* relativizations. History is thus ultimately conceptualized as *the unity of its differences,* and this unity is a product of active acts of synthesis and integration by linguistic subjects.

The standpoint, perspective, priorities, and vocabulary of the respective subjects are thus definitive for the operations and objectivations of historical consciousness. A subject achieves something when it thinks and speaks historically. Jeismann characterizes these acts as follows. "History" as a subject-dependent construct has three preconditions, namely, the "analysis of past processes and relations," the "interpretative organization into historical contexts," and last, but not least, the "creation of an evaluative relationship to the present."[22] The operations of the historical consciousness produce a construct that Jeismann, in an often-cited phrase, defines abstractly as an "inner coherence of interpretation of the past, understanding of the present, and perspective on the future."[23] Of course, as subject-dependent constructions, these operations, as well as their products, are socioculturally mediated, that is, they are fundamentally connected to the cultural and social background of an agent, to a group practice, and, not least, to an intersubjective situation.

Rüsen essentially concurs with the preceding conceptual definitions when he understands the historical construction of meaning as "those mental procedures in which the past is interpreted in such a way that the present is thereby understood and the future anticipated. Here the three temporal dimensions are integrated into a comprehensive idea of temporal process, by which past experiences are presented in the form of a history, and remembered for purposes of orienting action and forming social and personal identities in the present."[24] Elsewhere he provides a similar definition of historical consciousness as "the quintessence of the mental (emotional or cognitive, unconscious or conscious) operations by which the experience of time is processed through the medium of memory into an orientation for life practice…. History is here conceived quite simply as interpreted time.... What is important is the past that is somehow still present, or can still be made present."²⁵

For Rüsen, memory is a "necessary condition" of historical consciousness, though clearly "memory" should be understood metaphorically here. No one can "remember" *(erinnern)* history understood as subsequent reconstruction in the same way that one remembers an experience—an agonizing toothache, a sunny day, a terrified night in a bomb shelter at the height of the war—even if the memories of contemporary witnesses provide an important source for the reconstruction of history, a source that has gained considerable importance with the emergence of oral history. When it comes to "the operations of historical consciousness," one can only speak of "the medium of memory" (Rüsen) in a metaphorical sense. "Memories," then, would be far more discursive constructs (based on knowledge), than constructs supported by experience. The discussion of a collective historical memory, an external memory next to the internal memory of persons, is obviously metaphorical, which in no way means absurd, unintelligible, or misleading.²⁶

The recommended terminological specification allows us, in contrast to Pandel, to speak metaphorically of the memories of historical consciousness. However, I will diverge from Rüsen's definition in another respect. For Rüsen, historical consciousness is *necessarily* mediated by memory. The relation to the past is therefore constitutive for historical consciousness, and the future plays a role only as a period into which expectations, orientations, and plans for the shape of the next day's practice extend. I would prefer to speak of historical consciousness even in cases where the past and memory play no role in the construction of reality—or at least no explicit role—and instead the only question is how to relate the present to the future (where, strictly speaking, the present is also present to the subject in a fashion characteristic for that subject only in memory, that is, it is bound somehow to memories). Historical consciousness is not necessarily connected to the past, but rather can more generally be conceived as a construction of temporal differences and temporal relations, as the consciousness of continuity or of difference and contingency, variability, and mutability—in short, as the consciousness of the continuity and variability constituted by change. Even this variability is present to historical consciousness as a unity, as the temporal form of process, called, precisely, "history."

Once again, this exposition makes clear that the concept of historical consciousness designates the mental operations or speech actions that produce an internal coherence between interpretations of the past, understandings of the present, and perspectives on the future, while it also designates this internal coherence. The latter can then be defined not only in terms of "content"—as a conception of concrete historical events and connections as they are affirmed by particular subjects. This temporal coherence can also be regarded theoretically, and thus as a specific, cognitive and symbolic, predominantly verbal structure. The concept of historical consciousness describes "constructions of meaning through temporal experiences," and at the same time, their result and their cognitive-structural preconditions.

To summarize the idea most important for the following exposition: the essential and specific result of the operations of historical consciousness consists in establishing qualitative, temporal distinctions and *at the same time* in constructing temporal coherences. We also encounter analytic and synthetic acts whenever we deal with historical consciousness. In every case, something present is being differentiated from something past, or from something future as it is presented, "remembered," or anticipated by a subject, *and* thus brought into a differential relation. One might designate the latter, as we have done, a *relational* act. This act can have various results (often causal relationships, but relations based on intentions or on rules). Especially important, however, and central to the theoretical definition of "historical consciousness," is some kind of connection of previously unconnected conditions, events, or acts leading to the creation of a temporal unity in the stricter sense. Of course, I am thinking of *narrative* connections, of the construction of coherence, in other words, that begins with temporal differentiations and sequentializations, which is finally only possible—can finally only take shape—as narrative, as a story.[27]

The "folding" of the three temporal dimensions into a unity implied in the concept of historical consciousness is inevitably connected to narrative acts. Historical consciousness is thus immediately dependent on narrative competence, whatever else it may also be. We can now define historical consciousness as the *orientation-forming, narrative construction of a unity of temporal differences conceived as a meaningfully structured processual form, in which fundamentally collectively significant experiences and expectations are articulated*. The concept of historical consciousness understands these constructions *simultaneously as the result of actions, as a symbolic practice, and as the cognitive-structural preconditions that individuals must fulfill to participate in this practice;* individuals who meet these preconditions thus possess *historical-narrative competence.*

The preceding account leads up to what I consider central to a psychology of the historical construction of meaning. In my opinion, such a psychology has to be built on the concept of "narrative competence." Contributions to the heterogeneous, and in the German language, somewhat underdeveloped field of *narrative psychology* suddenly take on a new interest. Various contributions to the present volume are in this tradition; others have a critical relationship to it. In any case, no further references should be needed here. Of course, we should observe that narrative psychology is extraordinarily diverse, as the essays by Donald E. Polkinghorne, Jerome S. Bruner, Kenneth J. Gergen, and Donald P. Spence show. In fact, this domain is so diverse that it might be somewhat risky to speak of "a" tradition.

At least this much is clear: from a psychological perspective, too, an inquiry into the structure, logic, functions, and development of historical consciousness leads fairly directly to the human practice of telling stories.[28] This raises the question, What exactly is the ability to tell stories, and to understand them in turn, especially stories that have to do with historical situations, events, and the orientation and identity formation processes that relate to them? What is historical-narrative competence, and how does it develop ontogenetically and biographically? What functions do historical acts of meaning-construction fulfill in the lives of individuals and of groups? What is a narrative in the first place?

In the next section, I would like to substantiate and explain the narratological approach to historical consciousness.

Narratological and Temporal-Theoretical Assumptions: A Cognitive-Psychological Approach

From a narratological perspective, terms such as "history," "historical consciousness," and "the historical construction of meaning" represent the products and procedures of the psychological and social formation, transmission, and reception of stories. Narratology considers history as narrative, or, better: fundamentally, as an integrated heterogeneity of narrated and narratable stories and episodes. We can retain this definition without necessarily ignoring the so-called non-narrative elements of the historical construction of meaning.[29] Disregarding momentarily all the pragmatic-interactive aspects of narrative competence, we are basically dealing with the linguistic and cognitive ability "to structure a text as a story."[30]

If below we often discuss "texts," the reason is a pragmatic one: unlike narrative texts, or any other objectivations of narrative activity, we cannot analyze narrative competence properly. Narratives are thus verbal or textual units with an identifiable formal structure. We assume that this structure "correlates" to a cognitive or mental structure, a *schema* that subjects possess or do not possess, depending on their level of cognitive development. Of course, this correlation should not be conceived as a strict reproduction. A narrative schema is abstract, like any other cognitive schema. It is a comparatively quite decontextualized and generalized cognitive structure.[31] A narrative schema incorporates generic as well as highly abstract knowledge; it mirrors what Nancy L. Stein and Tom Trabasso call "the prototypical properties of various experiences encountered by an individual."[32] As Stein and Trabasso demonstrate, the psychological processes by which such schemata are created and applied are unconscious to a considerable extent. Once learned, they also remain relatively stable.

The psychological concept of a "story schema" represents the cognitive aspects of narrative competence. This includes not least all those acts of memory and recall that, as more recent scholarship has shown, have a narrative structure, that is, that need to embed things in a mentally represented story.[33] The story schema is often constitutive for memory; moreover, it also enables the recipient of a story, as listener or reader, to discern narrative structures of meaning even where texts, by the standards of an ideal-typical story grammar, are incomplete. In such cases internal cognitive structures make it possible to replace gaps in texts, to work with assumptions that allow texts to be read as stories in terms of the grammar of narrative, even where such stories are, in fact, narrated only incompletely. Consider, for example, cases in which certain aspects of a story, such as a protagonist's emotions, remain implicit, and so have to be deduced by the listener or implied by the teller.[34] Or recall the ability to understand and to provide summarized presentations of a story, which also presupposes the availability of an abstract schema, in addition to more specialized acts.[35] Of course, "complete" narratives or narrative texts have to be assumed if the discussion of internal and external narrative structures, and, in particular, the concept of an "internalization" of prior external structures is to make sense. As we know, this term often appears in theoretical or empirical accounts of the acquisition of the story schema, that is, in the development of narrative competence.

The important point is that the following exposition is based on the idea of a correlation between the structure of (verbal) action as it is expressed in objectivations such as texts, and the structure of a cognitive schema available to the actors. Conclusions about an underlying competence on the evidence of performative expressions are, of course, always risky; such evidence is never conclusive. The reconstructive hypothesis to which our perspective leaves no alternative is admittedly such a conclusion. Yet empirical observations do, under certain conditions, indicate that "the structural transformations that appear in the texts must actually be understood as expressing a change in the corresponding mental concepts and schemata."[36]

If we connect a psychology of historical consciousness with the concept of narrative competence, we must first describe binding general criteria for the structure of a narrative, that is, a cognitive story schema. This is the purpose of the following paragraphs. I will be guided primarily by certain findings of Dietrich Boueke and Frieder Schülein's research group.[37] In their studies on the development of narrative ability in particular, Boueke and his colleagues have developed criteria for a "narrative" that are, in my opinion, generally acceptable with respect to the concept of narrative competence. Even if the concept of *historical*-narrative competence requires certain specifications and additions, it can still be built on these general definitions. We should point out beforehand that a great deal depends on what criteria we establish for a "narrative." If we connect competence in making and understanding historical meaning-constructs precisely to the capability of telling and comprehending stories, that much will become evident. The more complex such theoretical constructs, the "older" the "narratively competent" subjects must be. Concerning the individual criteria:

1. Every story must organize a "series of related events into a coherent sequence."[38] A story exists through particular events that should ideally be pre-

sented completely, but in any case, in sufficient detail. The "verbal units" that "express these events" must thus be "linked together into a verbal chain."[39] Of course, every text fulfills this condition, which is why the ability to produce coherence can developmentally be considered a necessary condition of narrative competence, but hardly a sufficient one.

2. The purpose of a story is to involve listeners in the narrated events, to let them take part emotionally in the drama. Of course, narrators themselves can become involved in the emotions connected with what they are representing, particularly in the case of historical-narrative representations and reflections. In any case, the narration of stories goes along with *emotional and evaluative qualifications* to the described conditions, events, changes, and consequences. These can be expressed to different degrees: from explicit qualifications to entirely implicit qualifications only discernible after extensive acts of interpretation; anything is possible here. Such qualifications can also be undertaken from different perspectives, and related to different aspects of the narrative.[40] Hence, they could place the self and the world of the narrative's protagonist at the center, for example, thereby involving listeners by providing them with opportunities to identify with the protagonist. They thus participate emotionally in the sequence of narrated events and actions, as Boueke et al. write, in the course of the narrative elaboration of *psychological proximity*. Emotional and qualitative qualifications may also take the form of an *amplification of the basic emotional quality* of entire "clusters of events," that is, not just individual events, actions, and so forth. In this way, a *valence* is articulated, and, indeed, above all in the form of a contrast between horizons of comparison. To use an imaginary example: "Before the National Socialists seized power, many people had had difficult lives, particularly because of an employment shortage, but it became far more difficult, even dangerous afterward"; this is how one might explicitly amplify basic emotional qualities. Finally, the emotional and evaluative qualifications may fasten on the unexpected, surprising elements in a story, stressing them or commenting on them. In this connection, Boueke et al. write of the *amplification of the unanticipated,* or, more tersely, of *abruptness*. The abrupt elements of a story also spellbind listeners, and perhaps even the narrator. What is important is that the listener's and perhaps the narrator's involvement, elicited by the dramatization of an event, and especially by its "affective marking," is connected not least to a criterion that is equally constitutive for stories, namely, that it has a triadic structure.

3. Stories have a beginning, a middle, and an end. We can consider this the simplest version of the basic structure, normal form, or basic schema of a story. This schema, irrespective of the details, reappears in many and otherwise very different theoretizations. Consider, for example, Bremond's structuralist functional triad of "initial situation," "basic course of action," and "outcome of the action," or William Labov and Joshua Waletzky's enormously influential model, along with other variants of the "climax analysis,"[41] all of which have an "ori-

entation" followed by some kind of "complication," and then a "resolution." One should also recall that some story grammaticians with a text-linguistic or cognitive-psychological orientation have taken Labov and Waletzky's basically triadic model more or less into account. This is the case for those authors who had criticized David E. Rumelhart's initially influential hierarchic constituent model of narrative precisely for its lack of a triadic structure, and revised it accordingly.[42] Finally, those textual analysts interested in the pragmatics or the psychological, social, and cultural functions of narrative often enough stress the dramatic structure articulated by a triadic form, and orient their work by this model.[43] The middle of the story is generally conceptualized as something special, and as definitive for the very concept of a story: the middle represents the experience of *contingency*, something unanticipated or extraordinary, an unexpected event, a crisis or complication, a rupture in normality, a disruption in plans, or something in the same line. The extraordinary event, which temporally and objectively divides the "before" from the "after"—whether positive or negative, *critical* and *contrastive*—is central to every narrative representation of change. It is the axis and the platform of the transformation by narrative of an initial condition into a final condition, the outcome of the story. Of course, this triadic structure can be combined with other methods of organizing narrative tension. Brigitte Boothe distinguishes the possible formal sequences in narratives in terms of this organization, where stories with *no complications at all* represent an interesting limit case for her model.[44] Although I would still not designate such instances "stories," Boothe identifies the following permutations of the triadic model: in those "stories" that illustrate a *uniform and monotonous continuity*, everything remains as it was. Complications in such instances acquire no significance. The story structure consisting of beginning, middle, and end, where the organization of suspense is concerned, can be represented as a *climax* or as an *anticlimax*, as a *restitutio in integrum* after a disintegration or after a climax, as *approbation, frustration, chance, antichance*, and, finally, as *enigma*. Kenneth J. Gergen offers a simpler, though somewhat comparable, typology.[45]

These criteria provide the general defining features of a story schema that subjects with narrative competence should possess. Narrative competence is the linguistic and cognitive ability to create stories in the sense delineated here, to tell them, and to understand them in turn. In connection with the development of this capability, we should suggest the following.[46] Generally speaking, what all the developmental models known to me have noticeably in common is a certain logic extending from the prosodic elements of speech and wordplay, to the mere enumeration of fragmentary and isolated events and "theme and variations" stories, to the increasingly elaborate use of temporal markings and connections, as well as logical, final (including intentional and motivational) and causal connectors, and ending in the production of sequentially coherent stories with a regular *plot*. At the midpoint of the plot stands a complication, a *skandalon*, that emotionally affects the protagonist or protagonists, as well as the narrator and recipient; the "dramatic" structure ultimately acquires its energy from this center of the story, as does the "moral of the story" and its evaluation by the narrator and listener. We should again emphasize that *plot* is not only a sequential, chronological arrangement, but some kind of transformation impelled by contingency or complication, and having a particular outcome.

Numerous studies have demonstrated that the development of narrative competence already begins at an early stage of verbal development. If we apply our criteria, however, then this capability is usually only achieved, consolidated, and fully articulated between the age of seven and ten. According to Boueke et al., children of about nine narrate like adults—in short, they possess the story schema. According to experiments by this research group, there are exceptions where children of kindergarten age prove capable of structuring a story narratively, that is, in terms of our criteria. However, the development clearly tends in a certain direction:[47] while the observed kindergarten group produced texts primarily of the "isolated" or "linear" type, and children in the second year of school produced texts classifiable as "linear" or "structured," among children in their fourth year of school, the "narratively structured" accounts unequivocally predominated over the "structured" kind (the ability to narrate and understand stories in the precise, complex, and rigorous sense could first be demonstrated as a stable and general factor for this age group).[48]

These results have at least one benefit for the narrative psychology of the historical construction of meaning. The more specific and substantially more complex *historical-narrative competence* should only completely evolve in the transition to adolescence. There are still no adequate empirical studies on the emergence of this capability, despite some promising beginnings. This is also true of a competence that is, in many respects, related to the historical-narrative competence, and perhaps represents its psychological precondition, namely, the capability of narratively (re)presenting and reflecting on one's own life.[49]

In any case, the study of the development of historical-narrative competence would require additional inquiry into the construct considered above, namely, a *general* narrative capability. Thus, it seems inappropriate simply to equate "narrative competence" with historical consciousness.[50] We do not ascribe just any stories to historical consciousness, after all, but only stories of a particular sort. Historical consciousness necessarily operates, as was explained above, with stories in which the experiences, expectations, and transformations are *collective,* that is, socially or culturally significant. Historical consciousness exceeds an individual's experiential horizon, in principle. Historical-narrative constructs place the narrator and possibly the (imagined) audience (through the aforementioned emotional-evaluative and, of course, also through cognitive qualifications) in a *relationship* to the thematized experiences, expectations, and developments. There may be several coexisting, cooperating, or antagonistic groups (groups, organizations, institutions, nations, etc.).

To sum up, if we start from the thesis that history, as a symbolic, primarily verbal-symbolic construction of an inner coherence between interpretations of the past, an understanding of the present, and expectations of the future, is constituted and communicated narratively, then the concept of "narrative competence" logically becomes central to a psychology of the historical construction of meaning. This centrality is assured by a particular property of narrative: narrative, from our perspective, expresses *change as such* in language, in a comprehensible and subject-bound form. Change, however, is here simply synonymous with historical time: history basically *is* change; historical-narrative representation is, as has already been explained, the thematization and management of change. It should be emphasized that change cannot be reduced to a concatenation of discrete moments expressing or suggesting merely different, qualitatively or quantitatively comprehensible conditions of or development of some aspect of a situation or subject. The *description* of changes, that is, "temporally complex" phenomena, already necessitates narrative language. The reason has been demonstrated by numerous authors: narrative language is the language that corresponds, specifically and uniquely, to the temporal character of human practice, or somehow gives it this character.[51] We could justifiably assert that everything expressed in narrative acquires a temporal quality and a temporal structure. Narratives concern coming and going, emergence and disappearance, permanence and mutability. They open a diachronic framework where everything must have a place. Where there is narrative, it is becoming, permanence, and transience that set the tempo.

In Ricoeur's work, based on an anthropological theory of action,[52] temporality appears as that existential structure to which only narrative language can correspond; conversely, narrativity appears as that verbal structure which has its fundamental referent in temporality. Thus, narrative and the experience of time are reciprocally constitutive, both theoretically and practically—a relationship that seems simultaneously inclusive and exclusive. For Ricoeur, time, in fact, becomes "human time to the degree that it is articulated narratively."[53] Perhaps Ricoeur's exclusive definition of the relationship of time and narrative as "necessary" goes too far. We can leave that question aside, however, as well as the question of other modes by which "human" time might be configured, if the narrative configuration is not, in fact, the only one.[54] In the present connection, however, we can leave these questions aside for a single, and, in my opinion, very good reason: *history* as a symbolically represented, intelligible coherence between the temporally different seems to me to be inevitably bound to the *narrative* structuring of what is represented. Narrative, precisely with respect to history, properly serves as a unique "language of time, a language affected by time, a language that outlines time," in Emil Angehrn's formulation.[55] Narratives open those dimensions of the human world in which historical consciousness operates and can articulate itself. In Angehrn's apt formulation:

Only through the opening of temporal space, through the rupture of the now by the past and the future, is the present constituted as the space of experience, where what is outside the subject can become "present" to it, and where the subject becomes "present" to itself. The present thus acquires a tension between presence and absence, between near and far, and it first acquires it temporally, as a conquest over the abstract, unreal punctuality of the moment. Only in reference to the not-present does the "here and now" become the experienced present, and only thus is something like a "historical space" produced where the subject acquires its "own" space, its history. Narrative always already relates to this temporal space, by presenting its object in the process of taking place.[56]

In summary, we could say that the specific reference time of the events, actions, encounters, and changes thematized in a respective narrative is preceded by that fundamental and general temporal dimension that narrative speech alone creates. Narrative as a particular form of language creates and treats realities that are in flux, which, to the modern consciousness of contingency, is a matter of course. Perhaps one could generally say that modern narratives are distinguished from traditional narratives by the radically different way they treat the narratively developed consciousness of time and of change. In the traditional understanding of self and world, time and change, as Dewey once put it, are conceived as something that damages true, and therefore, immutable Being, whereas modern, properly historical consciousness conceives true and real Being in precisely the opposite way, as Becoming.[57] Traditional narrative must thus finally *immobilize* the change it thematizes, by, for example, deploying some "eternal" origin of the All-One, some singular principle remaining, and remaining valid, beyond all change—in other words, by revealing changes as the surface phenomena of the permanent structure that constitutes reality, and at the same time, incorporates it. In contrast, modern consciousness depends on change as a mode of reality—in fact, as the decisive one, especially in narrative. Changes, as narrated time, are precisely not there leveled into a horizon of immutability, but rather are treated in such a way that they can be overcome without having to disappear. This is what distinguishes historical thinking from forms of the construction of reality that, in comparison to the modern historical consciousness and measured by its standards, operate basically ahistorically.[58]

That narrative reconstructs *(nachvollziehen)* the progression of a story as such means not least that narratives cannot be reduced to merely the outcome of the story. As soon as we regard temporality as narrative's immanent referent, it becomes evident that narrative has to be *performed (vollziehen)* as a complex verbal action if it actually intends to reconstruct the genesis and evolution, the reconstitution, and perhaps the disintegration of its "object." What is narrated remains inevitably bound to the narrative development, to the act of narration itself, and thus to the time this act requires.[59] That certainly does *not* mean that a detailed and somehow complete narrative would be absolutely necessary *to open the temporal dimension*. This can also happen when narrative is not explicit in the form of a narrative, but is "present" only in rudiments, or, more precisely, in the form of narrative abbreviations.[60] Narrative abbreviations contain stories or suggestions of other stories without themselves being stories. They can be hermeneutically explicated only by recourse to the stories that they contain or suggest. Isolated terms or concepts that simply become semantically invalid as soon as their inner relation to the past, or even the future, is ignored should be mentioned here, along with symbols in the stricter sense, or metaphors. Of course, this hardly exhausts the variety of narrative abbreviations that operate with implicit stories.

It should be clear why narrative can be regarded "as the basis of the language of history, and, in a certain sense, as its horizon and broadest frame," even if, as Angehrn rightly emphasizes, it does not comprise the whole of it.[61] The same may be said of historical consciousness, and of the historical construction of meaning generally. Rüsen has recently presented an attempt to identify the "prenarrative elements of the historical question," "protonarrative elements of historical experience," "nonnarrative elements of the question of history" and of "historical experience," as well as "postnarrative elements of historical orientation"—all likewise important for historical consciousness. Throughout, Rüsen continues to maintain that the narratological paradigm is indispensable to the theory of history.[62]

In our view, objections to the real limits of the narratological paradigm do not affect the constitutive and central function of the narration of stories and of the comprehension of narrative for the creation, transmission, and reception of history. History, we have seen, is connected to narrative temporality; history is fundamentally a narrative construct. If historical consciousness is defined as the entirety of the psychological and social structures, practices, and operations through which meaningful historical narratives, that is, stories or *narrative constructs,* are created, transmitted, and received, then clearly we *must* discuss narrative if we are significantly to understand the historical construction of meaning. History, from our perspective, that is, the historical consciousness of subjects, is necessarily bound up with a basic competence in telling and understanding stories. If we do not consider these fundamental "cognitive operations of narrative understanding" (Ricoeur), we will be unable to adequately conceptualize and investigate instances of the historical construction of meaning.

The Functions of (Historical) Narrative

Although I cannot claim to offer an already adequately reflected, systematic classification, or even a comprehensive one, I would like to present some of the important functions of historical narrative. By historical narrative, I mean both a scholarly, but above all, an everyday practice. Psychologically, the focus of interest is the narrating subject itself—its meaning-structuring acts. Historical realities, particularly in a psychological analysis of the potential functions of historical narrative, appear as subjective constructs in which the contours of a person's self and world can be discerned—and naturally not just the contours, but, insofar as sufficiently subtle analytic methods are applied, precisely also details of the qualitative certainty and of the form of the relationship that a person has to herself and her world. Since such narratives are always *directed at someone,* or when they are part of a conversation, have one or more listeners, the psychological analysis of the possible functions of narrative includes its pragmatic and social dimensions. Where narrative takes place within a group or a collective, this much is already obvious.[63]

Historical narratives as specific verbal acts sometimes fulfill functions that *they alone* can fulfill. Sometimes, however, particularly on the functional view, they are obviously related to other narratives, not only to (auto)biographies, but also to everyday, conversational narratives. Here they can be considered functionally but not contentually equivalent to other narratives. The following enumeration of the functions or functional types of (historical) narrative includes some repetition of earlier material.[64]

Temporalization and the Constitution of Reality

This function, treated in the last chapter, is fundamental, since it first creates the idea of self and world as temporally structured realities, realities that have become, can change or disappear—realities that are, in other words, properly historical realities. Within the framework of this temporally structured ideational space, actors begin imperceptibly to be oriented historically in everything they think, feel, do, or fail to do. Historical narratives construct and shape reality as a system with particular qualities. This system, connected with claims to reality, is, as narrative system, always a temporal structure in the above sense, too. Where something real is treated in terms of becoming and change, then the communication of such realities is bound to the narration of stories and the use of narrative abbreviations. From the perspective of a poetics, aesthetics, or rhetoric of the historical, not to mention a biographical perspective, storytelling appears not least as a verbal form in which the facticity claims of historical constructions of reality are necessarily clothed. Historical narrative shares the temporalization function with every other kind of narrative. Historical narrative's reality and facticity claims connect it with biographical narrative, even, for example, if the latter is concerned primarily with individuals and with the authenticity of recollection, whereas the former, of course, is also concerned with collectively meaningful experiences and expectations; this nevertheless distinguishes it from fictional narrative. This difference is no more invalidated by similarities of form, structure, and function between fictional and factually supported narratives (emphasized by Hayden White, among others) than by the fact that "factual assertions" involve a rhetoric of facticity that suggests rather than guarantees their empirical basis.[65]

Information, Knowledge Creation, and Knowledge Communication

These terms already make clear that properly historical narrative, too, is misunderstood when considered *only* in its informative function. Of course, it has this function, thus also serving the creation, reproduction, expansion, intensification, and communication of knowledge about the world. But this knowledge is not so much knowledge *about* a reality that could exist independently of subjects as something objective and observable, as rather a knowledge that lends the world it *describes, understands, and explains* the character of reality in fulfilling its informative function. Historical narrative *uno actu* creates and articulates a world; it incorporates a view of the world *(Weltanschauung)*, an image of the world *(Weltbild)*, and a knowledge about the world *(Weltwissen)* that informs, shapes, and orients the person who appropriates it.

Identity Formation, Reproduction, and Presentation

Historical narrative and reflection do not simply shape subjects cognitively. Narratives, especially historical narratives formulated from the perspective of the present, are unique articulations of a continuity that creates and maintains *coherence*. This coherence is generally perceived as a meaning-structured unity of events, occurrences, and acts. Narratives are important constituents of subjective identity in a contentual-qualitative as well as in a formal-structural sense insofar as subjects "situate" themselves in the temporal coherence presented by narrative.[66] Historical narratives also articulate or thematize—directly or indirectly—who a person is or would like to be.

Generally speaking, narratives present a form by which subjects can mark out the temporal depth dimension of their identity in particular. Historical narrative is also always concerned with reference groups relevant to identity to which the subject feels it belongs, or from which it withdraws. The historical construction of meaning is grounded not least in a subject's identifications with collectively meaningful experiences and expectations, actions and life orientations. Such identifications, as they are performed and made explicit in the course of the narration of historically meaningful stories, are (re)identifications in the consciousness of contingency experiences, as narratives happen to thematize them. As we have seen, that narratives articulate a *coherence* naturally does not mean that they necessarily "fuse" present with past. History may serve reflection on commonalities between past and present, and so contribute to the formation of tradition. It may conserve a heritage. It can just as well draw attention to differences between life then and now. Somehow, narrative, understood as synthesis and integration, establishes coherence and unity; it clarifies what has remained of the past and it explains what has changed. The narrating self places itself in some relationship to this historical-narrative assessment, thus explaining more than just itself, and giving itself form and definition (always bound to context, always just provisional). Identity formation and identity presentation make as much use of the self as they do of the other; they require identification as much as differentiation and demarcation.

From precisely the psychological perspective, the formation, consolidation or transformation of identity, and its presentation, can be considered as perhaps historical narrative's most complex acts. Such function should therefore be considered as incorporating and comprising numerous others. If we analyze it more precisely, we could discern an entire series of additional, subordinate or implicit functions, so to speak, some of which will be discussed below.

Practical Functions, Orientation Formation

Anyone who imagines and represents a reality is opens up a system of orientation, thus creating a temporal space where certain actions become conceivable, advisable, valuable or even commendable, while others become inadvisable or even ridiculous. Historical narratives disclose and close off options for action; they imply the possibility or necessity of action; they structure the space of action for people who are somehow situated within this narratively represented history. It is not least the narrative interpretations, as James Young, for example, emphasizes, that define present action.[67] The present does not only create narrative representations of the past in order to help explain the present from the narrator's perspective; narrative representations also lead into a future by suggesting certain actions to subjects. In terms of the psychology of morality, we could say that they impose responsibilities on subjects. It may be true that an excess of historical memory cripples action, obscures our sense of the present, and deprives us of the strength to shape the future.[68] On the other hand, where historical memory is deficient or entirely absent, responsible action becomes a vain hope. We can finally say that narratives regarded as complex verbal acts can be understood functionally as an orientative horizon and framework of orientation, as a means to justify or legitimate actions in the past or the present.

Moral and Pedagogical Functions

The preceding sentences touched on the moral-normative dimension of historical narratives, and thereby the (possibly) implicit historical pedagogy. Action, Charles Taylor has argued, is not simply human behavior within a physical, material space, but within a valorative and normative space as well.[69] It is *oriented* behavior in precisely this sense as well. Subjects understand themselves through acts of the historical construction of meaning, which thematize more than just temporal differences; they always involve differences on the valorative and normative level as well. Values and norms are necessarily part of the substance of the historical construction of meaning. The by now formulaic "moral of the story" can also be, in fact, the moral of history. One can critically investigate that face, as Hayden White does, and in the present volume, as Kenneth J. Gergen does, or simply approve it, but one can never completely evade the moral implications and connotations of historical narratives. As long as stories are told, and as long as these stories concern human actions, valorative and normative standpoints and objectives will play a role. Of course, narratives can themselves reflect on this fact, and listeners can do so in any case. Beyond that, historical narratives need not always provide *a single* moral resolution *(Lösung)* or maxim *(Losung)*. Narratives are oftentimes considerably more ambiguous than such critics of the narrative paradigm as Hayden White generally suppose. In any case, where morality is predominant, or even implicit, pedagogy obviously cannot be far away. Historical narratives communicate experiences and expectations, values, rules, norms, and orientations, and possibly present them with educational intent. Understood as complex speech acts, they can sometimes really serve as pedagogical calls to action.

Social Functions, Including Phatic Functions

Historical narratives do more than articulate the narrator's subjectively appropriated reality, or *his* representation of history, and thus aspects of his own identity. They also invite others to share a conception of reality. When this invitation is accepted, historical narratives create a *mutual world;* they create a basis for consensual judgments and coordinated, cooperative action. Naturally, every historical narrative also represents a response to such an invitation—it is part of a discourse. Where the topic is history, subject, agreement or rejection, consensus or dissent, are already implied. We all grow up with sociocultural representations of history. In this way, historical narratives contribute to the socialization of individuals, to social integration as well as to distinction, to the formation of tradition and cultural reproduction.[70] Precisely the stories in which history takes shape fulfill functions of sociocultural cohesion and coordinate action or interaction. They create a common present and common perspective on the future by showing the past as something shared. Of course, historical narratives are also capable of establishing sociocultural differentiation, as we indicated, by potentially ascribing different, and even radically heterogeneous, pasts to different persons or groups. Contrasting constructions of the past bring conflict to expression. Historical narratives do not just create social unity and differentiation; they also document, indicating sources of solidarity and struggle. They may occasionally treat representations of difference and help bridge them.

Particular social functions are connected to the presence of narrator and listener within a narrative situation. Historical narratives can certainly serve as *entertainment,* as amusement, as admonition, and so forth. Like all narrative embedded in concrete, interactive situations, historical narrative can fulfill *phatic* functions: the act of telling and listening can create a social bond between speaker and listener largely irrespective of the verbal content. By signaling interest, narrative creates contact, proximity: the presence and attention of one person for another. One need hardly consider this to be the basic function of conversational narrative, as does Rainer Rath.[71] This aspect, the initiation and intensification of relationships, is certainly important, however—not least when we are dealing with historical realities. Thus, historical narrative can also attempt to overcome social isolation, in at least two ways: within the concrete narrative situation, speaker and listener are no longer alone, and intensify their relationship; certainly this may take place with respect to a story symbolizing a history that from now on will be shared.

Psychological Functions in the Stricter Sense

Obviously, all these functions are psychologically significant; some, certainly, are significant for social and cultural psychology. The functions we understand as more strictly psychological have to do especially with "inner" or internal states and processes. Irrespective of how psychological realities may be constituted or expressed, or to whom they may be addressed, we are dealing with what takes place within/inside subjects themselves—*their* thoughts, feelings, intentions, and wishes. What was obviously true above is even more obvious here: the psychological investigation of the functions of historical narrative must begin with the subjects and their social reference groups. The narrative incorporation of empirical fact, its truth or accuracy, is not our primary focus here; in fact, it will concern us only peripherally.[72]

Psychological analysis, of historical narratives or otherwise, attempts, above all, to determine and understand what speakers say *about themselves and about their world,* even when they are speaking about others. Such analysis attempts to discern a subject's present situation and condition in her representation of past realities. It reads her recollection of historical scenes and events as her current *staging of her self.* Precisely this focus on the *scenic character* of narrative, or at least of certain episodes, is of the greatest significance for a psychological investigation. Historical narrative lives in the presentation of scenes and connections; the subject matter may even become secondary to the dramatization.[73]

Boothe's psychoanalytic investigations of the narratives produced by clients in therapeutic sessions apply at least partially to the interests pursued here. This is certainly valid as a point of departure: narratives of every kind can be analyzed as the scenic-dramatic modeling of either one's own experiences and expectations, *or those of others.* Someone speaking of others is also giving expression to himself, by deliberately placing himself in relation to these others, or by unconsciously bringing such mechanisms as identification or projection into play.

Like other authors in this volume, Boothe, like Freud in his time, takes a critical position vis-à-vis narrative rhetoric and the "communicative strategies of narrative persuasion."[74] Naturally, this skepticism is only a starting point. Psychoanalysis, in particular, cannot be content simply with the analysis of narrative structures and representational forms typical for cognitive psychology. It is far more important

> to disclose the subjective fantasy life that motivates and shapes the narrative staging.... In a differentiated analysis, not only ... an individual's ideologies and ver-

sions become clear, but also fantasy-driven personal models for handling conflict and for psychosocial compromise formation as results of repeated attempts to avoid mental contents laden with fear, shame, or guilt, or to repress certain intentions.[75]

The psychoanalytical approach, according to Boothe, along with other approaches, looks for "elementary structures of the scenic" precisely also in the area of narrative analysis, for "identified figures" as they emerge from the assimilation of experience, both one's own and that of others.

Historical-narrative stagings and dramatizations may, in terms of their "objective" informational content, approach zero, indicating a possible knowledge deficit on the part of the narrator, who would certainly fail to meet the methodological standards of the profession. In addition, such stagings may additionally put into play arguments for or against certain actions, orientations, and lifestyles that recipients will find unpersuasive, even implausible. None of this needs to concern psychologists, for the aforementioned reasons, insofar as they are interested (at least initially) in "scenic self-design," in the "narrator's world of desires and anxieties,"[76] which, from our perspective, can be expressed in historical narratives as well. In contrast to at least some research in the area of oral history, such narratives should also interest psychology, not as supplying data about past events, at least not primarily, but rather as the creative, scenic modeling of experiences and expectations, as psychological articulations that must repeatedly be regenerated.[77]

For psychology, historical reality provides access to the subject and its world: the narrator, along with his reference group, is central to psychological analysis. What the narrative is about is interesting primarily in reference to the speaker and his "anticipated" reception. Only in exceptional cases is it interesting as historical knowledge, to be judged by the factual and methodological standards of the historical profession. Applying such standards would be a misunderstanding of the status of psychological truth. "The products of the psyche," wrote Freud, "possess a kind of reality."[78] This certainly holds, and not just for the neurotics Freud was discussing. Every narrative, of whatever kind, represents "psychological realities." The following are only some examples of the function of historical constructions:

1. They can serve as *self-justification* and *self-defense*. As a rule, these functions are connected to the repression of obligation or shameful involvements. Exculpatory stories often appear precisely where the subject's involvement in collective history is at issue.[79]

2. Equally common is the *alleviation of conscience* through something like a confession. Here, too, one can see a form of psychological self-regulation.

3. Historical narratives can serve to *idealize the self or reference group* relevant to identity, as in heroic epics, for example, but also as means of *self-criticism* and *self-reflection*. *Self-reproaches, self-accusations,* or the *denigration of others* are sometimes connected with self-idealizations, which suggests the following function.

4. Narratives can serve to *displace aggression*.

5. *Managing* or *reducing anxiety* is a narrative function that is particularly significant to psychoanalysis. This function includes the handling of anxieties and needs located in the present by means of a consolatory nostalgia about the past.[80] Hence, someone isolated in the present might ally himself with those long dead, and so escape his isolation, at least in the short term. Where the past contains the terrors that still afflict the subject, a narrative may serve to manage anxiety by means of narcissistic reorganization. The same could be said about past "critical turning points" and "destabilizations" in the positive direction:

> As an act of reorganization is how we designate the strategy of integrating some upheaval, some psychological destabilization by subsequently narrating in a negative, traumatizing sense or a positive, euphoric sense, indeed narrating it again and again. For narrative, as an elementary technique of self-ascertainment often helps achieve psychological reorganization after situations that caused an inner destabilization.[81]

Something one has suffered can be given shape through the narrative medium; passivity, writes Boothe, following Freud, is thus transformed into activity. One might say that psychoanalysis regards the narrative function of managing anxiety (and the conflicts behind them) as central:

> Narrative, as an externalizing act of modeling, has as its primary task the neutralization of destabilizations that arose as a loss of belonging, a reduction in the feeling of identity, from the realization of a desire or conflict. In order to achieve that neutralization, it installs the narrator as director, that is, as the central channel of guidance and control.[82]

These anxieties need not necessarily be connected with the kind of historical experiences the narrator understands as somehow his *own,* those to which he was witness. Every historical experience communicated and appropriated by a subject can become the object of identifications and projections, anxious or otherwise. That the narrator always *gives direction to the action* when representing the past (in its relationship to the present and the future), and so constitutes a narrative order, is more important here than what position the narrator occupies in the history being narrated. In historical narrative, the narrative need not have an active role, and yet because of the inevitably subject-bound, "exocentric" perspective of such representations, he will say something about himself.

6. With respect to traumatic experiences, Gabriele Rosenthal emphasizes the *healing* function of narrative.[83] One should not, however, ascribe as much efficacy to narrative as Rosenthal does. Narrative's power to reorganize experience has limits. Narrative may be unable to incorporate and integrate serious traumas, such that the suffering subject can find peace and adopt and accept her suffering as a component of her life story. Trauma in this case becomes a taboo, a disconnected zone; to trespass on it may renew the pain and cause a repeated loss of orientation. Such proscription and exclusion takes place completely under the sign of psychological functioning; in other words, as psychoanalytic experience has shown, it is often unavoidable and even necessary, but

in any case, it is not to be classified pathological.[84] Narrative can have a regenerative function, but it does not have such a function always or everywhere. If it fails to wait for the right moment, the *kairos,* narrative too runs the danger of repeating or even worsening those injuries and anxieties it had wanted to avert or relieve.

7. As some of the aforementioned functions may suggest, narratives can serve functions of *wish fulfillment,* and create, *uno actu, stability and certainty* where instability and uncertainty had predominated. This aspect, too, is emphasized by psychoanalytically oriented authors in particular:

> The narrator as dramaturge first employs externalization, in the sense of a wish fulfillment in effigy: emotional motives are relocated to some external event, and there organized as a conflictual event. This external event can then be perceived discretely, as enclosed in a punctuated process. The narrator thus gains control by making perceptible the whole process or "story." This control, however, hardly results in a damping of the emotions: on the contrary, the process of narration itself mobilizes, releases emotionality in the form of participation in the events presented. The motives of wish fulfillment and the attainment of security are, for both speaker and listener, embedded in a scenery which follows real events.[85]

Boothe, on the other hand, writes about narrative in the psychoanalytic context. Obviously the present function is significant in both ordinary as well as academic historical narrative. It goes without saying that wish fulfillments staged in narrative can turn out in quite different ways. Nevertheless, we are dealing with the shaping of experience in terms of the pleasure principle (which in narrative, too, can gain the upper hand over the reality or rationality principle—which happens often enough, allowing the id to triumph over the ego and superego in the narrative world as well). We are consequently dealing with narratives that somehow present what was in the direction of past or present needs and desires.

8. The tendency toward wish fulfillment is, of course, effective not only with respect to missed opportunities in the past, but to expectations for the future. Historical narrative can inspire *hope* or depict *utopian horizons,* to *inspire interest or motivation.* Psychological functions may be not only motivational, volitional, and emotional, but naturally also *cognitive,* among them the aforementioned formation of knowledge, judgments, and orientation through narratively structured recollection and retrospective, imagination and anticipation. I will discuss this special and yet extraordinarily complex and interesting cognitive function in more detail below. What I mean is *the cognitive management of contingency.* The analysis of this function leads into the core of narrative thought, and, more precisely, *historical*-narrative thought. This function, the management of contingency, is why narrative should properly be designated a specific form of *thought* or of human *intelligence.* Naturally, the management of contingency through narrative language is no purely cognitive matter, insofar as it always attempts to *manage* contingency, at least when it is experienced as problematic.

Narrative as the management of contingency is thus an emotionally and motivationally consequential attempt to live with accident perceived as heteronomy, with experiences that threaten one's autonomy of action. In general, the psychological restitution and reorganization through narrative that follows upon crucial occasions or experiences of psychological destabilization, whether of a positive or negative tendency, can be understood as the management of contingency. Narrative involves not only the perception, but also the acknowledgement and psychological integration of contingency. The following section will explain why Bruner designates narrative as a mode of thought, and Ricoeur as a specific form of human intelligence, as well as how this perspective offers a basis for connecting historical consciousness and historical rationality.

Historical Narrative, Contingency, and Narrative Intelligence

Narrative makes it possible to thematize contingency, and at the same time, to manage it. Historical narratives create an awareness of contingency *while* reducing it. They make something meaningful of contingency in the practical world, as well as of the contingency of action; they transform it from a mere incident, meaning nothing to anyone and entirely external to human life.[86] Ricoeur, in his definitive analysis of this narrative function, writes that narratives put "a new face" on contingency.[87] I will summarize, comment upon, and expand on those results of Ricoeur's inquiry that are important for our project.

Ricoeur explains first that every narrative brings contingency to language by dealing with events in some particular way. He understands an event first as something that happens—indeed, something that happens without respect to its relevance or consequence for a subject, irrespective of whether these events are natural events or human actions, whether they are unique, repeatable, or even repeated events: "The event considered outside of history is nothing but an *incident (Vorfall)*, that is, something that takes place in some way, but could have taken place differently or not at all, which is the very definition of contingency."[88]

Events are moments that, as soon as they are "taken up" by a narrative, become *definite and meaningful* (as a natural occurrence or as some kind of action) and transposed or *integrated* into a narrative. The latter is the essence of the narrative function. Narrative, to relate different events, places them in diachronic order where the various elements are fixed temporally *and* related by temporal connectors, as well as connected in other ways. It is precisely the complementary operations of distantiation *and* relation of pasts and futures from the perspective of the present, as well as their integration into a narrative that create a representation of a dynamic sequence of previously discrete realities in order to make them plausible (Leitner), that is, that make what might be called *narrative sense*. Narrative can thus generally be understood, in Ricoeur's felicitous phrase, as *a synthesis of heterogeneity,* and finally as a structure of meaning perceived as a *dissonant consonance.* All this is accomplished by narrative, by the way it makes events of incidents, presents and reshapes them, that is, through the act of emplotment that in all the relevant theories is the crux of narrative acts of the construction of meaning. Emplotment, corresponding to the English "plot" in either sense, as well as to the German *Fabel* and the French *intrigue,* should be understood simply as that shaping or modeling of the story structure that differentiates, sequences, and integrates events into a totality with beginning, middle, and end.[89]

The operation of emplotment represents reality *as pervaded by contingency,* in order to manage this reality and, thus, contingency. Ricoeur goes on to stipulate how through emplotment, an event *loses* the status of *mere incident,* that is, an incident conceived without regard for its possible human consequences, importance, or meaning. As components of a temporally structured context of meaning, that is, a story, events *codetermine* the advance of the narrative. This means, among other things, that the "narrative operation" transforms "irrational contingency into ordered, meaningful, intelligible contingency."[90] We should already note the role that narrative as a form-bound verbal or poetic act plays in constructing an order within reality, of which we can then say, this shows insight, understanding, intelligence. Conceiving an incident as an event, and integrating it into a unified structure, is the decisive aspect here. Articulating contingency and processing it cognitively—in other words, narratively—is a *mental act.* Such an act "reckons" with contingency, operating with chance such that chance finally, in Reinhart Koselleck's formulation, becomes a "motivational trace in historical writing."[91] "History" here can mean what happens, as well as the narrative about it. In this form, chance impels history, and moreover intelligibly, as every narrative reveals that manifests, integrates, and transforms contingency. Thus, chance, without being attributed to a law or a rule, becomes, on the verbal level, an element of an ordered, that is, narrative structure.

The transformation of unordered into ordered contingency may take place in different ways. A narrative not only integrates the most various circumstances and happenings, but does so in a way that can account for the qualitative differences between them. This means, above all, that along with specifically narrative acts of meaning-construction and explanations operating with the category of chance in Cournot's sense, with the contingency and coincidence of conditions, occurrences, and actions, that intentional and rule-based explanations also have a place.[92] Nevertheless, what is and remains central to narrative acts of meaning-construction is that they operate with *coincidences;* this is just what gives contingency "a new look." A related fact is "that a well-threaded intrigue organizes heterogeneous components as wholeness or totality and evokes a particular sense-effect."[93] We can now formulate: by the placement, according to a narrative logic, into a diachronic order of causes, purposes, goals or intentions, rules, and above all, coincidences, the lawless contingency, characteristic of pure occurrence of a plain, incomprehensible succession of occurrences becomes ordered, intelligible contingency.

In historical narrative, contingency is thus no longer what it was on the level of mere incident, because the beginning *chosen* by the narrator and the ending *set* by him create a temporal frame in which the beginning and ending, however apparently contingent, acquire a "narrative coloration," in Ricoeur's words. There can, after all, be a contingent beginning *without a "before"* and a contingent end *without an "after"* only *through the act of emplotment,* in other words, only in a narrative world. Nevertheless, the most important aspect of the narrative expression of contingency must be seen "in the role that contingency plays in what Aristotle called the *middle*."[94] A narrative's middle is indeed free of the contingency typical of the beginning and end set by the narrator's "poetic act," in Hayden White's words. It is not, however, free of contingency, as explained above—in fact, quite the contrary. Precisely this is narrative's specific and definitive function, then: in its middle section, contingency is acknowledged and represented as peripeteia in the Aristotelian sense, as the frustration of either the protagonist's or the audience's expectations—as a rupture in the situation and in the advance of the story up to that point.

Narrative compels a reconception and a revision of structures of experiences and expectation. It reorganizes existing symbolic systems. From a psychological view, this is, in all its essential aspects, a creative act. Narrative manages contingency; it adapts disruptions in order to be able to preserve an endangered orientation, or even restore a lost one. Narrative restitutes the order ruptured by change; it reconstructs it, creating a new order that assimilates this particular experience of novelty or surprise. In the same breath, then—and here is where Ricoeur's analysis properly begins—insofar as

> contingency is acknowledged, emphasized, given its due, it is also—thanks to narrative—placed in the service of the advance of the story: chance as *peripeteia* is embodied in the art of weaving and unweaving, which is why we speak of the stories as webs, as tangles, and so on.[95]

We can now see more clearly what the operations of narrative bring about: *narrative creates understanding* by creating connections and contexts, in different ways, but as a whole, in a unique way, and articulates all this in a unified form that makes the course of events as they are articulated plausible. Narrative describes what happens after a certain point, and where it finally leads. Narrative does not, however, describe only *what* happens, but rather makes clear and plausible, and explains, *uno actu, how* and *why* something had to happen, or should, or at least could have, happened.[96]

Such acts are necessarily retrospective, that is, they are only possible after what is to be described and explained and made intelligible has already come about. Narrative acts of the construction of meaning presuppose that we already know, or at least anticipate, the outcome of the story, thus allowing an "anticipated retrospective." The intelligibility characteristic of narrativity develops every narrative possessing a beginning, middle, and end as described above, and reconstructs the process of the transformation of beginning into end. This explanatory act is not somehow external to the narrative; it does not take place alongside it. Narrative is autoexplanatory. Prognoses in the strict sense are logically impossible within such a "field of contingency." We can therefore say that while there may be narratively justified expectations, such expectations do not exhaust the potential of narrative competence as it consists in the meaning-constructive integration of contingency. Contingent events can therefore, by definition, not be expected concretely.

Through the narrative management of contingency, the accident of peripeteia, order and understanding are constituted or restituted, stabilized or restored, only thereby orienting our actions (again). Orientation presupposes order. Historical orientation requires an ordered reality where contingency, novelty, and change can be "reckoned with." Acting *with a historical orientation*, and thus, in a particular sense, *with a rational orientation*, means not least to adapt, cognitively and practically, to the fact that something is no longer what it was, that pretty much everything could become different. To let one's desires and one's actions be guided by this radically temporal conception of reality without falling into overwhelming emotional and motivational despair is what it means to think historically, and finally to live historically, along the horizon of such thinking. By now it should be clear that every narrative-temporal structure of order far exceeds the image of a mere succession. Ricoeur speaks of the constitution of a *meaningfully* structured *configuration* and links this finally, again in connection with Aristotle, to catharsis, in the sense of relief from the emotion and suspense produced by the narrative. This is, again, entirely consistent with the kind of functionalist definitions one encounters more often in narrative psychology.

Clearly, this exposition, momentarily disregarding the psychological-pragmatic effects of historical narrative, is concerned primarily with narrative's *cognitive results and functions*. Narrative transforms contingency within "history" as a series of incidents into *coincidence within narrative*. This is an essential aspect of the cognitive and verbal "conversion" of history as incidents still not understood, into a history to be understood as symbolic order:

> Contingency, I would like to say, becomes *peripeteia* on the basis of narrative intelligence. It is the ability to "compose a plot," to connect consistency and inconsistency.... We are applying the same intelligence when we *follow* a story. Following a story is a very complex operation, which is carried out by the listener or reader and led by the expectations awakened by the unfolding of the story. These expectations are unceasingly corrected by the listener or reader as, in accordance with the development of the story, he comprehends *why* some *peripeteia had to* lead to some result—"with necessity or probability," Aristotle added—the point at the very least is to understand how it was *possible* for that to happen which did in fact

happen. In Ricoeur's words again: "The specific correlate of narrative intelligence is, briefly, the 'dissonant coherence' produced by the 'composition of the plot.' Contingency raised to the status of *peripeteia* is not external to this intelligence to the extent that it becomes part of the narrative sense."[97]

Narrative discloses insights into reality, oriented by rationality and orienting action, into a reality conceived as pervaded with contingency, as contingent reality, a reality that persists as such, and yet whose level of contingency must be reduced. This act of treating contingency, bound to reflection and to understanding, creates possibilities for both thought and action. Historical, and certainly also biographical, consciousness create a consciousness of contingency; indeed, they are formative for the modern consciousness of contingency, and are, at the same time, modes for reducing and managing contingency. When we conceive reality as contingent, when we can deal with the frustration of expectations, with variability and unintended variation, then we acquire new ways of thinking and acting. We might say that there is a certain sense of reality that is closely followed by a sense of potentiality. Specifically, historical consciousness and historical action exploit a space of potentiality first disclosed by the reflexive presentation of "history." In its "positive" tendency, it looks for opportunities for freedom of action that are only first created by a specific kind of temporalization of reality. Temporal orientation, and the kinds of action that correspond to such orientation, only become possible in the way delineated here through and in historical (as well as biographical) reflection and communication.

Ricoeur's inquiry suggests that we can presuppose that composing a plot and integrating contingency into the narrative development of the plot already expresses, and results from, a specific kind of—I will already hazard the term—rationally supported act. The performance and reconstruction of narrative constructions of meaning should be understood as acts of intelligence, whether these acts have a simple structure, like the shortest, everyday narratives, or the complexity evinced by elaborate historical, biographical, or literary texts. Narrative competence in this sense can be defined *formally* as an ability developed by subjects in the course of their overall, socially mediated verbal development.

Ricoeur would agree not only with certain work on historical pedagogy and the theory of historical consciousness that, in order to understand the processes by which we learn history, relates these learning processes, from the perspective of a theory of the subject, to the inception and development of narrative competence. Literary and psychological studies have taken a similar approach, even if they seldom discuss specifically *historical*-narrative. I have already mentioned Bruner's influential distinction between paradigmatic (or logical and scientific) and narrative forms of thought.[98] Bruner is also concerned to rehabilitate narrative as a form of thought, of intelligence. In this respect, he clearly continues the differentiation of thought by domains promoted by Piaget in particular.

In the section on "Narratological and Temporal-Theoretical Assumptions," I suggested a concept of narrative competence that could also be the basis for a psychology of historical consciousness. If we also consider the preceding discussion of the specifically *historical*-narrative construction of meaning, then the *outline* of a formally defined concept of historical thought becomes clearer. However, a more exact formalist or structuralist explication of this form of thought is very obviously still needed. It should be necessary to indicate the structural characteristics of historical consciousness that would not least allow a distinction in terms of *developmental* psychology between more and less complex structures of historical rationality. Only on this condition would our imprecise reliance on Piaget's genetic and structuralist conception of the different forms of thought or of reason be properly justified.

I am far from being able to present a formalist or structuralist model that would be persuasive from the standpoint of developmental psychology as well. This would require not only additional theoretical reflection, but, above all, empirical study. Apparently no such model yet exists, not even where the most gifted theoreticians have offered suggestions on the definition of historical thought. Rüsen's very interesting differentiation of different types of historical consciousness never exactly defines the *formal or structural* features that could constitute and substantiate his differentiation between the traditional, exemplary, critical, and, finally, genetic types.[99] Rüsen does, indeed, say quite aptly that in these types of thought, "the human past is recollected, a coherence between past, present and future is assumed, human communication is ordered, practice is oriented and historical identity is formed in entirely different ways." Nonetheless, the formal and structural criteria that, in my view, would be indispensable for a (psychological) theory of historical consciousness are nowhere apparent. These alone would allow the differentiation and hierarchization, in terms of developmental psychology as well, of variously complex cognitive abilities to *think* historically. This deficit is evinced not least in Rüsen's attempt to place types of historical consciousness into a developmental-psychological series.[100] This attempt makes it clear, though his title is already an indication, that the typology he has conceived as an ontogenetic model actually relies on moral criteria to such a degree that the (supposed) specificity of historical thought is occasionally lost to sight. The "relationship" between the power of moral judgment and historical thought tends to become a substitution and a subsumption, and the properly interesting theme of *historical* rationality in its various developmental stages is obscured. We might say, if I am not mistaken, that Rüsen here reduces historical argument far too readily to its *function* of justifying or suggesting moral values, orientations, and decision in situations of conflict. The different types of historical argumentation are *prejudiced,* as his examples show, by value judgments and action orientations determined by content.

Neither the functional nor textual characteristics of the different types of historical thought, however, could initiate the developmental theory that

Rüsen intends, which would be analogous to the genetic-structuralist developmental theories in the area of theoretical and moral-practical reason. In addition to the criteria that differentiate his types (logical operations, degree of implicit experience and implied knowledge, empirical frequency of the different types), Rüsen does suggest some that are intended to allow a ranking of the types according to their "degree of complexity; however, these remain too vague, in my view, or are defined from the outset as other than formal-structural. This defect recurs in a more recent study.[101]

Here, again, next to an abundance of suggestions and implications, there is no formal or structural concept that alone could answer the question Rüsen raises: "What does it mean to 'think historically'?"[102] The question remains open for a psychology that could take into account so much productive research into the structure and development of theoretical thought and moral judgment to develop an empirically grounded (developmental) theory of historical rationality. Although we cannot go more deeply into this issue here, I should still mention that Jeismann's typology also fails to satisfy what is, in my view, the unavoidable requirement for a formal or structural definition of historical thought and its potential developmental stages.[103]

Terminologically, Jeismann understands acts of historical consciousness as basically cognitive acts of reflection and as normative-practical, moral judgments under the sign of reason, where especially the systematic rationality of historical writing provides the standard. Of course, Jeismann hardly ignores noncognitive modes of the historical construction of meaning, that is, those not bound to rationally oriented reflection; *conceptually*, however, he does not comprehend them within the category of historical consciousness. Rather, his theoretical outline differentiates the different modes of historical consciousness terminologically, and speaks of *the desire* for history, the *image* of history, historical *understanding* as well as, finally, historical *consciousness* that somehow assimilates the other modes of the historical construction of meaning (in different form), by integrating them into one rationally oriented, self-reflexive form. As Jeismann's language indicates, his conception of "historical consciousness" requires rational inquiry into factual assertions and moral judgments, as well as systematic rationality—against exhilaration and against the overwhelming and magical power of need and feeling. The formal and structural criteria that could demonstrate what historical thought is, and what its different developmental stages as rational faculty are, are absent from his interesting proposal, as well as from the other relevant literature.[104]

The preceding reflections and references will have to suffice for a formal or structural definition of historical-narrative competence as a rational ability of subjects who learn to narrate and think historically in the course of their socioculturally mediated development. The reason is that historical thought cannot be described only in formal or structural terms. When we think historically, we are not simply applying a formal model. The analysis, to use the language of cognitive psychology, of the formal structure, the development and the application of story schemas will be an important part of the psychology of historical consciousness, but cannot comprise the whole of it. Thinking historically requires more than just competence in narrating stories about collectively meaningful experiences and expectations in the formally correct way. Historical rationality is obviously not just a matter of structural or formal narrative grammars.

In this connection, I would like to take up an old idea that has been adapted and expanded by Paul Ricoeur. Ricoeur speaks of the intelligibility of narrative, in order to argue that all narrative acts of the construction of meaning create the potential for understanding in the sense indicated above, and, as he then *also* says in connection with Aristotelian poetics, for *instruction*. The allusion to the instructive character of narrative obviously points beyond its formal structure. *In its content,* such understanding is "far closer to practical cleverness and to moral judgment than to science, or, more generally, theoretical use of reason."[105] Ricoeur immediately explains that through the medium of narrative, we learn "how our destinies change because of some behavior, just as it is construed by the plot. We learn thanks to familiarity with the ways our culture has developed of 'composing a plot.'"[106] Ricoeur connects the changes in destiny depicted in narratives to the (ethical) concept of the good life, to the various conceptions of happiness by which we evaluate both experience and narrative. Stories, of course, have a *moral;* they are inextricable from a normative code. This is not an objection to stories or to narrative language generally as I conceive it. Theoretically, narrative constructions of reality, whether scholarly or ordinary, can meet with objects or counterconstructions. Even the implicit values, the normative standards and orientations that stories somehow carry can become the objects of criticism by an audience. It is not in itself a problem that stories are bound to normative ideas about the world and about human beings; other forms by which one thematizes the self or the world are not free of moral-normative implications, either.

This much is certain: narratives deal with joy and sorry, fortune and misfortune, success and failure, satisfaction and longing, assent and rejection. Narratives propose how the situations in which human beings find themselves, by chance or their own doing, might be understood as the outcome of stories that can, as a whole, be *typified*. Even when stories deal with individuals and their particular experiences, they (also) present and treat transindividually meaningful and obligatory circumstances of some kind; they facilitate understanding, especially of the connections between the practical world and the mental structures of subjects, connections that are understood as being of a more *general* type. As Ricoeur writes, we are, of course, dealing here with "generalities of a lower order than those of logic or of theory. Nonetheless we may speak of intelligence here, albeit in the sense which Aristotle gave to *phronesis*."[107]

Even where narrative involves a conception of the good life, intelligence and rationality play a role. Practical-phonetic intelligence, and specifically, historical-narrative intelligence can also raise arguments for or against certain intentions, actions, or practices, by relating them to the experiences of joy or sorrow treated in narratives. Narrative intelligence in this sense operates with distinctions that bring narrative, as we have said, closer to moral reason and probably also to a kind of aesthetics of existence. Such intelligence has precisely the experience-dependent form that contemporary psychology has also begun to investigate more deeply.[108] Of course, the qualitative criteria with which this variant of phronetic intelligence operates are specific to a culture, subject to historical change, and possibly highly differentiated within a culture.

Obviously, this new way of speaking about "narrative thought" risks forgetting its specificity. It is not only narrative that operates with contrastive and evaluative conceptual dichotomies such as correct and false, success and failure, and so on. We can, nevertheless, assert that *narrative alone vividly concretizes* its evaluations *and develops them and renders them plausible within a temporally structured context of meaning.* This seems to me to be decisive in the present connection. *Only* narrative, and not, say, moral judgments à la Piaget or Kohlberg, *show,* for example, what speaks for or against certain actions, because these are bound up with the experience of successful or unsuccessful *developments,* developments that have a good or bad outcome. We can hardly ignore that the narrative form of phronetic intelligence is not least a *psychological* intelligence. For what is therapy, after all? For all the diversity among therapists, they clearly understand others on the basis of experiential knowledge that they structure primarily narratively, and gain through a professionally mediated practice of listening and sympathizing. They advise and assist others in reconstructing their narratively structured knowledge of the world and the self.[109]

Only narratives develop experiential or "practical" knowledge in its *temporal* structure—in other words, as "knowledge in stories." When we have gained and are able to transmit such knowledge, then we know and can say something generally significant about *how to act* and *how to live,* about how individuals have come to experience sorrow or joy, new possibilities for action or more restrictions on their self-determination. Such knowledge is always bound to the particular and yet generalizable conditions under which it was gained and to which it applies, and naturally also to the normative standards by which we characterize a certain experience as unfortunate or fortunate. Narrative intelligence lets us think *in* time; indeed, it is the necessary condition for *thinking time as experienced and expected.* For the historical-narrative construction of meaning, time is therefore always the time of collective or shared experiences, expectations, and developments.

The structuralist or formalist definition of narrative intelligence is thus clearly intertwined with a definition based on narrative's instructive character. Narrative intelligence, as a kind of thought *specific to a domain,* basically operates in and with "time," by telling stories. Historical narrative, or at least narrative that not least articulates historically significant experiences and expectations, can now be related to another "aspect of rationality." Of course, here we are leaving the sphere of specifically narrative thought, and turning to the general validity criteria of scientific rationality.

Every temporal and narrative order that includes forms of process, as well as connections of meaning and causality, is formed from the standpoint of the present, from a narrator's perspective, and according to the current priorities and interests of human agents. This hardly means, however, that the past, the future, and their interrelations with the present can be constructed arbitrarily. At least where such constructs are to achieve *validity* in a sociocultural context, in other words, where they are *recognized* by others, they are subject to *rules* that guarantee just this validity. Of course, such rules are historical, and so may change over time. In addition, they may be socially differentiated. In any case, such rules, insofar as those who use them are even aware of them, cannot simply be avoided. Recollections of past and anticipations of future realities are subject to sociocultural rules that determine whether they can achieve consensus or even become compulsory. This fact, and ultimately *only this* fact, removes the historical forms by which the self and the world are thematized from personal idiosyncrasy. Those who simply can not or will not follow such rules, whatever *they* might be in this case, may, indeed, live in "their" time, in "their" present, past, and anticipated realities, but they must do so alone, cut off from the experiences and expectations that first constitute sociocultural realities, that is, collective human practices. They will be excluded from at least that communication and interaction with others which is characteristic for subjects *equally capable of action,* and which stabilizes and revitalizes the participants' ability to act. This may hold as much for the supposedly "insane" as for minorities who can hardly be pathologized simply because they are committed to historical conceptions of reality that are denied broader recognition. Questions of reality are not least questions of power, questions of the practical enforcement of measures for the construction of reality, whether rational grounds can be given for such measures or not.

Depending on the sociocultural standards and rules, there can be "obviously valid," arguable, and meaningless constructions of the past, present, and future, as well as arbitrarily complex temporal systems. One might for example connect such standards to the demands for truth, accuracy, and veracity more or less familiar to everyone in our culture, to the more formal criteria for a successful story, or finally to the specialized principles and methods known to historians since Droysen as *Historik*.[110] Every *concrete* construction of temporally meaningful facts and complexes is thus a product, which no reality somehow independent of human perceptions and actions somehow prove or disprove. The standards, criteria, forms, rules, and procedures a culture supplies its members for producing temporal systems of meaning are themselves products specific to a culture. A "past," as a narrative construct shaped from a present perspective, is inextricably bound to the intellectual, linguistic, and communicative bases of its production.

When we consider reality in a particular way, in order to be oriented and able to act in reality, then nothing outside the limits of the culture, society, and community to which we just happen to belong compels us to do so in this very way. Recourse to so-called "general mental structures" would only help here if these could be conceived as "pure nature," anthropological universals, and if there were empirically persuasive reasons to do so. In any case, particular cultures impose rational requirements for the rules and procedures by which they construct historical realities—requirements for intersubjective supervision, argumentative substantiation, and general acceptability. It is not difficult to see that historical-narrative competence relies on the systematic rationality of scholarship, and may be judged by its standards. This is at least true where we accept scholarship as the ideal and an embodiment of rationality. Whether and to what extent one should do so in the framework of a *psychology* of historical conscious, or whether one even needs to, will not be considered here. Such questions would, of course, be central to a theory of meaning for *all* the interpretive disciplines, irrespective of their subject matter.

Narrative Competence and Other Aspects of the Historical Construction of Meaning

At the end of our discussion it remains to be said that a theoretical psychology of historical consciousness obviously cannot be based solely on the concept of historical-narrative competence. When the narration and reception of stories is oriented by rational requirements, it requires something more. Historical consciousness comprises far more than competence in configuring and reconfiguring time, or lending order and meaning to (collective) experiences and expectations from the narrator's view. This ability necessarily incorporates other abilities. In terms of developmental psychology, it builds on and invokes other abilities whenever a subject thinks historically.

This discussion was restricted by more than just pragmatic considerations, of course. I believe that a theory of historical consciousness should begin with the points outlined here, and should at first persist there if it is adequately to comprehend and investigate historical-narrative competence as a cognitive ability specific to a domain. I emphasize this point because, in my view, every attempt to theorize historical-narrative competence has lacked precisely this persistence. It still remains unclear, if I am not mistaken, what narrative *thought,* and especially a *historical consciousness* that operates with the means of historical rationality, properly is or should be. There is certainly no way to avoid this requirement if we expect the degree of precision that distinguishes Piaget's or Kohlberg's work on the forms of thought specific to other domains. This lack of clarity is due, first of all, to the aforementioned lack of persistence. If historical-narrative competence is simply the "sum" of other abilities, then it cannot be specific to a domain. If we consider it merely a "structure" for integrating other abilities, we will never understand the historical construction of meaning and historical rationality as something autonomous. If we want to thoroughly test the idea of *specifically historical thought* before employing it, we cannot speak of historical-narrative competence as an "epiphenomenon," a "metastructure," or some other "aggregate." Nevertheless, such a reduction is quite common in the literature.[111]

Moral judgment, indeed, requires several other abilities without being merely a sort of addition or integration of them. Like moral competence, historical-narrative competence must be irreducible and particular, to a certain extent, more than and qualitatively different from merely a "sum of parts," or this competence would hardly deserve the name. Narrative, and especially historical-narrative, thought must be clearly demarcated from other forms of human intelligence. The present study is intended as a contribution to such demarcation and definition.

Of course, it makes sense and, in fact, is necessary to clarify the various *psychological preconditions and implications* of historical-narrative competence. The concept of historical consciousness is, as everyone acknowledges, extraordinarily complex. The obviously provisional list below (see figure 3.1) provides, in its upper section, an overview of the abilities that need to be considered, from a psychological point of view, as the preconditions and implications of "historical consciousness." At this point it is little more than an enumeration; it hardly claims to be a theory of how each concept indicated might be defined individually, and in its objective and developmental context.

This list, of course, includes narrative or historical-narrative competence, which would be theoretically central to a psychology of historical consciousness. This alone can specify, as we have explained, the specificity of what we might call the *thought of human time,* which can and must be demarcated from practical-moral thought. It is related to moral thought by also having a relation to practice, to right action and to the good life, which is why we designated it a form of phronetic intelligence. Yet it is distinct from moral thought insofar as it is not concerned with the discursive justification of moral judgments from an abstract perspective, whatever role such judgments and justifications may play in historical thought. Its particularity and specificity have to do, as explained, with its management of contingency and its construction of temporal differences and relations, and not least with placement of lessons from experience into more encompassing stories, in other words, with their narrative representation. It is particularly closely related to biographical thought: what biographical thought does on the level of an individual's life is what historical thought does with respect to collective experiences, changes, and developments.

The diagram complements the present study, though not only in the direction indicated up to now. The necessary theory of historical consciousness is here placed into the framework of a *psychology of the historical construction of*

Basal Competence in Action, Interaction
Fundamental Functions of Memory and Recollection
Verbal Competence
Differentiation of "I" and "We," Concept of "We"
Availability of the Concept of "Experience"
Cognitive Competence (Piaget)
Concept of Temporality (Piaget, others)
Attributive Capability (Heider, others)
Relational and Explanatory Competence
Empathy
Social Adoption of Other Perspectives (Mead, Flavell, others)
Moral Judgment (Piaget, Kohlberg)
Narrative Competence (Bruner, Mandler, others)
Self-Distancing, Self-Reflexivity
Historical-Narrative Competence

|

Historical Consciousness
Historical Thought, Historical Rationality

|

HISTORICAL CONSTRUCTION OF MEANING
HISTORY AS SYMBOLIC CONSTRUCT

|

Latent Dimensions of Historical Meaning-Construction and of Historically Mediated Actions

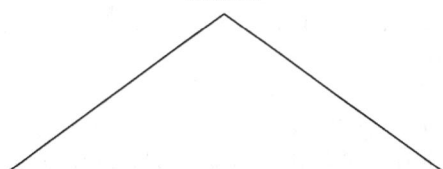

social-collective unconscious, language, worldviews, lifestyles, perspectives, interests (various behavioral, social, and cultural sciences)

individual unconscious, biography, current situation (psychoanalysis as the science of the subject)

Figure 3.1: Conceptual Structure for the Systematic Development of a Psychological Theory of the Historical Construction of Meaning.

meaning. The psychology of historical consciousness outlined here is a cognitive psychology. "Historical consciousness" as theoretical concept belongs to the vocabulary of a psychology of historical thought, of historical-narrative intelligence. If we define the concept of historical consciousness as summarized here, then we are ready to draw an *accentuating* and *analytical* distinction. This distinction demonstrates historical consciousness to be simply *one of two* sides from which the operations, acts, and results of *historical construction of meaning* can be analyzed. The historical constructs of symbolic agents are never products of rational intentions or motivations. It goes without saying that no practice that takes place under the sign of the historical construction of meaning, of a historical construct, can be perfectly rational; in fact, it is often enough not even rationally oriented.

I would like to *analytically* separate these aspects, which obviously break the framework of a psychology of historical consciousness, from the rationally motivated cognitive construction of a meaning-structured historical world, thus expanding the psychology of historical consciousness into a psychology of the historical construction of meaning that can also deal with latent dimensions of meaning in historical narrative. Seen *practically*, the intentional, manifest, conscious and "rationally controlled" meaning of historical constructs can not neatly be separated from the latent, "unconsciously motivated" meanings accessible only after extensive interpretation. A completely rational, self-transparent, and reflexively controlled historical construction is as much an ideal as a thoroughly latent structure of meaning, completely inaccessible to "thought at a distance," asserting itself in subjects' thoughts, emotions, and actions completely and irresistibly "behind their back."

Every act of the historical construction of meaning is partly determined by contexts and motives over which subjects have limited control, if any. Almost every historical construction is open to various complementary or conflicting readings, as well as to "deep" readings. The construction of historical realities always and everywhere has significance and meaning that escapes the "author's" consciousness. Different methods are available for illuminating the latent aspects of a historical construction of meaning depending on their nature and type. Our model distinguishes two options. On the one hand, it includes the concept of an *individual unconscious*. This refers to the idiosyncratic and unconscious motives of individuals that lend their historical constructions a significance and a meaning rooted in their own biography and current situation. Psychoanalysis as a "science of the subject" provides methods to analyze such motives. Methods equipped especially for the narrative stagings of individual subjects are suggested by Boothe's study mentioned above. However, the psychology of the historical construction of meaning is concerned not only with the individual unconscious, but with the *collective unconscious* as well. An explication of collectively unconscious meanings in historical-narrative texts is not the preserve only of psychology and psychoanalysis. These disciplines may be especially competent in the elucidation of latent structures of meaning, insofar as this latency is due to a socially or culturally specific psychological dynamics. The psychoanalytic study of society and culture, for example, might offer procedures appropriate for the analysis of the collective unconscious.[112] There are other behavioral, social, and cultural sciences that investigate the hidden sociocultural horizons, constellations, and contexts for acts of historical meaning-construction. An example of such a critical analysis of the construction of historical representations, conducted without psychological tools and methods, is suggested by Roger Chartier.[113]

Brief as these concluding remarks necessarily are, they should at least suggest how a psychology of the historical construction of meaning might advance. The schema presented here locates this study in a program of research upon which a psychology of historical consciousness would have to be specified and amplified in the indicated directions.

Notes

This chapter was translated from the original German by Anthony Nassar. Unless otherwise noted, all translations of quotations are also provided by Anthony Nassar.

1. [Both *Geschichte* and *Historie* mean "history" in German—"history" in the aggregate as well as the history "of" something; *Geschichte*, however, can also mean "story." Trans.]

2. Numerous contributions to the journal *Bios: Zeitschrift für Biographieforschung und Oral History* bear out this claim.

3. Jerome S. Bruner, "Two Modes of Thought," in *Actual Minds, Possible Worlds* (Cambridge, Mass., 1986), 11–43. For different variations on the recurrent distinction between two irreducible modes of thought, compare Gisela Labouvie-Vief, "Modes of Knowledge and the Organization of Development," in *Models and Methods in the Study of Adolescent and Adult Thought: Adult Development,* ed. Michael L. Commons et al. (New York, 1990), vol. 2, 42–62; see also David Olson, "Thinking about Narrative," in *Narrative Thought and Narrative Language,* ed. Bruce K. Britton and Anthony D. Pellegrini (Hillsdale, N.J., 1990), 99–111.

4. Compare Jerome S. Bruner, *Acts of Meaning* (Cambridge, Mass., 1990). On the theory, methodology, and methods of an interpretative psychology of action and of culture, see also Jürgen Straub, *Handlung, Interpretation, Kritik: Grundzüge einer textwissenschaftlichen Handlungs- und Kulturpsychologie* (Berlin, 1999). The latter work develops a typology of action that goes beyond the narrow frame of an intentionalistic or teleological model. It also brings up a point that will be significant for the present investigation: as the reader will already have seen, I designate speech (and all other acts of symbolization) as an action, in agreement with those relatively broad definitions of the concept of action, which do not link "actions" simply to observable physical movements or changes to the physical world. Practical and intellectual-imaginative acts can be differentiated by type or by emphasis; see also Ernst Boesch, *Symbolic Action Theory and Cultural Psychology* (Berlin, 1991), 96.

5. On the other hand, I do not connect these concepts, as is often customary with respect to individual historical consciousness, to the criterion that they should "exceed" the moment of an individual's birth: von Borries and Rüsen, for example, recommend that *Geschichte* or *Historie* by definition should always begin "before" one's own life. "Properly historical statements," then, are only "those about epochs before one's own lifetime" (Bodo von Borries, "Geschichtsbewußtsein, Lebenslauf und Charakterstruktur: Auswertung von Intensivinterviews," in *Geschichtsbewußtsein*

und historisch-politisches Lernen, ed. Gerhard Schneider [Pfaffenweiler, 1988], 163–183). In their influential theoretical work, Rüsen, Fröhlich, Horstkötter, and Schmidt write that historical consciousness "exceeds the biological time limits of subjects; it inscribes a social or cultural time into them, so to speak, through which they then have far more past and future that that section of life measured out to them biologically"; compare Jörn Rüsen, Klaus Fröhlich, Hubert Horstkötter, and Hans-Günther Schmidt, "Untersuchungen zum Geschichtsbewußtsein von Abiturienten in Ruhrgebiet," in *Geschichtsbewußtsein empirisch,* ed. Bodo von Borries, Hans-Jürgen Pandel, and Jörn Rüsen (Pfaffenweiler, 1991), 232.

Of course, historical consciousness expands the individual's life and biographical temporal horizon; after all, biographical consciousness already operates with social and cultural time. Doubtless one could describe differences between the consciousness of *contemporaneity* and the kind of *historical* consciousness that can move through other centuries, and even millennia. The former can be directly involved with individual experience, the latter by its nature cannot; the sources that nourish *contemporary* consciousness are often fundamentally different than those of the historical sense or historical consciousness. Notwithstanding any such differences, we are speaking in either case of historical consciousness. If we were to use a definition like von Borries and Rüsen's, we would involve ourselves in serious terminological and practical problems: by their definition, the period of National Socialism could potentially be an object or the content of historical consciousness for someone born after 1945; for someone born before 1945, such as the authors themselves, it could not. For someone, let us say, born in Berlin in 1960, and raised there, the student movement, which she will essentially hear about only later, and which she will only comprehend subsequently as "social movement" or whatever else, could never be the object or the content of historical consciousness—but what should it be, then, if autobiographical recollection can obviously not accomplish anything here, either? Clearly, the concept of historical consciousness cannot be fixed to biographically determined dates. Rather, its definition requires reference to the deliberate acts of distantiation, reflection, and construction by which history is constructed, that is, made present.

6. Herbert Schnädelbach, "'Etwas Verstehen heißt Verstehen, wie es geworden ist'—Variationen über eine hermeneutische Maxime," in *Vernunft und Geschichte: Vorträge und Abhandlungen* (Frankfurt, 1987), 125. Hegel and Marx, Droysen, Dilthey, and many others share this view, which seems like the reflection of a perhaps still even more influential ontological dogma. It means, as Dewey once said, that time, change, and motion are indications that Being is being besieged by its antagonist, that it is, in fact, about to collapse. The one and true reality, according to this traditional conception, is changeless; it remains one and the same. The epistemological implications of this view should be evident. I am not attempting below to absolutize this or that, but only *a* possibility of constituting, constructing, and understanding reality. The historical, and thus, narrative conception of reality interests me from both a theoretical and an empirical perspective here. The conception should absolutely not be normatively singled out, and even less, too hastily devalued.

In his very interesting critique of the aforementioned hermeneutic maxim and its narrativistic foundation, Schnädelbach tends toward such a devaluation when he all too indiscriminately accuses narrativism of a "conservative" hostility to modernity and reason. This accusation might be justified occasionally, but it is incorrect generally, as demonstrated by versions of the narrativist paradigm that are formulated entirely in the spirit of Enlightenment rationality, and eluding any overly simple contrast between narrative and theoretical discourse, between understanding and explaining, between universality and particularity or relativity, between the narrative and the non-narrative elements of historical thought. Rüsen's theory of history offers a particularly obvious example—see, for example, Jörn Rüsen, *Grundzüge einer Historik,* 3 vols. (Göttingen, 1983–1989); Rüsen, *Zeit und Sinn: Strategien historischen Denkens* (Frankfurt, 1991); and, "Historische Sinnbildung durch Erzählen: Eine Argumentationsskizze zum narrativistischen Paradigma der Geschichtswissenschaft und der Geschichtsdidaktik im Blick auf nicht-narrative Faktoren," *Internationale Schulbuchforschung* 18 (1996): 501–543.

7. Compare, for example, Gerhard Bauer, *'Geschichtlichkeit': Wege und Irrwege eines Begriffs* (Berlin, 1963), 2; Hartmann Leitner, "Gegenwart und Geschichte: Zur Logik des historischen Bewußtseins," unpublished *Habilitationsschrift,* Trier, 1994, 14.

8. Karlheinz Stierle, "Geschehen, Geschichte und Text der Geschichte," in *Geschichte—Ereignis und Erzählung,* ed. Reinhart Koselleck and Wolf-Dieter Stempel (Munich, 1973), 530–534.

9. Bauer, *Geschichtlichkeit,* 2.

10. Karl Heussi, *Die Krise des Historismus* (Tübingen, 1932); Paul Ricoeur, *Time and Narrative,* 3 vols., trans. Kathleen McLaughlin and David Pellauer (Chicago, 1984–1988), vol. 3, 143.

11. Ricoeur, *Time and Narrative,* vol. 3, 143.

12. For an overview of these tasks and themes, see Christoph Conrad and Martina Kessel, "Geschichte ohne Zentrum," in *Geschichte schreiben in der Postmoderne: Beiträge zur aktuellen Diskussion,* ed. Christoph Conrad and Martina Kessel (Stuttgart, 1994), 9–36; Hartmut Eggert, Ulrich Profitlich, and Klaus S. Scherpe, eds., *Geschichte als Literatur: Formen und Grenzen der Representation von Vergangenheit* (Stuttgart, 1990); Gerhild Scholz Williams, "Geschichte und die literarische Dimension: Narrativik und Historiographie in der anglo-amerikanischen Forschung der letzten Jahrzehnte. Ein Bericht," *Deutsche Vierteljahresschrift für Literaturwissenschaft und Geistesgeschichte* 63 (1989): 315–392. See also Roger Chartier, "Zeit der Zweifel: Zum Verständnis gegenwärtiger Geschichtsschreibung," in Conrad and Kessel, *Geschichte,* 83–97; Roger Chartier, *Die unvollendete Vergangenheit: Geschichte und die Macht der Weltauslegung,* trans. Ulrich Raulff (Frankfurt, 1992); Hayden White, *Tropics of Discourse: Essays in Cultural Criticism* (Baltimore, 1978); idem, *The Content of the Form: Narrative Discourse and Historical Representation* (Baltimore, 1987), especially the chapter "The Question of Narrative in Contemporary Historical Theory." Obviously, much of what these authors have to say about professional historiography holds for our everyday historical constructions as well.

13. Compare also Chartier, *Die unvollendete Vergangenheit,* as well as *Zeit der Zweifel,* where the concept of representation is defined as follows, beginning on p. 91: "This concept namely allows us to indicate three important facts." The role of power in historic-narrative representations assumes great importance in the contemporary debate, as in the aforementioned work of Hayden White.

14. On the distinction between verbal and presentative symbolism, see Susanne K. Langer, *Philosophy in a New Key: A Study in the Symbolism of Reason, Rite, and Art* (Cambridge, Mass., 1942).

15. Karl-Ernst Jeismann, "Geschichtsbewußtsein als zentrale Kategorie der Geschichtsdidaktik," in *Geschichtsbewußtsein und historisch-politisches Lernen,* ed. Gerhard Schneider (Pfaffenweiler, 1988), 1–24, here, p. 7. Compare also Jeismann, *Geschichte als Horizont der Gegenwart: Über den Zusammenhang von Vergangenheitsbedeutung, Gegenwartsverständnis und Zukunftsperspektive* (Paderborn, 1985), in particular, the essay first published in 1977, "Didaktik der Geschichte: Die Wissenschaft von Zustand, Funktion, und Veränderung geschichtlicher Vorstellungen im Selbstverständnis der Gegenwart," 27–43. On definitional issues, see Rolf Schörken, "Geschichtsdidaktik und Geschichtsbewußtsein," *Geschichte in Wissenschaft und Unterricht* 23 (1972): 81–89; Joachim Rohlfes, "Geschichtsbewußtsein: Leerformel oder Fundamentalkategorie?" in *Geschichte: Nutzen oder Nachteil für das Leben?* ed. Ursula A.J. Becher and Klaus Bergmann (Düsseldorf, 1986).

16. Hans-Jürgen Pandel, "Dimensionen des Geschichtsbewußtseins: Ein Versuch, seine Struktur für Empirie und Pragmatik diskutierbar zu machen," in *Geschichtsdidaktik: Projekte, Perspektiven* 12 (1987): 130–142.

17. Compare Leitner, "Geschichte und Gegenwart," 82, 99.

18. George Herbert Mead, *The Philosophy of the Present,* ed. Arthur E. Murphy (LaSalle, 1932); compare, for example, Hans Joas, *Praktische Intersubjektivität: Die Entwicklung des Werkes von G. H. Mead* (Frankfurt, 1980), 164; Jürgen Straub, *Historisch-Psychologische Biographienforschung: Theoretische, methodologische, und methodische Argumentationen in systematischer Absicht* (Heidelberg, 1989), 85.

19. Arthur C. Danto, *Analytical Philosophy of History* (Cambridge. U.K., 1968). Bunzl regards Danto's account as merely contemporary dogma, to which objections ought to be raised; see

Martin Bunzl, "How to Change the Unchanging Past," *Clio: A Journal of Literature, History, and the Philosophy of History* 15 (1995): 181–193. Bunzl argues that not all history can be conceptualized in terms of a narratological philosophy of history, and, in any case, certain points of orientation are indispensable: "It is also a bold soul who will not search for landmarks in the past that *can be treated* as fixed and unchanging" (181). I have emphasized what particularly interests me in the quoted passage: what can or must be treated as permanent and constant in the past has to be negotiated and agreed on; nothing in the past is immutable there in the strictest sense. Bunzl is correct when he writes that the conclusions Danto draws are not dependent on a narratological standpoint; rather, they are rooted in more general ideas from the theory of language. These ideas could be subsumed under the label of "hermeneutics," in my view. Our epigraph from Nietzsche might serve as an example of such an hermeneutic interpretation.

20. Aleida Assmann, "Stabilisatoren der Erinnerung—Affekt, Symbol, Trauma," in *Die dunkle Spur der Vergangenheit: Psychoanalytische Zugänge zum kulturellen Gedächtnis,* ed. Jörn Rüsen and Jürgen Straub (Frankfurt, 1998). The efficacy of such stabilizing factors is, however, as we indicated, not a fact of nature—in other words, not entirely independent of sociocultural conditions and practices.

21. Leitner, "Geschichte und Gegenwart," 82.

22. Compare Jeismann, "Geschichtsbewußtsein als zentrale Kategorie der Geschichtsdidaktik," 15.

23. Jeismann, *Geschichte als Horizont der Gegenwart,* 15.

24. Jörn Rüsen, *Historische Sinnbildung: Interdisziplinäre Untersuchungen zur Struktur, Logik und Funktion des Geschichtsbewußtseins im interkulturellen Vergleich* (Konzept der Forschungsgruppe) (Bielefeld, 1994–1995), 1.

25. Jörn Rüsen, *Historische Orientierung: Über die Arbeit des Geschichtsbewußtseins, sich in der Zeit zurechtzufinden* (Cologne, 1994), 6; see also Rüsen et al., "Untersuchungen zum Geschichtsbewußtsein," 226.

26. For an analysis of these metaphors, see my reflections on theories of memory: Jürgen Straub, "Kultureller Wandel als konstruktive Transformation des kollektiven Gedächtnisses: Zur Theorie der Kulturpsychologie," in *Psychologische Aspekte des kulturellen Wandels,* ed. Christian Allesch, Elfriede Billman-Mahecha, and Alfred Lang (Vienna, 1993), 42–54.

27. These "relational" forms lead to the creation of coherences to which we can generally ascribe *explanatory* force. The aforementioned forms of explanation—the intentionalist or teleological model, the model of explanation by reference to rules, the narrative model—are, according to the conception I am presenting, not just important for the psychology of the historical construction of meaning. They are also more generally significant for the psychology of action and of culture. If we concede this point, we will have to abandon models that understand scientific explanation exclusively as deductive-nomological subsumption (see Straub, *Handlung, Interpretation, Kritik*).

28. General arguments for combining the theory of history and the theory of narrative are presented in numerous sources, such as Emil Angehrn, *Geschichte und Identität* (Berlin, 1985); F.R. Ankersmit, *Narrative Logic: A Semantic Analysis of the Historian's Language* (The Hague, 1983); idem, *History and Tropology: The Rise and Fall of Metaphor* (Berkeley, 1994); Paul Ricoeur, *Time and Narrative,* vols. 1 and 3; idem, *Oneself as Another,* trans. K. Blamey (Chicago, 1992); Rüsen, *Zeit und Sinn;* Hayden White, *Metahistory: The Historical Imagination in Nineteenth-Century Europe* (Baltimore, 1973); and other works by Hayden White referred to above. Compare also Scholz Williams, "Geschichte und die literarische Dimension."

29. Compare Rüsen, "Historische Sinnbildung durch Erzählen."

30. Dietrich Boueke, Frieder Schülein, Hartmut Büscher, Evamaria Terhorst, and Dagmar Wolf, *Wie Kinder erzählen: Untersuchungen zur Erzähltheorie und zur Entwicklung narrativer Fähigkeiten* (Munich, 1995), 16.

31. More strongly dependent on context, although similarly generalizable cognitive representations of concrete sequences of events, actions, or interactions (for example, taking a meal, washing, taking a walk, etc.) are the so-called scripts that are present on an earlier level of cogni-

tive development than such more abstract structures as the story. Scripts are cognitive representations more closely bound to practice and to context, which make it clear that children are capable of practical acts of understanding of the most various kinds well before they master the ability of verbal symbolization.

As context-bound representations, scripts always relate to *particular* types of scenes and events (active and interactive models); a script is thus defined by its content, even if it does not relate to just a single experience, but only to its generalizable aspects. A script, of course, shows features that make it interesting as a predecessor of precisely the abstract narrative schema, in particular its functions of temporal and causal sequentialization, its aforementioned acts of generalization and its unified structure. It should be noted that they remain important as context-related, contentually concrete structures even after the abstract narrative schema becomes available. Scripts, one might say, remain significant as context, that is, situation-related *general event representations* (Nelson and Gruendel) for the narrative recall of realities.

For a social-constructivist approach to scripts, see the short overview by Tilmann Sutter, "Entwicklung durch Handeln in Sinnstrukturen: Die sozial-kognitive Entwicklung aus der Perspektive eines interaktionistischen Konstruktivismus," in *Soziale Kognition und Sinnstruktur,* ed. Tilmann Sutter and Michael Charlton (Oldenburg, 1994), 56. A basic work in the field is Roger C. Schank and Robert P. Abelson, *Scripts, Plans, Goals, and Understanding* (Hillsdale, N.J., 1977). The authors define a script as "a structure that describes an appropriate sequence of events in a particular context. A script is made up of slots and requirements about what can fill those slots. The structure is an interconnected whole, and what is in one slot affects what can be in another" (41). For an overview of the concept of the story schema, see Nancy L. Stein and Tom Trabasso, "What's in a Story: An Approach to Comprehension and Instruction," in *Advances in Instructional Psychology,* ed. Robert Glaser, (Hillsdale, N.J., 1982), vol. 2, 213–267, which also references the relevant studies by Anderson, Kintsch and van Dijk, Mandler, Stein, Thorndyke, and others.

I am disregarding the fact that much of the research relating to schema theory pursues goals related to particular applications. In the context of instructional psychology, the goal is often to improve learning and teaching processes on the basis of cognitive-psychological insights, as, for example, in the context of school, where stories have to be understood and created. This is immediately understandable as soon as one assumes that processes of comprehension and memory are dependent on the structural features of narrative representations. Thus, textbooks could be written on the basis of insights from cognitive psychology so that they begin with students' age- or development-dependent narrative competence and then deliberately stimulate them to further developmental steps. Such undertakings are unquestionably stimulating for a practically oriented theory of the historical construction of meaning of the kind that would interest teachers of history.

32. Stein and Trabasso, "What's in a Story."

33. Fredric C. Bartlett, considered the forerunner of contemporary schema theory approach, postulated as early as 1932 that memory and recollection operated with story schemata or scripts; see his *Remembering: A Study in Experimental and Social Psychology* (Cambridge, U.K., 1932). Of course, Bartlett did not consider the inner structure of stories more closely, which is why his references turned out rather vague and general. For Mandler, and many other authors who study questions of memory, in contrast, the concept of the schema relates to clearly stated *expectations* as to how a story, at least a simple one, normally proceeds. It is these expectations that then guide acts of memory and recall. An arbitrary selection from the numerous studies includes Jean M. Mandler and Nancy S. Johnson, "Remembrance of Things Passed: Story Structure and Recall," *Cognitive Psychology* 9 (1977): 111–151; Jean Matter Mandler, "A Code in the Node: The Use of a Story Schema in Retrieval," *Discourse Processes* 1 (1978): 14–35; for a more detailed account of Mandler's schema-theoretical approach, see Mandler, *Stories, Scripts, and Scenes: Aspects of Schema Theory* (Hillsdale, N.J., 1984).

I should point out that a psychology of the historical construction of meaning would have to problematize to what extent traditional models from the theory of memory, which all present some sort of storage model, could do justice to the creative and transformative aspects of memory. Mandler's model, like almost all current approaches in psychology, including the newer studies on autobiographical memory, are tied to models that conceptualize the functions of memory and recall in terms of an ideally pure, reproductive mechanism for the reception, storage, and retrieval of information. In connection with constructivist approaches, we should consider in what way memory and recall functions could still be modeled as form- or schema-bound operations in terms of narrative structure without thereby losing sight of the creative and transformative aspects of every present- and context-dependent representation of past realities. As the fundamental constructive performance could then be regarded the narrative formalization itself, by which an event or process becomes a narrated story. On constructivist approaches in research into memory, see, for example, Siegfried J. Schmidt, ed., *Gedächtnis: Probleme und Perspektiven der interdisziplinären Gedächtnisforschung* (Frankfurt, 1991).

34. Compare Stein and Trabasso, "What's in a Story," 221. The finding they outline holds, of course, for the memory and the recall of children—in fact, more so for children, as their cognitive representations depend even more strongly and less flexibly on the use of schemata and scripts: compare, for example, Charles Glenn, "The Role of Episodic Structure and of Story Length in Children's Recall of Simple Stories," *Journal of Verbal Learning and Verbal Behavior* 17 (1978): 229–247; Jean Matter Mandler, "A Code in the Node"; Dorothy Poulsen, Eileen Kintsch, Walter Kintsch, and David Premack, "Children's Comprehension and Memory for Stories," *Journal of Experimental Child Psychology* 28 (1979): 379–403.

35. Compare, in particular, Nancy S. Johnson, "What Do You Do If You Can't Tell the Whole Story? The Development of Summarization Skills," in *Children's Language,* vol. 4, ed. Keith E. Nelson (Hillsdale, N.J., 1983). Johnson shows that the beginnings of the ability to present a story in summary form appear early on. This ability is nevertheless only completely articulated in early adolescence.

36. Boueke et al., *Wie Kinder erzählen,* 177.

37. The criteria presented below build on Jürgen Straub, "Biographische Sozialisation und narrative Kompetenz: Implikationen und Voraussetzungen lebensgeschichtlichen Denkens in der Sicht einer narrativen Psychologie," in *Biographische Sozialisation,* ed. Erika Hoerning (Stuttgart, 1977). With respect to the narratological basis of a psychology of the historical construction of meaning, I would observe that it should coincide largely with the basis of the psychology of the biographical construction of meaning. In both cases, we are dealing with a narrative psychology.

38. Boueke et al., *Wie Kinder erzählen,* 15.

39. Ibid.

40. Ibid., 109.

41. Compare the overview in ibid., 26, 40, 43–49. Perhaps the best-known model with a basic triadic structure is provided by William Labov and Joshua Waletzky, "Narrative Analysis: Oral Versions of Personal Experience," in *Language in the Inner City: Studies in the Black English Vernacular,* ed. June Helm (Philadelphia, 1972). This essay offers a more extensive presentation of the basic schema, along with certain differentiations concerning types of evaluations, extensions to the underlying narrative syntax (functional forms of intensification, of comparison, correlations, explications) and reflections on the ontogenetic development of this syntax.

42. We should at least indicate that a "critical middle" in the sense of the triadic structure might be considered already inherent in David E. Rumelhart's model, and, indeed, because of his contrastive, syntactical structural categories, which already imply a transformation. Compare David E. Rumelhart, "Notes on a Schema for Stories," in *Representation and Understanding: Studies in Cognitive Science,* ed. Daniel G. Bobrow and Allan Collins (New York, 1975), 211–236. Jean Matter Mandler, for example, follows Rumelhart in the aforementioned critical sense (see idem, *Stories, Scripts, and Scenes: Aspects of Schema Theory*).

43. I would again just like to point to the clarifications in Boueke et al., *Wie Kinder erzählen,* 27 and 49–56, which discuss the important work of Ute Quasthoff, among others.

44. Brigitte Boothe, "Die Alltagserzählung in der Psychotherapie," *Berichte aus der Abteilung Klinische Psychologie* 29.1 (Zurich, 1992): 13.

45. Compare Gergen's paper in this volume, as well as Mary M. Gergen and Kenneth J. Gergen, "The Social Construction of Narrative Accounts," in *Historical Social Psychology,* ed. Mary M. Gergen and Kenneth J. Gergen, (Hillsdale, N.J., 1984).

46. Compare as well Polkinghorne's suggestions in the present volume. He raises a problem we are completely disregarding, namely, the problem of theoretical *principles* of development, which, of course, no developmental psychology of narrative competence can do without.

47. Compare Boueke et al., *Wie Kinder erzählen,* 177. The textual and structural types important for the developmental sequences described there are explained on p. 130. To summarize, in the *isolated* account of an event there is no contentual, meaningful connection between events; the *linear* account is a sequentialization of equivalent events achieved by additive and temporal connectors; in the *structured* account there is at least one marked event leading to an episode; and I have already described the *narrative* type more extensively. The research findings of Boueke et al. are considerably more conservative than other work that I do not need to cite separately—work, for example, by Applebee, Botvin and Sutton-Smith, Kemper, Haslett, Peterson and McCabe, Stein, Glenn and Trabasso, as well as Meng—with respect to the age at which children possess narrative competence. This has to do with a more difficult concept of the story and with more sensitive methods of evaluating the evidence. Of course, there are several studies that support the view suggested by Boueke et al.; compare the descriptions in the latter, on p. 185.

48. Compare also the overview by Susan Kemper, "The Development of Narrative Skills: Explanations and Entertainments," in *Discourse Development: Progress in Cognitive Development Research,* ed. Stan A. Kuczaj II (New York, 1984), 99–124. Kemper attempts a comparative analysis of the structural developmental theories and studies by Applebee, Botvin and Sutton-Smith, Maranda and Maranda as well as Stein and Glenn, and, finally, an assessment of the research, especially on the development of the causal concept of explanation. The latter is regarded as an important component of narrative competence (and thus, as a rule, broadly defined). Kemper places the development, after her overview of the relevant research, at the age of two, and comes to the conclusion that children of ten "can tell novel and complex stories about a wide variety of topics. Mastering the art of storytelling involves three separate processes. First, there is the gradual accretion of characters, roles, themes, and symbols from which stories are created.... Second, there is the differentiation of complex plot structure as children learn to create well-structured, dyadic episodes, to coordinate these episodes, and to subordinate certain episodes to others. Finally, there is the substitution of initiation, motivation, and resultant causes for simple enablements. The causal structure of children's stories gradually conforms to an adult's causal taxonomy as children learn to explain why characters act as they do."

49. Compare Straub, "Historische Sozialisation und narrative Kompetenz."

50. As Pandel does; see, for example, "Dimensionen des Geschichtsbewußtseins."

51. Compare the work of Angehrn, Ankersmit, Danto, Ricoeur, and Rüsen cited above.

52. We should precisely consider Aristotle's definition of *plot* as the *imitation of an action:* "Whatever the innovative force of poetic composition within the field of our temporal experience may be, the composition of the plot is grounded in a preunderstanding of the world of action, its meaningful structures, its symbolic resources, and its temporal character" (*Time and Narrative,* vol. 1, 54). Entirely within the theory of action founded by Aristotle, Ricoeur, of course, concentrates his concept of action on the teleological model. We should incidentally note that a preunderstanding of the basic structure of *goal-directed* action thus becomes the basis of narrative temporality. Studies are needed to test whether this suffices as an explanatory foundation for narrative competence. It is also questionable whether the teleological model of action in the sense it has in Ricoeur's work is even tenable as a *universal* model. Naturally, the universality claim of Ricoeur's theory of time and narrative stands or falls not least on this question. A test of this model's claims should *not* consider whether "we"—in other words, those to whom teleological interpretations of action are *a matter of course*—could understand the behavior of every "normal" person, independent of historical and cultural particularities, as goal-directed action. Rather, what should be tested is whether *the preunderstanding of the world of action* assumed by Ricoeur can be attested always and everywhere.

A final observation on Ricoeur's work: Only the action-theoretical grounding of the thesis that time and narrative are necessarily connected allows Ricoeur to say that we are always "entangled in stories," even when these stories are in no way verbalized or otherwise narratively articulated. When the plot is understood as the imitation of an action, it becomes clear that the essential structural features of plot would have to be demonstrated for *action itself;* otherwise, how could the narration of a story in this sense be understood as imitation? Only Ricoeur's circular definition of time, narrative, and action allows him to conceive human existence independently of explicitly narrative acts of meaning-formation—along with Wilhelm Schapp—as an entanglement in stories. An existence defined in this way is, where its temporality is concerned, never anything but a multitude of *expressed or unexpressed stories.* It possesses, as one might say, an implicit dramatic structure, which can be made explicit through narratives, and only through narratives. Of course, sometimes such acts of explication are not even readily possible. Psychoanalysis, for example, might be understood as the enterprise of articulating, in certain cases, the stories implicit in, that is, underlying a concrete existence, yet hidden from the subject.

53. Ricoeur, *Time and Narrative,* vol. 1, 3.

54. The question is, nonetheless, worth considering. Narratologically based conceptions of time and history of the type outlined here assume an enormous burden of proof if they are not uncritically to universalize and absolutize the conception of narrative temporality. The hermeneutic circle that leads to the elucidation and definition of the relationship of time and narrative indeed might not be a vicious circle, as Ricoeur emphasizes. It is obviously structured, however, so that only the concept of *narrative* temporality can even appear as long as one moves within this circle.

55. Angehrn, *Geschichte und Identität,* 36. One could make analogous claims for biographical consciousness: this, too, is a consciousness of time—in principle, in the sense of narrative temporality.

56. Ibid., 35.

57. In this sense, modern consciousness can also be called the consciousness of contingency. Compare, for example, the studies by Leitner, *Gegenwart und Geschichte;* Michael Makropoulos, *Modernität als ontologischer Ausnahmezustand? Walter Benjamins Theorie der Moderne* (Munich, 1989). This need not mean, on the other hand, that other conceptions of reality are unconscious of contingency. What is modern, however, is the consciousness that contingency is universal and experienced nearly continuously, and that it can change everything—not only some particular part of a given system, but the system itself; not just some part of the world, but the world as a whole.

58. Leitner's sociological study *Gegenwart und Geschichte* makes it absolutely clear that there can be no point in playing historical against ahistorical forms of understanding reality and of thought. The first thing is to recognize what is even *possible.* Moreover, the differences between these options should not be prematurely effaced. Of course, different forms of conceiving reality can be investigated for, and judged according to, their specific functionalities, but such analyses cannot, finally, be used to justify claims to cultural superiority. "In itself" it is neither true nor false, good nor bad to think historically, but at most advantageous or disadvantageous.

59. Compare Angehrn, *Geschichte und Identität,* 37. The time of the narration can be different than the narrated time, which, especially in literary texts, allows a skillful play with time, a play that, of course, can also be important in everyday narratives. It is often of considerable psychological interest how long a subject takes to relate something; the relationship between the time of the narration and the time of what is narrated might indicate its subjective relevance and significance. On this distinction, see, for example, Gérard Genette, *Narrative Discourse: An Essay in Method,* trans. Jane E. Lewin (Ithaca, 1980), 20.

60. On this concept, compare Rüsen et al., "Untersuchungen zum Geschichtsbewußtsein," 230.

61. Angehrn, *Geschichte und Identität,* 14.

62. Rüsen, "Historische Sinnbildung durch Erzählen."

63. On the collective narration not least of historical experience, compare Jürgen Straub, "Zur narrativen Konstruktion von Vergangenheit: Erzähltheoretische Überlegungen und eine

exemplarische Analyse eines Gruppengesprächs über die 'NS-Zeit,'" *Bios: Zeitschrift für Biographieforschung und Oral History* 9 (1996): 30–58.

64. Such systematizations have, of course, already been suggested, though not, as far as I know, for historical narrative in particular. Uta Quasthoff offers one example, in which the functions that interest us here are delimited from "interactive" functions and designated "communicative," and then subdivided into (primarily) speaker-oriented (relief through communication, self-presentation), primarily listener-oriented (amusement, conversation, and information), and context-oriented (proof and explanation). See Uta Quasthoff, *Erzählen in Gesprächen: Linguistische Untersuchungen zu Strukturen und Funktionen am Beispiel einer Kommunikationsform des Alltags* (Tübingen, 1980), 146. For additional discussion, see also Gabriele Michel, whose work examines war stories narrated by Germans about experiences during the time of the Second World War, which represents a special case in other ways, not least under functional aspects (Gabriele Michel, *Biographisches Erzählen—zwischen individuellem Erlebnis und kollektiver Geschichtentradition: Untersuchung typischer Erzählfiguren, ihrer sprachlichen Form und ihrer interaktiven und identitätskonstituierenden Funktion in Geschichten und Lebensgeschichten* [Tübingen, 1985], 12, 77, 98), and the empirical-narratological section. Michel discusses the following functions in particular: information, communication of the judgments and attitudes of contemporary witnesses, conveying a particular self-image, conversation, justification, group formation and the creation of solidarity. On this subject, compare also Hans-Joachim Schröder, *Die gestohlenen Jahre: Erzählgeschichten und Geschichtserzählung im Interview. Der Zweite Weltkrieg aus der Sicht ehemaliger Mannschaftssoldaten* (Tübingen, 1992). By the same method of analyzing autobiographical narratives, Barbara Keller studies the experiences of contemporary witnesses to the period of National Socialism from a psychological point of view in *Rekonstruktion von Vergangenheit: Vom Umgang der 'Kriegsgeneration' mit Lebenserinnerungen* (Opladen, 1996).

These examples all touch on the theme of the historical construction of meaning, even if they are concerned exclusively with autobiographical narratives. The connection between autobiographical self-thematization and the historical construction of meaning certainly represents a particularly interesting approach for the psychology that interests us here, though it is not the only one. When history is shaped and communicated in light of individual experience, the subjective aspects of historical representation are relatively easily accessible. However, where merely "academic" historiography is being absorbed and then repackaged into statements having no relation to the experiences, orientations, and expectations of the speaker, the functions that interest us here may not be apparent, at least not in a methodical way.

65. In his contribution to the present volume, as well as elsewhere, Spence discusses this problem in detail with respect to personal experience. On the problem of the empirically convincing representation of past realities, see also James Young, *Writing and Rewriting the Holocaust: Narrative and the Consequences of Interpretation* (Bloomington, 1988). Young's numerous examples reveal the following dilemma: someone who recognizes that language, and therefore the formalization of the past, is constitutive for memory as such might despair that the experience of the Holocaust could *never* enter *directly* and be assimilated into *any* description, could be preserved as something irrevocable, in particular, as an inviolable truth. We know that for survivors of the Holocaust who attempted to tell of their experiences, this realization became agonizing, for what but an uncertain struggle for words could remain for all those who recognized, on the one hand, that they must tell (or give their experiences expression and form in some other medium) if they would attest to and preserve the memory of these experiences and the "historical truth" connected with them, and, on the other hand, that no medium and no form can restore these experiences "as such." There can be no return by this rendering, but always just shaping, transformation, change, distance, difference, and loss.

66. On the theoretical concept of identity, compare my explanations in Jürgen Straub, "Identitätstheorie im Übergang? Über Identitätsforschung, den Begriff der Identität, und die zunehmende Beachtung des Nicht-Identischen in subjekttheoretischen Diskursen," *Sozialwissenschaftliche Literatur-Rundschau* 14 (1991): 49–71; idem, "Identität und Sinnbildung: Ein Beitrag aus der Sicht einer handlungs- und erzähltheoretisch orientierten Sozialpsychologie," in *Jahres-*

bericht ZiF 94/95 (Bielefeld, 1996), 42–90; idem, "Personale und kollektive Identität: Zur Analyse eines theoretischen Begriffs," in *Identitäten,* ed. Aleida Assmann and Heidrun Friese (Frankfurt, 1998).

    67. Young, *Writing and Rewriting the Holocaust.*

    68. That was, of course, why Nietzsche diagnosed history, or rather historicism, as the fatal sickness of his age; see, for example, "Unzeitgemäße Betrachtungen, Zweites Stück: Von Nutzen und Nachtheil der Historie für das Leben," in *Sämmtliche Werke,* vol. 1, ed. Giorgio Colli and Mazzino Montinari (Munich, 1988). A different view of the excess of memory is found in Paul Ricoeur, "Gedächtnis—Vergessen—Geschichte," in *Historische Sinnbildung: Problemstellungen, Zeitkonzepte, Wahrnehmungshorizonte, Darstellungsstrategien,* ed. Jörn Rüsen and Klaus E. Müller (Reinbek, 1997). A psychological critique of Nietzsche's essay can be found in Jürgen Straub, "Geschichte, Identität und Lebensglück: Eine psychologische Lektüre *unzeitgemäßer Betrachtungen,*" in *Historische Sinnbildung,* ed. Klaus E. Müller and Jörn Rüsen (Reinbek, 1997), 165–194.

    69. Charles Taylor, *Sources of the Self: The Making of the Modern Identity* (Cambridge, Mass., 1989). Compare also Straub, "Identität und Sinnbildung."

    70. Compare also Jan Assmann, *Das kulturelle Gedächtnis: Schrift, Erinnerung und politische Identität in frühen Hochkulturen* (Munich, 1992), 144–160.

    71. Rainer Rath, "Zur Legitimation und Einbettung von Erzählungen in Alltagsdialogen," in *Dialogforschung, Sprache der Gegenwart* no. 54: *Jahrbuch des Instituts für deutsche Sprache,* ed. Peter Schröder and Hugo Steger (Düsseldorf, 1980), 265–287; Rath, "Erzählfunktionen und Erzähllankündigungen in Alltagsdialogen," in *Erzählforschung. Ein Symposion,* ed. Eberhard Lämmert (Stuttgart, 1982), 33–50. Rath investigates the phatic function, in particular with a view to the relationship between adults and children. One could say this about this relationship: When adults tell about history, they not only initiate and intensify their relationships with children, but expand their horizons by familiarizing them with what came before them. The significance of phatic function is obvious, not least for the developmental psychology of the historical construction of meaning. On the tendency of narrative to bring speaker and listener closer, compare also Brigitte Boothe, "Die Alltagserzählung in der Psychotherapie," 37.

    72. Truth and accuracy here designate two kinds of validity claims related to qualitatively different domains of truth; compare Jürgen Habermas, *Handlungsrationalität und gesellschaftliche Rationalisierung,* vol. 1 of *Theorie des kommunikativen* (Frankfurt, 1981), 114. Next to these claims, related to the objective and to the social world, respectively, we recognized claims to honesty and authenticity, related to the subjective interior world of dramaturgical agents. But psychology is certainly not always concerned with evaluating validity claims of this kind. More important than evaluating validity claims of whatever kind is, in every case, a hermeneutic analysis of the subjective or social constructions of reality in question, whether these happen to be true, correct, or honest or not.

    It is certainly a difficult, and in my opinion, still unresolved question whether an interpreter, psychologist or not, nevertheless—in other words, independently of his central objective—ought even to react implicitly or explicitly to such validity claims. Habermas is of this view, assuming, after all, that a rationality claim inheres in *all* statements. Speakers thus somehow always make claims, depending on how their speech relates to the world, for the truth and correctness or honesty and authenticity of their words, and so everyone who wants to understand this speech, according to Habermas, must take a position. The rationality claims built into language finally make the problem of understanding in behavioral, social, and cultural sciences a highly difficult undertaking, which moves between criticism and appreciation of others. The danger of absolutizing one's own standards and expropriating the other in the name of a supposedly universal rationality is obvious. For a discussion of the problematic of understanding, see Jürgen Straub, *Handlung, Interpretation, Kritik,* part 3, and idem, *Verstehen, Kritik, Anerkennung: Das Eigene und das Fremde in der Erkenntnisbildung interpretativer Wissenschaften* (Göttingen, 1999).

    73. The concept of the "scene" is central to Alfred Lorenzer's psychoanalytic conception of scenic understanding. Boothe's "Die Alltagserzählung in der Psychotherapie" is also systematically based on the scenic character of language and especially of speech. She accordingly analyzes four basic processes modeled by narrative, namely, social integration, wish fulfillment or psycho-

logical restitution, the reorganization of the psyche in order to integrate what had been dissociated, and, finally, the recollection or re-presentation of memory. Space does not permit a more thorough discussion of the subject, or the related methodological issues, with reference here only to my discussion of Lorenzer's ideas in Straub, *Handlung, Interpretation, Kritik*. It should also be mentioned that the scenic content of narratives has been of interest not only to psychologists (compare, for example, Michel, *Biographisches Erzählen*, 10, or Uta Quasthoff, *Erzählen in Gesprächen: Linguistische Untersuchungen zu Strukturen und Funktionen am Beispiel einer Kommunikationsform des Alltags* [Tübingen, 1980], 27).

74. Boothe, "Die Alltagserzählung in der Psychotherapie," 4.
75. Ibid.
76. Ibid., 10.
77. Ibid., 42. Boothe considers everyday narratives to be generally less "objective" and informative, as far as "external events" in the past are concerned, as well as "imprecise, superficial, and inadequate in their observations" (24). Despite good reasons for such skepticism, her judgments seem to me to be overdrawn. The same holds for the claim on the next page: "Everyday narrative is obviously no description of an action, not even an inferior one"; narrative representations of the past *absolutely do not serve purposes* of "ascertainment, assertion, information." As accurate as it may be to say that everyday narratives of the most diverse kind are structured *egocentrically*, and emerge from the personal and emotional involvement of the speaker, this can hardly completely exclude an objective orientation. We leave aside the question of *how often* narratives may fail to guide future action, but here, too, Boothe's verdict seems untenable.
78. Sigmund Freud, "Vorlesungen zur Einführung in die Psychoanalyse" [Complete introductory lectures on psychoanalysis], in *Studienausgabe* (Frankfurt, 1978), vol. 1, 359.
79. This function of biographical narrative has been well investigated, not least in the context of research concerned with collective experiences and expectations; compare, for example, Albrecht Lehmann, "Rechtfertigungsgeschichten: Über eine Funktion des Erzählens eigener Erlebnisse im Alltag," *Fabula* 21 (1991): 56–69. The exculpatory aspect plays a role in investigations in entirely different disciplines, not least in studies dealing with experiences during Nazi Germany (see Michel, *Biographisches Erzählen;* Schröder, *Die gestohlenen Jahre;* Keller, *Rekonstruktion von Vergangenheit*.
80. Nostalgic retrospection can also be regarded as one of the possible forms of the past, as one of the relationships people can have to the past from their position in the present; compare Mario Bretone, *Dieci modi di vivere il passato* (Rome, 1991). Bretone touches here and there on the question of the function of the historical construction of meaning while pursuing basically quite other goals. It would be interesting, though too far outside the frame of the current inquiry, to ask what function each of the ways detailed by him for living with the past (dream, invention, duplication, identification, amalgam, isolation, nostalgia, skepticism, utopia, history) might have psychologically.
81. Boothe, "Die Alltagserzählung in der Psychotherapie," 46.
82. Ibid., 61.
83. Gabriele Rosenthal, *Erzählte und erlebte Lebensgeschichte: Gestalt und Struktur biographischer Selbstbeschreibungen* (Frankfurt, 1995), 167.
84. Boothe, "Die Alltagserzählung in der Psychotherapie," 39; see also 47.
85. Ibid., 41.
86. On the difference between experiences of contingency in general and the contingency of action in particular, compare Straub, *Handlung, Interpretation, Kritik*.
87. Paul Ricoeur, *Zufall und Vernunft in der Geschichte,* trans. Helga Marcelli (Tübingen, 1986). [This lecture was published in French as *Contingence et Rationalité dans le Récit* (Tübingen, 1986). A different version appeared in French as "Contingence et Rationalité dans le Récit," in *Studien zur neueren französischen Phänomenologie: Ricoeur, Foucault, Derrida,* ed. Ernst Wolfgang Orth (Freiburg, 1986), 11–29. It has not yet been translated into English. Trans.]
88. Ricoeur, *Zufall und Vernunft,* 11. Ricoeur's definition involves a modal-theoretical version of the concept of contingency. It is important to note that from the perspective of subjects,

the contingency of *their own actions,* as a rule, coincides with their experience of scope for action and chances for freedom, while the contingency of events they did not intend or cause (including the actions of others), on the other hand, is experienced as risk and uncertainty, as the danger, in other words, that their own expectations and desires will be disappointed. Of course, there are exceptions to this rule: on the one hand, one can fail to understand one's actions, or how one could have acted thus; on the other side, there are happy accidents, heteronomously caused surprises that the one is happy to accept as the blessing of fate. On the concept of contingency, compare also Niklas Luhmann, "Generalized Media and the Problem of Contingency," in *Explorations in General Theory in Social Science: Essays in Honor of Talcott Parsons,* ed. Jan Loubser (New York, 1976), vol. 2, 507–532; on the history of the concept, see the entry on "Contingency," by numerous authors, in *Historisches Wörterbuch der Philosophie,* ed. Joachim Ritter and Karlfried Gründer (Darmstadt, 1974), 1027–1038.

89. Ricoeur's concept of "emplotment" is, as mentioned above, oriented to Aristotle, who in the *Poetics* designates a complete action as a structure composed of incidents, that is, precisely, as "plot." This definition makes clear why Aristotle, as well as Ricoeur, designate conversely the plot as the imitation of an action; compare Paul Ricoeur, *Time and Narrative,* vol. 1, 31–87. Hayden White defines the narrative integration of events into culturally accessible conceptual and narrative structures also as "the encodation of the facts contained in the chronicles as components of specific *kinds* of plot structures" (idem, "The Historical Text as Literary Artifact," in *Tropics of Discourse,* 88). Concerning the culturally available conceptual and narrative structures, White thinks of a "*complex* of *symbols*" which gives us directions for finding an *icon* of the structure of these events in our literary tradition" (88). In particular, White is interested in the narrative structures we already know as romance, comedy, tragedy, and satire. For a critical discussion of White's narratological reflections, see for example, Jörn Stückrath, "Die 'Wendung' wider das Chaos: Zur Rekonstruktion und Kritik von Hayden Whites tropologischer Theorie der Geschichtsschreibung" (paper delivered at the conference "Narrativität und Fiktionalität," Bielefeld, June 1995); see also, Straub, "Zur narrativen Konstruktion von Vergangenheit," 34.

90. Ricoeur, *Zufall und Vernunft,* 14.

91. Reinhart Koselleck, *Futures Past: On the Semantics of Historical Time,* trans. Keith Tribe (Cambridge, Mass., 1989), 116–129.

92. Ricoeur, *Zufall und Vernunft,* 15. The allusion to rule-based explanations, which one might connect to Winch's philosophy of the social sciences, complements Ricoeur's account. We need to consider that narratives, next to causes, purposes, and accidents, also integrate (sociocultural) rules in order to lend events and developments in the social world intelligibility. Compare Jürgen Straub, *Die Prinzipien der historischen Forschung,* vol. 2 of *Rekonstruction der Vergangenheit: Grundzüge einer Historik* (Göttingen, 1986), 22.

93. Ricoeur, *Zufall und Vernunft,* 15.

94. Ibid.

95. Ibid., 18.

96. Ricoeur's formulation, according to which narrative explains *post facto* why something necessarily or probably had to happen thus, is entirely Aristotelian. In my view, this formulation does not quite do justice to the narrative treatment of contingency. It should therefore be expanded as indicated, so that, expressed in the terminology of newer theories of explanation, next to conditions that allow an event to seem necessary or probable, it also brings into view conditions that allow it to seem (merely) *possible.* In other words, not just answers to "why," but also answers to "how likely" represent explanations. Narrative acts of explanation need to be understood precisely in this latter sense as well. Compare Jürgen Straub, "Handlungsbegriffe und Handlungserklärungen: Typologische Unterscheidungen unter besonderer Berücksichtigung des narrativen Modells," in *Handlungstheorie: Begriff und Erklärung des Handelns im interdisziplinären Diskurs,* ed. Jürgen Straub and Hans Werbig (Frankfurt, 1999).

97. Ricoeur, *Zufall und Vernunft,* 24.

98. Bruner, "Two Modes of Thought."

99. On this typology, see, for example, Rüsen, "Untersuchungen zum Geschichtsbewußtsein," 237. This typology is most likely indebted to the analysis of the different stages of historical consciousness.

100. Jörn Rüsen, "The Development of Narrative Competence in Historical Learning: An Ontogenetical Hypothesis Concerning Moral Consciousness," in *History and Memory* 1 (1989): 35–59, reprinted in Rüsen, *Studies in Metahistory,* ed. Pieter Duvenage (Pretoria, 1993), 63–85.

101. Rüsen, "Historische Sinnbildung durch Erzählen."

102. Ibid., 4.

103. Karl-Ernst Jeismann, "Geschichtsbewußtsein als zentrale Kategorie der Geschichtsdidaktik."

104. See, for example, the contributions to Mario Carretero and James F. Voss, eds., *Cognitive and Instructional Processes in History and the Social Sciences* (Hillsdale, N.J., 1994); Gaea Leinhardt, Isabel L. Beck, and Catherine Stainton, eds., *Teaching and Learning in History* (Hillsdale, N.J., 1994).

105. Ricoeur, *Zufall und Vernunft,* 22.

106. Ibid.

107. Ibid.

108. The "pragmatic" intelligence that is so highly dependent on individual life experience is of great interest to the so-called study of wisdom, which one might not least understand as a corrective, from the standpoint of developmental psychology, to the conventional study of intelligence. See, for example, Ursula Staudinger and Paul Baltes, "Weisheit: Gegenstand psychologischer Forschung," *Psychologische Rundschau* 47 (1996): 57–77. Their definition of "wisdom" suggests, in my opinion, how useful the narrativist paradigm can be, not least for psychological inquiry. To the best of my knowledge, however, no one is making these connections with respect to terminology, nor in empirical methods of research.

109. In theoretical writing about psychotherapy and psychotherapeutic research, a narrative turn has quite rightly become the subject of discussion (see, for example, Donald Spence, *Narrative Truth and Historical Truth: Meaning and Interpretation in Psychoanalysis* [New York, 1982]; Roy Schafer, "Narration in the Psychoanalytic Dialogue," *Critical Inquiry* 7 (1980): 29-53; idem, *Narrative Actions in Psychoanalysis* [Worcester, 1981]).

110. Rüsen formulates a contemporary version of such a *Historik* in his *Grundzüge der Historik,* 1–3.

111. See, for example, Pandel, "Dimensionen des Geschichtsbewußteins." Pandel divides the concept of "historical consciousness" as an "individual mental structure" into single, systematically interdependent categories. This cognitive system of relations then consists of the consciousness of time, the consciousness of reality (as the ability to distinguish historical reality from products of the imagination), consciousness of historicity, the consciousness of identity, and political, economic, and moral consciousness. Hans Günter Schmidt's proposal, following Rüsen and others, derives historical consciousness essentially from narrative competence, and defines the latter as the ability "to instrumentalize, integrate, and coordinate the different affective, cognitive, and conative competences, so that first, temporal differentiations can be experienced, second, these experiences can be interpreted, and third, these experiences and interpretations can be made communicable with respect to the orientation of subsequent, individual and group action" (idem, "'Eine Geschichte zum Nachdenken': Erzähltypologie, narrative Kompetenz, und Geschichtsbewußtsein: Bericht über einen Versuch der empirischen Erforschung des Geschichtsbewußtein von Schülern der Sekundärstufe I (Unter- und Mittelstufe)," *Geschichtsdidaktik: Probleme, Projekte, Perspektiven* 12 (1987): 30. Seixas's conceptualization of historical understanding, oriented by the model of historiographical thinking, can be read in part as a competence-theoretical attempt. This becomes obvious where historical consciousness's acts of understanding are explicated not only by reference to the structural-qualitative aspects of historical texts, but are attributed to the integrated abilities of subjects capable of action and speech, namely, to such competences as the competence to create meaning-structured realities, to make narrative and

causal connections, or the faculty of empathy, or moral judgment (Peter Seixas, "Conceptualizing the Growth of Historical Understanding," in *The Handbook of Education and Human Development,* ed. David Olson and Nancy Torrance [Cambridge, U.K., 1996], 765–783).

112. See, for example, Jürgen Belgrad, Bernard Görlich, Hans-Dieter König, and Gunzelin Schmid Noerr, eds., *Zur Idee einer psychoanalytischen Sozialforschung: Dimensionen szenischen Verstehens* (Frankfurt, 1987); Hans-Dieter König, "Die Methode der tiefenhermeneutischen Kultursoziologie," in *"Wirklichkeit" im Deutungsprozeß,* ed. Thomas Jung and Stefan Müller-Doohm (Frankfurt, 1993), 190–222; Thomas Leithäuser and Birgit Volmerg, *Psychoanalyse in der Sozialforschung: Eine Einführung am Beispiel einer Sozialpsychologie der Arbeit* (Opladen, 1988); Alfred Lorenzer, ed., *Kultur-Analysen: Psychoanalytische Studien zur Kultur* (Frankfurt, 1986).

113. Roger Chartier, *Die unvollendete Vergangenheit,* in particular, the introduction.

CHAPTER 4

Narrative, Moral Identity, and Historical Consciousness
A Social Constructionist Account

KENNETH J. GERGEN

Two decades ago, inquiry into narrative played but a minor role in scholarly deliberation; the relationship between narrative analysis and historiography was little explored; the term "narrative" had scarcely entered the vocabulary of psychological science. Today, the study of narrative concatenates throughout the humanities and the social sciences, and the problems raised by such analyses for our conception of history, along with the historical consciousness of the individual, are profound. Further, there are now many distinct and well-articulated orientations toward narrative: realist, phenomenological, psychodynamic, cognitive, textual, and rhetorical among them. Each raises different implications for our understanding of history, identity, and the place of historical consciousness in contemporary society. My aim here is not to review, contrast, or compare these various approaches, but rather to elucidate the rudiments of but a single orientation, recent in its emerging self-consciousness, but bold and exciting in implication. I wish, then, to outline a social constructionist account of narratives, and to explore several of its implications with respect to both identity and history. Of ultimate concern will be the role of historical consciousness in the achievement of moral identity.

Social constructionist dialogues have long played a role in human sciences deliberation, with the classic work of Berger and Luckmann fostering lively and broadscale debate.[1] However, contemporary constructionism has largely abandoned the social phenomenology and social structural analysis of former years. Rather, it draws its primary sustenance from recent history of science, social

---

Notes for this section begin on page 118.

studies of science, ideological critique, post-structural literary theory, and the renaissance of rhetorical study.[2] As many now see it, social constructionism serves as the principle successor to empiricist foundationalism—now a moribund relic of "high modernism"—as the chief means of understanding the acquisition and generation of what we as human scientists take to be knowledge of the world. For purposes of illuminating the social constructionist view, and providing a platform for contrasting other modes of approach, I shall proceed seriatim to develop a number of rudimentary assumptions regarding narrative, personal identity, and the achievement of moral consciousness through historical narration.

The Structuring of Narrative Discourse

At the outset, social constructionism brackets the problem of individual minds as the locus of origin, comprehension, or storage of narrative. The initial focus, then, is on narrative as a linguistic phenomena, typically spoken or written text (but not to the exclusion of pictorial or other expressive media). For purposes of the present analysis, we shall consign narrative to the domain of discourse. In this sense, narrative accounting in the present era gains its character from long-standing traditions of storytelling, oral history, accounts of personal memory, and a variety of literary genres (including historical writing, the novel, and scientific accounts of cross-time change). How can we characterize contemporary conventions of narrative accounting; what are the requirements for an intelligible story within the present-day culture of the West? There have been many attempts to identify the characteristics of the well-formed narrative. They have occurred within domains of literary theory,[3] semiotics,[4] historiography,[5] and certain sectors of social science.[6] From these various analyses, we may synthesize a variety of common agreements. In particular, the criteria outlined in the paragraphs that follow are central in constructing an intelligible narrative in significant segments of contemporary culture:

Establishing a Valued Endpoint

An acceptable story must first establish a goal, an event to be explained, a state to be reached or avoided, an outcome of significance, or more informally, "a point." To relate how one walked North for two blocks, East for three, and then turned left on Pine Street would constitute an impoverished story; if this description were a prelude to "finding at last an affordable apartment," the account begins to approximate an acceptable story. The selected endpoint is typically saturated with value, that is, understood to be desirable or undesirable. For example, an acceptable endpoint may be the protagonist's well-being ("how

I narrowly escaped death"), the discovery of something precious ("how Jones discovered the phenomenon"), personal loss ("how I lost the debate"), and so on. Thus, if the story terminated upon finding 404 Pine Street, it would lapse into insignificance; it is when the search for a much-desired apartment is successful that we participate in the tradition. In MacIntyre's terms: "Narrative requires an evaluative framework in which good or bad character helps to produce unfortunate or happy outcomes."[7] It is also clear that this demand for a valued endpoint introduces a strong cultural component (traditionally called "subjective bias") into the story. Life itself is scarcely composed of separable events, especially of events which constitute endpoints and are saturated with value. Rather, the endpoint and its value are determined by the teller of the tale. Or more generally, it is only within a cultural tradition that "valued events" become intelligible.

Selecting Relevant Events

Once a goal is established, it serves to dictate the kinds of events that can subsequently figure in the account. The myriad candidates for "eventhood" are greatly reduced by establishing the endpoint. An intelligible story is one in which selected events serve to make the goal more or less probable, accessible, important, or vivid. Thus, if one's story is about the winning of a football match ("how we won the game"), the most relevant events are those that bring the goal closer or make it more distant (e.g., "Tom's first kick bounced off the goal, but on the next attack, he deflected the ball into the net with the twist of his head"). Only at the risk of inanity would one introduce into the story of the soccer match a note on fifteenth-century monastery life or a hope for future space travel, unless it could be shown that such matters were significantly related to winning the match (e.g., "Juan got his inspiration for the tactic from reading about fifteenth-century religious practices"). An account of the day (e.g., "it was crisp and sunny") would be acceptable in the narrative, as it makes the narrative events more vivid, but describing the weather in a remote country would seem whimsical. Again, we find that narrative demands have ontological consequences. One is not free to include in the story all that takes place, but primarily that which is relevant to the story's conclusion.

Systematic Ordering

Concomitant with establishing a goal state and selecting relevant events is the arrangement of these events in a systematic sequence. The random ordering of events relevant to "winning a war" would be nonsensical by current standards. As Walter Ong suggests, the bases for such order (e.g., importance, interest value, recency) may change with history and culture.[8] However, perhaps the most widely used convention of narrative ordering in the contemporary West is that of linear, temporal sequence. For example, certain events are said to occur at the beginning of a war and these precede events taking place toward the middle and the termination. It is tempting to say that the sequence of related events should match the sequence in which the events *actually* occurred. However, this would be to confuse the rules of intelligible rendering with what is the case. Linear temporal ordering is, after all, a convention which employs an internally coherent system of signs; its features are not required by the world as it is. The linear orientation may be applied or not to what is the case depending on one's purposes. Clock time may not be effective, for example, if one wishes to speak of one's "experience of time passing in the dentist's chair"; nor is it adequate if one wishes to describe relativity theory in physics, or the circular rotation of seasons. In Michail Bakhtin's terms, we may view temporal accounts as *chronotopes,* that is, as literary conventions governing space–time relationships, or "the ground essential for the … representability of events."[9] That yesterday preceded today is a conclusion demanded only by a culturally specific chronotope.

Stabilizing Identity

The well-formed narrative is typically one in which the characters (or objects) in the story possess a continuous or coherent identity across time. A given protagonist cannot felicitously serve as a villain at one moment and a hero in the next, or demonstrate powers of genius unpredictably interspersed with moronic actions. Once defined by the storyteller, the individual (or entity) will tend to retain his or her identity or function within the story. There are obvious exceptions to this general tendency, but most are cases in which the story attempts to explain the change itself—how the frog became a prince, or the impoverished young man struggled to financial success. Further, causal forces may be introduced that bring about change in an individual (or entity), and for dramatic effect, a putative identity may give way to "the real." However, the well-formed story scarcely tolerates protean personalities.

Causal Linking

By contemporary standards, the ideal narrative is one that gives an explanation. As Ricoeur puts it, "Explanations must … be woven into the narrative tissue." Explanation is typically achieved by selecting events that by common standards are causally linked. Each event should be a product of that which it has preceded ("Because the rain came, we fled indoors"; "As a result of his illness, he couldn't meet his class"). When events within a narrative are related in an interdependent fashion, the outcome approximates more closely the well-formed story. As it is said, "The king died and then the queen died" is but a rudimentary story; "The king died and then the queen died of grief" is the beginning of a plot.

Narrative Demarking

Most acceptable stories employ signals to indicate their existence as stories, beginning at one point and terminating at another. As Katherine Young has proposed, the narrative is "framed" by various rule-governed devices that indicate when one is entering the "tale world," or the world of the story.[10] "Once upon a time," "Did you hear the one about," "You can't imagine what happened to me on the way over here," or "Let me tell you why I'm so happy" would all be signals to the audience that a narrative is to follow. Endings may also be signaled by phrases (e.g., "That's it," "So now you know"), but need not be. Laughter at the end of a joke may indicate the exit from the tale world; often, relating the story's point is sufficient to indicate that the tale world is now evacuated.

Variations in Narrative Form

By using these conventions of narration, one can generate a sense of coherence and direction in life events. Life acquires meaning and happenings are suffused with significance. However, we also find that certain forms of narrative are broadly shared within the culture. They are frequently used, easily identified, and are highly functional. In a sense, they constitute a ready vocabulary for rendering cross-time intelligibility. What account can be given of these more stereotypic tellings? The question here is similar to that of literary theorists concerned with fundamental plot lines.

Since Aristotelian times, philosophers and literary theorists, among others, have attempted to develop a formal vocabulary of plot. As sometimes argued, there may be a foundational set of plots from which all stories are derived. For example, relying heavily on the Aristotelian view, one of the most extensive accounts of plot within the present century is that of Northrop Frye.[11] Frye proposed that there are four basic forms of narrative, each of which is rooted in human experience with nature, and most particularly, with the evolution of the seasons. Thus, the experience of spring and the uprising of nature gives rise to *comedy*. In the classic tradition, comedy typically involves a challenge or threat, which is overcome to yield social harmony. A comedy need not be humorous, even though its ending is a happy one. In contrast, the free and calm of summer days give inspiration to *romance* as a dramatic form. Romance, in this case, consists of a series of episodes in which the major protagonist experiences challenge or threat, and through a series of struggles, emerges victorious. Romance need not be concerned with attraction between people; however, in its harmonious ending, it is similar to comedy. During autumn, when one experiences the contrast between the life of summer and the death of coming winter, *tragedy* is born; and in winter, with one's increasing awareness of unrealized expectancies and the death of dreams, *satire* becomes the relevant expressive form. In contrast to Frye's four master narratives, Joseph Campbell has proposed a single "monomyth," from which myriad variations can be found across the centuries.[12] The monomyth, rooted in unconscious psychodynamics, concerns the hero who has been able to overcome personal and historical limitations to reach a transcendent understanding of the human condition.

Although possessing certain aesthetic appeal, these quests for foundational plots are ultimately unsatisfying. There is simply no compelling rationale for why there should be a limited number of narratives. Rather than seeking a definitive account, the culturally based view favored here suggests a virtual infinity of possible story forms, with differing forms favored in various historical periods. In the same way that fashions of facial expression, dress, and professional aspirations shift with time, so do modal forms of narration. If we extend the preceding account of narrative characteristics, we can generate a way of appreciating existing norms along with infinite variations.

To elaborate, as we first saw, a story's endpoint is weighted with value. Thus, a victory, a consummated affair, a discovered fortune, or a prize-winning paper can all serve as proper story endings. On the opposite pole of the evaluative continuum would fall a defeat, a love lost, a fortune squandered, or a professional failure. Further, we can view the various events that lead up to the story's end (the selection and ordering of events) as moving through two-dimensional, evaluative space. As one approaches the valued goal over time, the story line moves in an upward direction; as one approaches failure or disillusionment, the story descends. All plots, then, may be converted to a linear form with respect to their evaluative shifts over time. This shift allows us to isolate three rudimentary forms of narrative.

The first may be described as a *stability narrative,* that is, a narrative that links events in such a way that the trajectory remains essentially unchanged with respect to a goal or outcome. Life simply goes on, neither better nor worse with respect to the conclusion. The stability narrative may be contrasted with two others. One may link together events in such a way that either increments or decrements characterize movement along the evaluative dimension over time. In the former case, we may speak of *progressive,* and in the latter, *regressive* narratives (see figure 4.1). The progressive narrative is the Panglossian account of life, ever day an improvement over the preceding. The progressive narrative is captured with the surmise, "I am really learning to overcome my shyness and be more open and friendly with people." The regressive narrative depicts a continued downward slide. The individual may confess, "I can't seem to con-

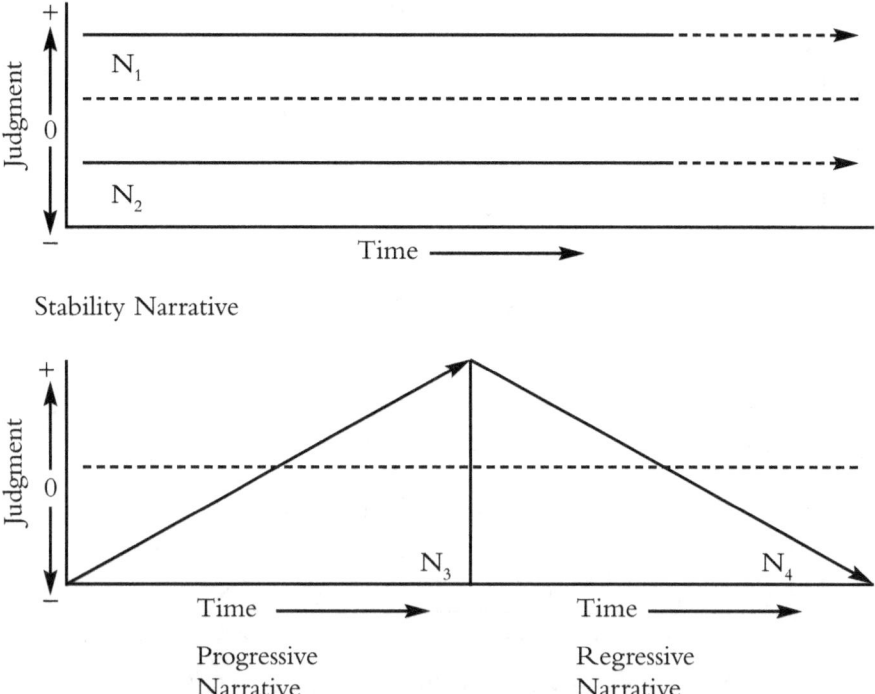

Figure 4.1. Rudimentary Forms of Narrative

trol the events in my life anymore," "It's been one series of catastrophes after another." Directionality is also implied in each of these narratives, with the former anticipating further increments and the latter further decrements.

As should be clear, these three narrative forms, stability, progressive, and regressive, exhaust the fundamental options for the direction of movement in evaluative space. As such, they may be considered rudimentary bases for other more complex variants. Theoretically, one may envision a potential infinity of variations on these rudimentary forms. However, as suggested, in various historical conditions, the culture may limit itself to a truncated repertoire of possibilities. Consider, for example, several prominent narrative forms in contemporary culture. There is first the *tragic narrative* as represented in figure 4.2. The tragedy, in this sense, would tell the story of the rapid downfall of one who had achieved high position. A progressive narrative is followed by a rapid regressive narrative. In the contrasting narrative (the comedy-romance) a regressive narrative is followed by a progressive narrative. Life events become increasingly problematic until the denouement, whereupon happiness is rapidly restored to the major protagonists. (The narrative is labeled comedy-romance in its conflation of the Aristotelian forms.) Further, if a progressive narrative is followed by a stability narrative (see figure 4.3), we have what is commonly known as the *happily-ever-after* story, which is widely adopted in traditional

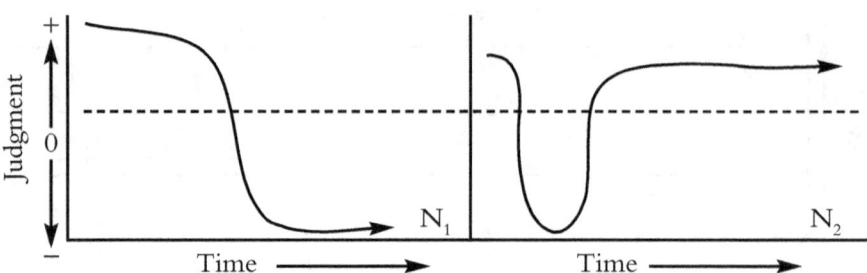

Figure 4.2. Tragic Narrative and Comedy Romance

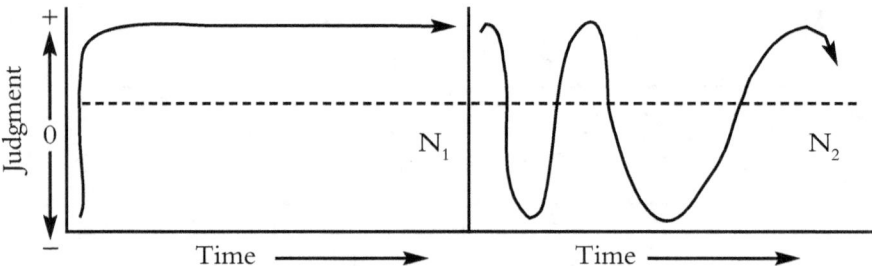

Figure 4.3. The Happily-Ever-After Story and the Heroic Saga

courtship. And we also recognize the *heroic saga* as a series of progressive-regressive phases (figure 4.3). In this case, for example, the individual may characterize his or her past as a continuous array of battles against the powers of darkness. Other narrative forms, including unification myths, communion narratives, and dialectic theory, may also be charted.

The Sociocultural Lodgment of Narrative

Because narration is chiefly a discursive mode of generating intelligibility, it shares with other linguistic formations a lodgment within particular sociocultural circumstances. In the same way that we confront enormous variations in language practices throughout the world, so we must be prepared for broad variations in narration, both in its existence, and in what counts as a well-formed story. This is most obviously the case in terms of fictional narratives.

The emergence of the novel in the nineteenth-century, its twentieth-century transformation in the hands of modernists such as Proust and Joyce, and the dislocation of continuity, time, and authorial standpoint in the work of various postmodernists, are only a few emergent properties. In postmodern writing, narratives may also turn ironically self-referential, demonstrating their own artifice as texts, and the ways in which their efficacy depends on their structure as narratives.[13] However, such sociocultural variations in narrative conventions are equally the case in the writing of both autobiography and biography.[14] As Mary Gergen's explorations of contemporary autobiography suggest, for example, men are far more likely to accommodate themselves to the prevailing criteria for "proper storytelling" than women.[15] Women's autobiographies are more likely, for example, to be structured around multiple endpoints, and to include materials unrelated to any particular endpoint. Further, as Hayden White's work makes clear, the narrative structure of historical writing itself has changed across the centuries.[16]

Narrative Truth as Cultural Convention

Although language is typically treated as representational—as capable of corresponding to or representing the world as it is—this view has virtually succumbed in recent years to a spate of criticisms from all branches of the humanities and social sciences. Such critique has obvious relevance to the possibility of narratives as conveyances for truth. Given the above account of narrative criteria and structure, the possibility for truth in narration is already obscured. As we have seen, there is nothing about the world that demands our singling out endpoint events and investing them with value. Similarly, because the well-formed narrative places requirements over what events may be included in a proper story, there is an enormous suppression of description. And too, the choice of "chronotropes" and the isolation of beginnings and endings are not matters that can be determined by recourse to "the world as it is."

At the same time, these limitations on objectivity do not necessarily apply to the events, actions, or entities making up the narrative. If we bracket consideration of the requirements for proper storying, can we conclude that narrative content is subject to empirical evaluation? For many, the arguments of Popper and Quine, in particular, give substantial reason for doubt.[17] The former argued that in science there was no logical means of inducing general theoretical statements from observation, that is, of moving in a logically grounded way from the level of observed particulars to a general or universal account of classes. This led Popper to embrace Reichenbach's distinction between a "context of discovery" and a "context of justification." The context of discovery—that space in which the scientist makes initial claims to correspondence—was, for Popper, "irrelevant to the logical analysis of scientific knowledge."[18]

In effect, the means by which the scientist establishes the ontological claims to be put to study, are not in themselves rationally justified. Quine's critique raised havoc with even the possibility of solid grounding in the context of justification. What is the possibility, he asked, of ostensive definition, that is, of defining scientific terms through public designation of material referents? Can the terms of a scientific ontology be grounded by the stimulus characteristics to which they refer? In his famous *gavagai* example, Quine demonstrated the impossibility of doing so.[19] If such a term is used by natives to refer to a running rabbit, a dead rabbit, a rabbit in a pot, or simply the signs of inferred rabbit presence, then what precise stimulus configuration secures the translation of the term as "rabbit"? In the extreme case, each time the native uses the term, he may be referring to an assemblage of rabbit parts, and the translator to the rabbit as a whole. We find, then, no means of ostensively linking the "facts" as narrated to the world as it is.

This is not to say that truth conditions cannot be established for narratives. However, these conditions must be established as specific cultural or subcultural achievements. In the same way that our reports of the weather, or the balance in our bank account can function for all practical purposes as "true" or "false" with respect to some form of datum, so can narrations of a crime, a space flight, or of a war be subjected to tests of veracity. It is critical, however, to realize that these forms of "objective" appraisal are a communal achievement. That is, the languages of description do not reflect or mirror what is the case; rather, the language functions to index a state of affairs for all practical purposes within a given community. Interlocutors come to assign words to given conditions, and if one remains within the community of agreement, it is possible to achieve a sense of objectivity within that community. We shall return to this point again in treating the function of historical accounting.

Narration as a Relational Achievement

Although the preceding account draws significantly from semiotic and literary theory, the social grounding of textual intelligibility must be underscored. If language is fundamentally a derivative of social interchange, then we are drawn to consider the ways in which narratives function within relationships—how and why they are used by persons in the course of their daily lives. In effect, the stance I am taking here is counterposed to the psychological, in which scholars are concerned with the mental function of narrative (e.g., the way in which narratives cognitively convert chaos to order). From the present standpoint, all that is meaningful to the individual privately is lodged within a meaning-generating process that is inherently social. Thus, individual mind gives way to social process as the central domain of concern. In this context, central attention turns to the social functioning of narrative accounts.

To appreciate the social pragmatics of narratives, it is useful to consider the quotidian functions of several narrative forms outlined earlier. Consider first the primitive narrative of stability. Negotiating social life successfully requires that one is capable of making him- or herself intelligible as an enduring, integral, or coherent identity. For example, in certain political arenas, it is essential to demonstrate that in spite of extended absences, one is "truly rooted" in the local culture and part of its future. Or, to be able to show on the more personal level how one's love, parental commitment, honesty, moral ideals, and so on have been unfailing over time, even when their outward appearances are suspicious, may be essential to continuing a relationship. In close relationships, people often wish to know that others "*are* what they seem," that certain characteristics endure across time. A major means for rendering such assurance is the stability narrative.

Consider the progressive narrative in this light. Society places a strong value not only on stability, but also on change. For example, every stabilization may also be characterized, from alternative perspectives, as problematic, oppressive, or odious. For many, the possibility of progressive change is of major significance. Careers are selected, hardships endured, and personal resources (including one's most intimate relations) sacrificed in the belief that one is participating in positive change—a progressive narrative. Further, the success of many relationships depends importantly on people's ability to demonstrate how their undesirable characteristics (e.g., unfaithfulness, quarreling, self-centeredness) have diminished over time, even when there are many reasons for doubt. As Kitwood's research suggests, people make special use of the progressive narrative in early stages of a relationship, seemingly to invest the relationship with increased value and promise for the future. In effect, the progressive narrative plays a variety of useful functions in social life.

Let us finally consider the social value of regressive narratives. Consider the effects, for example, of tales of woe in soliciting attention, sympathy, and intimacy. To relate one's story of depression is not to describe the onset of a mental state, but to engage in one or more relationships. The narrative may simultaneously solicit pity and concern, excuse oneself from failure, and deliver punishment. Within Western culture, regressive narratives can also serve a *compensatory function*. When people learn of steadily worsening conditions, the description often operates, by convention, as a challenge—to compensate or seek improvement. The decline is to be offset or reversed through renewed vigor; intensification of effort may turn a potential tragedy into a comedy-romance. Regressive narratives furnish an important means, then, of motivating people (including oneself) toward achieving positive ends. This compensatory function operates on a national level when a government demonstrates that the steady decline in the balance of payments can be offset by grassroots commitment to locally manufactured products. On the individual level, one may bolster his or her enthusiasm for a given project: "I am failing at this, I must try harder."

Narrative and Cultural Value

A final point must be made before treating the issue of identity. Although the groundwork has been amply laid, it is important here to underscore the extent to which narratives function both to reflect and to create cultural value. In part, the value-sustaining and generating function of narrative is textually derived. That is, in establishing a given endpoint and endowing it with value, and in populating the narrative with certain actors and certain facts as opposed to others, the narrator enters into the world of moral and political action. Value is placed on certain goals (e.g., "winning," "achieving"), certain individuals (e.g., individual heroes as opposed to communities), and particular modes of description (e.g., the world as material as opposed to spiritual). When a news commentator reports a local fire or describes a turn in the stock market index, she is also reasserting the topoi that unite the culture within a tradition. Typically, the culture's ontology and sense of values is affirmed and sustained.

However, narrative tellings do more than create a discursive world of value; such tellings are themselves constituents of ongoing and often institutionalized patterns of societal conduct. In this sense, they function so as to generate and sustain (and sometimes disrupt) traditions of action. In Austin's terms, we must not only pay attention to the *constative* character of narrative discourse (its portrayal of the world as being like this as opposed to that), but to its *performative* dimension—what it achieves as an action within a relationship.[20] When a child tells her parents the story of her day in school, she is simultaneously constructing an image and sustaining a relationship that links the parents to her daily pursuits outside the home. In the telling, her parents are constituted as guardians; their evaluative function is asserted; and the parent–child reality (and comfort) is extended from beyond the face-to-face context into the region of spatio-temporal absence. The simple story, then, makes an integral contribution to the sustenance of the family as such. In the same way, the family's telling stories of their past (e.g., how we survived the war, how we came to live here) serves to define and unite them as a unit. Narration inescapably functions, then, to create, sustain (and possibly disrupt or transform) traditions of value.

Narrative and the Achievement of Identity

Not only does narrative play a central role in structuring reality and relationship, but to an important degree, the very conception of self as an individual agent is lodged within narrative action.

Here we must first consider the extent to which "identity," is a discursive achievement. To be identified as this or that person (Kurt, Sarah, or Wilfred), to be in possession of various attributes ("kind," "honest," "intense"), and to be self-referential ("I said," "I went,") are fundamentally moves in language. It is largely through discourse that we achieve the sense of individuated selves with particular attributes and self-referential capacities. To be sure, there is "something" beyond discourse, but what there is makes its way into the practices of cultural life largely through linguistic interpretation. With the discursive construction of identity thus foregrounded, there are significant ways in which identity is importantly fashioned through narrative. At the outset, the very categories by which we understand individual identities are largely a by-product of discursive elaboration. The sense of a self possessing the faculty for rational and objective deliberation, for example, can be traced in a significant way to the texts (and conversations) of seventeenth- and eighteenth-century educated society.[21] An appreciation of the individual's capacity for genius and inspiration, the recognition of deep passions, and the suspicion of deep disturbance were made possible largely by the discourses (both arts and letters) of the nineteenth-century romanticists.[22] Further, these concepts of the person—as rational, passionate, inspired, and the like—are embedded within broader narratives. They are not simply names for existing entities, but discursive creations requiring extensive narration. For example, in order to acquire credibility as an existant, the concept of rational process requires a story world in which subject and object are separated, objects in the external world impinge on the subject, and the subject's rational deliberation influences action—essentially a narrative in which rational process gains its meaning through its function in the story world.[23]

However, it is not only the conceptual components of the narrative that bestow identity on individuals; the narrative forms themselves are a chief means of self-portrayal. As we inherit traditions of storytelling, individual actors play a major role in emplotment; we distinguish between heroes and villains, damsels desirous and dangerous, and so on. Further, these individuals play out their lives within culturally specific forms of narrative, such as comedy, tragedy, and the happily-ever-after story outlined above. These forms of emplotment and narrative structure serve as major resources available to persons in detailing their lives to others. One may intelligibly describe one's life in terms of early hardship and then, with continued striving, eventual success—a common progressive narrative. Yet, to depict one's life as a series of daily rises and falls, each day bringing one back to the level at which the day was begun, would place severe demands on our sense of credulity. There are no common conventions for this form of accounting, and thus one cannot achieve an intelligible identity in its terms. To paraphrase Wittgenstein, the limits of our narrative traditions serve as the limits of our identity.

In this context, it is useful to consider the process of personal memory—one's means of identifying oneself through reports of personal history. Traditionally, psychologists have treated memory processes as lodged within the individual. As it is typically argued, memory is a central ingredient of human makeup; its functions and potentials are genetically provided and are universal within the human species. In contrast, the social constructionist proposes that the very concept of human memory, as a specific process within human minds, is a discursive artifact.[24] We have no means of identifying a particular psychological state associated with or responsible for producing various actions that we publicly index as "memory." The conditions for ascribing memory are not then signaled by the existence of a mental event, but are socially designated. That is, under circumscribed conditions we collectively treat certain actions as "remembering." We treat the words one writes in an exam as "indicators of memory," while most words spoken in everyday conversation do not count as such. By saying that memory is a discursive achievement, is also to propose that "having a memory" is to participate in a cultural tradition. To speak of one's past is to enter into a tradition of talk for which the rules of well-formed storying are apposite. One cannot speak of last week's adventure by recalling a random patch of color, a breeze, a word, and an itch. Rather, one must identify oneself as a particular identity, moving through time, in certain directions with certain endpoints being prominent. To "remember properly" is to generate a story replete with all the earmarks of the well-formed narrative.[25]

Lived Narratives as Forms of Relationship

Although personal identity is essentially a discursive achievement, we must remember that discourse is also lodged within the realm of relations. Thus, the discursive creation of identity is more fundamentally a social undertaking. To underscore the significance of the social, it is useful here to explore forms of *lived narrative,* that is, forms of social interchange that we understand or index in narrative terms. For example, in the case of an athletic contest, we have no difficulty in telling a story of the fortunes of each team, recounting perhaps the climax of the game, and the final victory of one side versus the other. As we watch or play the game, it appears to us as narrative in itself; we feel we are witnessing or participating in an unfolding story. Rather than conceptualizing the game as a "narrative in itself"—prior to discourse—it is more appropriate to understand it as action that is indexed in terms of a narrative forestructure. We articulate the kinds of rules that establish victory as a valued endpoint, divide the world into antagonists, and index various actions in terms of their contribution to victory. In this sense, various patterns of interchange, such as debates, careers, sales transactions, seductions, and the like will carry the sense of lived narrative.

Lived narratives are also essential to the achievement of identity. Consider, in particular, the importance of emotional expression in determining the character of identity. The identification of a person's feelings, passions, or sentiments is often critical in determining what sort of person he or she is. In present terms, emotional discourse gains its meaning not by virtue of its relationship to an inner world (of experience, disposition, or biology), but through the way it figures in patterns of cultural relationship. Some forms of action—by current Western standards—are indexed as "emotional expressions." Following Averill, the actions themselves are properly viewed as social performances.[26] In this sense, one isn't "incited to action" by emotions; rather, one *does* emotions, or participates in them much as he or she would in a stage performance. From a constructionist standpoint, to ask how many emotions there are would be similar to asking a theater critic to enumerate the number of roles found in the theater; to explore the physiology of different emotions would be to compare the heart-rate, adrenaline surges, or neural activity of actors who play Hamlet as opposed to King Lear. Emotions do not "have an impact on social life"; they constitute social life itself.

Moving further to understand emotions as lived narratives, it is important to realize the ways in which emotional performances are circumscribed by or embedded within broader patterns of relationship. We tend to view emotional performances as events *sui generis,* primarily because they are frequently more "colorful" (e.g., more or less animated, voluble) than actions in their surrounds. In the same way, we may fasten on the impressive extension of the ballerina during a pas de deux with little consciousness of the essential role played by the male counterpart. However, without the actions of others—preceding, simultaneous to, and following the performance of emotion—the emotion would be unintelligible as such. If cut away from ongoing relationships, emotional performances would either not occur or would be nonsensical. For example, if the hostess at a dinner party suddenly bolted from her seat in rage, or began loudly sobbing, guests would undoubtedly be unsettled or abashed. Further, if she could not make it clear how such outbursts were related to a series of preceding and/or anticipated events (essentially a narrative account)—if she announced that she was moved to such outbursts for no particular reason—they might consider her a candidate for psychiatric care. To achieve intelligibility, the emotional performance must be a recognizable component of an ongoing chain of actions. There is good reason, then, to view emotional performances as constituents of larger or more extended patterns of interaction.

As I am proposing, emotional expressions are meaningful (indeed, succeed in counting as legitimate emotions) only when inserted into particular, crosstime sequences of interchange. In effect, they are constituents of culturally patterned forms of lived narrative. Consider the emotion of jealousy. Expressions of jealousy must be preceded by certain conditions. One cannot properly express jealousy at the sight of a sunset or a traffic light, but jealousy is appropriate if one's lover shows signs of affection toward another. Further, if the jealousy is expressed to the lover, he or she is not free (by current cultural standards) to begin a conversation about the weather or to express deep joy. The lover may apologize, for example, or attempt to explain why jealousy is unwarranted, but the range of options is limited. And, if the apology is offered, the jealous agent is again constrained in the kinds of reactions that may intelligibly follow. In effect, the two participants are engaged in a form of cultural ritual. The expression of jealousy is but a single integer within the sequence; the ritual would be unrecognizable without it, but without the remainder of the ritual, jealousy would be nonsensical. These patterns of relationship can be viewed as *emotional scenarios*—informally scripted patterns of interchange. The emotional expression, from this standpoint, is only the possession of the single individual in the sense that he or she is the performer of a given act within the broader relational scenario; however, the emotional act is more fundamentally a creation of the relationship, and even more broadly, of a particular cultural history.

Moral Identity, Narrative and Community

The final entry into the present treatment of identity draws heavily from two preceding points: first, the arguments for the pragmatic function of narrative in cultural life, and second, from the value-generating capacities of narrative. By conjoining these arguments, we may say that narratives of the self are used within daily life as a means of creating or sustaining value—the value of both oneself and all other protagonists who feature in the quotidian tellings of a life. In the case of self, the value-generating function may be linked in particular to what may be called "moral identity," that is, one's definition as a worthy and acceptable individual by the standards inhering in one's relationships. In Western culture, for example, to intelligibly narrate oneself as a stable and coherent individual (stability narrative), who is attempting to achieve a standard of excellence (progressive narrative), and is fighting against earlier setbacks or injuries (regressive narrative), is to approach a state of moral identity, of communal decency in its broadest sense. Heroes and villains are such by virtue of their narrative encasement. As MacIntyre also points out, we are accountable for these narrative portrayals: "To be the subject of a narrative that runs from one's birth to one's death is ... to be accountable for the actions and experiences which compose a narratable life."[27] To portray oneself as striving for noble ends is to generate expectations, and to open oneself to reproach should the narrative not "ring true" in terms of subsequent actions. By one's narratives, then, one's moral status is negotiated, and the result is one to which the person can subsequently be held responsible.

At the same time, narratives of the self form the basis of what we might view as "the moral community." This is so not only in terms of the mutual accountability generated by a community in which each is known by their life stories. Rather, the incidents woven into one's narrative are seldom the actions of the protagonist alone; others are included as well. In most instances, others' actions contribute vitally to the events linked in narrative sequence. For example, to justify his account of continuing honesty, the individual describes how a friend unsuccessfully tempted him to cheat. However, in the same manner that individuals usually command privilege of self-definition ("I know myself better than others know me"), others also demand rights in defining their own actions. Thus, as others' actions are used to make oneself intelligible, so does one become reliant on others' accord. If others are not willing to accede to their assigned parts, then one cannot rely on their actions within a narrative. If another fails to see his actions as "offering temptation," the actor can scarcely boast of continued strong character.

Narrative validity, then, strongly depends on others' affirmation. This reliance on others places the actor in a position of precarious interdependence. For in the same way that self-intelligibility depends on others' agreement as to their place in the story, so does their own identity depend on one's affirmation of them. An actor's success in sustaining a given self-narrative is fundamentally dependent on others' willingness to play out certain pasts in relationship to the actor. In Wilhelm Schapp's terms, each of us is "knitted into" others' historical constructions, as they are into ours.[28]

History, Identity, and Cultural Value

As historiographers from Mink and White to the present have made clear, we inherit a tradition of historical accounting in which history approximates the well-formed narrative.[29] What separates history from, let us say a record of events (a chronicle), is its approximation to the Western storytelling tradition. In effect, the writing of history could scarcely proceed today without the narrative features outlined above: (1) such writing is thus structured around a valued endpoint (e.g., economic, political, or technological power; cultural dominion; individual success or failure); (2) events are selected insofar as they bear on reaching this endpoint (e.g., the *rise* or *fall* of a given culture, religion, or government; the *winning* and *losing* of wars; the *development* of a technology); (3) a singular temporal trope generally prevails (namely, the Western calendar); (4) the players of history are not protean (e.g., we come to "understand the true character" of Pope Leo X, Napoleon, or Stalin); (5) we are given a sense of unified cultures, such as "the Greek," "the Norse," or "the Chinese"; (6) causal linkages are frequently elaborated (e.g., the linkage between natural resources and a nation's prosperity; trade routes and cultural dispersion; technological advances and military power); and (7) we typically find the beginnings and endings of historical accounts well marked (often by the covers of books). To be sure, there are historical accounts that violate one or more of these rules of narrative.[30] However, the noteworthiness of the exceptions in this case essentially vindicates the rules. To understand the structure of narrative, in a broad sense, is to comprehend the limits and potentials of historical understanding.

In this same sense, the truth-bearing capacity of history must be viewed as culturally circumscribed. That is, we inherit first a range of literary and rhetorical devices for generating a sense of the real and the objective.[31] Second, we inherit myriad traditions, each favoring different deployments of these devices. Thus, what a physicist would describe as "the real," would differ dramatically from the descriptions of, let us say, a spiritualist, an artist, a humanist, or the man on the street. Within these various traditions, one can "tell the truth." Because of the way in which the cultural language has been used to index various "events," people can reach satisfying agreements as to "what actually happened," and such accounts can be challenged to an extent by various "findings." However, these standards of veracity are community-specific, and the extent to which they can be sustained depends on the continued capacity of the community to negotiate reality together. As communities or societies become fragmented and their argots diffused, and as the "facts of the matter," are temporally dissociated from the practice of negotiation (as is necessarily the case in historical writing), then the path to *the* truth about history is progressively occluded.[32]

More broadly, we can say that history and community are inextricably intertwined. The beginning of narrative intelligibility signals the beginning of community. It is when two or more persons join together in creating an intelligible story of "what happened" that we locate important seeds of community. And, when communities of intelligibility are formed, so do they more effectively generate the kinds of stories that confirm their intelligibility and their relations with each other. As histories become sedimented—part of the taken-for-granted past—so do they serve as implicit guarantees of community solidarity.

History and the Achievement of a Moral Identity

Let us finally draw together the various strands of this analysis to speak cogently to the problem of historical consciousness today. As I have proposed, narratives are vital both to the creation and sustenance of value, and to the achievement of individual identity. To the extent that historical consciousness is inherently consciousness of narrative, we are sensitized to the ways in which the conversational realities created by historical accounts perform functions within the culture. They can be valuable constituents of long-standing cultural traditions, serving to demark (construct) a particular tradition, to invest it with honor, and to articulate a rationale for its future. In effect, historical narration is inevitably linked to cultural values and morality. To lend intelligibility to a given tradition, is to lend silent affirmation to the sense of the good that it embodies.

At the same time, because individual identity is configured or implicated in historical narratives, so is the achievement of moral being sustained (or impeded) by historical accounts. For good or ill, we each live within and are constructed by particular historical narratives—of our people, culture, nation, region, family, and so on. These historical narratives serve as a foreground for achieving moral identity within relevant communities. To paraphrase the logic, "People with our history do not engage in x; we uphold the ideals of y; as you chose y over x, you are one of us; you are a good and worthy person, a moral being." My capacity to achieve moral identity today is intimately linked to my relationship with the narratives of the past.

Let us apply these arguments to the hotly debated case of Holocaust history. The controversy over the "facts of the holocaust"—its magnitude and extensity—has, indeed, been intense. From a constructionist standpoint, we may view this controversy as problematically grounded but vitally important in implication. The controversy is problematic in its realist premises, that is, that an examination of the "facts of the case" will ultimately reveal the truth of history. As we find, there are myriad means of describing "what actually happened," multiple stories, each felicitous within its own community of intelligibility. Further, each history will inevitably select "the facts" necessary to sustain its existence as an intelligible story. There is, in this sense, no impartial history, no story that transcends community, context, and discursive tradition. And, because the conversations have become increasingly remote from the indexed particulars necessary to sustain their "objective" truth, there is little means by which the sense of objective grounding can be secured. In effect, the quest for the truly true of the Holocaust can never achieve satisfactory closure.

At the same time, the significance of the history for ongoing cultural life cannot be underestimated. For Jews and non-Jews alike, this history has largely been negotiated in terms of a regressive narrative in general, and a morality tale in particular. We have the loss (or negation) of a highly valued endpoint (humane conduct), as represented in the needless slaughter of millions. In the mourning of the loss, the cultural value is vindicated. In effect, the telling of the tale represents the continuation of a long-standing cultural tradition, a humanistic tradition that for most participants in the tradition, is beyond question. To tell the tale is to participate and sustain this tradition, and in terms of social pragmatics, to achieve moral identity within its terms. Moral identity is also at stake in terms of one's place within the narrative implicature. For Jews, the Holocaust plays a major role in a history in which their present-day identity is the outcome, and in a tradition from which their moral identity is inextricably wed. To question this history, is to challenge the intelligibility, identity, and one's standing as a moral being.[33]

For those who would argue against the Holocaust story, the question is not whether the facts can fully sustain the story. Here we enter the portals of indeterminacy. However, it is of profound importance to inquire into the moral implications of placing the story in question. What is lost to Western culture by doing so? To be sure, we must not simultaneously lose sight of the possibility that there are other traditions, other values, and other moral identities that may be placed in jeopardy by the dominant history. Under these conditions, sustained dialogue is essential, not on the adequacy of the facts, but in terms of our vision of the moral society. In the broadest sense, then, historical accounts are only manifestly "about the past." The creation of this past gains its chief significance in terms of its contribution to contemporary cultural life and the range of values that it instantiates. And it is the manner in which we achieve the sense of the good in contemporary life that establishes the forestructure of intelligibility by which we determine our collective future.

Notes

1. Peter L. Berger and Thomas Luckmann, *The Social Construction of Reality* (New York, 1966).
2. For a more complete account of contemporary social constructionist theory, see Kenneth J. Gergen, *Realities and Relationships* (Cambridge, Mass., 1994).
3. Northrop Frye, *Anatomy of Criticism* (Princeton, 1957); Robert Scholes and Robert Kellogg, *The Nature of Narratives* (New York, 1966); Wallace Martin, *Recent Theories of Narrative* (Ithaca, N.Y., 1986).
4. Vladimir Propp, *Morphology of the Folktale* (Austin, 1968); Shlomith Rimmon-Kenan, *Narrative Fiction: Contemporary Poetics* (London, 1983).
5. Louis O. Mink, "History and Fiction as Modes of Comprehension," in *New Literary History* 1 (1969): 556–569; Walter B. Gallie, *Philosophy and the Historical Understanding* (London, 1994).
6. William Labov, "Speech Actions and Reactions in Personal Narrative," in *Analyzing Discourse: Text and Talk,* ed. Deborah Tanner (Washington, D.C., 1981); Brian Sutton-Smith, "Presentation and Representation in Fictional Narrative," in *New Directions for Child Development* 6 (1979): 37–60; Jean Matter Mandler, *Stories, Scripts and Scenes: Aspects of Scheme Theory* (Hillsdale, N.J., 1984).
7. Alasdair MacIntyre, "Ideology, Social Science and Revolution," in *Comparative Politics* 5 (1981): 321–341.
8. Walter Ong, *Orality and Literacy* (London, 1982).
9. Michail Bakhtin, *The Dialogic Imagination* (Austin, 1981), 250.
10. Katherine Young, "Edgework: Frame and Boundary in the Phenomenology of Narrative," *Semiotics* 4 (1982): 277–315.
11. Frye, *Anatomy.*
12. Joseph Campell, *The Hero with a Thousand Faces* (New York, 1956).
13. Elizabeth Dipple, *The Unresolvable Plot: Reading Contemporary Fiction* (London, 1988).
14. See, for example, Herbert Liebowitz, *Fabricating Lives: Explorations in American Autobiography* (New York, 1989).
15. Mary M. Gergen, "Life Stories: Pieces of a Dream," in *Storied Lives,* ed. Georg C. Rosenwald and Richard L. Ochberg (New Haven, 1992).
16. Hayden White, *Metahistory: The Historical Imagination in Nineteenth-Century Europe* (Baltimore, 1973).
17. Karl R. Popper, *The Logic of Scientific Discovery* (London, 1959); Williard Van Orman Quine, *Word and Object* (Cambridge, Mass., 1960).
18. Popper, *Logic,* 31.
19. Quine, *Word,* 26–57.
20. John L. Austin, *How to Do Things with Words* (New York, 1962).
21. John O. Lyons, *The Invention of the Self* (Carbondale, 1978).
22. See Kenneth J. Gergen, *The Saturated Self* (New York, 1991).
23. For further explication of the self as a discursive achievement, see John Shotter and Kenneth J. Gergen, eds., *Texts of Identity* (London, 1989); B. Davies and R. Harre, "Positioning: 'The Discursive Productions of Selves,'" *Journal for the Theory of Social Behavior* 20 (1990): 43–63.
24. Gergen, *Realities.*
25. For more on memory as a by-product of social interchange, see David Middleton and Derek Edwards, eds., *Collective Remembering* (London, 1990); Kenneth J. Gergen, "Mind, Text and

Society: Self Memory in Social Context," in *The Remembering Self,* ed. Ulric Naisser and Robyn Fivush, (Cambridge, Mass., 1994).

26. James R. Averill, *Anger and Aggression* (New York, 1982).

27. Alasdair MacIntyre, *After Virtue: A Study in Moral Theory* (Notre Dame, 1984), 202.

28. Wilhelm Schapp, *In Geschichten verstrickt: Zum Sein von Mensch und Ding* (Hamburg, 1953).

29. Mink, "History"; White, *Metahistory.*

30. See, for example, Susan Griffin, *A Chorus of Stones* (New York, 1992).

31. See, for example, Gergen, *Realities.*

32. For specific discussion of the problems of objectivity in historical writing, see Peter Novick, *That "Noble Dream": The "Objectivity Question" and the American Historical Profession* (Cambridge, U.K., 1988).

33. See also Dominick La Capra's related discussion of "redemptive reading" of the Holocaust in *Representing the Holocaust* (Ithaca, N.Y., 1994).

CHAPTER 5

Narrative Truth and Identity Formation
Abduction and Abuse Stories as Metaphors

Donald P. Spence

Early in the *Culture of Narcissism,* Christopher Lasch calls our attention to the way in which unremitting self-awareness has become the bane of modern society. We long, he suggests, for the "suspension of self-consciousness." Modern man, "imprisoned in his pseudo-awareness of the self ... would gladly take refuge in an *idee fixe,* a neurotic compulsion, a 'magnificent obsession'—anything to get his mind off his own mind."[1] A similar idea can be found in a recent book by Christopher Bollas titled *Being a Character: Psychoanalysis and Self-Experience.* Believing that mental health demands a tolerance for a variety of inner states, he makes the argument that for many people, it is easier to do away with the conflicting voices and settle on what he calls a fascist state of mind—one voice, one thesis.[2] Unanimity of this kind can be found, in extreme cases, by merging with another or, more commonly, in such familiar states as being in love, absorbed in a piece of work or a hobby, or in belonging to a special interest group (stamp collecting or scuba diving). "Given the ordinary unbearableness of this complexity [of modern living]," Bollas writes, "I think that the human individual partly regresses in order to survive, but this retreat has been so essential to human life that it has become an unanalyzed convention, part of the religion of everyday life." In this essay, I want to discuss some of the scars we bear by being the victim of this complexity—in particular, the result of being beseiged by many voices. I will then go on to discuss some of the solutions we have found to simplify this kind of noisy internal chorus.

A recent memoir by a devoted motorcycle rider may be a good place to begin because it gives us a sample of what it is like to have found an answer,

---

Notes for this section can be found on page 132.

even if only temporarily. Once underway on her machine, she writes, "there is no room in the brain for idle thoughts ... and a biker can go for miles and miles without waking up to any sudden realization, including the one that nothing at all has been thought for miles and miles. The faster you ride, the more closed the circuit becomes, deleting almost everything but this second and the next, which are hurriedly merging. Having no past to regret and no future to await, the rider feels free, though that is hardly true; it's just that here, in this tight, charged world, the other world left behind seems sham, outworn."[3] I would guess that such an experience is shared by surfers, sky divers, skiers, and anyone who spends time in a partly dangerous sport.

A single-minded story line not only eliminates past and future; it also eliminates the disturbing press of other voices. Free speech is presently under mounting attack in our country, and the outcry about its dangers, starting from such slogans as "words can kill" and moving on to lists of forbidden terms, ranging from *buxom* to *nigger,* has been called the most "uncontroversial social movement in America" at the present time.[4] When many voices are disturbing the peace, one solution is to silence the messengers; another is to retreat into a single-voice world by one of the ways I just described. When only one message is running through your head, there is no space for hearing anything else; the inner world with its single voice effectively drowns out the outer chorus.

This thirst for a consuming passion—a Single Story line that may or may not be devoid of content—is not only an escape from too much self-awareness and a retreat from messages you do not want to hear. Certain internal scripts may also provide us with a new identity as a result of belonging to a recognized group with a certain kind of status. This kind of visible identity is only too often lacking in modern life; all too frequently, we are deprived of a clear sense of who we are or what we stand for. Our culture is marked by what might be called a cult of anonymity that makes it increasingly difficult to characterize a person by his occupation or his background; it has become increasingly difficult to form meaningful social interactions between individuals.

All too often, what deserves to be turned into a stable and significant relationship (e.g., the connection between doctor and patient) is transformed into an interchangeable encounter, either because the doctor has neither the time nor the inclination to become interested in this specific individual, or because the demands of the health-care system impose a different agenda on the two parties. The patient in the typical health-management program sees an array of different doctors, depending on who is available when he calls; the illness may be treated, but not the person. In similar fashion, a telephone request for information, more and more often, is greeted by an automated menu of choices that subverts the conversation into an exercise in branching logic; as we work our way through the choice hierarchy and normal conversation disappears from our experience, we lose a piece of our sense of self. Or consider the consequences of early retirement. As the choice of this option increases, more and more workers cast off their work identity at an ever-earlier age, and this loss adds to their confusion about who they are.

We can extend Lasch's formula by saying that Yes, modern man is uncomfortably aware of himself and at the same time, almost paradoxically, does not know who he is. He is like the improvising piano player who is concentrating so hard on chord patterns that he is not aware of what song he is playing (an experience I've had more than once). Modern man can readily describe his feelings or his dreams or his Medicare number, but he has more difficulty in identifying a sense of who he is as a person in a way that would make him instantly recognizable to someone who had never seen him before.

Modern man is also bothered by his ever-changing view of himself. Plagued by a lack of constancy from one moment to the next, sensing that he views himself one way in the office and another way at home, he would like to silence the competing voices that have come to dominate his inner world and settle for one self, one me, one I. Gergen has argued that one source of these inner voices are the personaes and values of the people in our e-mail, fax and telephone networks, and that it is our ever-expanding technology that has led to this new diversity of voices. "As we become ever more saturated with relationships," writes Gergen, "we become increasingly populated with *fragments of the other,* each of us harboring expanding congeries of potentials for relating and replacing the other.... Further, because each fragment we incorporate from others is also an acquisition of value ... any stabilized pattern of being treads on the sensibilities of myriad ghosts within."[5]

E-mail and fax may be one source of this confusion; constant television watching may be another. We are still coming to terms with what the constant exposure to television images has done to our inner world and our sense of who we are. There is an immediacy about television stimuli, brought about by their instant translation into here-and-now talking heads, that must contribute significantly to our sense that we have many people inside our head, each speaking with a slightly different voice. When we think back to a simpler time when only the print world existed, we were somehow protected from many of these voices; the translation from print to speech somehow protected us from too much invasion of privacy, and for some, they were never able to make the transition from language to image. With the advent of television, that protection disappears.

Whatever the cause of these inner voices, it seems likely that the growing increase in talking heads has led to an increase in selves, and this increase has a direct connection to the popularity of MPD (multiple personality disorder) as a diagnosis. Believing that too many inner voices is a psychiatric symptom and not a simple mark of how the brain works when exposed to the variety of stimuli found in our multifaceted modern environment, we have shifted from a benign fondness for imaginary companions (once celebrated in children's stories) to a search for ways to eradicate the many competing voices. It is probably no accident that one of the popular explanations for MPD rather conveniently replaces a chorus of voices with a single cause—that the victim was sexually abused as a child.

This brings me to my central theme. Many of the stranger stories circulating in the public media these days can be seen as attempts to give us an all-consuming personal scenario that is authored by one voice and will almost inevitably drown out the many other messages we do not want to hear. In these stories, furthermore, in contrast to the thoughts of the motorcycle rider or sky diver, content is crucial. The right kind of single-minded message will not only dominate our waking existence; it may also elevate us to a special place in the world, and in the process, counter our fear of anonymity and facelessness.

Consider the victims of spaceship abductions or early child abuse. A single story now dominates their life; their entire existence has been transformed and is now invested with a mission. They have become a certain kind of victim, and in the process, have joined a highly visible and readily defined group that we have all heard of and can relate to. The new identity, what is more, can never be challenged; more than that, it gives the holder a way of explaining his or her present status, view of life, continuing bad luck, and any number of other features that had formerly seemed baffling and beyond explanation. It also gives him or her a claim to a special kind of distinction; consider the fact that many victims of alien abductions say that they have been specially chosen to donate sperm or eggs to the visitors from outer space. Presumably, they were not chosen at random.

We should not lose sight of the fact that the new identity/explanation/narrative is remarkably successful as a piece of causal reasoning. Tell someone that you were abused as a child and their attention is immediately captured; from that moment on, they are a slave to your story and will frequently reinforce your reasoning; whatever links you want to form between the early abuse and your present condition, their imagination will do your bidding. Just as a tour of duty in Vietnam was once seen as a likely cause of substance abuse, violent behavior, nightmares, unemployment, and a wide range of other miseries, so an experience of child abuse (or somewhat less readily, abduction by aliens) is now seen as an equally valid cause of present unhappiness. The more mysterious the initial cause, the more our imagination sets to work spinning out its possible effects. (We may also be secretly congratulating ourselves that we are not in the victim's shoes, and in our efforts to be charitable and sympathetic, we may grant them lapses in their reasoning that we would probably not allow under other circumstances.)

Not only are the stories mysterious and compelling; they are also, by definition, impossible to argue with because acts of seduction or abduction, almost by definition, take place without witnesses. If you doubt any details of my claim, reasons the survivor, so much the worse for you because I was there and you were not. Thus, the structure of the average report, pointing up the absence of witnesses, makes it certain that the survivor's authority can never be challenged; as a participant in some extraterrestrial event or bedroom scene from the distant past, he or she gains an authority and a power of persuasion that is simply not present in civilian life. It may be this feature in particular that makes the stories so inviting for those who feel they are never listened to or believed in; as UFO (unidentified flying object) or abuse survivors, they have replaced their day-to-day anonymity with a kind of out-of-this-world notoriety. And we can now see more clearly why reason and argument have so little impact on the details, because one of the main reasons for telling an abduction story is to become an authority, and in so doing, become immune to revision, emendation, and second-guessing.

It is partly because of the spell cast by this new identity that it becomes addictive in its own right. Bollas has described his work with a particular lying patient who was able to explain the sense of intoxication that comes from being able to make up stories at will and hold the listener in thrall. The same power accrues to the victims of child abuse or UFO abduction. I am not suggesting that they are lying, but I suspect that they are tempted to take advantage of their story to maximize its dramatic effect and to increase their power over their listeners. As the listeners show their fascination and awe, the survivor becomes gradually more convinced that he or she really was a victim and the story becomes more embellished; what started as a vague hypothesis gradually turns into certainty. It also becomes clear how a two-person encounter (such as psychotherapy) is the perfect petri dish for growing the new narrative.

We now begin to understand the consequences of challenging the victim and threatening to dismantle his story. You are not only robbing him of a secret source of power and influence; you are also taking away an identity that gives him special status and was granted with almost nothing required in the way of preparation or apprenticeship (the American equivalent of an inherited title). We begin to see why the victims are so reluctant to consider other explanations of their unhappiness and why the arguments in this field are so polarized.

Sources of the Narratives

I have suggested that one of the functions served by these stories is to drown out competing messages from either inside or outside the head and replace them with a single story line that is so compelling that it is always running through our mind. Another function seems to be the replacement of an anonymous identity with an out-of-this-world notoriety. Let me now turn to some possible explanations for the content of these new stories and suggest some possible answers to the question of why it is that we are hearing so much about child abuse and UFO abductions.

First off, I think there may be a link between the prevailing culture of enforced anonymity (caused in part by the population explosion and various kinds of new technology) and the new identities of abuse or UFO survivor. If the new stories are hard to believe as reports of real-time adventure, perhaps they can be better understood as metaphors for an ongoing cultural crisis. The quiet desperation that Thoreau suspected lay hidden in the life of the average nineteenth-century citizen seems to be surfacing more and more frequently in current accounts of the cultural and political scene.[6] As the modern individual, for a wide variety of reasons, feels less empowered, more alienated, and less able to predict the course of the next two, five, or ten weeks (much less years), he or she may become aware of feelings that no one can reasonably explain or acknowledge. Some of these concerns may become transformed into stories of imaginary aliens or sexually active relatives.

I make this suggestion because both abuse and abduction stories are dominated by feelings of powerlessness, uncertainty, and alienation. The point is particularly clear with respect to UFO survivors, as L.S. Newman and R.F. Baumeister make clear. "In the typical account [they write], the person is a helpless pawn of powerful, superior beings who inflict degrading and painful experiences on him or her." What is more, the stories are dominated by the loss of self. In any number of stories, the individual feels that after being abducted, he or she has lost a sense of individuality or uniqueness, a "sense of destiny and of individual achievement."[7] What better metaphor to describe our current condition? As established structures such as family and church and profession are losing their influence, the nature of present life and future existence becomes increasingly unpredictable. As new diseases emerge or threaten to emerge, and as established drugs and other medical procedures seem to lose their effectiveness, our sense of mortality is significantly affected. As warfare changes its pattern from the traditional clash of massive armies by night into unpredictable outbursts in the middle of commuter trains or shopping malls or Harvard dorms, our vulnerablity necessarily increases. Could it be that many of these fears are encapsulated in the standard UFO abduction and return?

One reason to suspect that these reports may be an outgrowth of our current sense of vulnerability and alienation is the notable difference between current stories and what was being claimed in the 1950s and 1960s. Newman and Baumeister make clear how the earlier reports were more benevolent, all-knowing, and supportive. "None of these early contactees were kidnapped or assaulted like today's abductees, and the aliens they met have even been characterized as 'jolly fellows.'"[8] Even if many of these early "victims" were deliberate hoaxers, as the authors assert, their stories can still be read as projections of the cultural and political conditions obtaining at the time. The Eisenhower and early Kennedy years were marked by a strong sense of certainty about the future and the reassuring feeling that America was still the strongest nation on earth. The dollar was still strong; inflation had been kept in check; the population was still relatively small; and the established structures of church and family were still intact. As the political and cultural climate have changed in the intervening years, the abduction stories have become more ominous and more focused on helplessness and loss of identity.

Particularly striking is the way in which both sets of scenarios portray the victim as helpless and vulnerable to the influence of a superior being (parent or alien). Both flying saucer reports and memories of early child abuse are dominated by a loss of choices; a sense of powerlessness, immobility, and indoctrination; and by a sense of inevitability and loss of control. If free will has become too much of a burden in modern life, it may be a relief to be turned into a prisoner (or a child) and reduced to obeying orders. A close study of the population that believes in early child abuse or UFO abduction might reveal an unusually low tolerance for modern-day hassles and a predominant sense that the support system is often just out of reach.

By this way of thinking, the flying saucer and the child abuse scenarios may provide the kind of escape from freedom, that Erich Fromm identified in the Germany of the 1930s, and many features of his analysis of democracy and authoritarianism can be fitted to the current situation. Fromm began by arguing (at a time when World War II had already begun) that "the crisis of democracy is not a peculiarly Italian or German Problem, but one confronting every modern state." Is there, he wondered, "an instinctive wish for submission?" Fromm was one of the first social thinkers to identify the oppressive burden of freedom, which often leads to what he called the "first mechanism of escape ... the tendency to give up the independence of one's own individual self and to fuse one's self with somebody or something outside." He identified the unbearable feelings of aloneness and insignificance that could overpower contemporary man, and argued that these could be overcome by an annihilation of the individual self in the course of becoming part of an external power—for example, an institution or a nation. "One surrenders one's own self and renounces all strength and pride connected with it, one loses one's integrity as an individual and surrenders freedom; but one gains a new security and a new pride in the participation of the power in which one submerges."[9]

Our postmodern society adds a special wrinkle to the problem of individual freedom because of our increasing preoccupation with multiple selves. Not only does each new identity add its voice to our sense of who we are, but Gergen has noted how "each mode of being ... becomes a small prison from which freedom of expression must be sought."[10] But there may be no escape. Moving from one identity figure to another, I find myself acting in contradictory ways, and I end up not knowing who I am or what I want. Fromm's original escape from freedom has now become an escape from a variety of inner voices; because there is no one answer inside the head, we are tempted to look for a single message on the outside that will organize all our waking minutes and eliminate the intrusive, fleeting, internal identities. Free will, as it has come to be grounded on ever-increasing possibilities, has become too great a burden for many, and they find themselves seeking a simpler path with fewer branches. In an almost paradoxical manner, the best cure for the bedlam of multiple selves may be a loss of self that carries with it a loss of self-consciousness and a regressive merging with an external authority—seducing parent or visiting alien.

The recent phenomenal growth of UFO abduction, child abuse, and other survivor stories suggests that they may offer a more effective way to solve the feelings of helplessness, alienation, and life choices that have only increased since Fromm's time. I would agree with Newman and Baumeister that masochism and loss of self are two key ingredients in the stereotypical abduction story, but both these features may be secondary to the primary cause—the modern sense of powerlessness, helplessness, and lack of a single identity that has increased in direct proportion to the growth of modern technology.

Hard Facts

Against these growing feelings of alienation and uncertainty, it is not surprising that both the abuse and abduction reports are characterized by an emphasis on specific features of the adventure; it is as if uncertainty and ambiguity have been replaced by hard facts. In a series of reports quoted by Newman and Baumeister, we find such details as a "diaper-like cloth," a "planetarium projector," a "needle-like device," a "warm beam of light," a "needle in her navel," and similar, hard-edge referents. Similar features can be found in the stories of early child abuse (quotes from child abuse stories). The tone of the stories, moreover, tends to be uncritical and unforgivingly serious, almost totally lacking such words as *maybe* or *perhaps,* and it is tempting to believe that, here at last, the survivor has found the kind of certainty and lack of ambiguity that is so noticeably absent in present-day life on earth.

The current upsurge of abduction and abuse stories not only suggests that our high-tech world may come at too high a price for many of our citizens; it also tells us something about the relative standing of rationality versus a sense of well-being. For many of the UFO survivors and abuse victims, it may seem more important to find an explanation that fits the facts, even if it strains credibility, than to continue to be perplexed by anomalous experiences just because the standard explanations are no longer sufficient. We begin to realize that feelings are, in many ways, more important than reasons, and that the teachings of the Enlightenment and the overriding importance of rationality that we have celebrated since the Renaissance are starting to give way to another kind of message. As we move into the twenty-first century, we find that escape from freedom is also accompanied by escape from reason and a plunge into sensation.

The stories may also provide us with a comment on modern medicine and its dominating scientific base. One reason why the newest drug or radiation treatment makes you feel better can no longer be put into simple human terms; to really understand the newer miracles of modern medicine, you need a background in microbiology and cell chemistry. The rise of abduction and abuse narratives to account for current symptoms may be our way of returning explanation to a level that everyone can understand, even if it flies in the face of high-tech science. The abuse and abduction stories seem to operate as myths, engaging us on a deeper and more emotional level than accounts based on DNA or T-cells can ever hope to achieve. And it is partly because they serve a role not filled by modern science that these stories persist, and may be expected to increase. It is probably no accident that along with the proliferation of new high-tech treatments, a widespread interest in alternative medicine is also emerging. There may be a close connection between the search for new kinds of healing and reports from outer space.

Narrative Ethics

There is another feature of the new narratives that I now want to focus on: the implications that telling these stories have for the narrator. On the question of what has been called narrative ethics, I think we have more to learn from literature than from psychology, and it may be time to become acquainted with a different genre—traditional and modern literary criticism.

In his preface to *The Spoils of Poynton,* Henry James reminds us of one of the important distinctions between life and art:

> Life persistently blunders and deviates, loses herself in the sand. The reason is of course that life has no direct sense whatever for the subject and is capable, luckily for us, of nothing but splendid waste. Hence the opportunity for the sublime economy of art, which rescues, which saves, and hoards ... thus making up for us, desperate spendthrifts that we all naturally are, the most princely of incomes.[11]

By turning their life into a story, the UFO and abuse survivors learn something of what James knew all along. What seemed meaningless or ambiguous or impossible to talk about in its raw form—a piece of life itself—gets transformed into a focused narrative with a compelling story line with beginning, middle, and end, a clearly defined contrast between good and evil, a story with a hero and one or more villains. But this very narrative smoothing also makes it somewhat suspicious. "A chief part of the inauthenticity of narration," writes Lionel Trilling,

> would seem to be its assumption that life is susceptible of comprehension and thus of management. It is the nature of narration to explain; it cannot help telling how things are and even why they are that way.... The tale is not told by an idiot but by a rational consciousness which perceives in things the processes that are their reason and which derives from this perception a principle of conduct, a way of living among things. Can we, in this day and age, submit to a mode of explanation so primitive, so flagrantly Aristotelian?[12]

I have stressed the helplessness of the hero; I now want to turn to his or her unreliability as a storyteller because the temptation to turn your life into a piece of art begins a process of change that may never end. Details are adjusted to meet the demands of the genre rather than to bear witness to the past; narrative momentum may sweep away a bland piece of historical truth that would, if included, tend to slow down the story and confuse or bore the listener. Caught up in the Storytelling moment, the survivor becomes a performer rather than a historian, and this shift in identity cannot fail to affect his or her credibility.

We are caught up in the problem of the unreliable narrator first posed by Wayne Booth in the early 1980s (in a book titled *The Rhetoric of Fiction*); we are starting to realize that many of the issues he raised with respect to the credibility of the Storyteller in literature can also be raised with regard to the stories of the abuse and abduction survivors. Are they giving us a simple, straightforward account of a moment from the recent or distant past or are they, with a mixture of deliberation and naivete, putting together a story that is part fact but carefully crafted to produce a particular impression? We need to know their motives in order to know how to listen; it is useful to repeat one of Booth's early comments about the narrative structure of *The Turn of the Screw*:

> Though no one will deny to James his right to develop his original ideas as he discovers new complexities in his narrators, few of us feel happy in a situation in which we cannot decide whether the subject is two evil children as seen by a naive but well-meaning governess or two innocent children as seen by a hysterical, destructive governess.[13]

Parallel questions can be asked of the typical child abuse story. Is the victim innocently recovering the encounter from out of the distant past and putting it into story form for the first time, or is she (the victims are mostly women) partly creating a child abuse scenario to mollify her therapist and revenge herself on her parents? Is the victim speaking as the bearer of an early memory that is only now becoming conscious or has she become an unreliable narrator with mixed motives, telling less than she knows (and more than she believes) in an effort to make a lasting impression on her audience? Notice the ethical issues contained in all this. The fiction writer has a perfect right to be as ambiguous as he likes; his narrator can quite easily withold known facts from the reader to reinforce a certain impression (of, say, an untrustworthy observer). But the survivor of abuse or abduction is expected to be truthful, particularly when speaking in court, and the possibility that she is an unreliable narrator does not easily fit into our ethical and moral frame of reference. It is partly for this reason that much of what Booth had to say about unreliability in the early 1960s is only just now being heard in conferences such as this. And we clearly have much to learn from Henry James who had thought a good deal about how to present an untruthful narrator in a believable manner while still being true to his central character; how to withold a part of the story and still earn the reader's trust; how to tell a doubtful story and still retain the reader's respect; and similar, vexing issues of pace and openness and point of view.

If we read the abuse and abduction tales through the eyes of Henry James and Wayne Booth, what can we learn? Consider the following sample:

> Under hypnosis, he remembered that two lights descended from the sky and landed nearby. He felt a foreboding that something would happen if he stopped, but his car suddenly veered off the road as if pulled by a magnet, and when he got out he saw a light all over the area. A sound like leather rubbing together attracted his attention to four or five beings who apparently came over a fence along the roadside and approached him, at which time he was unable to move.... A clamplike device seized him by the shoulders, causing him pain in the back. The beings turned him towards the craft.... He entered a white room, rounded and domed and seemingly without an angle, and glowing with a misty luminosity. Though he did not remember undressing, he next found himself seated on a table wearing only a diaper-like cloth. A large and intricate device like a planetarium projector came down from the ceiling and ran a needlelike device along his back.[14]

We are first impressed by the obvious veracity of the narrator, a sense that is reinforced by the hard-edge detail of his account ("like leather rubbing together," "clamplike device," "diaper-like cloth," etc.). We are also struck by the passive nature of the encounter—since it all happened to him, we conclude, it must be true. But the clearly defined detail and the passive voice may only be devices to convince us that this is, indeed, a true story and as we noted above, there is a kind of precision in the reporting that is characteristic of stories from this genre. The tendency for this trait to occur in the vast majority of survivor stories should make us suspicious.

We are also struck by the fact that the narrator behaves as if he has no free will; despite his early foreboding, he shows no signs of resistance and complies with all orders. Does this strong sense of compliance and giving in have anything to do with our contemporary belief that we have too many choices in our everyday life and need more specific guidance, some relief from the existential problem of too much free will? Is the passive victim of a UFO abduction enacting a modern version of Fromm's escape from freedom? Is the abduction story, in all of its strangeness, also describing a kind of refuge, a retreat from decisions and a return to a childhood time when we were told what to do and did not need to make plans or think about the future? One of the abductees said as much: "If I could give up my autonomy to another, I might experience not only fear but also a deep sense of rest. It would be a little like dying to really give myself up in that way."[15]

To the extent that the spirit of the UFO story captures something that is true of our present cultural condition, we cannot accuse the narrator of being willfully misleading or capricious. Unlike Bollas's lying patient, he may be telling us something that is true of his feelings and thus qualifies as something more than Booth's unreliable narrator. We make the mistake of ignoring his feelings and attending to the details; because these strike us as false, we tend to discount the complete package. But the narrator's insistence on being heard and his relief after finding a sympathetic listener suggest that there is a piece of what he is saying that goes beyond simple make-believe.[16]

Coda

Let me conclude with some tentative hypotheses. First, it would seem as if the abduction and the child abuse narratives are related phemomena and may serve many of the same purposes, even though they differ in content. It is probably no coincidence that they combine a strong sense of helplessness with a moment of notoriety—the survivor has been singled out for a specific reason (sexual or cosmic), and this decision leads to a fatal turn of fate that has affected the survivor ever since. Like the wedding guest in the *Ancient Mariner,* the survivor cannot stop telling his or her story, and it may be this preoccupation with what happened once (and was never forgotten) that silences all the other voices—inner and outer—that many of us find so troubling. Obsessed by something that may never have happened, modern man has finally found the solution to his perpetual self-consciousness, the answer to Lasch's question. The need to drown out other voices may help to explain the stubbornness of the average survivor to resist any attempt to change his or her story; it may be better to believe wholeheartedly in something false than to be at the mercy of many voices and not always know who you are and what you stand for. Second, we are beginning to recognize, in the wake of countless abuse and survivor stories, all more or less alike, the dangers of the persuasive narrative and the unreliable narrator. Widespread disgust with repeated messages that are inflicting an enormous toll on blameless parents may have brought us to the end of what might be called the Uncle Remus or the Will Rogers era in American history. Tall stories were traditionally seen as harmless pieces of folklore, quaint specimens of local culture; now we see a more sinister side to narrative make-believe and narrative truth. We are reminded once again of the dangers of rhetoric, which

> subordinates knowledge to action and reason to will. It aligns persuasion and passion. It takes its place next to the arts, but claims for itself some of the functions of philosophy. It enjoins orators to feel passion, but does not forbid them to feign it. It does not require passion, even if actually felt, to be genuinely justified by the facts.... Indifferent to the truth, it is associated with speech or writing elegant in form but empty in content, or with modes of communication which, by means of clever linguistic devices, mislead their audience into unjustified conclusions or decisions.[17]

Now that narratives have started to lose their golden voice, other means of persuasion may have to be found.

Notes

1. Christopher Lasch, *The Culture of Narcissism* (New York, 1978), 96, 99.
2. Christopher Bollas, *Being a Character: Psychoanalysis and Self Experience* (New York, 1992).
3. M.H. Pierson, "Precious Dangers," *Harpers* 290 (1995): 69–78, here p. 70.
4. J. Rauch, "In the Defense of Prejudice," *Harpers* 290 (1995): 37–46, here p. 37.
5. Kenneth J. Gergen, *The Saturated Self* (New York, 1991), 127–173 (italics in the original).
6. P. Cushman, "Ideology Observed: Political Uses of the Self in Daniel Sterns Infant," *American Psychologist* 46 (1991): 206–219; Lawrence L. Langer, *Admitting the Holocaust* (New York, 1994); Lasch, *Culture*.
7. L.S. Newman and R.F. Baumeister, "Toward an Explanation of the UFO Abduction Phenomenon," *Psychological Inquiry* (1999): p. 31, 49.
8. Newman and Baumeister, "Explanation," 31.
9. Erich Fromm, *Escape from Freedom* (New York, 1941), 5–6, 141, 156.
10. Gergen, *Self,* 173.
11. Henry James and Bernhard Richards, *The Spoils of Poynton* (Charlottesville, 1984), 120.
12. Lionel Trilling, *Sincerity and Authenticity* (Cambridge, Mass., 1971), 135–136.
13. Wayne C. Booth, *The Rhetoric of Fiction* (Chicago, 1983), 346.
14. T.E. Bullard, *Catalogue of Cases,* vol. 2 of *UFO Abductions: The Measurement of a Mystery* (Mount Reinier, 1987), 39–40.
15. Whitley Strieber, *Communion: Encounters with the Unknown—A True Story* (New York, 1987), 101.
16. See John E. Mack, *Abduction: Human Encounters with Aliens* (New York, 1994).
17. A. Nehamas, "The School of Eloquence," review of "In Defense of Rhetoric" by Brian Vicker, *Times Literary Supplement* 15 (1988): 771.

Part 2

ON THE DEVELOPMENT OF NARRATIVE COMPETENCE AND HISTORICAL CONSCIOUSNESS

CHAPTER 6

The Concept of Time and the Faculty of Judgment in the Ontogenesis of Historical Consciousness

MICHA BRUMLIK

Historical consciousness originally appeared in human beings, from both the phylogenetic and the ontogenetic perspective, as narrative consciousness. Even myths and cosmologies embedded in a cyclical conception of time require narratives, accounts of things, actions, and events connected with adverbial particles such as "before" and "after," "later" and "earlier," "in the beginning" and "in the end."

If we are not simply to ascribe the human ability to articulate narrative, and thus express temporal consciousness, to an a priori kind of anthropological constant, we cannot avoid the empirical study of all the cultural connections where particular forms of narrative were invented, developed, and realized. The study of historical and cultural semantics alone, however, can no more explain the emergence of temporal consciousness than a comparative cultural history of visual semantics—from the Romanesque and medieval frontal view, through the early modern central perspective, up to the decentered mode of representation exemplified by Cézanne's *Mont Sainte-Victoire*—could explain how human beings in the early Middle Ages, in the Renaissance, and in the late nineteenth-century actually saw, or more important, how they learned to see that way. Visual semantics is no more identical to optical physiology than the latter is with the developmental and social processes by which individuals learn the active use of their physical organs.

It is no different with our peculiar ability to perceive time. This ability, too, can only be expressed within a particular semantics—whether a high-cultural semantics or a purely quotidian one—it, too, must have a physical basis within

---

Notes for this section can be found on page 140.

the human organism, and like every other human competence, human beings acquire it through socialization, through interactions with their material and social environment.

In spite of groundwork by Konrad Lorenz, among others, it was the special achievement of the Geneva biologist, cognitive theorist, and developmental psychologist Jean Piaget to have made the a priori abilities postulated by Kantian "cognitive theory" the object of empirical investigation, and thus to have pursued a genetic method. Piaget, who is today known above all as a developmental psychologist, was interested in children's perceptual abilities less from a pedagogical than from a cognitive-theoretical impulse.

Jean Piaget, forming a complement to the early twentieth-century French sociology and ethnology of Marcel Mauss and Lucien Lévy-Bruhl, among others, sought primitive thought where, in his opinion, it persisted in his own culture, neither remarked upon nor even noticed: in its infants and children. After studying the formal aspects of children's thought from 1923–1924,[1] he turned to particular contents of children's thought in 1926[2] (i.e., to children's animism or children's conceptions of the origins of the heavens, the seas, and plants). These and other investigations were followed in 1946 by the study *La genèse du temps chez l'enfant,* where Piaget presented the clinical results produced by his method.[3]

This method consisted of precise observation of the responses by a small, select group of children to simple physical experiments such as the flow of a liquid into flasks of different shapes but equal volumes. To simplify somewhat, the children in this experiment were then told that the liquid represented different volumes at different times as it flowed from one flask into another; they were asked to mark these volumes, draw the flasks, and sort the drawings. Finally, the drawings were shuffled, and the children were asked to put them back into the "right" sequence. Piaget's meticulous analysis of such experimental situations ultimately led him to propose a typical sequence of developmental stages, in which temporal and spatial series are initially differentiated. It turned out that children were initially unable to understand that two bodies that covered different distances in the same amount of time could arrive simultaneously. Similarly, very small children measured others' ages by their size, thus believing that one could accelerate one's growth and so overtake someone who had been born earlier.

Today, more than fifty years after these few studies—studies that are methodologically still controversial and in no way representative—there is no reason to examine them in detail. What is more important is to clarify the model of temporal consciousness, of the experience of time, that Piaget developed.

Here, as elsewhere, Piaget favors a strictly "operationalist" understanding of perception and experience. On this account, the cognitive structures that enable an adequate representation of the extraphysical world arise neither through a direct reproduction of externalities existing in themselves—as empiricism would have it—nor, as idealist speculations claim, through volitional construction, but rather through the equilibration of accommodation and assimilation, of decentering and recentering. In other words, the initially physically bound, then symbolically and verbally mediated and structured actions of the human organism encounter the discrete structures of the social and material environment, and modify them accordingly. The operational theory of the emergence of temporal perception sees it as a complex interrelation between perceived physical time and the perceived, humanly attributed time of human action. Piaget's experiments demonstrated that in our culture, it is only with great difficulty that children younger than six can reassemble a temporally indexed sequence of observed events (each represented by an image) into a new narrative, and give these events new causal attributes. Piaget thus concluded that the various operations of seriation, of the encapsulation of smaller temporal sequences into larger ones, and of causal attribution only lead to an understanding of the irreversibility of the passage of time, and thus of the absolute transitivity of "before and after" determinations, when the child understands the fundamental reversibility of actions. This insight into the basic reversibility of actions requires a prior act of decentering—the insight that individually experienced, perceptual time is not identical to the passage of "real" time:

> Understanding time means detaching oneself from the present: not only anticipating the future on the basis of regularities unintentionally constructed in the past, but extending a series of conditions, none of which resembles another, and which can be connected only by a movement from member to member—without hesitation, without pause. Understanding time, in other words, means overcoming space by means of mental mobility! That means reversibility above all. Following time only in terms of an irreversible sequence of events means not understanding time, but only experiencing it without becoming conscious of it.... The characteristic of thought in its early stages is after all that it absolutizes the momentary perspectives to which it is bound, and thus does not "group" them in terms of connections between reciprocal relations. This primitive realism is egocentric insofar as it always places a momentary state of consciousness at the center.... In the area of psychological time, this attitude means living always in the present, and knowing the past only in terms of its results.... In short, egocentrism and irreversibility are the two complementary aspects of the same inability to coordinate that explains the characteristic of primitive thought itself, that is, that it does not differentiate temporal order and spatial order, both of which are then subject to the limitations of an immediate perspective.[4]

In Piaget's conception, an individual's development of temporal experience requires a certain spatialization of time, that is, an attitude that a sequence of actions is at least tentatively reversible, as well as an ability to understand that the present one now experiences could be, from another's perspective, sooner or later. This developmental perspective, which Piaget regards as having been demonstrated by clinical experiments, corroborates George Herbert Mead's pragmatic conception of time as always the expression of social action, though without ever mentioning Mead. In 1932, Mead's reflections had converged on a theory of emergence from a cosmological perspective, as in the following passage: "The social character of the universe we find in the situation in which the novel event is both in the old order and the new thing which its arrival heralds. Sociality is the capacity of being several things at once."[5] The ability to discern simultaneity, to experience sociality, to decenter one's perspective and perceive the reversibility of action, thus all promote the development of temporal consciousness.

Comparing such reflections with the results of empirical research into the development of temporal semantics in children leads to this conclusion: children learn the use of the adverb "before" more easily and sooner than the use of "later." This effect, which would contradict Piaget, does not seem connected to the ability for logical inclusion. In fact, children seem to learn how to use "now" earlier than "then," and use "today" correctly before "yesterday" or "tomorrow," whereby "yesterday" is rather more familiar to them than "tomorrow." The first instance of temporal semantics in children of three or four years can, of course, be demonstrated by their knowledge of the opposition of "first" and "last."[6]

On these terms, the spatialization of time as a finite distance stands at the beginning of a distance that becomes accessible to the child's egocentric perspective primarily in retrospect.[7] Only the ability to understand that a distance can be traversed or represented over different durations, that is, to recognize a distance as the same even when different objects traverse it over different durations, constitutes a unified experience of time, in which an individual learns to situate himself, and by which he comes to understand the past as irrevocable. Conversely, without an understanding of the reversibility of actions, time will seem reversible. Piaget discovered this kind of temporal experience, or, more precisely, this schema of temporal experience, in his simple observations of children's interactions with their material environment. He investigated the semantics of social action in time, however, as little as his successors. Piaget, like Freud, was here encouraged by the traditional correlation of phylogeny and ontogeny, or the structural parallels between tribal and infantile animism, between the magical thought of preliterate cultures and that of small children.

One result of such reflections is his 1929 work, *The Child's Conception of the World*,[8] where, by means of the clinical method described above, that is, the conscientious transcription of children's statements, he was able to describe their speculations about the origins of the heavens, the seas, the mountains, the trees, and the earth. In every instance, Piaget arrives at the conclusion that the earliest cosmological schema, appearing at the age of five, consists in a childish "artificialism," that is, in a schema that assumes of everything that it is artificial, was created deliberately, even (or especially) when it has a discrete, final character. Piaget explains this attributive schema as children's egocentric and projective extrapolation of their experience of radical dependence on their parents, as well as their experience that the entire social world exists for their sakes. On the one hand, children's image of the world depicts it as a world of objects acting purposively: "The sun is there to warm us"; on the other hand, the world is the product of an active deity. Piaget expressly rejects the idea that this artificialism might be the expression or result of a semantics of action:

> It is evident that the verbs "to make," "to form," etc., that we apply to nature are pregnant with artificialism. But it is also evident that language is not enough to explain child artificialism, here, as usual, there is simply convergence between the regressive tendencies of language and child mentality. Moreover, as always, the child is original; it is not so much the word "to do" (*faire*) as the words "to get done" (*faire faire*) that he most often use.[9]

The brief and irritable rebuke with which Piaget brushes aside even the possibility that there might be semantic causes for children's artificialism, on the one hand, and their temporal sensibility, on the other, is due not only to his biologism, according to which organisms exist objectively, so to speak, in their own rhythms and regulations, that is, in a temporality that proceeds ecstatically, but also from his methodological insight, so to speak, that every genetic perspective, for its part, presupposes a concept of diachronicity, which in sociology requires explanations in terms of rhythms, regulations, and groupings.[10]

Whereas rhythms for Piaget are still subject to the interrelations of social life with physical and biological nature, society exists for itself when it can regulate its internal relationships by means of reciprocal interactions, to use contemporary terminology. Piaget speaks of "groupings" in cases where individuals recognize, through reflection, that the inadvertent effects of those interactions that grow into structures that they experience as objective are nonetheless alterable.

The value of Piaget's now rarely used, and by the standards of contemporary scholarship, often arbitrary, terminology can be contained in the generalization that every scientific conceptualization of the emergence of temporal consciousness requires a concept of time, which must be presupposed as a living being's movement through time, and which cannot semantically be analyzed. If we begin with movement through time by living beings who have the ability to assemble reflexive structures, then it must be purposive action—the internalized representation or assimilation of physical processes and social experiences by means of concepts of equivalence, repeatability, and reversibility—that transforms the human organism's "objective" movement through time into temporal sensibility. In other words, the experience of "time" is always connected to the potential for action, that is, to premeditated intervention in the world.

This research from the 1930s, though more or less terminated since, at least established a research perspective: if it subsumes the intersubjectivity of the semantics of action, which Piaget ignored, systematic research into the interrelations between physical operations, children's explanatory narratives, and the social experiences that lead to a decrease in dependency and an increase in autonomy might reveal whether temporal experience develops on a universal model, and whether the semantics used here is subject to cultural differences. If we could demonstrate that children's experience of time, independently of the cyclic or linear conceptions of time articulated by their cultures, is grounded in the understanding of a "before," that is, of a past, and that their ability to understand the past *as* the past is grounded in the insight into the reversibility of action—in other words, of the controllability of the exterior world in the framework of the experience of autonomy—we would have evidence of an ontogenetic origin of historical consciousness. This would therefore fail to develop in the absence of the experience of action and of the opportunity to displace authority. This thesis, too, is certainly capable of empirical investigation; the material for it would, of course, be furnished less by developmental psychology than by psychopathology.

Notes

1. Jean Piaget, *The Language and Thought of the Child*, 3rd ed., preface by E. Claparède, trans. Marjorie Gabain (New York, 1959) (first published in French as *Langage et la pensee chez l'enfant* [Neuchâtel–Paris, 1923]). Jean Piaget and E. Cartalis et al., *Judgment and Reasoning in the Child*, trans. Marjorie Warden (Totowa, N.J., 1968) (first published in French as *Le jugement et la raisonnement chez l'enfant* [Neuchâtel–Paris, 1924]).

2. Jean Piaget, *The Child's Conception of the World*, trans. Joan and Andrew Tomlinson (London, 1929) (first published in French as *Représentation du monde chez l'enfant* [Paris, 1948].

3. Piaget, *The Child's Conception of Time* (London, 1969).

4. Ibid.

5. George Herbert Mead, *The Philosophy of the Present*, ed. Arthur E. Murphy, with prefatory remarks by John Dewey (La Salle, 1932), 49.

6. Eve V. Clark, "Meanings and Concepts," in *Handbook of Child Psychology*, 4th ed., ed. Paul H. Mussen (New York, 1983), 813.

7. Leo Montada et al., *Die Lernpsychologie Jean Piagets* (Stuttgart, 1970).

8. See note 2.

9. Piaget, *Child's Conception of the World*, 384.

10. Jean Piaget, *Introduction à l'épistémologie génétique* [Introduction to genetic epistemology], 2nd ed., 3 vols., (Paris, 1973).

CHAPTER 7

Historical Consciousness
The Progress of Knowledge in a Postprogressive Age

PETER SEIXAS

A common complaint about history education in both North American and European schools is that it consists predominantly of the memorization of factual information. There is thus a huge gap between the practices of school history and the notions of "historical consciousness" that inform this volume. My purpose in this chapter is to articulate a conception of historical consciousness that might be of use in the reform of the practice of history in the schools, in order that pedagogy might serve more purposefully to develop students' historical consciousness.

Such a conception must do two things. First, it must recognize students' prior historical consciousness. That is, it must consider students' thinking, ideas, and orientation toward history upon arrival in school. Second, it must define a trajectory of development in that consciousness. That is, it must include some notion of what a more "advanced" historical consciousness might be. The conceptual work embodied in this chapter cannot proceed very far without empirical studies of students' and teachers' thinking. And yet, those empirical studies need a conceptual framework to be productively initiated.

In earlier work, I have proposed a set of seven core issues, suggested both by recent historiography and by British research on history learning, which must be confronted in order to think historically.[1] Each of these issues involves problems or paradoxes, not only for historians, but for all of us as historical thinkers in the late twentieth century. I suggested that we must address them, not only to begin to think historically, but also to gain expertise. In that work, however, I did not go far beyond defining the issues. That is, I did not take the next step to define a trajectory of development in historical consciousness. In part, of course, how historical consciousness develops in an individual is an

---

Notes for this section begin on page 158.

empirical question. But it is also a conceptual one: If the development of historical consciousness is something other than the accumulation of increasing numbers of historical facts, what *counts* as more "advanced"?

For a scheme of development in historical consciousness, we turn to the work of Jörn Rüsen. In chapter 4 of *Studies in Metahistory,* Rüsen outlines a four-stage scheme of development in historical consciousness.[2] He is particularly interested in moral values and the modes of moral reasoning, as they are connected with developing historical consciousness. To summarize his framework briefly, the first type is "traditional," where remembrance of the past exercises a binding quality on the present. The second is "exemplary," where the past is used to devise universal laws or rules about human activity and morality. This is followed by the "critical" type, which highlights the differences between past and present, offers counternarratives to traditional beliefs, and historicizes and relativizes human activity and thought. Finally, there is the "genetic" type, which embraces change and difference, but which uses both aspects of the past to orient the subject in a present "conceptualized as an intersection, an intensely temporalized mode, a dynamic transition."[3] Rüsen writes of "modes" or "types" rather than stages, but each of the four builds upon the last in what he calls the "principle of precondition." At least in this sense they represent increasing complexity and sophistication. The more basic stages are built upon, rather than discarded, by the more advanced stages.[4]

In the current chapter of this volume, I combine the two approaches to historical consciousness, using Rüsen's scheme to launch a reexamination of my own seven issues to provide them with a trajectory of development.[5] I then revisit some data that I initially collected to examine students' handling of three of the issues (significance, epistemology, and moral judgment) to test, in a very preliminary way, the utility of this combined scheme. I conclude with some observations about some problems and possibilities involved in using this synthesis as a basis for empirical research on historical consciousness. As Peter Lee reminds us, "Any comment on what can or should be taught in school history which is ignorant of the available evidence of children's ideas invites treatment as amateur speculation, or worse as empty pontification."[6]

Seven Issues Encountered by Historical Thinkers

In this section, I briefly define seven issues or paradoxes, more elaborated versions of which constitute the core of "Conceptualizing the Growth of Historical Understanding."[7]

Historical Epistemology

We can have no direct access to the past: it is gone. All traces from the past change over time, whether they are artifacts that decay (or get preserved) or documents, the meanings and connotations of whose words change over time. Accounts of the past are always written at particular times, with particular orientations. Moreover, as linguistic constructions, they are not the same kind of thing as "the past." In constructing our own accounts, what should we do with past accounts? To what extent do we believe what we do because of the accounts' modes of presentation, their persuasive qualities? If there is no "objective" account of the past, true for all times, what should we believe?

Historical Significance

The past is not composed of a finite set of "facts." We cannot possibly know everything about the past, so we select some things to study, learn, and teach. Our selections are based on criteria of historical significance. Historical significance thus involves us, our interests, and our concerns. The historically significant is not only different for different groups, but also changes over time. Feminism, for example, has redefined what is significant in history. But does this mean that *anything* is significant if someone says it is significant? If so, there is no such thing as "insignificant" or trivial, and the concept loses its meaning.

Continuity and Change

Continuity and change are fundamental to historical understanding, but only make sense in relation to each other. To identify historical change, one has to set a phenomenon against an unchanging, or continous, backdrop. For instance, to study change over time in "religious thought," one posits a continuous category, "religion," which is, for the moment, conceived ahistorically. Without such a transhistorical category, it becomes difficult or impossible to understand change within the category. Conversely, the concept of continuity of any phenomenon over time depends upon a backdrop of change elsewhere or in other phenomena. Highlighting any example of change in the foreground may inadvertently contribute to a set of ahistorical assumptions about the background to the change. Yet the more is brought into the changing foreground, the more complex the picture becomes. This is a problem both historiographically (as historians have historicized, for example, gender, childhood, death, the body, desire, leisure, work and knowledge, itself) and pedagogically (as young people live through an increased pace of historical change).

Progress and Decline

The discipline of history has been based largely on an underlying notion of progress. E.H. Carr explained historiography as a fundamentally progressive science built upon a fundamentally progressive phenomenon. The writing of history changes, he argued, as it provides "constantly expanding and deepening insights into [the] course of events which is itself progressive.... Modern historiography has grown up during the past two centuries in this dual belief in progress, and cannot survive without it, since it is this which provides it with its standard of significance."[8] Yet "progress" as a way of understanding our own time in history is up against serious challenge in contemporary popular as well as academic culture.[9] How do we (and our students) orient ourselves historically during a time when the progressive underpinning of the discipline is challenged in the culture at large.

Moral Judgment

In our moral judgments of historical actors, we constantly risk anachronistic imposition of our own moral frames of reference upon people whose circumstances and *mentalités* were very different from our own. Only by failing to understand the vast differences wrought by historical change do we dare leap to judgments on the past. Yet, historical knowledge that does not lead to moral orientation and moral judgments is useless history: why would we undertake the historical project at all, if not to orient ourselves morally?

Historical Agency

If there is potential for fundamental change in history, then who or what is responsible for that change? What kinds of collective agency do various groups exercise? When, how, and to what extent, are they constrained by the structures into which they are born? Historical agency is a way of recasting the question of historical causation that makes the question of deliberative human action both central and problematic.

Empathy

Empathy is often mistaken for an affective phenomenon. In the context of research on historical understanding, it is rather the ability to understand the motives, reasons, and actions of a distant actor who inhabits a very different world than we do. Lee prefers the term "rational understanding," whereas Matthew T. Downey uses "perspective taking."[10] Whichever we use, the paradox of historical empathy is very similar to that of moral judgments in history. Empathy involves an effort to confront difference, which, at every turn, tempts us to impose our own frameworks of meaning on others. The challenge, as Laural Thatcher Ulrich defines it, is one of negotiating between "affinity and distance," understanding human commonality without mistaking the contingent cultural constructions of our own time as transhistorical.[11] As with the issue of historical significance, however, we can only use our own frameworks through which to see and understand others.

Historical thinkers (historians, teachers, students, and "everyperson" who thinks about their own place in time) must achieve a resolution of the paradoxes or issues posed above. Are some resolutions better—more advanced—than others? If so, how? In the next section of this chapter, I use Rüsen's four types of historical consciousness to suggest how different types of historical thinkers might approach each of these seven dilemmas. I suggest, though not without the reservations articulated in the conclusions below, that moving students from type one to two to three to four would be a desirable goal for history education.

Four Types of Historical Consciousness

The Traditional Type

Rüsen explains the first type in this way: "Traditional orientations present the temporal whole which makes the past significant and relevant to present actuality and its future extension as a continuity of obligatory cultural and life-patterns over time."[12] Unlike David Lowenthal's past as "a foreign country," here the past is understood as events and incidents that have direct and unmediated relevance for us in the present.[13] In this way, it is unhistorical history. Tradition is the conservation of sameness over time. It is historical only in that it looks to the past to provide depth and significance to the present, hoping for a future that will continue to conserve. In popular culture, commemoration often serves this traditional function.

In the traditional mode, historical epistemology is simple: We know because we were told. Authority is the only grounds for belief. There are no grounds for critical revision of stories presented to us. Nor are there means for settling conflicting historical claims encountered between two accounts of the past. There is no idea that one might appeal to documentary sources to ground historical claims. On the other hand, the encounter with historical documents gives rise to fundamentalist readings. There is no need (and no ability) to contextualize documents from the past: they speak directly to the present as if there were no historical divide between them and us. In Dennis Shemilt's terms, there is no way to treat a source as "evidence," only as "information."[14] Of course, when a traditionalist account is challenged by a differing account, the need to resolve the conflict may give rise to a search for grounds on which to build an argument, and thus to the advance of historical consciousness.

The traditional mode of handling historical significance is similar: events that are handed down by authorities as being significant are so. As with questions of historical truth, there are no grounds for revising historical significance. Events achieve significance by having been remembered and commemorated (or written about) over time. Significant events provide the basis for annual holidays and celebrations—national, ethnic, or religious. But they also may be more personal, as when historian Michael Ignatieff writes: "I owe to [my grandparents] the conviction that my own life did not begin with my birth ... it is up to me to pass on their remembering to whoever comes after."[15] A similar traditionalist rationale emerges in some students' understanding of significant events: one student wanted others to know about wars because "so many people gave their lives and lost them and lost them in the war and it's fitting to give them some tribute for all the sacrifices they made, for all their efforts."[16]

The traditional orientation assumes ongoing continuity; it uses history to affirm continuity and remembrance in the face of change over time. History is used—though not necessarily consciously—as a bulwark against change. Commemorations provide meaning as if the past were living in the present. Because the past lives in the present, there is no awareness of change over time. Neither progress nor decline is a central trope in organizing human history.

Moral judgments are based on tradition, an "unquestioned stability of Lebensformen, cultural and life patterns over time."[17] Because basic life patterns, values, and mentalities are not conceived as changing significantly over time, there is no issue of historical agency. If these things don't change, there is no role for individuals or groups in bringing change about. Human activity is confined to acting out lives and roles, within the traditional givens.

Again, if people in past times acted with mentalities and motives fundamentally similar to those in our own times, then historical empathy cannot constitute a problem. In looking back at people in other eras, the traditionalist assumes that they acted for reasons like our own. If they acted in ways that are inexplicable in terms of our reasoning, then they must have been irrational or stupid.[18]

The Exemplary (or Progressive) Type

With exemplary historical consciousness, the past is useful for guiding the present, but not in the undigested and unchanging form of the traditional orientation. The exemplary type uses events from the past to derive laws or rules that can be applied to the present. This is history as positivist social science. In this orientation, particular events in the past may have a historicity, but the laws derived from them for the use in the present are timeless. This is a quintessentially Enlightenment use of history: history is science's twin.[19] The physical universe—as well as human affairs—function according to laws that can be learned and known through study. The study of history's particulars is useful insofar as it leads one toward universal knowledge. Because of the association of the exemplary mode with Enlightenment thought, and because of its deep association with faith in progress in history, it might also be appropriate to call this a "progressive" mode.

Whereas the traditional orientation was fundamentally unable to deal with conflicting accounts of the past, in the exemplary orientation, rational, empirical historical procedures enable the newer accounts to supplant older ones by overcoming prejudices and utilizing new sources of previously unavailable evidence. This is the process that J.H. Plumb celebrated as "the death of the past," that is, the transcending of partial, prejudiced, irrational versions of the past.[20] Peter Novick's "noble dream" of historical objectivity drives the enterprise.[21] The exemplary mode is driven by faith in the progress of historiography.

In the exemplary orientation, events derive their significance as evidence for, or examples of, rules and laws. The generalizations drawn from history guide us in our orientation toward the present and future. The largest events from history—those affecting the most people over the greatest length of time—are the most significant, because they teach us the most important things about what we need to know today. The exemplary mode understands that change occurs over time according to laws. Human beings can understand change over time, through historical study. What's more, the growth in knowledge that occurs over time, provides people with more control over their own histories. Thus, the study of history, itself, leads to progress.

With respect to moral judgements, universal rules and inalienable rights apply to people throughout history. Nevertheless, more primitive peoples in premodern eras may not have understood what we understand now. We (in the exemplary mode) are in a position to pass categorical moral judgments on them because of our superior understanding. Historical progress confers on us (in the modern era) the broad, universal vision that allows insight into the more limited, particularist, parochial views of people in the past (and the "people without history" in other parts of the world). Universal human rights always existed, though older societies did not always recognize or respect them.

In the exemplary orientation, human agency is mobilized to bring about progress, not only through science and technology, but through the study of history and other human sciences. Increased knowledge helps, in the exemplary orientation, to promote the increased rationality of modern life. People understand that their lives are shaped—or might be shaped—not by irrational forces, but by human agents, and see their own power to control their own destiny.

The exemplary orientation toward historical empathy is related to what has already been said about moral judgments and human agency. The belief in a universal human nature, a characteristic of the exemplary mode, both promotes and constrains empathy with people across the radical differences of time. It offers the possibility of broad generalizations about human thought and behaviour, but still maintains a barrier toward full recognition of the different other.

The Critical Type

"Here historical consciousness searches for and mobilizes a specific kind of experience of the past: evidence provided by 'counter-narratives,' deviations which render problematic present value-systems and Lebensformen."[22] The critical type simultaneously challenges the two previous paradigms (i.e., both the timeless relevance of traditional events, and the binding the universality of laws or rules derived from those events) by showing their historicity, that is, the "relativizing power of historical conditions and consequences.... 'History' [in this mode] functions as the tool by which ... continuity is ruptured, 'deconstructed', decoded—so that it loses its power as a source for present-day orientation."[23] Much of the new social history has a critical orientation.

The critical orientation problematizes knowledge about the past. It challenges historiography as a progressive science and questions the use of historical evidence to support historical arguments. The question of history as "proof or persuasion" comes to the fore. The faith that new history will be "better" than the old history is at least made problematic by the notion that there is no escaping ideology. In recent times, professional historians have engaged the challenges mounted by Hayden White and others.[24]

In the critical mode, significance inheres not in the historical events, but in what the historian makes of the events. The critical historian challenges the significance of those events and people that were previously thought to be most significant, in part by rendering previously insignificant events as significant. The historian's task is to unearth the previously insignificant, and show how important it was, rupturing the old stories of significance. Feminist history offers a prime example of writing that challenges older notions of historical significance.

If continuity was the hallmark of the traditional orientation, awareness of change moves to the fore in the critical orientation. Indeed, change is so pervasive that knowledge about the past is, itself, problematic. If "human nature" is no longer universal, but historicized—if language and knowledge are historicized—then we are separated from the past by chasms that are harder to bridge than formerly understood. Moreover, the ruptures with the past derail the story of "progress": the past is no longer a linear upward development. This mode of historical understanding moves beyond the uncritical faith in Progress and universalist norms of the exemplary mode. It frees the subject from strictures of the past, but threatens to leave her disoriented in a sea of cultural and historical relativism.

With respect to moral judgments, the critical mode of history is used to critique values handed down from the past. It may show the immoral origins of "moral" codes, or it may demonstrate the historicity or relativity of values previously considered to be timeless and universal. Critical historical consciousness inverts given power relations by affirming the agency of the subaltern. That is, it demonstrates the potential historical agency of those groups that were hidden and marginalized in traditional historical accounts. In so doing, it may lead to fragmentation of the grand narratives that organized the progressive past of exemplary history.

Because historical empathy depends upon some continuity in human reasoning, some commonality between how we function in the present and how others functioned in the past, the critical stage of historical consciousness throws the possibility of historical empathy into question. Jenkins offers an extreme example of this critical historical skepticism: "Given that there is no presuppositionless interpretation of the past, and given that interpretations of the past are constructed in the present, the possibility of the historian being able to slough off his [sic] present to reach somebody else's past on their terms looks remote."[25]

The Genetic Type

The genetic type provides the way out, in Rüsen's scheme. If the critical stage describes the new social and cultural history of the past ten or twenty years, then the genetic stage embodies the search for an epistemological ground after the challenges of postmodernism. In this type,

> it is change itself which gives history its meaning. Temporal change sheds its threatening aspect, instead becoming the path upon which options are opened up for human activity to create a new world. The future surpasses, indeed "outbids," the past in its claim on the present—a present conceptualized as an intersection, an intensely temporalized mode, a dynamic transition.[26]

In this stage, the consciously historicized subject undertakes the project of moral activity in the face of difficult odds, without the firm faith in Progress that motivated such activity in more optimistic times. Rüsen emphasizes the capacity for a pluralism of standpoints in this type.

In some ways, this type is, as Rüsen states, "shaped by the category of progress."[27] Yet it is a progress that lies beyond the subversion of Enlightenment Progress by the critical orientation, a "morality of values conceptualized in terms of a pluralism of viewpoints and the acceptance of the concrete 'otherness' of the other and mutual acknowledgement of that 'otherness,' as the dominant notion of moral valuation." Genetic consciousness takes neither an objectivist nor a relativist view of historical epistemology. Knowledge is constructed by a community of inquiry that exercises mutual checks and balances within itself. Historical knowledge changes over time, and yet, in any particular historical era, there are standards for valid historical accounts or arguments relevant for orienting life in that era. In the genetic orientation, significant events from the past are those that can be constructed into a narrative to help to contextualize the present in what has gone before. The narratives into which we arrange events tell us something important about our lives in the present and our choices for the future.

Rüsen says of the genetic stage, "our identity lies in our ceaseless changing." While ceaseless, profound change is a fact of life, an understanding of change leads not to disorientation but to hope with respect to the possibilities of change in the future. The universal grand narrative of Progress, which underlay the exemplary stage of historical consciousness, is gone. So to, is the metanarrative of decline from the critical stage. History is understood as both progress and decline for various groups at various times. Recognition of others with different perspectives and interests requires—and makes possible—a collective reworking of definitions of progress. Moral judgments, similarly, are constructed in the context of the "acceptance of the concrete 'otherness' of the other," engendering "procedures of mutual acknowledgement."[28]

Understanding the changing nature of the past opens up the possibility for collective action to shape the future, though not in a predetermined trajectory of Progress, technological or otherwise. Indeed, historical agency in the genetic orientation may set itself in opposition to the trajectories of Progress defined in the exemplary mode, opening the door to new futures.

The historical thinker is aware of differences across time that render historical empathy problematic. Nevertheless, the thinker in this stage attempts to construct a picture of life in the past that is both consistent with the available documentary traces, and to which she can exercise some human relationship.

Empirical Investigations

Students Confront Filmic Text

How might the synthetic framework sketched above help to analyze young people's reading of historical accounts?[29] Does it help us to distinguish among students' orientations to historical texts? In the first examination of this question, I revisit a study in which I investigated how students understand and interpret film that deals with the past.[30] It was undertaken on the premise that a significant element of young people's historical consciousness is shaped by their viewing of popular film and television. All seven issues are present, inextricably linked, in the process of students' viewing historical film. Yet the analysis presented here focuses primarily on students' epistemology and moral judgments when they view two films with radically contrasting interpretations of similar events. A small number (eleven) of tenth-grade students viewed segments from the revisionist Western, *Dances with Wolves,* which won an Academy Award for Best Picture in 1990 and was widely viewed and discussed among young people. The segments were drawn from throughout the film in order to not only offer close-ups of characters and dialogue, but also to convey the plot line of the film. The film portrays a brutal United States Army advancing westward in the 1860s, victimizing the Lakota Sioux who live decently and in harmony with their environment. Kevin Costner plays the main character, Dunbar, who deserts the army and joins the Sioux as they try, unsuccessfully, to escape the ravages of white civilization.

After viewing each segment individually, the students responded to questions from an interviewer. Next, they were shown segments from a 1956 Western exemplary of the genre of that era. *The Searchers,* also set in the 1860s, inverts the heroes and villains of Costner's film. At the outset, the happy frontier homestead of the Edwards family is devasted by the hostile Commanches. The remainder of the film is a quest, led by John Wayne as Uncle Ethan, not only to find the abducted daughters (Lucy and Debby), but to exact retribution from the "savages," and thus make the West safe for white families. The shift from *The Searchers* of the 1950s to *Dances with Wolves* of the 1990s is part of what Tom Englehardt (1995) has called "the end of the victory culture" in the United States. The interpretive discrepancy between the two films provided an opportunity to examine students' film-reading strategies: what do they believe, what do they question, what moral judgments do they make?

Generally, when they viewed the current film, *Dances with Wolves,* they assumed that they were confronting, for all practical purposes, a window on the past. Perhaps, in part, because it conformed to their understandings of the meaning of white Western settlement, and also, in part, because its social and cinematic conventions were so familiar to them, the medium, the filmic text, was rendered transparent, unproblematic. The "window on the past" became problematized, however, in their viewing of the second film, for it was so at odds with their beliefs and so divergent from familiar cinematic codes. Interesting differences among the students emerged at this point. The scheme developed in the section "Four Types of Historical Consciousness" (above) offers an analytical frame for understanding students' resolutions of the differences between the two films.

In some ways, there is nothing "traditional" about movies in general, and *Dances with Wolves* in particular. Moreover, the design of the film-watching exercise, with sharply contrasting interpretive viewpoints of the two films, almost forced students beyond the traditional type. Yet some student responses demonstrated aspects of a traditional historical consciousness as discussed above. A traditional reading sees historical text as if it provided a direct and unproblematic link between past and present. Near the beginning of the interview, one student said reflexively, "I'm what they call a stupid audience ... [I] just sort of follow how the movie goes." He offered this as a disclaimer: in case we were expecting him to critique the two films, he wanted to tell us that he just read them literally. He observed the fact that the films took opposing perspectives only fleetingly. Apparently, he entered the conflicting frames of both films relatively unproblematically. When asked to compare the two, he responded simply:

> in *Dances with Wolves* I thought it was sort of, it was more complete because it integrated Kevin Costner into the Indians from what he was. And similarly in the second, Debbie into the Indians, but it was more vague. So basically, the emphasis was different.

This student did not use what some of the others perceived as a stark contrast to explore moral dilemmas or make ethical judgments. Rather, adopting the stance of the white protagonists, he entered the interpretive frame of each film consecutively.

A second strain of student thinking resolved the interpretive dissonance between the films as an example of cinematic and moral progress. This strategy belongs to the exemplary or Progressive stage, not because these students use the historical film to derive universal laws of human nature, but because they express a faith in human progress over time.

> The difference is, I guess, in the 1950s, their opinions about the Indians and things like that were a lot different and that was, I mean, just like how American TV made Russians out to be so bad—like they're the worst, and you're scared of them.

And here they're presenting us the same thing, whereas in *Dances with Wolves* ideas have changed and stuff.

Here, the second student historicized the culture of the 1950s, which produced not only *The Searchers,* but also television's anti-communism. The fears upon which both played have faded as "ideas have changed." When asked explicitly to explain the differences between the two films, this student responded, "The first one was written with the old attitudes like ... sort of racism and badness towards people ... whereas *Dances with Wolves* is more, maybe, open-ended." The better values of the contemporary film result, in part, from its more recent production, in this view.

A third student's thinking exemplifies the critical stage. Her responses to the interpretive discrepancy of the two films were varied. Only by selecting certain moments in the interview do we capture a version of the destabilized postmodernist. In these moments, she grapples with the problems of a model of historiographic development as linear progress. After the first segment of *The Searchers,* she led herself to a sophisticated historicist disabling of her own moral judgment:

> S: I know we've changed a lot I guess.
> I: When you say we've changed a lot what do you mean?
> S: Well, not "we," but the way, well, society sort of. Like, that was in 1956 you said?
> I: Yeah.
> S: And now *Dances with Wolves* is 1990 or 91. But it seems like in both movies it's not equal representation. There's always one side that's the worst, the meanest, and then the other side seems perfect.
> I: Okay, what do you make of that? And you were saying before that you really liked *Dances with Wolves.* You found what the army was doing, you couldn't understand it, but you didn't say that that was unfair to the....
> S: No, I didn't think of it until I saw this, because this is totally placing or making it seem as though it's the Indians who are the problem, the ones who are "savages" and killing all the white people, and they're the ones who are the meanest. Whereas in *Dances with Wolves,* it made the army seem as though they were the ones that were the savages. I guess in both cases it is sort of unfair representation.
> I: So you would like to have a film that didn't show any....
> S: Yeah.... In both of these films they're sort of extremes.
> I: So is there any way of deciding ... one or the other?
> S: What do you mean?
> I: Now you're putting them of equal ... I mean they're both side by side—one has good guys and bad guys and the other has bad guys and good guys.... Is one of these more accurate than the other?
> S: I can't really say, well, if I had to say which one is more accurate I'd probably say *Dances with Wolves,* but I'd probably just say that because it's more modern.

Like the others, this student initially saw *Dances with Wolves* as a transparent and unproblematic window on the past. The juxtaposition of the two films, however, destabilized that view. When she saw the differences as the result of historical change, her moral bearings were loosened, and she acknowledged that she did not feel sure about the grounds on which she preferred Kevin Costner to John Wayne: perhaps she would "just say that" because the former "was more modern" (grounds which she saw as inadequate).

The fourth student provided responses of the genetic type. She was intensely involved with *Dances with Wolves*. She claimed to have seen it ten times and cried each time she watched it. Though she liked it, she also talked about it as a film constructed to convey certain messages. Yet, in her view, the messages were accurate: she had done school research on native peoples, and referred to that research to confirm the views portrayed in the film. She explained the discrepancy between the films, historicizing the mentality of the audience:

> I would say what's happening to society, you know, what is socially acceptable in society, what the majority of the society feels and how they see things. I mean thirty-eight years—that's a big difference. A lot of ideas change in thirty-eight years. People are becoming more aware now. They don't want to hide behind lies anymore, that they want to accept—or not necessarily accept—but deal with what happened, take our history for what really happened and try to deal with that instead of covering it up by making us look like the good guys and the Indians being the bad guys. They want to say, "Hey, that's not really what happened. We have to deal with what really happened."

This student showed elements of other stages, upon which her genetic understanding was built. There is unmistakable progress over thirty-eight years: people "don't want to hide behind lies any more." And yet, the films are less expressions of simple historiographic progress than they are moral acts with social consequences, part of an ongoing cultural dialogue about truth, knowledge, and power, in which historical accounts play an important part. This student's understanding of film as text did not destabilize the narrative for her. Rather, it enabled her to see it as an element in the moral politics of the present.

Students Consider Historical Significance

We turn now to a different student exercise, one which examined eleventh-grade students' understanding of historical significance.[31] The core of the exercise consisted of students drawing a diagram of the most significant "events, trends, developments, or themes" in the history of the world. They had approximately ten minutes to do so, forcing a highly selective choice. They then wrote a short answer in response to the following questions: "Why did you choose these events," and "Why did you organize them on the page in this way?" A series of written follow-up questions offered choices of "most significant" and "least significant" from a fixed list of historical events, with opportunities for students to justify their choices and add to the list.

In the traditional stage, the student takes the word of authorities as to what is significant, and has no means of criticizing or going beyond it. Historical knowledge is received already ordered in terms of significance. Students at this stage may have difficulty reasoning about historical signficance (as they do about historical evidence). The choices of student "W-14" may seem strikingly idiosyncratic for a question as wide-open as "the history of the world" (see figure 7.1). In fact, the elements of his diagram all came directly from topics in the current year of his social studies course. He chose these events, he said, because "this is all that I can remember." Eighteen of the eighty-two students (22 percent) offered a similar rationale for their diagrams, indicating that they felt they did not have enough of a range of historical phenomena at their disposal even to make reasoned choices about historical significance.

At the exemplary/Progressive stage, young people can reason about historical significance, and they do so by "objective" and universal criteria: significant events are those that affect the greatest number of people, in important ways, over the greatest period of time. Thus, another student selected "the invention of moveable type" from the fixed list of choices: "moveable type has entirely revolutionized the speed, range, [and] efficiency with which we are able to communicate. It has changed the world. So many more things are possible with increased communication." From the same list, she chose "rock music" as least significant, again, looking for broad historical impact: "I doubt it will have any long-lasting effects on anything." In response to the question that asked her to add to the fixed list of significant items, this student wrote:

> I think that the very first humans who developed ideas about life after death or spirits or gods or whatever was a monumental development in human history. I myself am not religious, but these concepts are what differentiate our minds from animals. From these first rudimentary beliefs, all of the religions in the world were eventually developed, and they have deffinately been very influential on the way the world developed [sic].

Contribution to human Progress is implicit here as a standard of significance. That is, innovations that contribute to human Progress are significant. By the same logic, events that retard human Progress would also be significant: both are part of a universal grand narrative of development.

Critical views of historical significance interrupt these grand narratives, challenging traditional and progressive notions of significance. In this exercise,

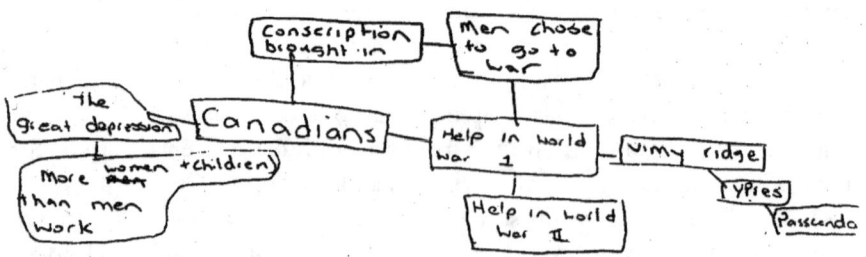

Figure 7.1

many students could be seen as doing this, as they mentioned events of personal, family, ethnic, or national significance rather than selections based on universal standards. Yet rather than challenging other, more "objective" definitions of significance, many of these students appeared to be ignorant of them. Students' responses are of the critical type only when they are able to explain how and why their choices challenge the traditional, progressive standards of significance. One student did offer such a challenge (see figure 7.2). She constructed a phallic tower of civilization arising from the "prehistoric base" and peaking in "technological boom." Yet she expressed fundamental doubts about the potency of Progress: "I see our progression as making us weaker, and the higher we get up, the weaker we become. A lot of uncertainty on how high we can go." The critical yields to the genetic in many aspects of her answers—in her sense of the present as the link between a morally complex past and an uncertain future.

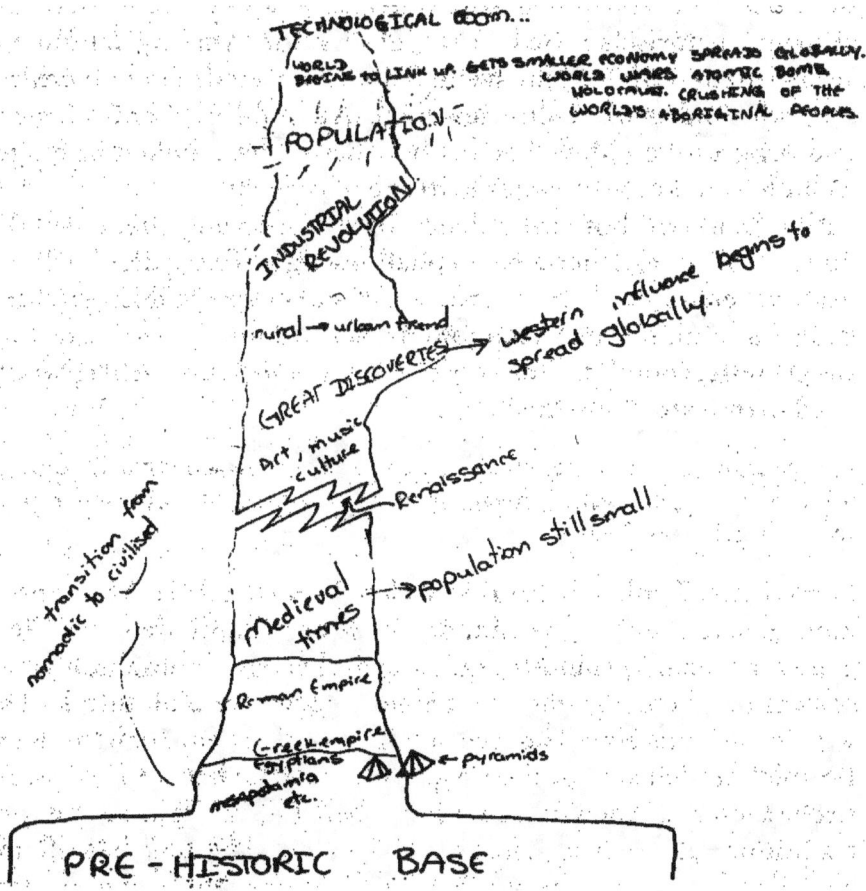

Figure 7.2

Yet we turn to another student for an even clearer example of the genetic type. The genetic takes any events—traditionally held to be significant or not—and consciously constructs them into a narrative that is meaningful for us and our concerns in the present. Our final student used a series of events, many of which could not have plausibly been found in the Progressivist's list because they are too small (see figure 7.3). For example, there are thousands of other events that might take the place of "CFC's [chlorofluorocarbons] are invented." Yet this student convincingly weaves them into a narrative that has meaning for our lives today. She chose these events and organized them this

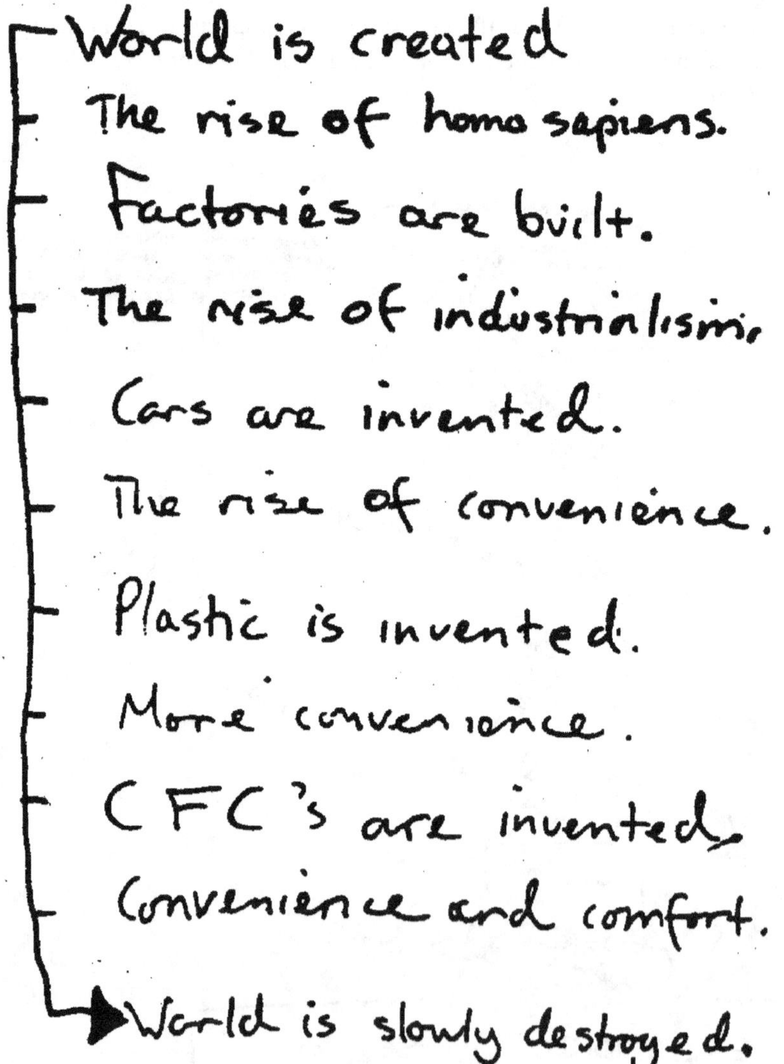

- World is created
- The rise of homo sapiens.
- Factories are built.
- The rise of industrialism.
- Cars are invented.
- The rise of convenience.
- Plastic is invented.
- More convenience.
- CFC's are invented.
- Convenience and comfort.
- → World is slowly destroyed.

Figure 7.3

way "to show reasons for the destruction of the world and the irony of human comforts." Eight of the eighty-two students in the sample used phrases similar to her "to show [x]....". This language demonstrates students' awareness of the constructed nature of their narratives of historical significance. Like the genetic type student, who understood *The Searchers* and *Dances with Wolves* as moral acts in a dialogue about the past that would help to shape the future, the students who put historically significant events together in a way such that they would *show* something important, had moved to the genetic stage of historical consciousness.

Conclusion

In this chapter, I have tried to fashion a synthesis of two different schemes of understanding historical consciousness: one that catalogues seven issues confronted by all historical thinkers, and another that provides a scheme for development in historical consciousness. The advantage of this synthesis is that it links all the issues together in global stages of development. It points to what may be important relationships, for example, between how one thinker may confront historical significance and historical evidence. It also points us toward empirical investigations that might test and flesh out this developmental scheme.

But serious limitations remain in using this as a single scheme for the development of historical consciousness. Alternative schemes of development may be more sensitive to the growth of understanding for particular issues.[32] Perhaps even more seriously, the scheme is based largely from historiographic (or what Rüsen calls phylogenetic) sources. The empirical work that comprises the section "Empirical Investigations" (above) merely suggests that these types are identifiable in students' historical reasoning; it does not provide evidence for individual development through these types, either as a result of simple psychological maturation, or as the result of a program of history teaching.

There is also a real question of whether the later types are indeed "more advanced" than earlier types. Because these types are derived from a highly foreshortened scheme of historiographic development, we may face the conundrum of expecting students to think in ways that are "more advanced" than the thinking of historians at the peak of the profession (e.g., E.H. Carr, J.H. Plumb) a mere twenty-five years ago. This leads us to question whether we are dealing in *different* types, not necessarily more or less "advanced" types. In a time when the notion of historiographic progress is in question, what counts, in history education, as "more advanced" historical thinking will continue to constitute a problem.

These qualifications notwithstanding, there are important attractions of a global scheme like the one laid out here. It becomes a starting point for new research on the growth of historical consciousness. And, perhaps most important, it opens up the question of the historicity of history education itself: perhaps even the most advanced types of historical understanding from another era are inadequate as the basis for history education—that is, the development of historical consciousness—in our own time.

Notes

This essay was written with support from the Spencer Foundation/National Academy of Education Post-doctoral Fellowship Program.

1. Peter Seixas, "Conceptualizing the Growth of Historical Understanding," in *The Handbook of Education and Human Development: New Models of Learning, Teaching and Schooling*, ed. David Olson and Nancy Torrance (Cambridge, Mass., 1996). Discussed below, the issues include epistemology, significance, continuity and change, progress and decline, moral judgment, agency and empathy. See also, Tim Lomas, *Teaching and Assessing Historical Understanding* (London, 1990).

2. Jörn Rüsen, *Studies in Metahistory,* ed. Pieter Duvenage (Pretoria, 1993).

3. Ibid., 75.

4. Ibid., 76–78.

5. There are a number of frameworks for examining the growth of historical understanding. The best researched of these grew out of the British Schools Council History Project (see Denis Shemilt, *History 13–16 Evaluation Study* [Edinburgh, 1980]; Christopher Portal, ed., *The History Curriculum for Teachers* [London, 1987]. While the British work is far ahead of any empirical work in North America, it is grounded in what might be called a static notion of historiography. That is, the standards for historical thinking are grounded, themselves, in an ahistorical (and philosophical) notion of historiography. The British do not comment on historiographic change or cultural changes over time. In contrast, Kieran Egan does pose a four-stage scheme of historical understanding, based on a reading of historiographic and cultural change (see idem, "Layers of Historical Understanding," *Theory and Research in Social Education* 17.4 (1989): 280–294). His reading, however, seems less plausible than that offered by Rüsen. On some of the difficulties of "stages," see the work of Martin Booth, "Ages and Concepts: A Critique of the Piagetian Approach to History Teaching," in *The History Curriculum for Teachers*, ed. Christopher Portal (London, 1987), 22–38, and Martin Booth, "Students' Historical Thinking and the National History Curriculum in England," *Theory and Research in Social Education* 21.2 (1993): 105–127.

6. Peter Lee, "Historical Knowledge and the National Curriculum," in *History in the National Curriculum,* ed. Richard Aldrich (London, 1991), 47.

7. See note 1.

8. E.H. Carr, *What Is History?* (New York, 1965), 165.

9. Christopher Lasch, *The True and Only Heaven: Progress and Its Critics* (New York, 1991).

10. Lee, "Historical Knowledge"; Matthew T. Downey, "Historical Thinking and Perspective Taking in a Fifth-grade Classroom" (paper presented at the meeting of the National Council for Social Studies, Phoenix, 1994).

11. Laural Thatcher Ulrich, *A Midwife's Tale: The Diary of Martha Ballard* (New York, 1990).

12. Rüsen, *Metahistory,* 71.

13. David Lowenthal, *The Past Is a Foreign Country* (New York, 1985).

14. Dennis J. Shemilt, "Adolescent Ideas about Evidence and Methodology in History," in *The History Curriculum for Teachers,* ed. Christopher Portal (London, 1987), 39–61.

15. Michael Ignatieff, *The Russian Album* (London, 1987), 20.

16. Peter Seixas, "Problems in Students' Understanding of Historical Significance," *Theory and Research in Social Education* 22.3 (1994): 281–304.

17. Rüsen, *Metahistory,* 71.

18. Rosalyn Ashby and Peter J. Lee, "Children's Concepts of Empathy and Understanding in History," in *The History Curriculum for Teachers,* ed. Christopher Portal (London, 1987), 62–88.

19. For a discussion of the links between the development of science and history in the Enlightenment, see Joyce Appleby, Lynn Hunt, and Margaret Jacob, *Telling the Truth about History* (New York, 1994), especially part 1. The organization of their volume into three parts corresponds closely to the exemplary, critical, and genetic types proposed by Rüsen.

20. J.H. Plumb, *The Death of the Past* (Boston, 1970).

21. Peter Novick, *That "Noble Dream": The "Objectivity Question" and the American Historical Profession* (Cambridge, U.K., 1988).

22. Rüsen, *Metahistory*, 73.

23. Ibid., 73–74.

24. Hayden White, *Tropics of Discourse: Essays in Cultural Criticism* (Baltimore, 1978); Novick, *That Noble Dream;* W. Cronon, "A Place for Stories: Nature, History, and Narrative," *Journal of American History* 78.4 (1992): 1347–1376; David Harlan, "Intellectual History and the Return of the Prodigal," *American Historical Review* 94.3 (1989): 581–609; Joyce Appleby, Lynn Hunt, and Margaret Jacob, *Telling the Truth*. Students may take a parallel position: there is no proving anything about the past; everyone is entitled to their own feelings about what happened. Lee argues that this position, among students, is closely related to a traditional orientation; that is, students who accept historical claims simply on the strength of authority, are more likely, when confronted by paradoxes, to flip to this radical subjectivist stance.

25. Keith Jenkins, *Rethinking History* (London, 1991), 40; see also Keith Jenkins and Peter Brickley, "Reflections on the Empathy Debate," *Teaching History* 55 (1989): 18–23; and Harlan, "Intellectual History."

26. Rüsen, *Metahistory*, 75.

27. Ibid.

28. Ibid., 76.

29. For literature on reading historical texts, see Samuel S. Wineburg, "On the Reading of Historical Texts: Notes on the Breach between School and Academy," *American Educational Research Journal* 28.3 (1991): 495–519; Charles A. Perfetti, M. Anne Britt, and Mara C. Georgi, *Text-Based Learning and Reasoning: Studies in History* (Hillsdale, N.J., 1995); Margaret G. McKeown and Isabel L. Beck, "Making Sense of Accounts of History: Why Young Students Don't and How They Might," in *Teaching and Learning in History,* ed. Gaea Leinhardt, Isabel L. Beck, and Catherine Stainton (Hillsdale, N.J. 1994), 1–26.

30. Peter Seixas, "Confronting the Moral Frames of Popular Film: Young People Respond to Historical Revisionism," *American Journal of Education* 102.3 (1994): 261–285; idem, "Popular Film and Young People's Understanding of the History of Native-White Relations," *The History Teacher* 26.3 (1993): 351–370.

31. These were initially presented in Peter Seixas, "Margins and Sidebars: Problems in Students' Understanding of Significance in World History" (paper presented at the meeting of the American Educational Research Association, New Orleans, 1994).

32. See, for example, Ashby and Lee's four stages of historical empathy, and Seixas's five categories of students' approaches to historical significance (idem, "Children's Concepts"; Seixas, "Margins and Sidebars.")

Part 3
Empirical Research / Case Studies

CHAPTER 8

Empirical Psychological Approaches to the Historical Consciousness of Children

ELFRIEDE BILLMANN-MAHECHA AND MONIKA HAUSEN

At that moment he read on the tomb the date of his father's birth, which he now discovered he had not known. Then he read the two dates, "1885–1914," and automatically did the arithmetic: twenty-nine years. Suddenly he was struck by an idea that shook his very being. He was forty years old. The man buried under that slab, who had been his father, was younger than he.
—Albert Camus, *The First Man*

Today, historical consciousness is frequently taken as a "central category of historical didactics."[1] There is nevertheless a lack of empirical investigations on how historical consciousness looks in different age groups and regions in concrete terms, and above all, on how it develops.[2] Current developmental and social psychological research includes the topic of historical consciousness mostly with reference to adults, and not, however, to children. Yet we have a comprehensive store of investigations that deal with basis competencies of historical consciousness, such as investigations on cognitive development in general, on moral development, on the development of the ability to change perspectives, and on the development of time concepts in children, to name a few. These basis competencies and their respective empirical findings will not be reviewed here individually.[3] Instead, different methods of data acquisition will be investigated from a *methodological-critical point of view* regarding what they can or cannot contribute to empirical psychological studies on historical consciousness.

Notes for this section begin on page 183.

Such an assessment requires, of course, a certain prior conceptual-theoretical understanding of the field to be investigated. All of the various conceptions analyzed by Martina Meyer and Jürgen Straub,[4] more or less amount to understanding historical consciousness as a psychical or mental structure that can be represented in a *competence model*—however it is drawn up theoretically. According to Karl-Ernst Jeismann, for instance, historical consciousness incorporates three forms of the relation of individuals, groups, nations, or societies to history: "It requires the basis of historical longing; it needs compositional performance, which finds expression in the historical image; it considers the methodological distance of an understanding of history imperative in the face of the dominance of current norms and needs over the interpretation of the past."[5]

Historical consciousness manifests itself in concrete material statements, but it cannot be reduced to such: "More than mere knowledge or pure interest in history, historical consciousness encompasses the interrelation between interpretation of the past, an understanding of the present, and a future perspective."[6] Thus, for empirical investigations of historical consciousness, it is not sufficient to ascertain knowledge of history; rather, an interpretative analysis of *individual patterns of interpretation* is necessary, which in a subsequent step can be elaborated into *types* of historical meaning construction. Jörn Rüsen has already submitted such a typology from a theoretical perspective.[7] He differentiates between the modes of traditional, exemplary, critical, and genetic historical meaning construction. Whether this typology can be sustained empirically remains a question open for future research.

In view of the complexity of the different attempts to determine the *theoretical construct* "historical consciousness," the difficulties of an empirical approach are obvious: *The* historical consciousness as such is not empirically accessible; rather, we only have available concrete utterances made by individuals in interviews or other forms of data acquisition. Arrival at patterns of interpretation or types of historical meaning construction requires either a series of interpretative steps based on these utterances, or theoretically founded "operational" definitions. The interaction between knowledge of history and historical consciousness also remains an unclarified problem for the conception of the respective instruments of acquisition, because without any knowledge of history, historical consciousness is, indeed, scarcely conceivable.

The empirical approach to the *development* of historical consciousness in the individual contains further difficulties, which are only insufficiently described by the known theoretical and methodological problems of longitudinal and cross-section studies. The development of historical consciousness is certainly to be understood as a life span process, which is dependent on the development of social-cognitive basis competencies, takes place in a social environment, is dependent on access to and exploitation of educational opportunities, and which also includes emotional and motivational factors. This list of essential components does not, of course, represent a developmental model.

It must be taken into account that the "developmental process is not a simple process of the accumulation of abilities, but rather it must be understood as the process of acquiring the competency of historical interpretation."[8]

Because empirical psychological research on historical consciousness is still in its beginnings,[9] it seems first of all to make sense to investigate the *whole* spectrum of methods of empirical social research with regard to its potential contribution to the recording of different *aspects* of historical consciousness. In this way, in subsequent studies, this could enable the closer application of theoretical considerations to empirical findings. The question of the nature of this relationship arises from the theory of science, and results from the fact that concepts of historical consciousness are ultimately *normative* models[10] with a series of educational implications that formulate the *ideally* founded approach of an individual to history based on certain of his or her views of the world and of human beings. Such models are naturally open to rational argumentation, but in a strict sense, they are irrefutable by empirical data. Nevertheless, empirical data promote rational argumentation about these models in that they can *support* certain arguments (or counterarguments, for that matter).[11]

The data acquisition methods introduced in the following will be discussed in an exemplary fashion against the background of empirical investigations. Because the focus here is on methodology as such, concrete empirical results assume a subordinate role in the argumentation, even if some of the results make important reference to certain basis competencies of historical consciousness. Due to the interest in developmental psychological aspects, only those investigative methods are mentioned that are potentially suitable for children.[12] Investigations relating to children up to the age of ten were chosen as examples. If they are not quoted from specific sources, they are examples taken from pilot studies we have been carrying out at the University of Hanover since 1995.

Experiment

At first glance, the experiment—the ideal way of scientific research—does not appear suitable for investigating historical consciousness. Nevertheless, sections of an experimental study that attempts to plumb the scope of autobiographical memory should be cited here. Eve M. Perris, Nancy M. Myers, and Rachel K. Clifton exposed two-and-a-half-year-old children, who at six months had participated in a twenty-minute perception experiment on auditory localization, to the same experimental situation.[13] A group of children of the same age who had not participated in the first experiment served as the control group. No differences emerged between the experimental group and the control group when the children were asked if they had been in the room before, or when they were observed selecting a plaything. However, when the actual experiment was carried out, during which the room had to be completely dark, there were significant differences. In the initial phase *without* instruction, those children who had already participated in the experiment exhibited the reactions they were expected to exhibit later in the actual experiment significantly more often than the other children. Furthermore, those children who had participated in the previous experiment appeared to have *less* feelings of fear or reluctance when the room was darkened than those who were participating in the experiment for the first time. "We conclude that the one unique experience at 6.5 months of age was sufficient to establish a memory of both action and meaning that became accessible upon reinstatement of the event in the third year of life."[14]

Based on its recent findings, memory psychological research assumes on the whole the much earlier development of memory and recollection functions than previously thought. For example, from analysis of the monologues of a child before falling asleep, Katherine Nelson was able to show how a girl of only eighteen months spontaneously recalled past events.[15] What is interesting, though, about the experimental study cited is its proof of how far back a child's autobiographical memory is able to reach. Even singular, nontraumatic events occurring in infancy and lasting only twenty minutes can obviously leave such a strong impression, that even after two years, a rudimentary form of memory is still present, even if this cannot be retrieved verbally and can only be indirectly deduced based on certain actions and situations.[16]

If we conceive of the development of powers of recollection as a significant basis competency for the development of historical consciousness,[17] experiments like the one cited above could supply arguments in support of autobiographical memory at least partially going back to the first year of life, though at a level not directly accessible linguistically. Based on the existence of certain memory content, such experiments are not, of course, suitable for making a statement regarding the possible meaning of this content for the self-reflexive subjective organization of the autobiographical memory. Verbal methods are indispensable for this, though they presuppose certain linguistic competencies and can "only" include content that is conveyed linguistically.

Survey

The heading "survey" combines different methodological approaches intended to ascertain stores of knowledge and attitudes or forms of argumentation regarding previously determined topics. These include, among others, guided interviews, the clinical interview after Piaget, and questionnaires with closed or open questions. As a rule, a high degree of standardization has been aspired to in order to achieve good comparability of the results. The problem of standardized surveys lies, among other things, in the necessary assumption that all persons surveyed have understood the instruction and the individual tasks in a comparable way. This can hardly be assumed to be the case, in particular, as regards younger children. Even so-called language-free tests require minimal, linguistically formulated instruction. If a task is processed incorrectly, it is often difficult to determine whether the instruction was not understood or whether the task would have been processed incorrectly even if the instruction had been understood correctly. This, along with further problems, shall be briefly outlined here using four different methodological approaches, all of which can be assigned to the area "survey" in the broadest sense.

Picture Stories

According to Rüsen, historical consciousness always expresses itself "in narratively composed linguistic stories."[18] In investigating the question of how children learn to tell a story, in a cross-section study, the linguists Dietrich Boueke, Frieder Schülein, and Dagmar Wolf showed a group of thirty-two children, which was divided into groups of five-, seven-, and nine-year-olds, picture stories from the series "Der kleine Herr Jakob" (Little Mister Jacob), subsequently asking the children to retell the respective stories.[19] The formal structure of these stories was then analyzed.

According to the authors, contrary to other narrative texts, stories distinguish themselves by their unique quality "that an unexpected event, which causes a break in the course of events normally to be anticipated, forms the focal point" of the story.[20] To this is added "the affective marking of the narrated events, which is intended to enable involvement of the listener."[21] The subsequently introduced hierarchical structural model of a story consists of elementary facts *(events)* at the lowest level, which are linked together linearly to form a *chain of events* at the next higher level. This is followed by the levels of episodic marking, and affective marking, as well as the setting: "In this way the *setting* becomes the *exposition,* the *episode* becomes the *complication,* and the *conclusion* becomes the *solution*—and thus the 'dramaturgy' of the story is complete."[22]

Based on this pattern of an elaborated story, the authors distinguish four narrative types, according to which the children's texts were classified: (1) the isolated representation of events, (2) the linear representation of events, (3) the episodically structured representation of events, and (4) the narratively structured representation of events. The empirical evaluation showed that preschool children primarily employed isolated and linear representations of events; among children in second grade (seven-year-olds), the linear and structured types of event representation occurred most often, whereas children in fourth grade (nine-year-olds) primarily selected the narratively structured representation of events, not once using the isolated representation of events. The authors inferred corresponding stages of development from these results.[23]

As already outlined, this interesting linguistic approach to the development of narrative competency is based on a normative model that determines how an elaborated story is structured. It has been empirically proven that among children, corresponding narrative structures can actually be identified dependent on their age. However, this empirical approach presupposes the children's (especially the five-year-olds') understanding of the scenic representation in the illustrations. Due to the problems children with no previous school experience can have with test situations, and particularly with understanding instructions, it would at least be conceivable that younger children also already have at their disposal elaborated narrative structures in accordance with the model used here that they cannot exhibit in empirical test situations. It would therefore be interesting to attempt to standardize—relying solely on empirical material—the structures of children's spontaneously related everyday stories and to compare the results with the narrative types derived from the model. The classification of children's stories into four types, which is strongly guided by theory, possibly distorts our awareness of further conceivable forms of child narrative.

Rolf Hänni and R. Hunkeler carried out a theoretically more open investigation of children's storytelling among children aged two-and-a-half to just under six.[24] First, the children were investigated in their usual family surroundings, and second, the children were asked to recount something they had experienced *themselves*. In individual tests, a Punch and Judy play was acted out for these children at home. After the researcher had left, they were expected to recount the play to their parents a few hours later. These stories were recorded on tape by the parents. The content-analytical and text-grammatical evaluation of the stories enabled identifying linguistic stereotypes that can be considered to be basis components of a narrative pattern (e.g., "and after that") among even the youngest participants. It now still remains to be tested which narrative structures young children choose on their own initiative—that is, without any prior formulation of the task by the researcher—to recount an everyday situation they experienced themselves. To record such stories, we must leave the methodological framework of the "survey" and turn to the method of participant observation (see below).

Picture Questionnaires

Standardized surveys of younger children can be carried out using pictures. We converted questionnaires originally designed for instruction in general science at the primary school level (so-called *Sachunterricht*) into picture questionnaires for answering the question of what preschool children know about the further development of technical products with which they should be familiar. The worksheet consists of fifteen pairs of objects (e.g., blackboard/notebook, pencil/ballpoint pen, letter/telephone, horse-drawn carriage/truck). The children were asked to mark the object in each pair that "came earlier." The one exception to the pair of "objects" was the pair cat/dinosaur.

The picture questionnaires were presented to twelve preschool children as well as to a second- and a fourth-grade elementary school class. Some of the preschool children required help because they were still unfamiliar with the medium "questionnaire." The purely quantitative evaluation revealed, among other things, the following: Whereas only one of the preschool children completed the questionnaire without error, nearly all of the children in grade four succeeded in doing so. The significantly lower error count among the fourth graders therefore reflects the increase in knowledge to be expected in the course of elementary school. More widespread sample surveys will certainly also confirm this tendency. For our line of questioning, what is interesting about such investigations is less the quantitative increase of knowledge that accompanies the years spent in school, but more the reference to the subject of historical consciousness.

Rüsen considers the comparison of images from the past and the present as a significant source for historical meaning construction: "Yesterday is 'different' than today. That is what matters. This difference can be a genuinely visual experience, for example when one sees the Church of the Virgin Mary next to the television tower on Alexander Square in Berlin."[25] The visual perception of a time difference, however, can only be a beginning. Historical meaning construction first occurs "when the difference as such becomes central in such a way that one can describe the narrative curve between that which is different, the one time, and the other time."[26]

Several individual observations made in the group of preschool children should be discussed against this background:

1. To describe a "narrative curve" between different times, certain minimal linguistic competencies are necessary. A six-year-old girl, for example, almost consistently marked the objects developed later, which raises the question of whether this child was adequately familiar with the linguistic representations of the concepts of "earlier" and "later" to begin with. This questionnaire could not be evaluated. Only a more detailed conversation with the girl could have clarified which linguistic representations she had at her disposal; these could have then been "translated" back into the original task. Other children, however, sometimes marked both objects of a pair, with the reasoning "they existed at the same time," whereby it is not quite clear whether these children erroneously believed that these objects originated at the same time, or whether they correctly assumed that both objects still exist today (as, for example, broom and vacuum cleaner). However, they added the linguistic concept of "at the same time" to the formulation of the task, which was not provided for but definitely makes sense if one looks at things chronologically. The cognitive competency to meaningfully arrange periods of time in accordance with our understanding of time, and to represent them linguistically, is certainly fundamental to describing a narrative curve between objects from both earlier times and today.

2. When the children were ignorant of the age of things, many of them marked those objects that were more familiar to them based on their own sphere of experience. As follows from their corresponding utterances, these objects then already existed "earlier." In view of the patterns of interpretation

they contain, such "errors" are of great interest for the question of the origin of historical consciousness. The link here is that which is familiar, as in, that is: What is familiar must have "always" existed (e.g., television versus radio). The unfamiliar or unknown is projected into a later time.[27] The temporal connection made in this way between the familiar and the unfamiliar is also not unknown to adults. Even in the social sciences, quite a lot of published observations are labeled "new" without further historical enquiry.[28] An important research question would be how the interpretational pattern "unfamiliar = new" is anchored in (early) childhood and how it can be overcome.

3. One girl supplied reasons for her choice, such as "You can make a broom yourself" (versus a vacuum cleaner) or "You could build the boat yourself" (she was referring to a sailboat versus a steamboat). Of course, this does not yet describe a narrative curve, but the beginnings of a "story" are discernible in roughly the following sense: Things that one can make oneself have existed for a long time; it was not until later that machines were invented with which one could manufacture other things. These few comments may have already served to illustrate the extent to which picture questionnaires, which can also be used with younger children, are quite useful for investigations in the field of historical consciousness. However, their usefulness does not rely so much on the quantifiability of the results (number of errors per age group); what is more revealing is the use of such questionnaires to initiate conversations with the children about the objects in the illustrations shown them. These conversations could serve to determine whether and the extent to which even preschool children are able to describe a "narrative curve"—in Rüsen's sense—between the times partially represented by the objects. This has not been attempted in this investigation, but supplementary observations contain reference to the possible productiveness of such a probe.

Completion Tests

Completion tests are familiar in language instruction, where, above all, they are useful for vocabulary and grammar exercises. We designed a completion test as a partially standardized method for the acquisition of children's notions about everyday life in earlier times and tested it with fourth graders. For this task, the children were asked to imagine having lived in a past age and to write a report about it for a children's newspaper. The text is entitled "A day in my past life," and begins with "My past name was.... The age in which I once lived is called.... This was about ... years ago." This is followed by expositions regarding the structure of the child's day, the living situation and the family, favorite activities, likes and dislikes, each with the corresponding blanks. This formally provided the children with a "narrative curve," which they were expected to fill in.

The epochs selected by the children themselves in our sample survey ranged from the Stone Age to the Second World War, and also included other cultures, such as Native Americans or the Egyptians. The corresponding ages the children assigned the epochs varied considerably. During the Middle Ages, for example, was assigned from "forty years ago" to "one million years ago." Hence, average ten-year-olds had still not yet developed notions of historical periods of time. This was also confirmed in other investigations (see below). In their organization, with regard to the content of the time of the "Second World War," the children apparently fell back on stories told to them by people in their social environment who had experienced the war themselves. They mentioned, among other things, the thunder of canons, bunkers, hunger, and cold. For the other periods of time, rudimentary stores of knowledge were combined with images out of fairy tales and other stories, or with a child's own everyday experiences. According to some children, for instance, during the Middle Ages one wore "velvet and silk," was a princess, and lived in a castle; in the Stone Age one might live in caves, but one had chairs, tables, and cupboards. According to one child, even eyeglasses existed at that time.

These kinds of completion tests require the ability to change perspective, which is an essential basis competency of historical consciousness, but which can at least be presupposed as a cognitive competency with older elementary school children. This method can most certainly be introduced from about third grade onward, when children are able to read and write with relative confidence. With a larger sample survey, the partial standardization of this completion test enables a quantitative evaluation (e.g., regarding the stores of knowledge brought in) as well as an interpretative analysis of the added constituents of the sentences. However, the structure of the presentation is prescribed, that is, the children are forced to organize their notions about earlier periods of time according to the prescribed structure and cannot develop them freely. The conceptualization of further completion tests therefore requires a certain amount of sensitivity in order to come as close as possible to the children's own narrative structures.

Questionnaire

Questionnaires and standardized interviews are probably the most common empirical approaches to historical consciousness, yet we are not familiar with one example of an investigation along those same lines among children. Bodo von Borries investigated the historical consciousness and political orientation of *young people* using a representative survey of over six thousand students in grades six, nine, and twelve in both eastern and western Germany.[29] The comprehensive statistical analyses provide a good overview of the levels of knowledge, attitudes, and opinions of these young people that are dependent on gender, type of school, and political party preference. Because, for methodological reasons, only "closed" questions were formulated, the young people were also only able to formulate their answers to fit within the prescribed framework.[30]

To observe how *children* use standardized questionnaires and to learn what historical knowledge one can anticipate among children who have not yet experienced systematic instruction in history, we designed a questionnaire containing nineteen multiple-choice questions regarding a wide variety of topics, which we selected on the basis of the historical topics contained in a children's dictionary. This questionnaire was presented to a fourth-grade elementary school class, and although these students enjoyed filling out the questionnaire, they showed no further interest in the correct answers.

With such a small number of cases, the purely quantitative results are, of course, insignificant. Interesting statements can be made about individual items, however. The only question that was answered correctly by all the children was the one concerning the discovery of America by Columbus. The only question that none of the children could answer was the one concerning the language of a sentence written in Latin, which is not surprising considering these were fourth graders. The second most difficult question was, "What or who are 'nomads'?" Only four children chose the correct answer. The following two questions were the only ones answered gender-specifically: (1) "From about what year to what year were the Middle Ages?" was not answered correctly by a single girl, but seven of the nine boys marked the correct answer; (2) "About how long have there been human beings?" was answered correctly by nine out of twelve girls, but by only two boys.

One boy's remark about the question correctly answered by thirteen children, "When did Martin Luther live?" is revealing. One of the choices was "Eight hundred years before Christ." This boy wrote, "Eight hundred years before Christ is not true, because Christ is in the Bible and the Bible was translated by Martin Luther." With his unsolicited remark, this boy shows us how he arrived at his correct answer—a piece of information that is substantially more interesting for the investigation of historical consciousness than an overview of the selective historical knowledge of children.

Despite these critical remarks about such questionnaires, there is, however, a potentially meaningful way to use them, namely, as a "preliminary test" for the selection of topics for subsequent group discussions (see below). One could, for example, select the question correctly answered by all of the children (the question about the discovery of America) as a topic for discussion and compare it with Peter Bichsel's children's story "Amerika gibt es nicht" (There is no America), thus encouraging the children to discursively examine this historical topic.

Participant Observation

In contrast to experiments and surveys, participant observation is an open method of data acquisition that allows the close investigation of a child's experience and behavior in an everyday setting. In an investigation of the ability to change perspective, we successfully tested this method with preschool children. Because the ability to change perspective can be taken as an essential basis competency of historical consciousness,[31] the concrete procedure and the most important results will be briefly summarized here. The entire investigation has been documented elsewhere.[32] The question of whether even children who have not yet entered school are in a position to recognize the perspectives of other people and to take these into account in their own behavior is a controversial issue in the relevant literature. Those who maintain the view that preschool children think primarily "egocentrically," that is, they cannot "decentralize" their own way of seeing an object and/or the facts, refer to Piaget and the "Geneva school." In this tradition, the investigation paradigm is the experiment and the "clinical interview"; the paradigm of theory formation is the structuralist approach.

Opponents of this view make reference to results achieved with the aid of alternative testing orders or from everyday observations, and which lead one to assume the presence of abilities in children that, according to Piaget's theory, they should not yet even have at their age. Alternatives with regard to theoretical constructions can be found, for example, within the disciplines of phenomenological psychology, ecological psychology, dialectical psychology, and the conceptions suggested by George Herbert Mead. We consistently based our investigations on the "interpretative paradigm," dispensed with the experiment as a method of data acquisition, and by employing the method of participant observation, selected an interpretative approach to the formulation of questions. A child's open behavior in everyday situations was first of all recorded on videotape in ten families. A large number of episodes indicating a connection to the ability to change perspective could be filtered out of this material. Together with the contexts out of which they stemmed, these episodes were transcribed in detail and individually interpreted with regard to the questions guiding our research.

The results presented a broad spectrum of behavior and speech, which suggests the ability to change perspective even among younger children.[33] Five different types of a child's performance that require the ability to change perspective could be extracted and verified with empirical examples: (1) conveyance of information, (2) consideration of the cognitions of other people, (3) acting from the perspective of another person, (4) conveyance of a personal need to communicate, and (5) consideration of several aspects of an object. The apparently relatively simple actions of younger children can also be assigned to these types, provided they are analyzed in their detail and with respect to their context. For the formation of a theory, this gives rise to the question of whether the construction of experimental investigation situations does not already in itself obscure our view of a child's performance, which cannot be recorded using experimental methods of data acquisition, but about which statements can be formulated in theoretical generalizations. In contrast, interpretative type formation enables doing justice to the complexity and the contextuality of everyday life, as well as formulating and substantiating comprehensive statements that go beyond the individual case. For purposes of theory formation, in the continuation of this approach it appears to be necessary to understand the ability to change perspective in its relation to social situations of communication.

Even if the method of participant observation requires a lot of time and effort, the results outlined above indeed encourage testing this method for the investigation of other basis compentencies of historical consciousness as well. As an example, the question of the narrative competency of younger children presents itself in particular, for which, as mentioned above, we have only few empirical findings.

Group Discussion (Focus Group)

"Historical consciousness not only enables, it requires the ability of controversial discourse, which is founded on the understanding of the partiality and susceptibility to error of one's own interpretations and assessments.... Historical consciousness of this kind makes the communication of different persons or groups, different peoples or religions possible; indeed it makes it necessary. And in these tensions and controversies it proves itself to be tendentially 'cosmopolitan' consciousness."[34] In view of these remarks, it is somewhat surprising that the group discussion method has scarcely been employed in the field of historical consciousness.

Group discussions are, above all, suitable for recording socially shared opinions, attitudes, orientations, and patterns of interpretation. In this setting, the social formation of cognitions in the exchange with others is "reproduced" in miniature through the establishment of a small group in which a particular complex of topics is discussed. Today, group discussions are primarily carried out within qualitative social research and primarily with adults and young people. From the field of philosophy for children comes the suggestion to hold discussions, oriented toward the Socratic method, about philosophical problems with children in groups. As an empirical method of acquiring data, group discussion with children is, however, also suitable for recording children's opinions and imagination and their formation within discursive interaction with other children. Are group discussions also suitable for clarifying questions about a child's historical consciousness?

The group discussion in relation to which the possible yield of this empirical approach shall be discussed was held with four children from a fourth-grade elementary school class in Hanover. To stimulate the discussion, a series of "historical" objects were spread out on the table, such as a lorgnette with a case, a box showing a scene from Hanover in 1850, copies of Gothic script, and the illustration of a scene from Hanover in 1800. Depending on the age of the children, there are, of course, other possibilities for evoking group discussions about historical topics (for example, by using short historical narratives with an open end).[35] For the purpose of first testing this method as such for the question of historical consciousness, the broad range of objects used to stimulate conversation in our children's group discussion facilitated an openness for the determination of relevance by the children themselves.[36]

After the children had looked at the objects and pictures and made spontaneous comments about them, a multifaceted discussion ensued, partially structured by questions from the leader of the discussion. At some points, the children constructed small historical scenarios based on their own selective knowledge. When the leader of the discussion asked questions, she oriented herself largely on aspects of the topics that the children had already touched on themselves in shorter sequences in order to discuss these again in more detail. Further, the leader of the discussion was responsible for gently guiding the dynamics of the group so that all of the children had relatively equal opportunity to speak and were also able to finish speaking. There was no further "didactic" intervention; the children were not corrected when, for instance, they expressed unusual opinions. Rather, the leader of the discussion largely limited her remarks to those that expressed interest (as, e.g., "aha" or "hmm") or to questions that reflected statements made by the children (as, e.g., "So, you mean human beings hunted dinosaurs?"), partially supplementing these with questions directed toward the other children ("What do the others think then?"). But it was mostly the children themselves who expressed their contrasting opinions. The discussion was so comprehensive that it cannot be presented here in its entirety.[37] The following provides a structured overview of the *main* topics that were addressed, immediately followed by the introduction of examples of those passages from the group discussion that could be empirically relevant for the question of historical consciousness. First, the list of topics:[38]

1. *Topics introduced by the children and dealt with in more detail:*
   - Were there birds in primeval times?
   - Were there human beings when dinosaurs existed?
   - What did Stone Age people have?
   - What did the Ice Age look like?
   - What about the hieroglyphs and the pyramids?
   - What purpose do museums have?
   - Are the objects in a museum authentic or replicas?
   - Are old objects valuable?

2. *Topics introduced by the children and dealt with in brief:*
   - What did people look like in primeval times?
   - Were there snails in primeval times?
   - Can frozen mammoth babies be revived?
   - How does a lorgnette work?

3. *Topics introduced by the leader of the discussion:*
   - Why do we deal with history?
   - What times could the objects I brought along be from?

The Joint Construction of Historical Scenarios

Although the children had only very selective knowledge about natural and cultural history, they nevertheless appeared to have an "idea"—however vague—of life in earlier times. Stimulated by a child's remark, at several points during the discussion, historical scenarios of sorts were developed together as a group. Each child contributed his or her "knowledge" acquired from books, pictures, television programs, and lessons in general knowledge, thus either continuing the "story" or changing the direction of the conversation by means of new questions and assumptions. "Historical scenarios" as we understand them here consist, then, of elements of knowledge that are combined *narratively* to create a communicable image, occasionally enhanced by descriptions (as, e.g., "But today they still have little hairs, but ... no fur ...") and historical arguments (see below).[39]

Such a scenario can be found, for example, in the topic "Were there birds in primeval times?" This topic quickly led to dinosaurs, which are extremely popular among today's generation of children, to the question of whether the archaeopteryx was a bird, and, finally, to early human beings, who, according to at least three of the four children, hunted dinosaurs and hid in caves. Another scenario was developed for the Ice Age. During this exercise, the children transferred their subjective notions of how Eskimos live to the Ice Age, and said, among other things:[40]

ANNE: The Ice Age, where there was only ice and things, where the people had to dress really warmly because, after all, and they had to stay in their houses sometimes, and they still had to try to find wood, or they always made holes in the ice so they, um, the fish get air and things, or so they don't, well so that they still get air.

TANJA: And could fish. The Eskimos do that, too. They eat frozen fish. So they fish and eat them at once.

ANNE: Then they always make a kind of little hole, they don't have real fishing rods, wooden fishing rods, and then they take a kind of regular rope, but they didn't have rope then, that's why ...

STEPHAN: Plants!

ANNE: Yeah, kinds of plants that are really flexible. Then they hung something on it, and then they always sat around the hole and tried to get something to eat, too. And then they couldn't always close the hole, and that's why it was good for both of them. They could fish there and the animals, well, the animals could get a little bit of air, too.

For the sake of vividness, a further example is cited here in more detail:

What about the hieroglyphs and the pyramids?
ANNE: Here, on this page is a kind of writing ...
STEPHAN: Hieroglyphs.
ANNE: ... only the Egyptians could read them. They always had a kind of brown map and ...
STEPHAN: You can ...

ANNE:	... and here, with the kind of pyramid, there were always kinds of secret maps, and they could only read them themselves, so that they, so that only they could read them. So that they could get out again.
INT.:	Stephan?
STEPHAN:	And then the kings and things were always buried in the pyramids, like a mummy.
TANJA:	Buried.
STEPHAN:	Yeah, there and inside there they were practically buried.
INT.:	And what do the others think about the pyramids then?
ANNE:	There are, well, there are kinds of, co-, coff-, no.[41]
TANJA:	You mean *saga - saga*.
ANNE:	Yes.
STEPHAN:	Coffins.
TANJA:	Coffins.
ANNE:	Where the mummies are inside, there's sometimes a kind of pattern on it, too.
(...)	
KATHRIN:	In a movie, no, I saw a kind of movie on TV once ...
STEPHAN:	Sphinx.
KATHRIN:	... there was a kind of ring on the top, and then he came alive.
INT.:	Aha.
TANJA:	I have a question. I want to know how they did that with the mummies. Did they just take people and wrap them up in toilet paper? [Laughs]
INT.:	In toilet paper?!
KATHRIN:	No!
INT.:	What do the others think then?
STEPHAN:	They used silk fabric.
INT.:	Aha, then there was ...
ANNE:	Yeah, they - when they were really old - well, when they were there in the pyramids for a really long time, then they also - so, well in kind of co ...
INT.:	Coffins?!
ANNE:	... then they put them in there so that not just anybody found the secret or anybody can steal the king.
INT.:	Aha.
ANNE:	And then they made a kind of map, and anybody who wants to visit the king knows right where the king is then.
INT.:	Aha. A kind of treasure map.
ANNE:	Yeah.
KATHRIN:	But the ...
STEPHAN:	They're painted on the walls.
Tanja:	Yeah!
INT.:	Hmm.
TANJA:	And there were some - um, scientists have - um, scientists have already reported, they, that they have already found kinds of drawings on rock faces. Well, with - with writing.
STEPHAN:	Yeah ...
INT.:	Stephan?
STEPHAN:	Those were old cave drawings. And that all pyramids, those there were, they were kinds of mazes where you could only orient yourself on such - such - on the walls ...
INT.:	Aha.

STEPHAN: ... or you needed a guide.
INT.: Aha. Anne?
ANNE: Or you had to, because, when you, there is, there are traps down there too, and that's why the treasure map was really good, wasn't it? That the ones who made the treasure map, so they didn't walk into their own traps.
INT.: Aha.
ANNE: That's really so big, the pyramids, and that's why they all couldn't, well ...
STEPHAN: ... know all the ways by heart!
ANNE: Yeah, and sometimes there are secret passageways there, too, where there's nothing inside.

Stimulated by Anne's reference to the hieroglyphs in one of the illustrations, the image of secret maps that guide one through pyramids was developed in this passage. Anne kept to her idea, supported by Stephan, who contributed his knowledge about pyramids, and Tanja and Kathrin, who referred to the mummies. Space does not allow for a more precise sentence-for-sentence analysis here. For this reason, we offer just a few interpretational comments: What is interesting is, for example, how the children attempted to understand historical facts as they see them in the form of adventure stories with which they were apparently familiar. Something similar can be found in the passages concerning the dinosaur hunt as well. This interpretational hypothesis would have to be scrutinzed in further group discussions with elementary school children. It is supported theoretically by the view held in recent work on historical consciousness that historical meaning construction is essentially founded on the ability acquired in everyday life to (re)construct, reflect, and interchange experience in the form of stories.[42]

Because reality and fiction cannot be sharply distinguished in any story,[43] the fictional content of the construction of historical scenarios is not a fundamental argument against the view that historical consciousness can develop out of reference to adventure stories. Children certainly reflect less—or not at all—on the possible fictional content of their constructions. However, the "stories" of our group discussion exhibit something like a social corrective when, for example, with respect to the dinosaur hunt, Stephan voiced his doubts about whether human beings had even existed in the age of the dinosaurs several times.

Historical Argumentation

Initial signs of historical argumentation could also be ascertained in the group discussion. We understand historical argumentation as such forms of argumentation that fall back upon historical knowledge—however rudimentary—to support the claims or opinions expressed and associate this knowledge in the form of an argument. Two examples from Stephan serve to illustrate this. Tanja answered the question about how long human beings have had eyeglasses with "ten million years." Stephan countered with a historical argument: "Well, I say it can't be ten million years at all, there was this early man, and he hadn't invented anything like that yet. He still lived on things he got from nature and all of that. And he hadn't built such things yet." After different guesses by the other children concerning what year the image of Hanover on the box could be from, Stephan said: "I don't think it can be 1900, otherwise we would also see the Town Hall in the background. Um, and, I mean the new one [town hall]. And I think maybe it's from 1500."

Identification with History

What was obvious in the discussion was the occasional use of the concept of "we" when historical times were being talked about, as the following three examples demonstrate:

> And this here is from *very* old times, we weren't even born yet, you weren't even born yet, birds weren't even born yet. [Tanja]

> But they [the primitive human beings in an illustration] really did look like that, we all really looked like that once! [Tanja]

> (...) Well, the town, like it looked in the war and things, they are there, too [in the museum]. And then you can see, when you see your house or something on it that you admire, you know, then you can see how well we copied it. (...) [Anne]

On the basis of such a rather inconspicuous, almost accidental use of the concept of "we," one could put forward the interpretational hypothesis that identification occurs insofar as the girls spontaneously and virtually naturally see or perceive themselves as a part of the history of humanity. This aspect, which requires more precise investigation, could be a prerequisite for the meaningful linking of past, present, and future. Jürgen Straub also regards the concept of "we" as one of the basis compentencies of historical consciousness.[44]

Time Concepts

As was illustrated in the examples on the construction of historical scenarios and historical argumentation, the children definitely exhibited a series of basis competencies of historical consciousness in the discussion. However, despite the argumentative interjections cited, in the considerations stimulated by the leader of the discussion on the age of the objects she brought along, we find estimates that appear very strange to us adults, estimates that extend in part over several million years. According to William J. Friedman, until children are about twelve years old, they refer to a "verbal list system" to conceptualize long periods of time.[45] This has been researched in detail for the order of days of the week and months. It is not until after about fifteen years of age that a spatial concept of historical periods of time successfully sets in. Children's concepts of historical periods of time have still scarcely been researched. At this point, the hypothesis that can be formulated is that in a child's mind, a hundred, a thousand, or a million years are not number concepts in the true sense; rather, they are simple lexical tags similar to the "verbal list system" investigated by Friedman.

The Aesthetics of Old Objects

Stimulated by the lorgnette case, the children also considered whether such things are valuable; within this context, they began to talk about the beauty of old things. During the discussion they mentioned silk fabric, which people had in the Middle Ages, several times, in addition to beautifully painted old pictures. Here are two examples from Anne:

> And with this thing here [the case], there's really - really fine fabric in it, too. Then - they took everything really carefully, because they thought it was really valuable then, that they even have something like that. And today, things are really - and today it is - and today these things don't even exist any more. And if you saw them, you might think they're really neat, but then you wouldn't like to have them.

> [About a painted picture]: ... but that's only valuable for some people, who know something about art or things. But the others, they think, that that's only a picture painted on there. Anybody can paint that. But when you look at it from far away or from way up close, then you think that - there's something in that.

One could interpret what the children expressed in these and other passages about old objects and illustrations as a certain "respect," even if the children were not quite sure of it. Rüsen makes the following comment about this kind of an approach to old things: "With apparent age they gain their own aesthetic quality. The aesthetic charm of the past appears on them. The objects become 'aural' solely because of their age.... Thus historical consciousness can initiate itself on an aesthetic level in the sense perception of time difference."[46]

What Purpose Do Museums Have?

In view of the recent discussion surrounding an appropriate museum education,[47] we will conclude by showing what the children themselves think about the purpose of museums. At one point during the discussion, the discussion leader introduced the question of what they were dealing with at that moment:

> INT.: Um, what do you call - What are we dealing with right now? With art, or ...?

ANNE: With, well - now we are kind of like a preview, too. Now they want to know something about it.
STEPHAN: Biology.
ANNE: Yeah.
INT.: Biology?
TANJA: No!
STEPHAN: Nonsense.
TANJA: Geography.
INT.: Geography you think? What do the others think? - - -
ANNE: Oh no.
INT.: Now I'm going to turn this over! What's the name of this book? [turns over the history book]
STEPHAN: History.
KATHRIN: History.
TANJA: Historical World Studies.
ANNE: That is history! And the chi - and we're still going to learn something about it, when we're in the ninth grade, or if we're already there before that.

Despite the fact that the children did not think of the term "history" themselves, they were still able to understand something by it. Later in the course of the conversation, Anne, Tanja, and Stephan, first of all, said that one needs knowledge about history to get good grades on history tests in school and possibly for one's future career (whereby only scientists and history teachers came to mind). Anne also said that one could be interested in history because it was fun:

> Well, I think that's great, because you might want to know, you live in Hannover now, then you also want to know how it looked before. Or how much money they spent to make this town new again.

Kathrin, on the other hand, said that she had no interest in history. When Stephan finally said that one pursues history "so that you go to the museum more," there ensued a longer unit of conversation about the purpose of museums. Whereas Tanja and Kathrin first held the view that museums take advantage of that in order to earn more money, additional aspects increasingly entered the discussion, such as "so that you are then more interested in history" (Stephan; note his circular view—he originally introduced the topic by saying that one pursues history so that one visits the museum more often); "so that you see their finds" (Stephan); "And then, when you go to the museum, then you also know, yes, what they wore and how they murdered him and everything" (Tanja); "and the people in the museum don't just want to earn money there. They also want to do something to please the people too" (Anne). Anne finally arrived at the following argumentation, in which she attempted to link dimensions of the past, present, and future, which, according to Jeismann, is a fundamental way of expressing an understanding of history:[48]

> We -, um, at most of them there are - at most museums there are always the city of them, too. Well, the town, like it looked in the war and things, they are there,

too. And then you can see, when you see your house or something on it that you admire, you know, then you can see how well we copied it and that the people don't just want to have money, but they want to do something for the other people, too, who aren't born yet too -, um, well, that they want to do something to please them, too. They had the pleasure of possessing that, but the others still have to possess it. But if there is a war now and everything is broken, then they can't do that at all.

Later in the discussion, the children thought about whether the objects in the museums are authentic or replicas. To find the solution to this, it appeared important to the children to find out how these got into the museum in the first place. A few excerpts are cited here:

KATHRIN: Some people, they still weren't even born yet then, and then they can't even get that so easily. They've probably read about that and things, they read it here and they read it there, and then they looked for all the paints and then somehow they, then they copied everything. Because now they ...
INT.: Aha.
ANNE: ... knew exactly everything about that.
INT.: Hmm. Stephan, what do you think?
STEPHAN: Hmm, read. Somebody else must have somehow found another colored one because there weren't any books then, and besides that, *found*, you can *find* it under the ground, researchers and such can *find* it too.
(...)
KATHRIN: But Stephan, how are you supposed to find the carriages? - - -
STEPHAN: Carriages?
KATHRIN: Yeah, the carriages.
ANNE: Yeah, the carriages are in the museum too, aren't they?
STEPHAN: Yeeaah, the carriages are, OK, but that is in the Middle Ages. From the Stone Age, there you find, you have to really find it.
(...)
TANJA: Well, I think they're copied too, um, because - because otherwise it would - they would - have already - they would have already stolen that. [Thoughtfully]
STEPHAN: They - but they have alarms.
(...)
ANNE: Well, I - at this - we were in the museum, too, and there are, where the things were - clothes and things, and all these brooches they had on, there -, you know, all the things they had, you know, and there was a kind of text there, they probably wrote it like out of a book or something. But, but I don't think it's real because, um, well, the clothes, they probably knitted them nicely like that or something, because - I think, they wouldn't hand over the brooches or anything.

Altogether, this group discussion supplies us with a number of references to different aspects of the historical consciousness of children, which, however, lie on different levels. Thus, we obtain references to basis competencies (as, for example, concepts of time), as well as references to more complex historical patterns of interpretation. The "construction of historical scenarios," in particular, but also other passages, already provide some insight into children's interpretations of the past. In our opinion, the few results of this one discussion presented here already exhibit the possible fruition of this new empirical approach to the historical consciousness of children. To test this impression, further pilot studies are required, of course, which, among other things, will clarify which initial stimuli are particularly suitable for such group discussions.

Summary

The journey through the different methodological possibilities in approaching the historical consciousness of children has, we hope, demonstrated some of the strengths and weaknesses of the individual methods. None of these methods appear to be completely unsuitable, especially when we are concerned with recording basis competencies of historical consciousness. With the aid of experiments, for example, the memory performance of very young children can be established, which suggests an autobiographical memory even in earliest childhood. Participant observation enables us to describe the ability to change perspective in everyday situations of communication, even in children as young as two years old. The participant observation method also appears to be suitable to assess the narrative competency of younger children. To find out what historical knowledge elementary school children actually possess prior to systematic instruction in school, standardized questionnaires—possibly combined with verbal questions—certainly make sense. Experiments, (partially) standardized surveys and participant observation can, however, only weakly elucidate which meaning children associate with the fragments of knowledge they already have, and whether and the extent to which they succeed in producing a "correlation between interpretation of the past, understanding of the present, and a future perspective" (Jeismann). For us, group discussion appears to be the more suitable method for pursuing such more complex questions. This approach cannot be employed with very young children, but, as already confirmed in other areas, such as concepts of nature, it can definitely be used with children starting at about the age of six or seven. However, as we were able to show in an investigation of the temporal consciousness of elementary school children,[49] a combination of several of the methods mentioned will ultimately be the most revealing.

Notes

This chapter was translated from the original German by Rebecca van Dyck. Unless otherwise noted, all translations of quotations are also provided by Rebecca van Dyck.

    1. Karl-Ernst Jeismann, "Geschichtsbewußtsein als zentrale Kategorie der Geschichtsdidaktik," in *Geschichtsbewußtsein und historisch-politisches Lernen. Jahrbuch für Geschichtsdidaktik,* ed. Gerhard Schneider (Pfaffenweiler, 1988), vol. 1, 1–27.

2. Cf. Bodo von Borries, Hans-Jürgen Pandel, and Jörn Rüsen, eds., *Geschichtsbewußtsein empirisch* (Pfaffenweiler, 1991); Jörn Rüsen, *Historische Orientierung: über die Arbeit des Geschichtsbewußtseins, sich in der Zeit zurechtzufinden* (Cologne, 1994).

3. See the overview in Martina Meyer and Jürgen Straub, *Literaturdokumentation und erste Hinweise zur Ausarbeitung einer Psychologie historischer Sinnbildung* (Bielefeld, 1995); see also Jürgen Straub in this volume.

4. Meyer and Straub, *Literaturdokumentation*.

5. Jeismann, "Geschichtsbewußtsein als zentrale Kategorie," 14. By "historical longing" Jeismann understands "an affective turn towards history with the awareness that opinion and judgement are inseparably intertwined with one another" (12).

6. Karl-Ernst Jeismann, "Geschichtsbewußtsein," in *Handbuch der Geschichtsdidaktik*, ed. Klaus Bergmann et al. (Düsseldorf, 1979), vol. 1, 42.

7. Rüsen, *Historische Orientierung*.

8. Ibid., 23.

9. Roth constitutes an exception: see Heinrich Roth, *Kind und Geschichte. Psychologische Voraussetzungen des Geschichtsunterrichts in der Volksschule*, 4th ed. (Munich, 1965).

10. Jeismann, for example, explicitly refers to the normative implications of his model (idem, "Geschichtsbewußtsein als zentrale Kategorie," 22).

11. For example, the discussion surrounding an adequate model of moral development is similar, particularly the argumentation surrounding Step 6 of Kohlberg's model, which is hardly accessible empirically. Compare, for example, Fritz Oser and Wolfgang Althof, *Moralische Selbstbestimmung. Modelle der Entwicklung und Erziehung im Wertebereich*, 2nd ed. (Stuttgart, 1994), chap. 8.

12. For this reason, the narrative interview, which, in addition to group discussions, is the method most well suited for investigating the historical consciousness of adults, will not be dealt with. Preschool and elementary school children have a difficult time keeping up with the special form of communication of the narrative interview, if such communication can even be conveyed to them in the first place. The participant observation method presents itself as an alternative here.

13. Eve M. Perris, Nancy M. Myers, and Rachel K. Clifton, "Long-term Memory for a Single Infancy Experience," *Child Development* 61 (1990): 1796–1807.

14. Ibid., 1806.

15. Katherine Nelson, "The Transition from Infant to Child Memory," in *Infant Memory: Its Relation to Normal and Pathological Memory in Humans and Other Animals. Advances in the Study of Communication and Affect*, ed. Morris Moskovitch, (New York, 1984), vol. 9, 103–130.

16. Compare Spear for a differentiation of the different levels of memory expression: Norman E. Spear, "Behaviors That Indicate Memory: Levels of Expression," *Canadian Journal of Psychology* 38 (1984): 348–367.

17. Cf. Rüsen, *Historische Orientierung*, 6. Hans-Jürgen Pandel holds a contrary opinion in this regard (see idem, "Dimensionen des Geschichtsbewußtseins. Ein Versuch, seine Struktur für Empirie und Pragmatik diskutierbar zu machen," *Geschichtsdidaktik* 12 [1987]: 130–142). Pandel assumes that "historical consciousness has nothing to do with 'recollecting.'… We do not *experience* a story or stories, rather they are handed down, recounted. We do not recollect them, rather they are conveyed to us in a cultural communication" (131; italics in the original). Here we must abstain from a discussion of this view regarding the significance of the powers of recollection for the development of historical consciousness.

18. Rüsen, *Historische Orientierung*, 10.

19. Dietrich Boueke, Frieder Schülein, and Dagmar Wolf, "Wie lernen Kinder, eine Geschichte zu erzählen? Zur Entwicklung narrativer Strukturen," *Forschung an der Universität Bielefeld* 11 (1995): 27–33.

20. Boueke, Schülein, and Wolf, "Wie lernen Kinder," 27.

21. Ibid.

22. Ibid., 29 (italics in the original).

23. For this interpretation, however, the influence of school should also be taken into account as a developmental factor, as picture stories are part of German lessons in the fourth grade.

24. Rolf Hänni and R. Hunkeler, "Von der Entwicklung der kindlichen Erzählsprache," *Schweizerische Zeitschrift für Psychologie* 39 (1980): 16–32.

25. Jörn Rüsen, "Geschichte sehen. Zur ästhetischen Konstitution historischer Sinnbildung," in *Auf der Suche nach dem verlorenen Staat. Die Kunst der Parteien und Massenorganisationen der DDR*, ed. Monika Flacke (Berlin, 1994), 32–33.

26. Ibid., 33.

27. Although they did not explicitly articulate this, this pattern of interpretation could have also played a role in the incorrect answers of other children.

28. To cite one example: In certain circles—even scholary ones—the "new" decline of the values of young people has recently (yet again) been the subject of complaint. Such complaints have existed since antiquity; within the area of ethnological field research, Klaus E. Müller also identified such complaints among so-called primitive peoples (see idem, *Prähistorisches Geschichtsbewußtsein*, report no. 1/94 der Forschungsgruppe Historische Sinnbildung [Bielefeld, 1994]).

29. Bodo von Borries, "Geschichtliches Bewußtsein und politische Orientierung von Jugendlichen in Ost- und Westdeutschland 1992," *Neue Sammlung* 34 (1994): 363–382; Bodo von Borries, *Das Geschichtsbewußtsein Jugendlicher. Eine repräsentative Untersuchung über Vergangenheitsdeutungen, Gegenwartswahrnehmungen und Zukunftserwartungen von Schülerinnen und Schülern in Ost- und Westdeutschland* (Weinheim, 1995).

30. Example: "What do you associate with the Middle Ages?" This is followed by five possibilities (e.g., "glittering tournaments," "bold knights"), which could be answered more in the affirmative or more in the negative on a scale from one to five.

31. Cf. Meyer and Straub, *Literaturdokumentation,* see also Straub in this volume.

32. Elfriede Billmann-Mahecha, *Egozentrismus und Perspektivenwechsel. Empirisch-psychologische Studien zu kindlichen Verstehensleistungen im Alltag* (Göttingen, 1990).

33. The youngest child in the sample survey was two and a half years old.

34. Jeismann, "Geschichtsbewußtsein als zentrale Kategorie," 22.

35. In the field of philosophy for children, comprehensive experience has resulted from this type of discussion stimulus. Compare, for example, Gareth B. Matthews, *Dialogues with Children* (Cambridge, Mass., 1984). In an investigation of the historical consciousness of secondary school children, Hans-Günter Schmidt selected historical narratives that included a dilemma, but not to stimulate group discussions; rather, this dilemma was included for individual written surveys (see idem, "Eine Geschichte zum Nachdenken. Erzähltypologie, narrative Kompetenz und Geschichtsbewußtsein: Bericht über einen Versuch der empirischen Erforschung des Geschichtsbewußtseins von Schülern der Sekundarstufe I [Unter- und Mittelstufe]," *Geschichtsdidaktik: Probleme, Projekte, Perspektiven* 12 [1987]: 28–35).

36. For qualitative social research, to which the group discussion method belongs, the possibility of the determination of relevance by the persons being investigated is an important principle.

37. For the evaluation of group discussions with children, compare Elfriede Billmann-Mahecha, Ulrich Gebhard, and Patricia Nevers, "Naturphilosophische Gespräche mit Kindern. Ein qualitativer Forschungsansatz," in *Mit Kindern über Natur philosophieren*, ed. Helmut Schreier (Heinsberg, 1979), 130–153.

38. We formulated the topic headings as summarizing characterizations.

39. The distinction between narrative, description, and argumentation is an ideal-typical one. The concrete, everyday forms of communication the children use here consists of a series of mixtures of these types.

40. The children's names have been changed. "Int." stands for the discussion leader; (...) means shorter, insignificant omissions; - stands for short breaks; - - - for longer breaks; ... stands for interruptions.

41. [Anne attempted to utter the German word for coffins, *Särge*, which is why Tanja suggested she might be searching for the word *saga*. Trans.]

42. Cf. Rüsen, *Historische Orientierung.*

43. Cf. Hans-Joachim Schröder, "Interviewliteratur zum Leben in der DDR. Das narrative Interview als biographisch-soziales Zeugnis zwischen Wissenschaft und Literatur," *Materialien und*

Ergebnisse aus Forschungsprojekten des Institutes für kulturwissenschaftliche Deutschlandstudien an der Universität Bremen, FB 10, Heft 5 (1993).

44. See Straub in this volume, chapter 3; figure 3.1.

45. William J. Friedman, *About Time: Inventing the Fourth Dimension* (Cambridge, Mass., 1990).

46. Rüsen, "Geschichte sehen," 33–34.

47. Compare, for example, Udo Liebelt, ed., *Museumspädagogik. Museum der Sinne. Bedeutung und Didaktik des originalen Objekts im Museum* (Hannover, 1990).

48. Jeismann, "Geschichtsbewußtsein als zentrale Kategorie."

49. Cf. Monika Hausen, "Zeitbewußtsein von Kindern am Beispiel einer zweiten Grundschulklasse" (diss., University of Hannover, 1998).

CHAPTER 9

The Psychological Study of Historical Consciousness

SAMUEL S. WINEBURG

School children the world over spend countless hours every year learning about the past. In Western countries, the block of the school day devoted to this study is referred to as "history," "social studies," "civics," "government," or a host of other names. Yet, despite this variety in nomenclature, in practically every case, students are taught something about what transpired before their births. Despite variations in context, different national traditions and curricu-luar customs, students from Tokyo to New York, Auckland to Berlin, and Tel Aviv to Toronto all learn something about a movement known as the Renaissance, an event known as the French Revolution, and a ruler known as Joseph Stalin.

The study of the past, an understanding, as Cicero once remarked, of "what happened before one was born," is thought to be the mark of a mature citizen the world over. Yet, for as along as educators have designed programs for teaching history, they have been faced with the problem of evaluating the effectiveness of their efforts. To what degree are educators successful in teaching the young about their history? How do students develop an understanding of "what happened before they were born"? Before this question can be considered, a prior one must be asked: How can we ensure that students' understanding of the past is more than the mere recitation of historical facts, the parroting of a litany of information that they little understand? How do we know whether students' knowledge of historical fact rests on something more than a supple memory? How can we get a fix on students' emerging understanding of history's "deep structure"? What, for want of a better term, might be called their grasp of "historical consciousness"?

Notes for this section begin on page 208.

My intent in this chapter is to provide a brief survey of the ways that "historical consciousness" has been approached by researchers in education. To some extent, this survey turns out to be an accounting of the ways that *psychologists* have tried to understand the nature of historical learning, for most educational research—particularly that conducted in English-speaking countries—has used the tools, conceptions, assumptions, and techniques of measurement native to the discipline of psychology.

Obviously, it is impossible to survey the full scope of this work in the space allotted. Therefore, my approach is to focus on some recent developments occasioned by the "cognitive turn" in psychological research in education.[1] Before doing so, however, I provide a brief context for these developments by examining the early history of psychological research on history. I then turn to an examination of a small number of studies that represent exemplars of different conceptual and methodological research traditions. The reader should bear in mind the following caveat: I restrict my scope to work conducted in English-speaking countries (principally, the United States, Great Britain, and Australia), leaving a survey of the extensive work conducted in Germany, France, Sweden, and elsewhere to my European colleagues.

Research on History: Some Early Investigations

To the pioneers of the emerging field of educational psychology at the turn of this century, history was a topic more of theoretical than empirical concern. In the 442 pages of Edward L. Thorndike's *Educational Psychology*,[2] history went unmentioned save for a single brief reference.[3] Only in *Education: A First Book*[4] does history receive more than fleeting attention, as Thorndike paused to speculate on the burning question of his day: Should history "be taught backwards," an approach that begins with the present and traces events back in time, or was the traditional chronological treatment best suited to the abilities and dispositions of youngsters? Despite the absence of data, Thorndike was certain of the right approach:

> The educational value of finding the causes of what is, and then the causes of these causes, is so very much superior to the spurious reasoning which comes from explaining a record already known ... that the arrangement of the ... course in history in the inverse temporal order ... deserves serious consideration.[5]

The developmental psychologist G. Stanley Hall shared Thorndike's speculative interests in history.[6] Hall saw history as a means for helping students place events in a "temporal perspective as products of growth and development," a subject that, especially during adolescence, should be infused with lessons that "inspire to the greatest degree ideals of social service and unselfishness."[7] Hall's history would be a moralizing force, "a thesaurus of inspiring ethical examples to show how all got their deserts in the end."

Among the founders of American educational psychology, only the University of Chicago's Charles Hubbard Judd dealt incisively with history. Judd's chapter in the *Psychology of High-School Subjects*[8] was a treatment that was impressive in scope, embracing in twenty-nine pages the nature of chronological thinking, the difficulties of causal judgment ("much more complicated" in history than in science), the dangers of dramatic reenactments, the psychological difficulties presented by historical evidence, and the motivational role of social (then called "industrial") history.[9] While drawing on the work of others, Judd's discussion contains flourishes of insight in its own right. One example comes in a section on the "Intricacy of Moral Judgments," in which Judd dealt with the ubiquity of presentism, the difficulty—perhaps even the impossibility—of understanding the past on its own terms:

> The modern student is ... guided in all of his judgments by an established mode of thought ... peculiar to his own generation. We have certain notions ... that are wholly different from the notions that obtained at the time that England was in controversy with her American colonies. When ... [the student] is suddenly carried back in his historical studies to situations that differ altogether from the situations that now confront him, he is likely to carry back, without being fully aware of the fallacy of his procedure, those standards of judgment and canons of ethical thought which constitute his present inheritance.[10]

In this short comment, Judd anticipated issues that would occupy psychologists' and philosophers' attention well into the final decades of the twentieth century.

It was not until 1917, the year the United States entered World War I, that history made it into the pages of the fledgling *Journal of Educational Psychology*. J. Carleton Bell, managing editor of the *Journal* and professor at the Brooklyn Training School for Teachers, began volume 8 with an editorial entitled "The Historic Sense." (A timely second editorial examined "The Relation of Psychology to Military Problems.") Bell claimed that the study of history provided an opportunity for thinking and reflection, the opposite of what went on in much instruction. However, to teachers who would aim at these lofty goals, Bell put forth two questions: "What is the historic sense?" and "How can it be developed?"[11] Such questions, he continued, did not only concern the history teacher, but were ones "in which the educational psychologist is interested, and which it is incumbent upon him to attempt to answer."[12]

Bell offered clues about where to locate the "historic sense." Presented with a set of primary documents, one student produces a coherent account while another assembles "a hodge-podge of miscellaneous facts." What accounts for this discrepancy? Similarly, some college freshmen "show great skill in the orderly arrangement of their historical data," while others "take all statements with equal emphasis ... and become hopelessly confused in the multiplicity of details." Do such findings reflect "native differences in historic ability," Bell wondered, or are they the "effects of specific courses of training"? Such questions opened up "a fascinating field for investigation" for the new field of educational psychology.[13]

Bell located questions that continue to occupy our attention: What is the essence of historical understanding? What determines success on tasks that have more than one right answer? What role might instruction play in improving students' ability to think historically? In light of this forward-looking research agenda, it is instructive to examine how it unfolded in practice. In a companion piece to his editorial, Bell and his associate D.F. McCollum presented an empirical study that began by sketching out the various ways historical understanding might be operationalized:[14]

1. "the ability to understand present events in light of the past";
2. the ability to sift through the documentary record—newspaper accounts, hearsay, partisan attacks, contemporary accounts—and construct "from this confused tangle a straightforward and probable account" of what happened (this is especially important, because it is the goal of many "able and earnest college teachers of history");
3. the ability to appreciate a historical narrative;
4. the ability to provide "reflective and discriminating replies to 'thought questions' on a given historical situation";
5. the ability to answer factual questions about historical personalities and events.[15]

Bell and McCollum conceded that this last aspect was "the narrowest, and in the estimation of some writers, the least important type of historical ability," but it was also the one "most readily tested." In a fateful move, the authors announced that the ability to answer factual questions was therefore "chosen for study in the present investigation." While perhaps the first instance, this was not the last in which ease of measurement, not priority of subject matter understanding, determined the course of a research program.

Bell and McCollum composed a test of names, dates, and events believed by teachers to be important facts every student should know. They gave their test to 1,500 students at the upper elementary (fifth through seventh grades), secondary, and college levels. In the upper elementary grades, students answered 16 percent of the questions correctly, in high school (after a year of U.S. history) 33 percent, and in college, after a third had exposure to history, 49 percent. Taking a stand that is customarily reserved for ministers of education worldwide, Bell and McCollum indicted the educational system and its charges: "Surely a grade of 33 in 100 on the simplest and most obvious facts of American history is not a record in which any high school can take pride."[16]

As subsequent research efforts turned increasingly to test development and refinement, historical knowledge, viewed as a menu of possibilities by Bell and McCollum, moved perilously close to only one of their entrees: the ability to answer factual questions about historical personalities and events. These advances carried with them a certain antipathy to traditional forms of assessment in history classes, like essay writing.[17] According to one study, essays were not only "distasteful" to students but also to teachers, because the "scrutinizing, marking, and correcting of the student products is the teacher's greatest bugbear."[18] What if it could be shown that written work, in addition to being laborious, produced little benefit? Worse, what if the essay produced "as much harm as it does good"?[19] This was precisely the claim of F.R. Gorman and D.S. Morgan's study, conducted in three U.S. history classrooms.

These classes, all taught by the same teacher, were assigned different amounts of written homework. Class I was assigned "three units"; Class II "one unit"; and Class III, none at all. Class III, indeed, did best on the factual outcome measure (181 points versus 175 for Class I, $n = 31$ and $n = 29$, respectively), but the authors failed to account for the wide disparity in the entering achievement levels of the two classes. Moreover, the researchers' homework assignments often looked more like directions for drawing up lists than for composing thoughtful written responses (e.g., "List Lincoln's cabinet with the offices held by each." "List the states which seceded in order, with the dates of succession"). When Gorman and Morgan concluded that "the popularity of written work with teachers may result from a confusion of busy work with valid learning procedures,"[20] one wonders where the confusion truly lay: with muddled teachers or with researchers hell-bent on demonstrating the ineffectiveness of written assignments? Advances in psychometrics fueled the movement toward objective testing, as did the spirit of Taylorism that swept American schools between the World Wars.[21] But the fact-based image of historical knowledge was not an educational invention; it fit cozily with prevailing views of knowledge in the discipline of history. As educational psychologists worked to produce reliable and objective history scales, university historians tried to extricate themselves from their humanistic roots to emerge as scientists who would, as the saying went, "cross an ocean to verify a comma." This doggedly factualist approach, as Peter Novick[22] has argued, helped distinguish professional historians from their amateur colleagues, a distinction necessary if history was to become a full-fledged member of the academic community. It is no coincidence, then, that at nearly the same time, L.W. Sackett was presenting his refinement of a world history scale in the pages of the *Journal of Educational Psychology*, a scale that would "nearly eliminate the subjective factor in grading history,"[23] the *American Historical Review*'s editorial policy was being formulated so as to exclude from its pages "matters of opinion" in favor of "matters of fact capable of determination one way or another."[24] This was not an age characterized by a breach between school and academy, but by a tightly woven nexus.

A Long American Drought, A Resurgence in Great Britain

The next four decades were a period of parched earth in American research on historical understanding. Behaviorism held sway in both the academy and in schools, and its fiercely anti-intellectual bent rendered irrelevant the kinds of concerns about historical understanding raised by previous psychologists. Furthermore, the school subject that had been known as "history" in American schools became lost in the unwieldy amalgam known as "social studies." Because this curricular catch-basin held everything from history and geography to newer upstarts such as political science, sociology, psychology, "life skills," citizenship, and "family life," just to name a few, any attempt to ask what it meant to "think in the social studies" was doomed to incoherence.

At the same time that the American curriculum became mired in social studies, a small group of researchers in Great Britain followed a different lead. Led by the psychologist E.A. Peel, these researchers began to apply the theories of Jean Piaget to the study of students' understanding. Some of the early attempts to apply Piaget's structuralist and hypothetico-deductive models to historical reasoning look quaint in retrospect, such as one attempt to study "pure historical reasoning" (untainted by prior background knowledge), which led to the odd creation of "fictionalized historical scenarios" on the part of researchers.[25] Nevertheless, these early forays into how children reasoned about history contributed to an atmosphere of experimentation and innovation, and led, by some curious twists and turns, to the most extensive attempt to reform the history curriculum in an English-speaking country—and perhaps the most successful.

The School's Council History Project began as a small grassroots effort at the University of Leeds in 1973.[26] By the 1980s, the curriculum materials of this project were used in approximately 20 percent of British schools,[27] and by the 1990s, the nonchronological approach of School's Council and its focus on historical epistemology, was one of the major influences on the development of the British national history curriculum.[28]

The approach of School's Council was unique in its emphasis on history as a distinctive way of thought. Deeply influenced by the "form of knowledge" approach of R.S. Peters and the "structure of the discipline" approach associated with the American psychologist Jerome S. Bruner, project founders sought to develop a curriculum that provided students access to history's underbelly—the nature of historical evidence, the warrant for conclusions, and the bounded and contextualized nature of historical interpretations.[29] Although the School's Council Project was primarily a school reform effort, the evaluation of the project, a major undertaking involving over a thousand students and extensive interview and "matched-pair" comparisons, offer an intriguing model for thinking about the development of students' historical thinking.

The primary means of evaluating the project was a series of comparisons between students whose teachers had used the School's Council materials and those who had not. But before comparisons could be made between Project and non-Project students, Project staff first had to invent measures and coding schemes to capture the "form of knowledge" approach to history. For example, students' responses about the nature of history from the matched-pair interviews were coded using one of four levels spanning the range of historical conceptualization. Level I responses were characterized by a "just because" quality. Events happened because they happened, with no inner logic other than their arrangement in temporal sequence. Level II responses viewed history with "an austere, Calvinistic logic,"[30] equating historical reconstruction to a process of slotting pieces of a puzzle into a preexisting form. At Level III, adolescents had a dawning awareness of a disjuncture between historical narratives and "the past," recognizing that the former involved selectivity and judgment, and could never reflect the latter in all its complexity. At Level IV, students transcended the search for overarching historical laws and came to understand historical explanation as being context-bound and context-sensitive.

The two highest levels of this typology were attained by 68 percent of Project students versus 29 percent of the non-Project students. The lowest level was occupied by 15 percent of non-Project students versus 1 percent of Project students. In each of the three evaluation components, Project students outperformed their counterparts from traditional classrooms. For example, 50 percent of non-Project students were unable to differentiate between historical and scientific knowledge, versus only 10 percent of Project students. And when students were asked to compare history to mathematics, 83 percent of the non-Project students saw math as more difficult than history, versus 25 percent of Project students. As one non-Project student put it, "In history you just look it up, in math you work it out"; another non-Project student added, "From one formula in Maths you get three or four others following, but History has no pattern."[31]

The overall picture emerging from the evaluation supported the idea that adolescents could be taught to understand history as a sophisticated form of knowledge different from other forms in the school curriculum. Yet Dennis J. Shemilt's evaluation is not the story of unqualified success, for as he noted, the difference between Project and traditional students may be compared "to the difference between stony, derelict ground barely able to support a few straggling weeds and a cultivated but undisciplined garden in which a few splendid blossoms struggle to show through."[32]

While offering a way to conceptualize children's development along a continuum of historical thinking, Shemilt's evaluation of the School's Council Project offered only periodic glimpses of children's actual words and thoughts. Most of the snippets of children's thinking presented in the evaluation report came in response to interview questions put to them by adult researchers. In some cases, these responses tell us more about children's ability to philosophize about their own thinking than the nature and texture of this thinking itself. Nonetheless, the School's Council Project and its evaluation stand out as the most successful attempt to date to influence how history is taught and learned in an English-speaking country.

The Cognitive Revolution

Every revolution inspires new hopes, and the "cognitive revolution" was no exception. Freed from behaviorist strictures that held them in thrall for decades, researchers in education and psychology took up with vigor questions about the nature of learning, the nature of consciousness, and how the teaching–learning dynamic is transacted in concrete social settings. New images of school learning promised to answer questions that had riddled researchers not only since the beginning of scientific psychology, but since humankind began asking itself what it meant to know and learn. During the 1970s and 1980s, cognitive researchers illuminated students' thinking in an array of school subjects, from traditional subjects such as arithmetic, biology, physics, and geometry, to newer additions to the curriculum such as computer science and economics. But amidst this efflorescence of research, the subject matter of history was ignored. Indeed, one of the first attempts to draw together the new work on school learning, Ellen Gagné's *Cognitive Psychology of School Learning,* contained over four hundred references but not a single one applied to history.[33]

In 1986, I began a series of studies that used empirical means to explore the nature of historical cognition. I was broadly concerned with how historians, teachers, and university and high school students come to an understanding of the past when evaluating historical evidence. What cognitive processes do they use as they piece together bits of evidence from the past? How do they discern patterns and make meaning out of the mixed bag of truths and untruths left from past ages? These questions have been explored in a veritable library of books on historical methodology, beginning with Langlois and Seignobos's handbook in 1898. However, it may be the case that we know far more about what historians say they do, and what they think they ought to do, than what they actually do.

There are at least four problems with taking the largely prescriptive literature on historical methods, a literature based almost exclusively on self-reports, at face value. First, we know from research on other professions that there is often a wide gap between the practices recommended by handbooks and textbooks and those carried out by practitioners. For example, in a study of the thought processes of physicians, Arthur Elstein, Lee S. Shulman, and Sarah A. Sprafka[34] found that while medical textbooks depicted the process of arriving at diagnoses as one of induction, in which the physician keeps an open mind while gathering the necessary data, expert physicians in practice approached the task *deductively,* generating multiple competing hypotheses in their first few moments with patients and then eliminating hypotheses as more information became known. The lesson from this work is clear: the fact that textbooks and guidebooks claim that experts go about solving a problem in a certain way is itself no guarantee that this is the case in practice.

Second, decades of psychological research has amply demonstrated that people can be woefully inaccurate in their reports of their own cognitive processes.[35] For example, R. Nisbett and Thomas Wilson[36] in a series of ingenious experiments demonstrated that although people were able to articulate the contents of their thoughts, they were often wrong about the processes they used to arrive at them.

Third, many of the cognitive processes used by historians have become automatic, so much so that they are inaccessible to conscious review and reflection. Processes such as those used to determine the stance or interest of a source may occur so rapidly that historians may be unable to describe the intermediate cognitive steps taken to arrive at judgments. This phenomenon is implicated in a section on how historians evaluate documents in Ward Gray's *Historian's Handbook*[37] in which the author describes documentary criticism as relying on a "sort of sixth sense that will alert you to the tell-tale signs." It may be that this ineffable "sixth sense," like other reports of spontaneous insights in the problem-solving literature, is the result of fleeting intermediate processes whose only trace is the conclusions they leave behind.

Finally, every discipline possesses implicit rules of evidence and argument, and history is no exception. In explaining the behavior of the men who stood on Lexington Green on April 19, 1775, in what became the outbreak of hostilities in the American Revolution, historians may refer to the actions of these particular men in other encounters,[38] draw on theories from the social science that account for crowd behavior, or even invoke everyday notions of human nature or common sense. But rarely do historians write about how their *own* lives—their *own* feelings, thoughts, emotions, and experiences—aid them in reconstructing the actions of people who lived in the past. This is because, as Donald N. McCloskey explains, the implicit rules of writing academic history limit the historian "in what sorts of evidence and what sorts of logical appeals he can make if he wishes to retain an audience."[39] Records of historians' personal experiences are not found in the footnotes of historical monographs, even if these experiences are essential to the points being made. Nor are they given prominence in the counsel of established historians in the handbooks they write for neophytes. Despite the importance of such personal experiences for understanding the experience of others, professional norms dictate that they remain hidden from view. Because such thinking rarely finds its way into historical handbooks, one would suspect that the picture such books present of historical thinking—and the processes that constitute it—is only partial at best.

The examples of historical thinking that I present below are drawn from two separate studies. In the first, a group of eight historians and eight high school students read documents and reviewed graphic illustrations of the Battle of Lexington, the opening volley of the American Revolution on April 19, 1775.[40] Participants in this study were presented with a series of documents about the battle, ranging from eyewitness accounts and recollections by contemporaries, to treatments in school textbooks and even an excerpt from a historical novel. In the second study, a group of historians and high school teachers reviewed a series of documents related to the debates between Abraham Lincoln and Stephan Douglas, both of whom vied for the right to represent Illinois in the U.S. Senate in 1858. The "Lincoln-Douglas" debates, as they are known to American school children, contain the major arguments for and against slavery, and are considered one of the major starting points for learning about these issues in the American school curriculum.

The methodology used in both studies is known as the "think-aloud" technique. Essentially, "think-aloud" asks people to verbalize their thoughts as they solve complex problems or read sophisticated texts, and it departs from traditional "experimental" research by focusing on the ongoing processes of cognition, not just on its outcomes. While the artificiality of this technique has drawbacks—for many, thinking aloud is a contradiction in terms and takes some getting used to—it offers a window into thinking provided by few other methodologies. The technique has proven to be particularly useful in understanding the writing process, and models of cognition based on the think-aloud protocols of experienced writers have been used to teach novices the skills of composition. Writing researchers John Hayes and Linda Flower, pioneers in using think-aloud protocols ("protocols" simply refers to the written transcriptions of think-aloud sessions) have likened the think-aloud process to following the tracks of a porpoise:

> Analyzing a protocol is like following the tracks of a porpoise, which occasionally reveals itself by breaking the surface of the sea. Its brief surfacings are like the glimpses that the protocol affords us of the underlying mental process. Between surfacings, the mental process, like the porpoise, runs deep and silent. Our task is to infer the course of the process from these brief traces. The power of protocol analysis lies in the richness of its data. Even though protocols are typically incomplete, they provide us with much more information about processes by which tasks are performed than does simply examining the outcome of the process. Knowing what answer people get in solving problems is much less informative than catching even fragmentary glimpses of the complex processes by which they arrive at the answer.[41]

At first glance, the think-aloud technique seems susceptible to the criticism that people have only limited access to their internal processes. Indeed, this is largely the claim made by Richard Nisbett and Thomas Wilson in the study referred to earlier. However, Nisbett and Wilson's criticism is most persuasive when applied to people's reports of the *processes* they went through to arrive at a particular decision. The think-aloud technique, however, asks people to report the *contents* of the conscious cognition, not to make inferences about the processes used to arrive at these contents. People are encouraged to give "on-line" reports of everything that goes through their mind as they read a text or solve a problem. Typically, these reports are telegraphic, elliptical, filled with hunches and missteps, and are often difficult to interpret conclusively. They do, however, open a window to people's active construction of meaning, and are useful despite their methodological shortcomings.

The foundation for my work on historical texts is the model of text processing proposed by T.A. van Dijk and W. Kintsch.[42] This model focuses on the representations, or private mental structures, that people build as they read written texts. According to this model, readers form two distinct cognitive representations: a representation of the *text base* and a representation of the *situation*. The representation of the text base rests on deciphering the literal meaning of a text and establishing coherence relations among its propositions. But successful readers must also form situation models, or cognitive representations of the situation described by the text. While a great deal is known about how text base models are formed, our understanding of "how situation models are formed and how they are used is still in its infancy."[43]

Researchers who study the processing of written texts must make decisions about the appropriate level of analysis for the questions they ask and the phenomena they investigate. My own goal in understanding the nature of historical reasoning was not to understand the act of reading in all of its perceptual and cognitive complexity, but to shed light on what psychologists called "controlled processes,"[44] those cognitive processes that remain under active cognitive control. But even among researchers who study controlled processes, there is a range of levels at which one can look at the reading process. At one end of the spectrum are researchers such as Walter Kintsch and T. van Dijk, whose goal is nothing short of a comprehensive model embracing all forms of discourse processing. In their analyses of text processing, these researchers break sentences down into their smallest meaning units, called *propositions,* in order to design computer simulations to test their models. At the other end of the spectrum are a host of literary critics and reading-response theorists less concerned with the processing of single sentences than with the processing of thousands of sentences in the form of whole novels and literary works. Bypassing the basic psychological processes of text comprehension, these critics ask questions about the global meanings attached to literary works and the validity of these meanings as they apply to the intentions of the author,[45] to one's "interpretative community,"[46] to the world of textuality that resides within the pages of the text,[47] or to the material conditions in society that frame the act of reading.[48]

My goal in undertaking a research program devoted to the empirical study of historical reasoning was not to create a computer simulation (however useful such an enterprise might prove), but to describe the cognitive processes that lead to the sophisticated interpretation of historical texts. Furthermore, I had an unabashedly practical goal in mind as well: I hoped that the study of skilled historical cognition could inform the instructional practices of teachers who used primary sources in their classroom. In view of these goals, the reduction of texts into propositions would be premature, for the amount of detail generated by such an enterprise would obscure the more global questions about historical interpretation that I wanted to ask. On the other hand, leaving texts whole would be equally intractable, given my goal of understanding the intermediate cognitive processes—the false starts and missteps and heuristics—that ultimately contribute to the construction of historical meaning. Therefore, the unit I use to discuss historical understanding lies somewhere between the atom-like proposition and the unwieldy whole text. In my work I discuss the construction of historical meaning in terms of *cognitive representations* of text. By "representation," I mean, simply, the private cognitive structures readers build in their minds as they read.

Learning about Lexington

Before readers can go beyond the literal text, they must first understand it. Extensive knowledge must be marshaled to understand the meanings of words and to establish the basic connections between clauses and sentences. Readers must be able to strip away surface features of the text to get at its main point. These processes occur when readers construct the *representation of the text*. Inferences are a part of the rT, but only those that are necessary for establishing textual cohesion and coherence, in short, for understanding who did what to whom.

Words and phrases in historical texts often convey different meanings from their modern usage, and the lexical knowledge automatically activated in memory may turn out to be inappropriate or misleading. For example, in a court deposition on the Battle of Lexington dated April 25, 1775, it says near the beginning: *By the clearest depositions ... it will appear that on the night preceding the nineteenth of April*. Professor O'Neil, an expert on Japan, paused at the phrase "it will appear" and commented: "He's trying to show objectivity, or—no no, he's not. He's saying it will be made manifest to you, that's what he means by 'appear.'" Professor O'Neil first represented "it will appear" as part of the subtext, not something the author really believed in, but which he placed in his text to look tentative and fair. But almost as soon as O'Neil rendered this subtextual reading, she retreated from it. "It will appear," she suggested, simply meant that "it will be made manifest," or that in the course of reading this document, the sequence of events will become clear to the reader. Indeed, the 1986 edition of the *Oxford English Dictionary* lists entries from this period that show "appear" as "made manifest" to be common usage.

The Representation of the Event

The fragmented nature of historical documents means that historians must go beyond what their sources offer. Inference is the vehicle that allows them to go from the *words* of the text to the *worlds* of the text, from formulating the gist of a text's literal meaning to reconstructing the mental and physical worlds of people who lived in the past. By using inference, and drawing on their own knowledge and experiences, historians build *representations of the event,* mental constructions of text that try to capture the physical and emotional qualities of historical actors and events.

"Event" is used broadly. It refers not only to *what* happened, but embraces questions of causality: *Why* did things happen? To illustrate aspects of this representation, consider Professor Astren's comments after reading the first line in a diary entry from a British officer at the Battle of Lexington: *At 2 o'clock we began our march by wading through a very long ford up to our middles.*[49]

> It must have been cold in April ... ooh yeh, they're going to be wet and cold.... So it means that they are really cold, from 2 o'clock in the morning—they may not have dried out all night. These guys may have been cold and wet all night.

Though the phrase "ford up to our middles" says nothing about the climate in eastern Massachusetts or the physical conditions endured by soldiers, Astren, a Medievalist by training, constructed a representation that rests on both elements. Nor was this a flight of textual fancy; three of eight historians used the same textual clues to erect representations of shivering men slogging through cold Massachusetts marshes. Despite the fact that the literal text said nothing about the soldiers being cold, wet, or tired, these elements became part of the "text" historians constructed from this document. So, for example, when Professor Astren later read in a later document that British troops had "advanced some miles on their march," he returned to his earlier representation: "Now remember [the soldiers'] legs were cold." For this historian, the coldness of the men's legs was not an adornment added to the text, but the key to understanding the British officer's unexpected admission that his troops ran amok. In Astren's words, the physical conditions the soldiers endured created a situation in which the firing of one or two shots was enough to make the soldiers "flip out." Here, the historian's representation of the event is not just a description of the event, but served as an explanatory framework for it.

In building representations of events, historians evaluate sources along a variety of dimensions. Some of these dimensions, such as deciphering the underlying bias or interest of sources, come under the *representation of the subtext*, and will be discussed in the next section. But other dimensions, such as the position of witnesses vis-à-vis the events they report, the quality of information available to them, their ability to tell the truth (provided that is their intention), as well as other situational factors that affect the quality of testimony, all contribute to how historians represent events. In other words, documents themselves become events.

Professor Jody, an Americanist who studied Native Americans, had an immediate reaction when he reviewed a purported diary entry from a British officer at Lexington. Jody immediately rejects Lt. Barker's claim that this text was a diary entry for April 19, the day of the confrontation at Lexington. He reasoned that it would be unlikely for Barker, awake since the previous evening, to record the day's events on the 19th. Hence, Jody created an elaborate scenario in which Barker returned to Boston worried about a probable inquest, and believing that he might be implicated for issuing the command to fire, crafted a diary entry to exonerate himself of wrongdoing. (Professor Evans came to a similar conclusion: "Even though [the diary excerpt] wasn't being written for publication or deposition, it's obviously written for later reference, simply because of the fact the he's exculpated himself.") In short, Professor Jody represents this document as a careful artifice that, while bearing the date April 19, was written later.

Representation of the Subtext

Language, as Bruner reminds us, is never neutral but "necessarily imposes a perspective in which things are viewed and a stance toward what we view."[50] The third major representation of the text, the *representation of the subtext,* focuses on these implicit perspectives of a text—a text of hidden and latent meanings. Subtexts can be divided into two distinct but related spheres—the *text as a rhetorical artifact* and the *text as a human artifact*. In the first sphere, historians try to reconstruct authors' purposes, intentions, and goals. But the subtext goes beyond a reconstruction of the *intentions* of the author, beyond the use of language as a linguistic technology for persuasion. In fact, many representations of the subtext include elements that work at cross-purposes with authors' intentions, bringing to the surface convictions authors may have been unaware of or may have wished to conceal. These aspects fall into the second sphere, the *text as a human artifact,* which relates to how texts disclose information about their authors' assumptions, worldviews, and beliefs.

Text as a Rhetorical Artifact

Consider Professor Jody's comment on the following sentence from a letter the colonists sent to Parliament describing the events at Lexington: *These brethren are marks of ministerial vengeance against this colony for refusing with her sister colonies a submission to slavery.*

> What I think of is a book I read by Jack Rakove talking about how one of the problems at the time was getting the colonies to hang together and to try to get some unity. So the "refusing with her sister colonies" is kind of an appeal to the other groups.

For Jody, this letter is more than a plea from the colonies to the crown. In Jody's reading, the author of this text deliberately frames the confrontation at Lexington, not as an isolated exchange between a group of soldiers and a handful of farmers, but as a fateful meeting between the representatives of the American colonies (Massachusetts and her "sister colonies") and the representatives of the crown. This "appeal," then, was only partially designed to stir passions in London; it was also intended to rally the forces at home.

The referent for Jody's representation is a linguistic world, a world of hidden or latent textual meanings. In representing the text as a rhetorical artifact, historians reconstructed the purposes and intentions behind documents: What do authors want their audiences to think? How do authors set the terms of the debate? What rhetorical techniques do authors use to convince readers of the rightness of their cause? What is the *polemic,* or underlying argument, of the text?

Representations of the text as a rhetorical artifact go on at various levels of generality. At the local level, these representations can be situated on what the linguist Roman Jakobson called the "vertical axis of selection." Along this axis, authors make rhetorical decisions among words that satisfy similar grammatical constraints. For instance, an American history textbook describing the events at Lexington recorded the following: *The English fired a volley of shots that killed eight patriots.* Using the vertical axis, a host of grammatically and logically correct alternatives could replace "patriots." However, the author's use of "patriots" carries with it different connotations from the use of, say, "criminals." For historians, words like "patriots" and "the English" are not labels for the combatants but descriptors that maximize the righteousness of one side at the expense of the other. In these readings, word choice is neither automatic nor whimsical, but guided by motive and design.

The representation of purpose also goes on at a higher level: the level of *information selection.* Professor O'Neil made the following comment on this line from the minutemen's account of events: *Several guns were fired upon the King's troops from behind a stone wall, and also from the meeting-house.*

> "Meeting-house" would be ... a church and therefore, it's very interesting that they are noting that shots would be fired from the church because ... you are not supposed to fire from a church. So the implication there is that there's something a little bit off, unfair, not kosher, about firing from a meeting-house.

Here an elaborate representation of the subtext rests on a "mere" detail. There is nothing in the text about a church or about the social strictures against using firearms in one: these are all part of the resources brought by the historian to the text. Whether shots were fired from a meeting-house may or may not be true, but O'Neil views its inclusion (as opposed to including details about the color of the buildings or the clothing of the colonists) as motivated by the author's goal to cast the colonists in the worst possible light.

Text as a Human Artifact

The second way in which the subtext is represented is by constructing the text as a *human artifact.* The representation is broader than the detection of bias or the determination of point of view. It is a representation that leaps from the words authors *use* to the types of people authors *are,* from the use of a particular word or phrase to inferences about authors' attitudes, convictions, and values. Texts vary in the degree to which they disclose their authors. One of the primary documents, a deposition of thirty-two colonists assembled on Lexington Green, elicited no comments reflective of the nature of its authors, save for a comment by Professor Astren that it was conceived by a "legal mind." On the other hand, a journal entry from Ezra Stiles, president of Yale College in the 1770s, elicited representations relating to the author's character by four of eight historians. The comments by O'Neil were the most elaborate:

> Ezra Stiles for all his, you know, supposed democracy, comes across ... as very kind of classist in a way.... Pitcairn comes in the same class as Stiles ... both are men of integrity because of their upbringing, so he's "a good man in a bad cause."... I don't know what Stiles' background is but I assume he's not aristocratic but he's educated, probably a man of the cloth if he was a president of Yale.... So he was educated even if not a noble.

In this representation, Ezra Stiles is a "classist" (based on his haughty tone and his use of the word "peasants"), a cleric (based on textual cues and this professor's background knowledge), well-educated but probably not a member of the aristocracy (again, background knowledge brought to the text along with aspects of Stiles's tone and diction), and a hypocrite (based on the discrepancy between Stiles's patriotism and his reference to his compatriots as "peasants"). It is not Stiles's intentions that O'Neil represents here, but the man himself, someone whose assumptions about the world can be discerned from his words. In this way, the reading of history moves from a reconstruction of past events to a reconstruction of past witnesses, in which authors, as well as texts, are decoded.

Study 2: Understanding the Creation of a Historical Context

It is one thing to think about how historians create a context for a group of shivering men en route to battle, which is a concrete and easily imagined scene. But how does one create a situation model for something more diffuse and less easily visualized? How does one create the context of an *intellectual* landscape, a nexus of ideas very different from our own? How do the readers who I am most intent on understanding—working historians whose livelihood depends on recreating mental universes of the part—create contexts for different intellectual worlds?

To study this question empirically, I designed a task around a set of documents about Abraham Lincoln and his stance on slavery.[51] The documents I assembled drew from a range of genres and sources-exchanges with Stephan Douglas, with whom Lincoln had a series of public debates as part of an 1858 run for the Illinois senate seat, a personal letter to the wife of a close friend, and an excerpt from a speech to a group of free blacks about the possibility of starting a colony in Central America.[52] I included, as well, documents that represented other views on slaves and slavery circa 1860, such as an excerpt from John Van Everie, a notorious racialist who appealed to God as providing a permanent sanction for slavery, to William Lloyd Garrison, the noted abolitionist, whose views, while modern in cast, were embraced by very few in his day. In recruiting historians for this study, I reacted to a certain whimsy in the psychological literature in defining who is and who is not an "expert" in studies of cognitive process tracing. Sometimes an esteemed professional, sometimes an advanced graduate student, sometimes even a college major, "experts" in these studies are frequently defined more by their juxtaposition to a population of novices than by any intrinsic quality they share. Therefore, I set out to design not an "expert-novice" study, but an "expert-expert" study, since both participants in it would be considered experts in extant studies of expertise.[53]

The first of my two experts was Professor Alston, a man who had written several books about Lincoln and authored countless articles—he was an experts' expert. Professor Pierce, on the other hand, had taught about Lincoln in undergraduate survey courses but his specialization lay in another time period of American history. After reading a series of ten documents by and about Lincoln and slavery, Professor Pierce was able, by the task's end, to build an interpretative structure that brought him to the point where Professor Alston, his senior colleague, began. The analytical question to me was, how, in the absence of detailed content knowledge about Lincoln, was Pierce able to regain intellectual footing, work through confusion, and resist the ever-present urge to simplify. In other words, how did he form a coherent interpretation of Lincoln's views on slavery?

Before we explore this question, several words about the expert's expert, Professor Alston, are in order. His think-aloud protocol was twice as long as Pierce's. Every document in the set was familiar to Alston—the think-aloud task was an opportunity to "profess aloud." A sense of the quality of Alston's comments can be found in his gloss on Lincoln's retort to Douglas in the debate at Ottawa, in which Lincoln makes the following comments in response to Douglas's assertion that he (Lincoln) is in favor of complete and immediate emancipation:

> the Negro is not my equal in many respects, certainly not in color, perhaps not in moral or intellectual endowment. But in the right to eat the bread which his own hand earns, he is my equal and the equal of Judge Douglas, and the equal of every living man.[54]

At this point in reading the document, Professor Alston made this long comment:

> In a way I'd say this passage as a whole sort of reflects, what shall I say, not necessarily the dilemmas, but the complexity of Lincoln's position. The first half is the

most pro-White/anti-Black side of the coin, the second half of the quotation seems to me to be the most pro-Black side of the coin or the pro-Black rights side of the coin. I believe that the first part is about the most severe anti-Black statement that Lincoln ever made that's recorded. The audience in Ottawa was very pro-Douglas and anti-Black. A staunch critic of Lincoln has cited this passage as [an] example of Lincoln's two-facedness. But I think that if you take the passage as a whole, it seems to me it's not. Only if you single out the first half of the passage, then can you say Lincoln is playing to the crowd here, opportunistic, trying to get votes.

Alston, in a word, sees Lincoln as neither an avowed abolitionist nor as a defender of slavery, and this primary document provides the historian with an opportunity to place Lincoln precisely on a scale of views toward slavery and emancipation. His reading conforms to images of expertise gleaned from other domains: he marshals extensive knowledge at an instant and he uses it to locate Lincoln in exact situations organized by a sequence of weeks in a series of months in 1863.[55] To a great extent, the documents that are presented to Alston are stimuli for issuing preset or fully formed interpretations.

For the other historian, Professor Pierce, the task served a different purpose. For him, the task was a learning experiment, an encounter with textual materials that led him to view the past differently. Initially, Pierce responded in ways that were reminiscent of some of beginning history teachers who participated in the task: both Pierce and the teachers responded to Lincoln's early statements by remarking that they knew less about Lincoln's views than they had assumed.[56] Often teachers were alarmed to find a Lincoln who seemed to be enunciating racist views, and in some cases, teachers came to the conclusion that they had been lied to in their previous history education. They concluded that instead of the "Great Emancipator" of history textbooks, Lincoln was a man filled with bigotry. On the other hand, Pierce's final vision of Lincoln dodges either/or distinctions. His Lincoln is nuanced, complex, and full of questions. An hour and twenty minute encounter with historical documents changed his thinking. The key question for an emerging science of cognition is, What did Pierce do that allowed him to form a new understanding of Lincoln?

Even though Pierce had taught about Lincoln in a survey course, had taken dozens courses in American history, and even entered the task believing that he had a general sense of Lincoln's views, it didn't take long for him to become unsettled. Pierce read a section from Douglas in which the Illinois senator charged that Lincoln advocated complete equality. After reading this document, Pierce remarked:

> I don't know as much about Lincoln's views as I think I do. I mean, as I read it and see Douglas, perhaps putting words in Lincoln's mouth, I'm not sure about what I do and don't know about Lincoln. Douglas makes it sound as if Lincoln believes they're equal, blacks and whites, on virtually every level, but I don't know to what extent Lincoln did or did not believe this. I know that he was very practically aware of the concerns of bringing the races together as if they were equal

in the same society at this point. But I don't know enough about Lincoln's views to make some other judgments I've been making.

In the next document presented to Pierce, his understanding becomes, on the surface at least, more murky. Pierce read the following words by Lincoln responding to Douglas's charges:

> I hold that he is as much entitled to these as the White man. I agree with Judge Douglas that the Negro is not my equal in many respects, certainly not in color, perhaps not in moral or intellectual endowment. But in the right to eat the bread which his own hand earns, he is my equal and the equal of Judge Douglas, and the equal of every living man.

Pierce re-read these words several times, and zigzagged between this document and the first document by Stephan Douglas. After a considerable pause, he remarked:

> Again, [Lincoln] says at the beginning, he wants not to interfere with slavery where it exists, but everything else thereafter, talking about the natural rights of Blacks and Whites being equal suggests that he is against slavery. If Blacks have the natural rights to life, liberty, and the pursuit of happiness one would assume that liberty and pursuit of happiness would indicate that they cannot be slaves at the same time. Similarly, if Blacks have the right to eat the bread which his own hand earns, that they have the right to the product of their labor, that is the pursuit of happiness or liberty, one form or the other, then if that is a natural right then slavery goes against those natural rights.

Pierce detects a contradiction. When a group of history teachers encountered this point, they located the source of this contradiction in Lincoln, or created in their minds, a series of duplicitous multiple Lincolns, each saying different things to different audiences. But Pierce's reaction differs: his response to contradiction is to call attention to it, but not to make an attribution that would dissolve it. In this case, the detection of a contradiction is a signal of a possible disjunction, not in Lincoln, but in the mental model of the historian, a signal that he may be lacking information that would make these historical statements consistent.

Indeed, Pierce's reading over the next five documents is something that I think of as a prolonged exercise in the *specification of ignorance*. My first inclination was to think of this as a kind of "weak method" (in the phraseology of cognitive science), the generic generalized problem-solving skills that fill the gap when knowledge is not present. On reflection, however, I believe that the characterization of Pierce's problem solving as "generic" misrepresents it. Indeed, it is a way of reading that is profoundly disciplinary. He is, at base, leery of words, particularly words that he is familiar with. When Lincoln says to a group of freed slaves that he wants to establish a colony in Central America, he tells them that he wants men *capable of thinking as White men*. Other people reading these words see them as a clear indication of a deep commitment by Lincoln to the intellectual superiority of whites. But to Pierce, the words do not transcend time and place. He cannot immediately "empathize," or "re-create a mental universe."

> "Capable of thinking like White men," this is a baffling statement! I have to think about it. I want to read that again. Clearly the condition of slavery in [Lincoln's] mind has clouded their thinking. It has given him, given the nation poor materials with which to work. Poor materials for what? For the nation to work with or for the colony to work with? I'm not quite sure.... "Capable of thinking as White men," does that mean that they have never been enslaved or that they are so far from slavery that they don't think as if they have ever been slaves? I've got to read it again. I think too much has been taken out of it for me to appreciate exactly what's going on.... I don't quite understand the context, I'm confused.

However, by the end of this task, some eighty-eight minutes and nine documents from the time he started, Pierce ends up in a different place. It is in the context of John Bell Robinson's appeal to God as providing sanction to slavery that Pierce makes the following comment:

> What I'm looking for is his discussion—the physical difference between the two and his discussion of natural rights, and see if [Lincoln] links those to God and the Declaration of Independence, but in this [a reference to the second document he read, Lincoln's reply to Stephan Douglas] ... I am looking here for a reference to God, I'm not finding it, but I haven't finished yet, he refers to the Declaration of Independence. But in the letter to Mary Speed[57] he [Lincoln] did say how true it is that "God renders the worst of human conditions tolerable." But God didn't render slavery [to be] the condition that Blacks ought to find themselves in, according to Lincoln.... He talks about natural differences but he does not bring God into it, other than to say that God makes, God allows people to make the worst of human conditions tolerable, and that's a form of mercy not of any kinds of restriction on their status or behavior.

By looking carefully at what Pierce does here we get a glimpse of historical expertise in its most fluid state. First, the Robinson document is used to establish a zeitgeist. John Bell Robinson's view, that God ordained slavery, becomes an anchor at one end of the continuum. Robinson's remark sends Professor Pierce searching back to the other documents he has read. He initially goes back to Lincoln's response to Stephan Douglas in search of Lincoln's invocation of God. Finding only a reference to the Declaration of Independence, Pierce then goes to the first document, Douglas's characterization of Lincoln's views. He then jumps back and forth from document to document trying to find references to the Almighty by Lincoln or his detractors. When the word "God" is found in the context of Lincoln's remarks, it is used with the opposite intent from its use by the racialist John Bell Robinson.

Professor Pierce's summary comment tells us much about the creation of new historical knowledge. This process is at base an intertextual enterprise: in this short passage, we can identify at least seven links with other texts in the document set. Lincoln is understood by aligning what he said in different contexts and comparing these to the ways in which these issues were viewed by others of his day. Pierce learns that while Robinson appeals to God to justify slavery as a lower form of manhood; Lincoln appeals to God to connect the races in common humanity. He learns that Lincoln justifies the Negro's equality, not by appeal to God, but by appeal to "natural rights," a view which comes remarkably close to the notion of the argument by definition developed by a school of historians that have devoted decades to the study of these documents. To develop this partial understanding, Pierce has marshaled every document read in the task, and the intertextual connections between documents are the seams that allow us to see how this interpretative fabric has been pieced together. The question that this study tried to reveal is how historians figure out not what "happened in the past," but what people *meant* in the past. It is an untidy question, particularly in a postmodern age suspicious of anything that ventures beyond solipsism. In common parlance, we talk blithely about putting things *into* context, as if historical understanding were akin to placing elements on the proper shelf. We speak of contexts being "located," much like the static border pieces we use to frame a jigsaw puzzle. But this is not what is happening here. A context is not "found" or "located." Words are not "situated." Rather, human beings *create* contexts in the full etymological sense of the word. Context, from the Latin *contexere*, means to weave together, to engage in an active process of putting threads together to make something new. This is what Professor Pierce does here. Historical understanding becomes, to paraphrase Quentin Skinner,[58] the creation of a linguistic context that helps us get closer to the meaning, the actual intention, of a historical figure.

Reading in this way is profoundly different from ordinary understanding. A historical reading begins with distrust of our own understanding, a recognition that words give rise to multiple mental models, and that the first one that comes to mind is one that tells us more about who *we* are than the meanings of the people we are trying to understand. It is this understanding that undergirds Professor Pierce's "specification of his ignorance," an understanding that allows him to "learn" from this encounter with textual materials from the past. And it is precisely the kind of understanding least taught in history classes, both at the secondary and university levels.

Summary

Psychologists interested in history have traditionally looked to the extensive body of historiographic writings for clues to the nature of historical thinking. This storehouse of essays and monographs, composed largely by historians, looks at historical works not for what they disclose about the American Revolution, daily life in the Middle Ages, or the demise of French Indochina, but what they say about historical knowing more generally. The strategy of looking carefully at written histories, and inferring from them the processes used in their composition, offers many insights to the interested psychologist. However, the problem with using this approach to inform the teaching and learning of history is that final products can be explained by appealing to wholly different intermediate processes. Historiography teaches us how to recognize skilled cognition but gives us scant advice for how to achieve it.

There is a second way to understand what it means to think historically. Less developed than the historiographic tradition, it examines the steps and missteps that lead to the formation of historical interpretations and conclusions. This work is carried out by psychologists (and increasingly, historians and philosophers)[59] who conduct empirical studies into how students, teachers, and historians come to understand history. It asks questions about what people know and how they come to know it. In doing so, this approach wrests questions of epistemology from the clouds and turns them into objects of psychological and historical inquiry

The pursuit of such research would return us to the beginning of this century, a time when the American Psychological Association and the American Philosophical Society held joint meetings because the psychologist and the philosopher were often one in the same. As a research strategy, this approach would claim intellectual ancestry not to the American behaviorist E.L. Thorndike, who displayed little patience with questions philosophical, but to Wilhelm Wundt. Contrary to the popular image of Wundt as a hard-nosed experimentalist singularly determined to establish psychology as an empirical science,[60] the lesser-known Wundt was a man whose empirical investigations informed—and were informed by—his writings on epistemology, logic, and ethics, a man who argued that psychology and philosophy were so interdependent that, separated from one another, both would atrophy.[61]

What I am advocating, in other words, is a research strategy that can best be termed "applied epistemology." It would be, at its core, an interdisciplinary enterprise, with contributions from historians, historically oriented psychologists, philosophers, educators, linguists, and cultural critics. It would view the empirical study of historical consciousness not as an ancillary to theorization, but as a part of a dialogue between the theoretical and the empirical, the idealized and the actual. Not only could it lead to a new understanding of how we might teach history to our young; it might even lead to deeper insights into our own understanding of the cognitive processes we use to decipher the past.

Notes

1. The best account of the changes in educational and psychological research in this century is provided by Howard Gardner, *The Mind's New Science* (New York, 1985).
2. Edward L. Thorndike, *Educational Psychology* (New York, 1923).
3. Ibid., 345.
4. Edward L. Thorndike, *Education: A First Book* (New York, 1912).
5. Ibid., 144.

6. G. Stanley Hall, *Educational Problems* (New York, 1911), vol. 2, 285.
7. Ibid., 286.
8. Charles Hubbard Judd, *Psychology of School Subjects* (Boston, 1915).
9. Ibid., 384.
10. Ibid., 379.
11. Carleton J. Bell, "The Historic Sense," *Journal of Educational Psychology* 8 (1971): 317–318.
12. Ibid., 317.
13. Ibid., 318.
14. Carleton J. Bell and D.F. McCollum, "A Study of the Attainments of Pupils in United States History," *Journal of Educational Psychology* 8 (1971): 257–274.
15. Ibid., 257–258.
16. Ibid., 268–269.
17. See, for example, the article by R.B. Weaver and A.E. Traxler, "Essay Examination and Objective Tests in United States History in the Junior High School," *School Review* 39 (1931): 689–695.
18. F.R. Gorman and D.S. Morgan, "A Study of the Effect of Definite Written Exercises upon Learning in a Course in American History," *Indiana School of Education Bulletin* 6 (1930): 80–90.
19. Ibid., 90.
20. Ibid., 90
21. See Raymond Callahan, *Education and the Cult of Efficiency* (Chicago, 1962).
22. Peter Novick, *That "Noble Dream": The "Objectivity Question" and the American Historical Profession* (Cambridge, U.K., 1988).
23. L.W. Sackett, "A Scale in United States History," *Journal of Educational Psychology* 10 (1973): 345–348, here p. 348.
24. See Novick, *Noble Dream,* 200.
25. M.F. Jurd, "Adolescent Thinking in History-Type Material," *Australian Journal of Education* 17 (1973): 2–17.
26. For a brief overview of this project, see L.W. Rosenzweig and T.P. Weinland, "New Directions of the History Curriculum: A Challenge for the 1980s," *The History Teacher* 19 (1986): 263–277.
27. Ibid.
28. See the article by Martin Booth, "Cognition in History: A British Perspective," *Educational Psychologist* 29 (1994): 61–70. This entire issue was devoted to the psychological study of the teaching and learning of history.
29. R.S. Peters, *The Philosophy of Education* (Oxford, 1971); Jerome S. Bruner, *The Process of Education* (Cambridge, Mass., 1960).
30. Dennis J. Shemilt, *History 13–16: Evaluation Study* (Edinburgh, 1980), 7.
31. Ibid., 20.
32. Ibid., 14.
33. Ellen D. Gagné, *The Cognitive Psychology of School Learning* (Boston, 1985).
34. Arthur Elstein, Lee S. Shulman, and Sarah A. Sprafka, *Medical Problem Solving: An Analysis of Clinical Reasoning* (Cambridge, Mass., 1978).
35. R. Nisbett and L. Ross, *Human Inference: Strategies and Shortcomings of Social Judgment* (Englewood Cliffs, N.J., 1980).
36. R. Nisbett and Thomas Wilson, "Telling More Than We Can Know: Verbal Reports on Mental Processes," *Psychological Review* 84 (1977): 231–259.
37. Ward Gray, *Historian's Handbook* (Boston, 1959), 17.
38. A.B. Tourtellot, *Lexington and Concord: The Beginning of the War of the American Revolution* (New York, 1959).
39. Donald N. McCloskey, "The Problem of Audience in Historical Economics: Rhetorical Thoughts on a Text by Robert Fogel," *History and Theory* 24 (1985): 1–22, here p. 1.

40. A fuller account of this work can be found in Samuel S. Wineburg, "Historical Problem Solving: A Study of the Cognitive Processes Used in the Evaluation of Documentary and Pictorial Evidence," *Journal of Educational Psychology* 83 (1991): 73–87.

41. John Hayes and Linda Flower, "Identifying the Organization of the Writing Process," in *Cognitive Processes in Writing*, ed. Lee W. Gregg and Erwin R. Steinberg (Hillsdale, N.J. 1980), 3–30, here p. 9.

42. T.A. van Dijk and W. Kintsch, *Strategies of Discourse Comprehension* (New York, 1983).

43. W. Kintsch, "Learning from Text," *Cognition and Instruction* 3 (1986): 87–108.

44. R.M. Shiffrin and W. Schneider, "Controlled and Automatic Human Information Processing: Detection, Search, and Attention," *Psychological Review* 84 (1977): 1–66.

45. E.D. Hirsch, *Validity in Interpretation* (New Haven, 1976).

46. Stanley Fish, *Is There a Text in the Class? The Authority of Interpretive Communities* (Cambridge, Mass., 1980).

47. Jacques Derrida, *Of Grammatology* (Baltimore, 1976).

48. Roland Barthes, *S/Z* (London, 1975).

49. For a complete version of the documents used in this task, see Wineburg, "Historical Problem Solving."

50. Jerome S. Bruner, "Narrative and Paradigmatic Modes of Thought," *Learning and Teaching the Ways of Knowing*, ed. Elliot Eisner (Chicago, 1985), 97–115, here p. 121.

51. For a more thorough introduction to this set of studies, see Samuel S. Wineburg and J. Fournier, "Contextualized Thinking in History," *Cognitive and Instructional Processes in History and the Social Sciences*, ed. Mario Carretero and James Voss (Hillsdale, N.J., 1994), 285–308.

52. See ibid., for full bibliographic references for the documents in this task.

53. The full methodology of this study, as well as additional analyses, appear in Samuel S. Wineburg, "Reading Abraham Lincoln: An Expert/Expert Study in the Interpretation of Historical Texts," *Cognitive Science* 22 (1998): 319–346. See also Samuel S. Wineburg, "Historical Thinking and Other Unnatural Acts," *Phi Delta Kappa* 80 (1999): 488–499.

54. Don E. Fehrenbacher, ed., *Abraham Lincoln: Speeches and Writings* (New York, 1989), 504–505.

55. For an overview of the cognitive literature on expertise, see K. Anders Ericsson and J. Smith, *Toward a General Theory of Expertise* (Cambridge, Mass., 1987).

56. For an overview of the research on beginning teachers who participated in this task, see Samuel S. Wineburg and J. Fournier, "Thinking in Time," *History News* 3 (1993): 26–27.

57. This letter was another document in the set.

58. See Quentin Skinner, *Meaning and Context*, ed. James Tully (Princeton, 1988).

59. See, for example, Michael Frisch, "American History and the Structure of Collective Memory: A Modest Exercise in Empirical Iconography," *Journal of American History* 75 (1989): 1130–1155, and David Lowenthal, "The Timeless Past: Some Anglo-American Historical Preconceptions," *Journal of American History* 75 (1989): 1263–1180.

60. One finds this characterization of Wundt especially in E.G. Boring, *A History of Experimental Psychology* (New York, 1929).

61. Steven Toulmin and David Leary, "The Cult of Empiricism in Psychology, and Beyond," in *A Century of Psychology as Science*, ed. David Leary and S. Koch (New York, 1985), 594–617.

CHAPTER 10

Biography—A Dream?
Self-Chronicling in the Age of Psychoanalysis

BRIGITTE BOOTHE

Story and Message

Psychoanalysis lives on stories: symptoms tell a story, Freudian slips in everyday life reveal stories, and jokes maintain a proverbial relationship to the unconscious. Poets' stories take their charismatic charm, says Freud, from silent liaisons with the most marvelous and most outrageous wish-fulfilling fantasies. Dreams, which are even closer to wish fulfillment according to the theory, present themselves as mystery stories and riddles.

Does psychoanalysis then see dreams, jokes, Freudian slips, and symptoms as *messages*? This conclusion may seem unnecessary, because, after all, "story" and "message" are distant relatives. With an emphasis on "distant," however, the conclusion proves worthy of study.

The poetic and hermeneutic tradition of text analysis seeks to interpret (consciously or unconsciously) a text's intended meaning. This activity addresses the whole of an available text that is to be deciphered as a message. The text is an announcement, and the text interpreter is an expert who presents the message to others in an intelligible form. Story analysis as the art of allegorical decoding corresponds to interpretation of the intended meaning; it examines how the story speaks to us in allegoric pictures.[1] Solemn ceremonial interpretation is an act of acknowledging respect for and honoring a text. This tradition continues to affect psychotherapeutic practice and dream interpretation. We like to believe that dreams, symptoms, pain, or physical distress *tell* us something, *communicate* something. They are sacred messages on higher or lower planes, or at the least, they are messages possessing dignity. Although Freud warns

---

Notes for this section begin on page 225.

us against viewing dreams as messages, he still honors them as the "royal path to the unconscious." And though Freud[2] warns just as insistently against succumbing to the pleasing rhetoric of impressive stories, he stands, as the founder of psychoanalysis, in the aura of a master thinker.

Moving from the dignified to the prosaic, from a "Chosen" text to the fleeting narratives of the everyday, we might ask whether text concepts are still appropriate. The systematic brevity of oral speech in the social context allows comprehension through means that differ from those used to decipher written language.[3] For example, everyday recounting usually includes evaluative elements and frequent explicit "morals."[4] The "moral" of an everyday narrative may be expressed in such phrases as "my mother always treats me unfairly like that" or "so you can see how easy it is to get into a fight with him." To call the message of a mother's unfairness the *intended* message of the narrative is shortsighted. The "moral" is much more the *consequence* or conclusion drawn by the teller from the experience communicated in the story. It is not the result of interpretation of the story, and it is not even the result of interpreting the situation the story refers to. Rather, the "moral" has the character of a *decision*. The teller decides (before, during, or after recounting an experience) to add his own standpoint to the story he presents dramaturgically. He puts his own personal stamp on the story: his personal conclusion.

The stories told in psychotherapies—stories told by psychoanalysts as case studies or by patients recalling their personal histories and life situations—also most characteristically follow the pattern of "episode + moral." However, the moral that the analyst draws from his own case study narrative very often unnoticeably becomes the *explanation*. And patients recounting the events of their lives in the narrative pattern of the sufferer or victim frequently offer the moral of the story as a *subjective theory of their pathology*.

It is not surprising that the morals of psychotherapeutic narratives, in the mouth of therapists and patients, do not stand up to critical examination, for the formulation of the moral of a story is a very biased conclusion. Nevertheless, they are very popular, both in psychotherapeutic circles and in the media. This is probably because these morals touch our emotions, such as the seemingly innocent feelings of indignation or outrage, but demand little thinking. At the same time, the complex and confusing ramifications of human life acquire cheap and easy meaning and conclusiveness.

If psychoanalysis views certain manifestations of everyday life as a matter of understanding stories, the conclusion is not justified that dreams, slips, fantasies, and symptoms should be seen as sanctioned texts to be decoded as messages. Although the practice of interpreting dreams or symptoms lends the dignity of deep messages to these productions, this does not reflect knowledge of the lawfulness of mental life. Instead, this practice is a *decision* that has social repercussions[5] and *prescriptive* consequences.

"Message" and "story" are bound together only by formal judgment and are only distantly related to each other. We can hardly expect to find compelling conceptual or theoretical reasons that justify the search for "messages" from the "unconscious." We do not know what messages from the unconscious are, or even how we should understand the term "message from the unconscious": apart from the enigma and mystery, can this lead to establishing anything that would allow further conceptual clarification? A deep treatment of this unplumbed question would go far beyond the scope of this paper. Let us return to our initial assertion: the psychoanalytical idea of the *story character* of certain manifestations of corporal existence, behavior and experience.

Story and Scene

Stories are linguistic stage productions, language *scenes*. Scenes are episodic happenings in a story framework. "Story framework" is used here in a broad sense. There is a story framework not only for scenes of heard or written stories, but also for action sequences and events. Action sequences and events are scenes in a story framework if they are designed by, or partially influenced by, participants who can recount the experience. This broad use of the concept of a story framework is important in terms of the perspective taken here. We are interested in the forms of interaction among those participating where at least one "member of the cast" enters into the arena as a potential storyteller. We speak of "scenes" only if the material can be recounted. Material can be retold if someone experiencing episodic events has taken part in or been affected by them.[6] In this sense, lightning striking a tree is material that can be recounted—on the condition that the episode is experienced by at least *one* involved person. The figures experiencing the event who appear in the scene construct the happenings on a narrative basis in various ways. Narrative construction of experiences can be realized in two fundamental ways: as *open or hidden narrative activity*. In open narrative activity, participants produce and formulate a story after the fact that articulates the outline and shape of an experience. Hidden narratives are nonformulated stories, or drafts of stories, in the minds of the actors who help to direct the lead-in to the real events or their course. The construction of narrative models has been seen as the cradle of human experiencing.[7] Experiencing always has both a self-referential and an episodic character.

The self-referential character of recounting deserves attention in the psychoanalytic perspective. Recounting is the construction of experience that models the facts in reference to the experiencing self.[8] In the act of retelling, events are presented as something to be acquired or learned subjectively. The narrative gives structure retrospectively to practical acting in the world. The experiencing self becomes a character presented: in the narrative process, the experiencing self constructs itself as a character in the story, or, if the self is involved in the narrative process only passively, the character is at least sketched out.[9]

Narrative models are determined by themes.[10] The psychologically interesting theme of a narrative becomes comprehensible as a subjective issue that depicts itself in the narrative process. In the retelling, subjective wishes are usually presented in a somewhat hidden form. This view of narrative activity as the articulation of a desire, directed toward the world of objects assimilated into the world of the mind, takes up Freud's definition of wish activity.[11] Wish activity, says Freud, is the creative ability (an ability that is difficult to establish in content) that regulates mental tension temporarily and pleasurably.[12]

Narrative Competence, Directing the Scene, Degree of Involvement

In a dramaturgical perspective,[13] a scene is made up of a repertory of characters and sequential organization forms, as well as a repertory of props and backdrops, and there is at least partial narrative competence available. This means that for characters, there are three principle cases: there are characters possessing narrative competence (in command of everyday speech), characters developing narrative competence (infants and small children), and characters without narrative competence (nonhuman life forms[14]). The analysis of scenes demands consideration of these three varying cases, for characters having narrative competence do not only enter into relationships with other narrative-competent figures, but also with infants and children.[15] Objects without language abilities can also be developed into characters (for example, cats, cars, the moon and stars, houses, laptops, brooks and rivers). The production of a scene requires at least one person having narrative competence. In such a constellation, this person takes over direction of the scene (for example, a child playing with a wooden block makes the block his friend, or a mother calms her crying infant). Stage direction in a constellation where there is only one narrative-competent character involves a high degree of imaginative and stage-managing activity in role casting and interpretation (for example, the mother assigns a role to the infant, interprets his bodily signs and expressive behavior, and imaginatively attributes various characteristics to the child). In scenes where there is only one such competent character, this aspect of stage managing shows as unbroken and uncontaminated. The character assigns roles to inanimate objects and performs an imaginative, dramatic play. In everyday scenes with many characters having the power of speech, there are competing directors with corresponding intricacies of plot in the real course of interactions. The degree of involvement in the events of the scene can vary: actors in a production, to name two extremes, may lose themselves completely in a scene or may place themselves in an audience position.[16] (See figure 10.1.)

	Scene Structure	
Controls		Narrative competence
Theatrical direction		
	Storyteller	Developing narrative competence
Is integrated into theatrical direction		No narrative competence

Figure 10.1 Illustration of Scene Structure

To analyze events as scene contexts, we need to consider the following:

- the narrative definitions of the situation imposed by those involved who possess narrative competence;
- dramatization requirements of those possessing narrative competence;
- dramatization conflicts among narrative-competent actors;
- dramatization activity of narrative-competent actors developed toward characters or objects having no narrative competence;
- the varying degrees of involvement in the events and the possibility of reflective self-withdrawal; and
- the differing versions of the narrative presentation of scene events by the various actors after the fact, based upon their diverse narrative definitions, dramatization demands and concerns.

"The Secret of Dreams"

The Interpretation of Dreams is one of Freud's most striking works.[17] The monumental significance of this *opus magnum* lies not just in its creator's genius in theory, clinical practice, and interpretative literary criticism, and not only in the authoritative boldness of the work's impenetrably magnificent chapter 7, "The Psychology of the Dream Processes." It is important also due to the solemn honor bestowed upon a work that places itself within an ancient tradition linked to the sacred art of priests and scribes, on the one hand, and, on the other, rejects the power of reason and the unity of the person. The book deciphers dream activity as the experimental stage for the pleasure-driven anarchy of thought. If you want/like, Freud of *The Interpretation of Dreams* was the first experimental dramatist of the twentieth century, but not one whose dramatic creations were a gesture of provocation. This was the solemn and bold gesture of the master thinker, and from this the work derives its suggestive tension. The unity of the person disintegrates, the rationality of thinking is discarded, and the continuity of personal biographies is based on infantile drives. But in spite of all this, we are told, insight and explanation are possible. Through deconstruction[18] and the help of the active interpretation of the analyst, these disintegrating things achieve a new and exciting form. Through ideas and combination, the bare and unwieldy dream report becomes a story filled with emotions.

Freud's method of dream interpretation remodels the dream *report* to become a highly suspenseful *story*. The process of interpreting becomes a suspense-filled scene. An example will show how this happens:

The dream of "Irma's Injection"[19] has received more attention in the psychoanalytical literature than any other.[20] The dreamer is Freud himself; the date is the night of July 23, 1895, and Freud writes that this was the first dream he ever subjected to an exhaustive interpretation.[21] Freud presents this dream as the center of focus at the start of the second section, "The Method of Dream-Interpretation." The dream is offered as proof of his fundamental thesis that complete interpretation reveals dreams to be wish fulfillment.[22] In a letter to Wilhelm Fliess on June 12, 1900, Freud refers to the Irma dream as the key experience that revealed to him the "secret of dreams."[23]

The dream report of Irma's injection is of particular value to Freud, because he relates his own research prowess to it. "Irma's Injection" has, indeed, found the recognition both within and outside the psychoanalytical research community that its author deemed justifiable. The work is a carefully written, even stage-directed, text. Its author is not a client seeking guidance, but one who has made himself a "patient" by subjecting himself programmatically to self-analysis.

The following excerpt is taken verbatim from A.A. Brill's translation of *The Interpretation of Dreams*, published in 1938 in *The Basic Writings of Sigmund Freud*. Following the original work, the dream is reported in cursive writing under the subtitle "Dream of July 23–24, 1895."[24] Freud presents the dream in a stylistically elaborated form, and we do not know when the report was written down in this manner. For the sake of clarity, the text is shown here in subject-predicate units.

The Dream of Irma's Injection

1/ a great hall—a number of guests/
2/ whom we are receiving/
3/ among them Irma/
4/ whom I immediately take aside, as though to answer her letter, and to reproach her/
5/ for not yet accepting the "solution"/
6/ I say to her/
7/ if you still have pains/
8/ it is really only your own fault/
9/ she answers/
10/ if you only knew/
11/ what pains I have now in the throat, stomach, and abdomen/
12/ I am choked by them/
13/ I am startled, and look at her/

14/ she looks pale and puffy/
15/ I think/
16/ that after all I must be overlooking some organic affection/
17/ I take her to the window and look into her throat/
18/ she offers some resistance to this, like a woman/
19/ who has a set of false teeth/
20/ I think/
21/ surely, she doesn't need them/
22/ the mouth then opens wide/
23/ and I find a large white spot on the right/
24/ and elsewhere I see extensive grayish-white scabs adhering to curiously curled formations/
25/ which are evidently shaped like the turbinal bones of the nose/
26/ I quickly call Dr. M./
27/ who repeats the examination and confirms it/
28/ Dr. M. looks quite unlike his usual self/
29/ he is very pale, he limps, and his chin is clean-shaven/
30/ now my friend Otto, too, is standing beside her/
31/ and my friend Leopold percusses her covered chest, and says: she has a dullness below, on the left/
32/ and also calls attention to an infiltrated portion of skin on the left shoulder/
33/ which I can feel in spite of the dress/
34/ M. says/
35/ there's no doubt that it's an infection/
36/ but it doesn't matter/
37/ dysentery will follow and the poison will be eliminated/
38/ we know, too, precisely/
39/ how the infection originated/
40/ my friend Otto, not long ago, gave her, when she was feeling unwell
41/ an injection of propyl ... propyls ... propionic acid ... trimethylamin/
42/ the formula of which I see before me, printed in heavy type/
43/ one doesn't give such injections so rashly/
44/ probably, too, the syringe was not clean

Stage Production, or the Organization of Scenes

In scene 1, we see a stage setting of a spacious interior. There is a crowd declared to be an audience (1). The "I" character and his wife present themselves in relation to the crowd as "we," who receive their guests (2). Irma (a female person familiar to the "I" character) appears in the crowd (3). Now the crowd and the couple disappear, and the "I" character develops threefold activity toward Irma (4): first, he takes Irma aside and leaves the scene with her. Then the dreamer gives Irma a signal in answer to a signal she has sent. Finally, the dreamer challenges and attacks Irma for her refusal to accept the "solution" the "I" character had suggested to her (5). The "I" character turns to Irma with a spoken signal: Irma is told that she is the recipient of physical tortures and is herself the cause of her pain (6–8).

In scene 2, there is a changeover (9–12): whereas in the first scene, the "I" character determines the course of action through his activity, now Irma sends a spoken signal and relates that she knows she is the silent sufferer of physical complaints that torture her (9–12). Irma's speech affects the "I" character, who has an affective reaction of fear and now looks at Irma (13), who displays her devastation (14).

In scene 3, this moment of horror demands a new view: first, the retelling "I" begins to think (15). The "I" reflects that his perception may have been wrong (16). He then moves into action and takes Irma to a space between indoors and outdoors ("window") and examines her mouth (17). Irma's gestures display hesitation (18), and then there is a break in the action as the "I" character evaluates Irma's resistance as being similar to that shown by women who wear dentures. The "I" character thinks that Irma has no need of such (19–21).

In scene 4, Irma, as a whole person, disappears (and remains hidden to the end of the retelling). She is active only physically (her mouth opens) (22). The "I" character achieves something (it finds something) and perceives various physical phenomena in the sick or devastated patient (23–24). Again, the "I" figure steps out of the action to evaluate: some tissue he has perceived is shaped in the form of a certain body part (the nose auricle) (25).

In scene 5, the retelling "I" returns to the action but calls for reinforcement. With a speech signal, he appeals to a man of higher status (26). This superior goes through the same motions the "I" had performed and confirms his results (27). The "I" figure again leaves the scene to evaluate and describes his superior as one who also shows signs of dismantling (28–29).

With this state of affairs, scene 6 shows the entry of new reinforcement in the form of two men equal in rank to the main character. The familiar figure of Otto takes a position next to Irma (30). Acquaintance Leopold engages in manipulations with Irma and sends a speech signal (31): shows some damage; shows that Irma has something damaged down below (32). The "I" character, just like Leopold, perceives this, despite Irma's concealing garments (33).

In scene 7, the higher status man shows up again and gives a speech outlining his diagnosis of the problem (34–38). He states (34) that there is no room for doubt (35). Bodily damage is mentioned (36), and the damage is unified (37): there will be more damage, and the damaging element will then disappear (38).

In scene 8, an undetermined number of those involved join to form a "we" group sharing the same knowledge: we know (39) the cause of the physical damage (40). One of the main character's friends of equal rank had given Irma a damaging substance (41). At this point, the "I" is removed from the scene. In the first part of the scene, as a perceiver, he perceives a "formula" (law) (42), but then he becomes one and the same with the law—through apotheosis, so to speak—and an impersonal, anonymous man makes a normative pronouncement of the injection of potentially damaging substances (43, 44).

Context of Action Development

The narrative sequence is embedded within a formal interior setting. The Ego appears before an audience together with a female escort (wife). The space,

Ego, and audience are enlarged and take on great dimensions. Within the audience, an individual takes on contours. This individualized character is female. The relation of the Ego to the audience is receptive.

Organizational Features of Action Development on the Basis of Freud's Theory of Wish Fulfillment

The dream as "protector of sleep"[25] regulates disturbing instinctual impulses. It generates wish-fulfilling scenarios in the service of prolonging bodily relaxation. Wish-fulfilling scenarios often undergo modification by the "censor," where wishes produce excessive arousal or negative tension.

Let us try to reconstruct the series of unfolding scenes in the dream report hypothetically as modeling the tension between wish fulfillment and censoring. Reconstruction takes the shape of a number of rounds in a fight: tension regulation must ensure that the hedonic gain in wish fulfillment is maintained and the critical voice of the censor is assuaged. Freud believed it was quite impossible to discover the wish-fulfilling aspect of a dream without taking into consideration the free associations of the dreamer. He saw the narrative organization of the dream product as the mere result of secondary elaboration, which must follow everyday conventions of communication. But according to the approach taken here, as an episodic form of the events, wish fulfillment itself possesses narrative structure and becomes the central formative aspect of the manifest dream report. The following example will illuminate this viewpoint:

1. The graphic nature of the dream stage-manages the initial *wish-fulfilling scenario*, a situation of extensive narcissistic gratification. The expanded Ego is the recipient of honor from the large crowd in an expanded, formal interior setting.
2. Within the ceremony of the reception by an up-to-now anonymous crowd ("guests"), a female figure takes shape.
3. The imagining of the female figure produces negative tension and is stage-managed as a *disturbance*, interfering with narcissistic gratification.
4. This negative picture has to be repressed. The Ego figure attempts to remove the female figure from the wish-fulfilling scenario through suppression.
5. Simple *radical suppression* becomes delayed, however (possibly because of a sexual aspect). The main character *initiates interaction with the figure,* by means of a communicative exchange and an aggressive demand for recognition from the female figure.
6. With this, radical removal of the disturbing figure from the scene *fails*. The demand for recognition takes up the scene of narcissistic gratification: if the female figure could be added to the group of honoring spectators, the ceremonial nature of the scene at the start would be reestablished. The demand for recognition *undermines* radical suppres-

sion, because, with its wish, the Ego figure is making itself independent of recognition through others.

7. The weakening of repression and removal activity on the basis of independence allows the disturbing figure to take on contours: the figure develops initiative, presents complaints and accusations, and *offers itself in its bodily being.*
8. At this point, the Ego figure begins *another* move toward ousting this, but nevertheless keeps up the threatening, possibly (covered up) sexually enticing confrontation.
9. The confrontation now becomes defused, however, and danger's dimensions change.
10. With the reduced danger and distancing, the Ego figure *approaches* the threatening Other physically, makes physical connection in the mode of examining, seizing hold in a penetrating manner.
11. But this approach does not take place without effort: the ideational image of the whole person is brought to disappear, in order to *accentuate* only physical being. The Ego figure is no longer stage-managed as an experiencing and feeling being, but as a mere perceiving and performing being.
12. Under this condition of *reducing* and limiting the Ego to perceptual and performance functions, damaging physical symptoms are registered.
13. Dynamic movement itself is again suspended; the Ego figure takes on a stance of distance and control (the diagnostician).
14. A return to dynamic movement is brought about through the personification of diagnostic judgment as an authority. At the same time, this *office* of a judging authority serves to form a link to the setting of narcissistic gratification: it bestows recognition.
15. The dynamics are again interrupted, this time in order to partially *dismantle* the office of authority. Dismantling the authority serves to weaken the threat contained in the diagnosis: the examination establishes that there are lesions on the female body. If the office of authority is put into question, then the threatening content of the diagnosis is also questionable.
16. A return to dynamic movement is caused by another approach to the ideational image of the female figure. This time, the Ego creates representatives in the place of his own direct approach. The activity of the Ego thus becomes, at least in part, alienated.
17. This retreat is *turned around radically,* however. There is even a direct fusion of sensations ("feel on my own body," p. 169).
18. This situation of fusing again calls up the inner authority, which now takes control of the scene with a diagnostic judgment, planned to be final.
19. But this completed judgment is opposed by a tendency toward circumventing the disturbing aspects connected with the female body pre-

sented. The diagnosis is formally pronounced, but it remains inconsistent in content. Two aspects remain disparate: the *registration of physical illness* and the *nonregistration of physical illness*.

20. This ambivalence remains unresolved; it is *skipped over*. Self-suggestion conjures up a diffuse, expanded ego and definitive knowledge, even to the point of fusion with the iron authority of the law. One aspect of the ego must, in the sense of personifying evil, become externalized as guilty.
21. This end to dynamic movement becomes, with all its force, depersonalized. Standing external to the "persons," the judging office is itself the expanded ego, which is now remote, distanced, and dissociated; it has definitive knowledge of the law at its disposal. (See figure 10.2.)

The reported dream and its analysis by Freud form the core of a staging of self before a reading public. The wish-fulfilling scenario becomes expanded

---

Wish:
- To receive ceremonial recognition and honor from a large public.

Disturbance of the wish-fulfilling scene:
- Disturbance occurs through a female figure. This figure fits the stage role of the "uninvited guest" who brings unrest (sexual danger, danger of sanctions). The uninvited guest is modeled as an atoning figure. The lesions on her body are signs of her accusation: you have harmed me and have, through me, become guilty.

Conflict:
- The wish to take a receptive stance toward the objects and to be "received" by them is made questionable by the threat of guilt that results from the bodily damage of a female figure.

Strategies of conflict resolution in the retelling process:
- The threat of guilt is not made precise, explained, or spelled out in detail.
- The object is reduced to the status of an object-like nonactor.
- A paternal authority is called upon.
- The paternal authority is dismantled (due to the danger of being sentenced by that authority).
- There is banding together of the brotherly gang (after the fall of the father).
- A brother figure is expulsed, who is made guilty of harming the woman.
- There is modified return to the expansive wish: the wish to become the authority and law-giving office oneself, so that the accusations will come to an end (Moses fantasy).

Figure 10.2. The Narrative Organization of the Dream as a Presentation of Wish Fulfillment

in communication with a reading public rendering homage to him. That which was shaped in the dream takes on new form as a communicative scene between the author and his public. Freud, to whom the secret of dreams was disclosed, becomes a figure receiving a large audience to honor this epochal achievement.

Incorporation of the Reading Public

The structure of the dream personifies both authority and a guilt fantasy. In *The Interpretation of Dreams,* Freud's own associations reported on the text have to do with guilt fantasy and the exoneration of guilt; they do not point to a wish for passive gratification or narcissistic aggrandizement and enlargement. At the same time, the author states clearly that he refrains from pursuing further associations, because, among other reasons, he has an understandable aversion to exposing too many private details.

For this very reason, we might well ask how Freud stage-managed the themes of concealment/revelation with the publication and exposure of his text. We find that the "secret of dreams" disclosed itself to him in a similar fashion: a passive perceiver becomes a remote possessor of knowledge, raised above all the entanglements. In the same way, the anonymous reading public of *The Interpretation of Dreams* becomes an astonished and admiring witness to the divine "revelation" given to the Chosen One. This ceremonial aggrandizement through the glowing eyes of an admiring and moved readership does, however, demand the payment of tribute: the stage-managing magician and arranger makes an open declaration of guilt. He puts the reader in a position of authority to pronounce judgment on the damage done to the female sex, damage that the Chosen One claims to be guilty of. In the psychoanalytic literature, the "damage" is usually viewed in connection with an instance of medical malpractice by Wilhelm Fleiss with a patient of Freud's, who is seen to be motivated by the interest, at the cost of the woman, of protecting his friend.[26] It is through Freud's insistent declaration of guilt that the female "uninvited guest" can be held in check. This disturber of the festivities (presented by means of her status as a victim) is not hidden, but exposed.

What is the point, really, of this female atoning figure as an obtrusive focus of the dream report? What is this "guilt" proffered so insistently and publicly to the reader's eye? Freud, as the Chosen One, presents himself to the world as the first person to whom the secret of dreams is disclosed. To mollify the "jealous gods" in the face of this enormous triumph, in the heart of *The Interpretation of Dreams* he stage-manages a self-accusation as a guilty party. For this, he chooses a female figure, a member of the (in his view) determinedly "jealous" sex. He succeeds, under the guise of his admission of guilt, in making fun of both the "false-toothed schoolmarm" and the masculine teaching authority, mainly Josef Breuer (who, as happened in the case of Anna O., met defeat with this woman). This is an artful, competitive attack in which the readership takes pleasure in joining through identification. The reader's reception outlined in this paper, however, takes its orientation from the decisive importance of the fulfillment of a grandiose wish presented in the dream report, which should have been staged as a ceremony of honor and testimony in a "great hall" with "many guests."

In this perspective, the supporting theme of the dream report is the honoring of the One to whom the law (of the dream) has been revealed, but One who, like Moses and Polykratus, must pay tribute. The deviousness of the dream report would be to convince the public that here a great confessor is at work—a male "rapist" even—who degrades the female "object" in alliance with other men. This seeming crime is presented openly and conceals the homage scene, hides the sexual aspects of the organization of actions, and veils as well the sense of triumph over Dr. M., the paternal authority. Dr. M. is dead, and Freud becomes the new administrator of the law. He is now the celebrated new discoverer. Of course, this triumph cannot be enjoyed without ambivalence, without self-confrontation with disloyalty. This is expressed strongly in Irma's accusation. Whereas Freud wished to leave the castrated and weakened old master behind, he returns as an "uninvited guest" in the form of a wounded woman to complain of her suffering and reveal the pain inflicted upon her. The "I" of the dream takes on a challenging stance to the female figure, silencing her complaints. He takes hold of her, not in a sexual way, but with the objectivity of the medical authority. Dr. M.[27] himself then appears on the scene. Weak and ill, Dr. M. recedes into the background—helpful, but with no fight in him. Dr. M. cedes the field to the capable young men.

Celebratory Self-Chronicling

Under the heading "A Leader is Born," Ronald W. Clark writes:

> Freud had reached the age of 40 when his studies on hysteria were published—nearly the age at which it is assumed that a scientist will no longer produce anything of great merit. But 1895 was the beginning of five years of extraordinary activity for Freud. While completing the last of the studies, he undertook the first exhaustive analysis of one of his own dreams, an undertaking of such enormous importance to his later work that Freud later, in 1900, jokingly suggested that one day, a plaque would be hung with the inscription "Here the secret of dreams was revealed to Dr. Sigmund Freud on July 24, 1895." Later in the same year, he wrote within a few weeks a brilliant article attempting to describe mental processes in terms of quantifiable forces. In this article, Freud just barely missed setting up the neuron theory, which was formulated one year later by Wilhelm von Waldeyer, and describing the nervous system on the basis of the neuron, the technical term for the nerve cell with its dendrites. In 1897, Freud began the tremendous task of self-analysis, which became accelerated through the death of his father. At this time, Freud made, in his own words, his "first big mistake": his theory of seduction. This theory, as unfortunate as it was, led on to the Oedipus complex, which

Freud soon came to view as the key to psychological development. And then he wound up the last year of the century with the publication of *The Interpretation of Dreams,* considered to be his most influential work.[28]

Sigmund Freud, a man flourishing at midlife, left a monument to himself: an unusual monument, through unusual means. His *opus magnum, The Interpretation of Dreams,* appeared under the auspices of a new century and was not simply a scientific or interpretative work, but was an original and influential form of self-chronicling that involved the emotional participation of his readership.

Psychoanalysis itself is a form of self-chronicling, a form of bestowing meaning that was new in a time when old forms of self-understanding were becoming questionable. The magic means are new and old. Old was the pattern of the great tragedies. Novel was the shifting of the conflicts to the metaphorical interior of a dark stage. Self-chronicling took on new form with Freud in the spirit of a withdrawal from one's self. The person no longer forms a grasp of his history from the fullness of a life lived and viewed. A person's individual history articulates the conflict between "body-linked wishes" and the world of social behavior.[29]

But this is not all that is new in Freud's mode of self-chronicling. New is the introduction of the *other* into one's self-understanding. The activity of designing the self becomes explicitly dialogic: there is an avenue into other lives. Who I am is always also a matter of dialogue.

Freud chronicles himself to the audience involved in his stage production in the heroic pose of the courageous scientist seeking truth and the liberator from mental immaturity that creates unconscious entanglements. But this staging, shown by the example of Irma's dream, requires an antagonist in the shape of the "uninvited guest." The uninvited guest enters the stage as a disrupter of narcissistic gratification and interferes with the attempt to position the self at the lofty heights of priests by presenting the challenges of sexuality and guilt. At the dream's onset, there is celebration of the great One. At the end of the dream, there is celebration of the impersonal great. In between, there is attack and defense toward the attack by means of mastering and laying down the law. There is an analogy to be found here in the way in which the psychoanalytic tradition, at least partly, continues to be handed down. This does not take place without the great masters, without expulsion of dissidents, without controversy over the question of the significance of historical influences and over openness to developments within modern scientific dialogue, or without controversy over the psychoanalytic theory of the sexes.

The problem is not at all that the controversies exist. Rather, our concern is the near ideological dogmatism that causes the barrenness of psychoanalytic discussion. It would seem that the fascination of psychoanalysis lies in the possibility of becoming the Chosen One, the privileged recipient of the law for all times, protected and supported by a community of loyal affirmation. The cult of authority, the forming of cliques, self-celebration in halls of fantasy made holy by childhood tragedies, the lack of cultivation of fruitful dialogue by the argumentative—all these are danger zones that psychoanalysis has not yet escaped.[30]

Notes

This Chapter was translated from the original German by Ellen Russon. Unless otherwise noted, all quotations are also provided by Ellen Russon.

1. Gerhard Kurz, *Metapher, Allegorie, Symbol* (Göttingen, 1982).

2. Sigmund Freud, *The Interpretation of Dreams* (1900), in *The Basic Writings of Sigmund Freud,* ed. A.A. Brill (New York, 1995), 149–517.

3. Rainer Rath, *Kommunikationspraxis. Analysen zur Textbildung und Textgliederung im gesprochenen Deutsch* (Göttingen, 1979); Rainer Rath, "Erzählfunktionen und Erzählankündigungen im Alltagsdialog," in *Erzählforschung. Ein Symposium,* ed. Eberhard Lämmert (Stuttgart, 1982), 33–50.

4. See, for example, the article about van Dijk in Elisabeth Gülich and Wolfgang Raible, eds., *Linguistische Textmodelle* (Munich, 1977), 267.

5. The following sentences express meaningfulness: "What is my wildly beating heart telling me?"; "What is the message of my dream last night?"

6. Peter M. Wiedemann, *Erzählte Wirklichkeit* (Weinheim, 1986).

7. Barbara Eisenmann, *Erzählen in der Therapie* (Opladen, 1995).

8. Peter Brooks, *Reading for the Plot: Design and Intention in Narrative* (New York, 1984); Jerome S. Bruner, *Acts of Meaning* (Cambridge, Mass., 1990); Walter A. Schelling, "Erinnern und Erzählen," *Wege zum Menschen* 35 (1983): 416–422; Peter Sloterdijk, *Literatur und Organisation von Lebenserfahrung* (Munich, 1978).

9. Daniel Stern, *The Interpersonal World of the Infant: A View from Psychoanalysis and Developmental Psychology* (New York, 1985).

10. Gernot Böhme, "Sinn und Gegensinn—über die Dekonstruktion von Geschichten," *Psyche* 44 (1990): 577–592; Lester Luborsky, "Measuring a Pervasive Psychic Structure in Psychotherapy: The Core Conflictual Relationship Theme," in *Communicative Structures and Psychic Structure,* ed. Norbert Freedman and Stanley Grand (New York, 1977), 367–395; Lester Luborsky and Horst Kächele, *Der zentrale Beziehungskonflikt: Ein Arbeitsbuch* (Ulm, 1988).

11. Freud, *The Interpretation of Dreams.*

12. Ibid.; see also Sigmund Freud, "Creative Writers and Day-Dreaming" (1908), in *The Standard Edition of the Complete Works of Sigmund Freud,* ed. James Strachey (London, 1953–1974), vol. 9, 143–153.

13. Erving Goffman, *The Presentation of Self in Everyday Life* (New York, 1959).

14. Here it may certainly be left open whether there is sense in viewing certain communicative practices of higher mammals as forerunners or early forms of scene direction.

15. Prototypical scene progressions have been described impressively by, for example, Stern, *Interpersonal World,* or Berry T. Brazelton and Bertrand G. Cramer, *Earliest Relationship: Parents, Infants and the Drama of Early Attachment* (Addison-Wesley, paperback reprint, 1991).

16. The classic psychoanalytic treatment setting, provides the opportunity to make unconscious role casting and fantasy dramas conscious.

17. Freud, *The Interpretation of Dreams.*

18. Böhme, "Sinn."

19. Freud, *The Interpretation of Dreams,* 164ff. A first, illustrated basic version of the narrative-analytical dream interpretation presented here is found in Brigitte Boothe, *Der Patient als Erzähler in der Psychotherapie* (Göttingen, 1994).

20. Among the many interpretations and treatments, Erik H. Erikson's "Das Traummuster in der Psychoanalyse," *Psyche* 8 (1954/1955): 561–604, stands out as being particularly important historically. Erikson's re-analysis makes a plea for the great psychoanalytical meaningfulness of the

so-called manifest dream: the shape of the retelling as a linguistic sequence. None of the other numerous publications on "Irma's Injection" can do without taking this gestalt of the retelling into consideration, as analysis in dialogue with the author is not possible. Programmatically, formalist approaches, such as Patrick J. Mahoney, "Towards a Formalist Approach to Dreams," *International Review of Psychoanalysis* 4 (1977): 83–98 and Adam Kuper and Alan A. Stone, "The Dream of Irma's Injection: A Structural Analysis," *The American Journal of Psychiatry* 139 (1982): 1225–1234, emphasize text structure as the central object of investigation. The results of Mahoney's analysis stress, in particular, Freud's wishes for passive-submissive self-abandonment, homosexual submission, and identification with feminine receptivity—wishes that must be defended against (idem, "Towards a Formalist Approach," 96). Similar treatments are found in Didier Anzieu, *Freuds Selbstanalyse und die Entdeckung der Psychoanalyse* (Munich, 1990), vol. 1, 1895–1898; Erikson, "Das Traummuster"; Alexander Grinstein, *On Sigmund Freud's Dreams* (New York, 1980); Hyman Spotnitz and Phyllis W. Meadow, *Treatment of the Narcissistic Neuroses* (New York, 1976). In "A Reappraisal of the Emma Episode and the Specimen Dream," *Journal of the American Psychoanalytic Association* 31 (1983): 555–586, Frank R. Hartman also emphasizes the experience of self-dependency. Kuper and Stone, in contrast, focus upon the dreamer's thought activity that develops a self-consistent and polished dialectic-based argumentation; in this way, the retelling of the dream models Freud's theory of hysterical disorders at that time.

Dreaming as problem solving and the dream report as the presentation of a problem-solving process necessarily play the decisive role in Ramon Greenberg and Chester Pearlman's ego-psychological dream analysis (idem, "If Freud Only Knew: A Reconsideration of Psychoanalytic Dream Theory," *International Review of Psychoanalysis* 5 [1978]: 711–775). For Max Schnur ("Some Additional 'Day Residues' of the Specimen Dream of Psychoanalysis," in *Psychoanalysis—A General Psychology,* ed. Rudolph M. Loewenstein, Lottie M. Newman, Max Schnur, and Albert J. Solnit [New York, 1966], 45–85), the interpretation focuses upon coming to terms with the traumatic Emma Eckstein episode and rehabilitation of friend Fliess, whose image had been ruined. (Emma Eckstein, a young patient of Freud's diagnosed as hysterical, at Freud's suggestion, had undergone a nose operation by Fliess. Subsequent complications were grave due to medical malpractice.)

Erikson places emphasis upon the dream's character of a male conspiracy against a woman sentenced to silence and reduced to an object. Even stronger is the focus on a "phallic defense maneuver" in Robert May, "Freud and Phallic Defense," *Psychiatry* 42 (1979): 147–156, and in Christa Rohde-Dachser, *Expedition in den dunklen Kontinent* (Berlin, 1991). Other authors (Anzieu, "Freud's Selbstanalyse"; Alan Elms, "Freud, Irma, Martha: Sex and Marriage in the 'Dream of Irma's Injection,'" *Psychoanalytic Review* 67 [1980]: 83–109; Grinstein, *Dreams;* and Hartman, "A Reappraisal") stress again the motive of forbidden sexual desires, to the point of "sexual megalomania," which Hartman (ibid., 579) bases on evidence in Freud's answer to a letter from Abraham (Hilda C. Abraham and Ernst Freud, eds., *A Psycho-Analytic Dialogue: The Letters of Sigmund Freud and Karl Abraham 1907–1926* [New York, 1965]).

Rivalry with father figures, or even with Freud's own father, is the significant theme emphasized by authors such as Harold P. Blum, "The Forbidden Guest and the Analytic Ideal: The Superego and Insight," *Psychoanalytic Quarterly* 50 (1981): 535–556; Johannes Grunert, "Freud und Irma. Genetische Aspekte zum Initialtraum der Psychoanalyse," *Psyche* 29 (1975): 721–744; and Hartman, "A Reappraisal." In fact, Freud's father fell ill in July 1985 and died in October 1896; Freud himself reported his impression that he could only begin to work with full productivity following his father's death. Swings between idealizing submission and rebellious revolt are obvious in the manifest content of the dream (Grunert, "Freud and Irma"; see also, Sigmund Freud, *Totem and Taboo* [New York, 1918]). But behind all this, the further grandiose fantasy of personal uniqueness, of standing out among the generations, of being one's own father becomes apparent (Grunert, "Freud und Irma").

These narcissistic fantasies stand in close relation to the theme of creative productivity and the "birth" of psychoanalysis (Anzieu, "Freuds Selbstanalyse"; Blum, "The Forbidden Guest"; Erikson, "Das Traummuster"; Hartman, "A Reappraisal"; Stanley M. Kaplan, "Narcissistic Injury and the Occurrence of Creativity: Freud's Irma Dream," *The Annual of Psychoanalysis* 12 [1984/1985]: 367–376; Robert Lang, "Freud's Irma Dream and the Origins of Psychoanalysis," *Psychoanalytic Review* 71 [1984], 591–617; Barbara Mautner, "Freud's Irma Dream: A Psychoanalytic Interpretation," *The International Journal of Psychoanalysis* 72 [1991], 275–286; Roy M. Whitman, Milton Kramer, and Bill J. Baldridge, "Dreams about the Patient: An Approach to the Problem of Countertransference," *Journal of the American Psychoanalytic Association* 17 [1969]: 702–727). These latter authors, as well as Robert Langs, "Supervisory Crises and Dreams from Supervisees," *Contemporary Psychoanalysis* 18 (1982): 575–612, view the Irma dream also—in light of psychoanalytic technique—as a "supervision" or "countertransference" dream.

21. Freud, *The Interpretation of Dreams*, 164.

22. Ibid., 175.

23. Jeffrey M. Masson, *Was hat man dir, du armes Kind, getan?* (Reinbek, 1984).

24. Freud, *The Interpretation of Dreams*, 164–165.

25. Ibid.

26. Of course, it is also viewed in a generalizing and anticipatory manner as being related to Freud's theory of femininity (a theory frequently criticized as discriminatory).

27. Had the guilty fantasy become predominant in the dreamer's conflict dynamics, Dr. M. may very well have become a figure of revenge, the "stone guest" of Mozart's opera *Don Giovanni* who, as a freeze-frame of the murdered father, challenges the anarchistic lord of the manor and seducer to take part in the banquet. The murder victim indeed then appears as "stone guest" at the banquet and demands regret and self-humiliation of the host, the loss of hubris, which is Don Giovannis's main trait. Don Giovanni, the feudal individualist, does not submit to this and risks his own demise. Freud, in contrast, the charismatic leader figure, is protected by the loyalty of his brothers and friends.

28. Ronald W. Clark, *Sigmund Freud* (Frankfurt, 1990), 169.

29. Not an easy undertaking under the power of the anarchy of the romantically "dark instincts."

30. A contemporary attack, though more emotional than sharp-sighted and culminating in veritable castigation, is found in Manfred Pohlen and Magarethe Bautz-Holzherr, "Der Fundamentalismus des psychoanalytischen Apparats und der Preis der Analyse," *Zeitschrift für Klinische Psychologie, Psychopathologie und Psychotherapie* 43 (1995): 164–174; see also, idem, *Psychoanalyse—Das Ende einer Deutungsmacht* (Reinbek, 1995).

CHAPTER 11

Authenticity and Authority
On Understanding the Shoah

ALEXANDRE MÉTRAUX

This essay arose from reflections on the question of, and then occasional irritation over, the particular language embedded in popular conceptions of the Shoah. We will first delineate the question, and briefly elaborate on it. In subsequent sections, that is, in the exposition of the theme (circumscribed by the posing of the question), various aspects of the Shoah's representation by authors, and its understanding in turn by listeners and readers, will be considered. As a next step, the narratives of Primo Levi, understood here as exemplary, will allow us to describe different models of reception, and to more easily conceptually clarify the different mnestic acts. Insofar as this exposition is persuasive, the term "historical consciousness" will then appear as a theoretical blank that, when used unspecifically, contributes little or nothing to illuminating the relation of event and memory.

The View from Inside and the View from Outside

The initial question could be formulated as follows, following James Young's monograph on writing the Shoah:[1] What defines the relationship between descriptions of the Shoah from the inside and descriptions from the outside, in particular historical representations of the destruction of European Jewry?[2] The question is hardly trivial, narratologically or historiographically. For one thing, it forces us to consider the degree of authority and authenticity ascribed to texts as mediating instances between past events and present conceptions—or to which the authors appeal, through the use of particular formal, stylistic, and semantic features in their statements.

Notes for this section begin on page 242.

No quantitative limits can be set on representation from the outside. This holds for representations of practically any event that leaves material traces. The representations of the Ming dynasty or the Thirty Years' War that became current in the twentieth century could be extended without limit, although such extension can culminate in irrelevance, not to mention become cumulatively redundant. The possibility should not be excluded that the destruction of the European Jews in the first half of the twentieth century[3] could still, three, four, or thirteen centuries from now, become the subject of learned treatments or even the object of bitter controversy. On the other hand, descriptions from the inside form a finite quantity of many but numerable parts (among these elements are diaries, memoirs, tape recordings of eyewitnesses, judicial and similar records of statements by witnesses, and similar documents[4]).

This difference is reflected in all the different forms of knowledge, tradition, communication, and representation. Constitutive for descriptions from the outside is second-, third-, and fourthhand knowledge gained from a source-critically refined and methodologically domesticated relation to empirical data. The plausibility of a representation is then measured by certain textual features, imposed primarily by the precisely obligatory methodological canon of the historical and sociological disciplines. In contrast, texts written from the inside themselves appear to embody the empirical relation between the writer and the named, recognized, and recollected events. This relationship is self-explanatory for the writer in its immediacy. In other words, it does not need to be carefully reconstructed and justified by means of textual crutches and conceptual prostheses. Young remarks:

> Especially for the diarist who reported events as they played themselves out before his eyes, the words he inscribed on a page seemed to be living traces of his life at that moment: his eyes, his engraving hand, and the ink on paper all appeared to be materially linked in the writing act itself. But it is just this perception of words being bodily linked to events that constitutes both the source of these words' evidentiary authority and the point at which they lose this same authority for the reader.[5]

In other words, for the reader who sees only letters on paper, instead of more or less continuously connected events, texts written from the inside lose evidentiary force:

> The words in a translated and reproduced Holocaust diary are no longer traces of the crime, as they were for the writer who inscribed them; what was evidence for the writer at the moment he wrote is now, after it leaves his hand, only a detached and free-floating sign, at the mercy of all who would read and misread it.[6]

Authenticity and authority, as one may guess from the preceding (however fragmentary) explanation, are not the complementary properties of a transcription of historical reality. Rather, transpositions of reports from the inside into representations from the outside can only be bought at the cost of shifts, defamiliarizations, or even distortions of meaning. Conversely, representations created in accordance with historical method simply cannot be integrated into imitations of the view from inside without fictionalization, for the experience of the observing individual is ontologically barred from mimetic duplication. What authenticity eyewitness reports possess does not equal the authority one would want. The high degree of authority attained by histories through the construction of empirically saturated data, as a rule, does not meet even the least requirement of authenticity.

On the Use of Descriptions from the Inside

The dilemma between authenticity and authority, which descriptions of the Shoah enter, is not without consequence for mnestic appropriation. It is no wonder that historians, persons with textual and/or narrative competencies, have asked culture and media workers, for example, how eyewitness reports from the ghettos and the death camps, and the memoirs of survivors, can (or should) be made used of. It is also no wonder that a similar question could be asked with respect to historical representations. On which model are research results communicated, with what linguistic, iconic, and other tools is this mediation accomplished, and to what purpose should the Shoah even be communicated, that is, impressed on the memory of those to whom, because of their family history or personal biography, it must remain a "strange story"?

In a discussion of the uses of documents written from the inside, Ball-Kaduri has formulated the hypothesis that eyewitness reports possibly only give "life and blood to otherwise dry facts known from other sources."[7] If that were always the case, the function of representations from the inside could be reduced to a rhetorical whispering—or to a subtext, in itself dispensable, that one lets resound as accompaniment when the inconceivable is supposed to become conceivable, the dry explanation narratively vivid, the historiographic objectivation, palpable life and death. Or, to express it more crudely: the descriptions left behind by the interior of the Shoah are at best reading aids for a discourse whose insights into historical relations could have been gained just as well without eyewitnesses.

I consider the question of use important. On the other hand, I consider the tendency to level all the formal, stylistic, and generic variations in the representation of the Shoah on the one side, and the different models of reception and understanding on the other side, in the search for an answer to this question, to be inadmissible. Not all eyewitnesses wanted simply to testify; not all were guided by the same models as they wrote (if such models were even determining); not all had the same knowledge of events; and finally, not all remembered, processed, and committed what they had seen to external memory (notebook, paper, or other medium) in the same way—not even to mention that some, such as Primo Levi, initially told and retold their stories face to face before they were ready for print.

Just as it is conceptually problematic to speak of nature (as such) or life (in general), and therefore advisable to begin with orders, genera, geological eras, phylogenetic regularities, ontogenetic particularities, and the like,[8] so it seems advisable, instead of theorizing generally on the description, understanding, and remembrance of the Shoah, first to work out a number of paradigmatic difficulties of certain limit conditions in the discussion of the destruction of the European Jews. For the use of eyewitness testimony and other expressions from the inside depends not least on who is speaking for whom, about what.

In a recent opusculum on the misuse of memorial celebrations, Tzvetan Todorov pointed to the tension between tradition and modernity as a factor in historical activity:

> In our general conceptions of public life, we have, as the philosophers say, completed the transition from heteronomy to autonomy.... The essential point, however, is that tradition can be contested in the name of the general will as of the common weal.[9]

The disenchantment with tradition, however, does not lead to the disqualification of historical consciousness,[10] though certainly of hermeneutic authorities, and along with it, their previous monopoly on interpretation, despite occasional contestation. The consequence of the transition from heteronomy to autonomy is not only a new multiplicity of understandings of the past, but the neutralization of previous historical representations. This multiplicity results from the different experiential constellations of groups and individuals, whereas the neutralization occurs because the mere proclamation of historical depictions no longer underwrites their plausibility: only through narrative consistency, verisimilitude, and plausibility of the interpretation offered can descriptions of the past attain a status distinct from fictional, mythical, moralizing, propagandistic, or hagiographic representations—not to mention from rumor. Todorov remarks:

> No state authority should be able to say: you have no right independently to seek out the factual truth—those who do not accept the official version of the past will be punished. Thus the definition of democratic life is at stake: individuals and groups have the right to know, i.e., to know and to publicize their own history. It is not the place of the state to forbid or allow them to do so.[11]

An imperative is unaffected by an empirical statement, since it does not express who did or is doing what. It also specifies no legal interest as long as it is not assimilated, in part or as a whole, into positive law. But empirical givens can be considered and judged from the standpoint of an imperative. They then assume a function related to the classical Aristotelian topos.

The constitutional equality of subjects under the law means, as we have suggested, that all individuals have the right to strive for knowledge for themselves as well as for others, that, in other words, they have the right to learn history or part of it, and to publicize this knowledge in the form of biography, historical frescoes, narration, interpretive or explanatory hypotheses, chronicles, commentaries, or any other sort of text. From this standpoint, the aforementioned dilemma of authority and authenticity likely cannot be resolved, but is nevertheless blunted to the extent that the use of eyewitness testimony in the recollection of the past (here, the Shoah) can then be considered under different aspects. If we think in terms of a republican constitution, we have to add to the historical canons of proof here and to the moving or shattering or illuminating testimony there, whose narrative basis is, however, always life experience, the equality of voices, including textual voices, as a point of view. And this point of view should not be bracketed out for convenience, for the simple reason that the remembrance of the Shoah is, after all, demanded by calling on concrete laws of justice. For a theory of understanding the past (the Shoah in particular, and above all) the imperative of equality is, of course, insufficient. This imperative alone will not demonstrate how the medium of representation (text, image, film, theatrical, or radio version of the narrative) influences the appropriation of the past. Nor can the imperative of equality be used to measure the corners and edges of "narratology," that is, the repertoire of different narrative forms and styles, such that the narrative problematic no longer is a theoretical obstacle. An interesting theory of historical understanding cannot avoid these two aspects with impunity. It should thus be clear that this essay proposes to offer neither a primer for understanding the Shoah, nor a propaedeutic of narrative communication. It does, however, claim to define, by reflecting on seldom considered and thus marginal aspects of the representation of the Shoah, a number of limit conditions of its understanding.

Of Names and Designations

Hebrew uses the general term *shoah* (destruction, annihilation) for the destruction of European Jewry. The day of remembrance for the Jews destroyed thus bears the name *yom ha-shoah*. The Hebrew word was originally used for Israel's destruction by its neighbors as well as for the Babylonian captivity; its root, however, has connotations of "despair" and "metaphysical doubt," which have been explored in Jewish history, literature, and theology.

In Yiddish, the word *churbn* (destruction, ruins) is used to denote the destruction of European Jewry.[12] This word also appears in the phrase *di churbn-zajt*.[13] The substantive *der churbn* derives from the Hebrew lexeme *churban*, referring to the destruction of the First and Second Temples. As Young emphasizes, the obvious religious resonance of *churban* and *churbn* are why the Labor Zionists, writing on the European situation from a vantage in Palestine, could find no use for the word. They therefore quite openly chose the alternative term *shoah* to designate the most recent and historically unparalleled murder of Jews.[14] In any case, from documents of the time, it is evident that the designation came at the same time as the event itself. A different designation in use in German, as well as in English-speaking countries, is *Holocaust,* usually pronounced by Germans not as a loanword from the Greek, but instead according to English phonemics. The term first acquired the particular meaning of "destruction = annihilation = the murder of European Jews" between 1957 and 1959.[15] Astonishingly, this term first began to denote a desecration in the German language with the television series *Holocaust,* produced by an American network and broadcast in 1979 in the Federal Republic. It should be noted that this series was not produced with the intention of creating historical awareness, but rather to counter the tremendous financial success enjoyed by ABC with the *Roots* series. The laws of the market and the competitive necessity to acquire a market share that would be attractive to advertisers thus dictated the content and construction of this fictional depiction of the Warsaw uprising.[16]

This new designation pushed aside the earlier ones, and with them, any Hebraic element. For example, the term "final solution [*Endlösung*] of the Jewish question" disappeared, which after the war had maintained euphemistic mystification through National Socialist bureaucratese; that this term might have been a malicious play on Theodor Herzl's recommendation for a Zionist "solution [*Lösung*] to the Jewish question" most likely never occurred to the speakers. The term *Völkermord an den Juden* (murder of the Jewish people) also disappeared, which had signaled the murderous intentions, but renamed the events themselves as a fact on which strict judgments about both the agents and the act itself would have to be dictated by general legal norms.

That it is precisely the German language which had no word for what would now be designated the Holocaust should be no surprise. For the Shoah had been planned from the beginning to leave no trace—and thus no name.[17] It is therefore understandable that the word for it had to come from another language. Why this particular word, however, and not a Hebrew name? Does the etymological resonance of "Holocaust" (*holokauston,* after all, is the word for a particular kind of burnt offering), with its primal religious conceptions of an offering, possibly preserve some metaphysical justification, perhaps meant to suggest that the Shoah was not meaningless? And why this name, which even the least exercise of judgment would find unjust, since it falsifies the experience of those who experienced it. Natalia Ginzburg, whose husband died of the effects of Fascist torture, found the name hypocritical: "It ennobles something that should not be ennobled. It means 'to bring an offering to God,' and in the concentration camps, there was no God. The annihilation was terrible and remains terrible."[18] Likewise, Georges-Arthur Goldschmidt, one of the best translators of Freud into French, sharply criticizes the use of the familiar term:

> The stupefying and certainly the ultimate stage: the negation of the genocide is equivalent to the genocide. This negation evacuates the object itself from its language, leaving nothing behind. For the object is so intolerable, one suppresses it. On the other hand, it all comes to the same thing; one speaks the language of

infamy—the Holocaust! ... What contempt: to say "holocaust" where there was only *industry,* the fabrication of death, bureaucratic terror! "Holocaust" presupposes an offering made to some god. Saying "holocaust" does honor to those who bring the offering.[19]

However, one does not even need to analyze designations such as *churbnzajt* in order to find an asymmetric relation between the view from the inside and the view from the outside in representations of the Shoah—in other words, relations that violate the equality of voices. In place of numerous possible examples, I would like to consider a passage from Primo Levi's novel *If Not Now, When?* (first published in Italian as *Se non ora, quando?* [1982]) and its German translation. The novel describes a group of Jewish partisans and their odyssey before and behind the Eastern European front lines. Levi himself at no place and in no way obscured the fictional quality of this text. In other words, it is not eyewitness testimony, but rather a synthetic description, in which material from different historical sources is being treated in a literary way.[20]

In chapter 10 of the novel, dated February 25, 1945, some silk stockings are under discussion that Pavel, one of the main characters in the novel, turned up somewhere. The female partisans try on the silk stockings; some fit, some do not. Then Pavel suddenly tells the group that he has found a truck in a Russian junkyard. In the German translation, the passage reads, "I have something else to tell you. I've found a truck [in German, *Lastwagen*]!"[21] Since Pavel understands nothing about demobilized rolling stock, junk, or broken machinery, he looks among his comrades for someone who can join him in returning to his discovery the next day. The short passage can be read either as description (i.e., a representation of the author's perspective) or as indirect speech (i.e., as the representation of speech acts to be ascribed to the characters). One cannot know, however, *who* is saying what. The question as to who knows something about trucks could have been raised by Pavel, or by one of the other partisans. The passage reads:

> Who knew about trucks [in German, *LKWs*]? Who knew how to drive them? The band had covered more than a thousand kilometers on foot: wasn't it time now for them to travel by truck [*LKW*]?[22]

The reader will not fail to notice that *Lastwagen* has become *LKW* in the translation. Levi's original, however, uses the same word each time, *camion*.[23] But why the substitution of *LKW* for *Lastwagen*? In other words, how could it happen that a word in the target language was changed into its seemingly equivalent acronym in that language, as though the history of this acronym would not color what Levi's pen had put in the mouths of his characters? The thoughtless, unnecessary, and—let us be charitable and suppose—benign replacement of *Lastwagen* by *LKW* provokes associations with the *lingua tertii imperii,* or, more precisely: with elements of the language of the Third Reich, which Victor Klemperer noted in his philology of the terror:

The will to action spawns new verbs. They want to get rid of the Jews, so they *entjuden* {dejew}, they want to make sure that all business life is in Aryan hands, so they *arisieren* {aryanize}, they want to re-establish the purity of their ancestral blood, so they *aufnorden* {nordify}. Intransitive verbs, to which technology has assigned new meanings, are reactivated as transitive ones: one flies {*fliegt*} a heavy machine, one flies in {*fliegt*} boots and provisions, one freezes {*friert*} vegetables with new techniques of deep freezing, where one previously had to refer, rather more long-windedly, to making something frozen {*gefrieren machen*}. Part of the aim is certainly to express oneself more stringently and briskly than is usually the case, and it is this same aim which turns a *Berichterstatter* {a man who makes a report} into a *Berichter* {reporter}, the *Lastwagen* {lorry} into the *Laster*, the *Bombenflugzeug* {bomber plane} into the *Bomber*, and which finally ends up replacing the word with an abbreviation. With the result that *Lastwagen, Laster, LKW* corresponds to a crescendo from positive to superlative.[24]

If there were actually a stylistic intention to vary *Lastwagen,* then the word *camion,* for example, still used in Switzerland, would have served, and *Lastauto* would have been generally understood. The use of the abbreviation, however, falsifies by paraphrase the author's message (through the characters): the sound represented by those three letters imitates not the voices of Jewish partisans, but the voices of the present. One might innocently argue that *LKW* and *Lastwagen* can be interchanged as synonyms with no loss of meaning, but this cannot account for the shift in perspective. A linguistic triviality? There are worse imaginable solecisms than the use of *LKW,* but as an unfortunate paraphrase that appropriates the message of one voice for another voice (or of one language for another), it is certainly symptomatic.

As with the assignment of names and the choice of designation, one can also violate the imperative of equality through the use of metaphors and evaluations. "Auschwitz" as synecdoche silences through repetition what occurred at the margin of the Shoah, and draws a border on the imaginary geography of both speakers and listeners between the continent of murder and the continent of exile, even though we are dealing with *one* continuum of persecution. The hyperbolic phrase about the "unspeakable suffering" inflicted on the victims dissolves the describable, the narratable, and representable into inexpressibility. In view of the expansion of the suffering into the numinous, corresponding to an evil posited as numinous, the detailed descriptions of episodes, or the attempts precisely to name and define things, events, deeds, and methods, become disturbances in the contemplation of the universal. How can we be surprised that eyewitnesses' reports, for whom the general phenomenon was not apparent (because human eyes *cannot* see it and human hands *cannot* grasp it) cannot be forced into the official rhetoric of generalities (and of generalized victimization) without dissonance? As long as European fascism, the social phenomenon of anti-Semitism in Poland, German, Austria, France, and other European countries, and the pogroms in the ghettos, the concentration camps, and the forest clearings in territories overrun by the Wehrmacht are described with the help of such synecdoches and hyperboles, dissociations will be unavoidable:

the dissociation between the innermost circle of the system of annihilation and the responsible authorities in the outer circles of this system; the dissociation between those destroyed and those increasingly safe from destruction; the dissociation between the ultimate things and the penultimate things. Initially, these rhetorical figures may have helped overcome verbal difficulties, or indicated general facts. After their petrifaction into figures of speech, they function only as convenient schemata of interpretation or emphasis. And as such schemata, they can be used as cognitive ready-mades, unaffected by particularities of context or their own semantic inertia.

Evocations of the universal certainly accommodate eschatological conceptions of history or metaphysical representations of evil. After their subsumption into generalities, the lives destroyed and the variety of inventive methods of destruction are no longer important. For the general concept of destruction is finally fulfilled in an arbitrary and vague "and so on." Certainly the acceptance of a "metahistorical myth,"[25] involved from now on only with the last things, summarily conceived as unfathomable, already decides the question to which Yosef Hayim Yershalmi was first led by his reflections on the relation between history and memory: "The choice for Jews as for non-Jews is not whether to have a past, but rather—what kind of past shall one have."[26] Such a question can only be meaningful, however, when alternatives are available, or at least conceivable—when, in other words, the imperative of the equality of voices in the recollection of the past is not violated. That such alternatives exist is empirically true. How we might activate memory with their help and the mnemonic functions they address will be presented in a short case study.

The Exemplarity of Primo Levi's Autobiography

On November 19, 1976, Primo Levi was the guest of the Venerdí Litterari. The sponsors of this literary evening had asked the writer to speak on new theories of writing. Instead, before a hall in Turin's Teatro Carignano filled to overflowing, Levi undertook an "Attempt at a Self-Portrait," into whose conclusion he interjected this remark: "I have said it often, and I will repeat it today. To whomever asks me, 'Why are you a chemist who writes?' I answer, 'I write because I am a chemist.' My profession helps me communicate my experiences."[27] Among these experiences are those of prisoner 174517, who on December 13, 1943, was arrested as a partisan by a fascist militia in the Val d'Aosta, admitted to being Jewish, was sent to the transit camp in Carpi-Fossoli near Modena, and was then selected by the SS for transport to the concentration camp system at Auschwitz.[28]

Levi's deportation, his confinement in the camp system up to his liberation by the Red Army in January 1945, and his odyssey from Eastern Europe back to Turin, the city of his birth, have been described in his *If This Is a Man* and *The Truce*.[29] The first text was written between December 1945 and January 1947, the second between December 1961 and November 1962. The subject of Nazi persecution itself, along with other biographically significant episodes, was treated in *The Periodic Table* (1982).[30] The Shoah, the problematic of memory, the relation between the survivors to the dead and between the nonpersecuted and the persecuted are in the thematic foreground of Levi's last book published in his lifetime, *The Drowned and the Saved* (1986).[31] Levi had already depicted the armed Jewish resistance in the aforementioned novel *If Not Now, When?* Finally, the author described his experiences at countless readings and public appearances, and presented his reflections on these experiences as well as on the Shoah.

It would be presumptuous to summarize the biography and historical analyses that Levi composed into texts. Such a summary would neither reveal the architecture of a life as chemist and writer, nor help illuminate the concrete work of memory by a survivor, not to mention that anyone who has read Levi's work would, for good reason, want to avoid such redundancies. Some remarks on the structure of the autobiographical narration, and how verbal intentions can be reconstructed from his self-portraits, will perhaps be found acceptable, however.

Levi frequently emphasized the realistic core of his autobiographical texts, as in an interview he granted Mario Miccinesi in the fall of 1982, for example. In the first of his two self-portraits,

> nothing was deliberately invented. There might be transfigurations, interpretations of facts, transpositions, but no inventions. I can remember stubbornly such a temptation [i.e., to invent]. The facts I reported were far too vivid and far too fresh. I did not want to contaminate them. I did not want to give the reader the least reason to suspect that I had left any room for embellishment, exaggeration, for "good writing." I allowed myself somewhat more freedom in *The Periodic Table*, especially in the two central stories, which were *admittedly* [sic] invented, but the book's intention is still documentary and autobiographical.[32]

In his testimony, then, Levi documents what he perceived with his own senses (though not only that), and what left mnestic traces on him. Seen thus, his testimony differs from a diary insofar as it was not written during the event or shortly thereafter, but only after an interval of several months, or even years, during which autobiographical memory also worked on these traces. Of course, Levi was quite aware of this; otherwise he would not even mention transpositions, transfigurations, or interpretations. The treatment of immediate experience by autobiographical memory, which functions in no one as a multidimensional recording apparatus for the storage of every extero-, intero-, and proprioceptive stimulus, should not be the author's burden, however.[33] For even transcription is based in every case on multiply nested coding algorithms, whether the result of this act is materialized in diaries, self-presentations (mnestic-verbal flashbacks), debriefings, or checklists.

Chronological transpositions of these kinds are not only the result of the functioning of autobiographical memory. The cause, especially for Levi, was also the loss of elementary spatial and temporal orientation: there was no clock time in the camp at Auschwitz, for the prisoners' watches had been confiscated; there were no calendars or similar objects; thus, the seasons remained the only natural relic of historical time, and this at a place where the arrival and departure of trains, the assignment of train numbers, the production of expense reports followed rules dictated by the camp's administrative machinery.[34] This also means, however, that the chronological errors of autobiographical memory in a desperate situation increase the authenticity of the narration, because the gaps, distortions, and transfigurations are expressed in the structure of the text itself, without the need to be explicitly indicated. Levi, in fact, named and described his textual models on numerous occasions: Ludwig Gattermann's *Die Praxis des organischen Chemikers* [1935; The practice of organic chemistry], which Levi described as part of a conceived "personal anthology" in chapter 10, under the suggestive title "The Word of the Father,"[35] and, above all, the laboratory report, "which has to be written at the end of every week. Clear, substantive, comprehensible. Presenting readers with a report that they cannot understand seems to me the apex of rudeness. That does not mean that the language of my unconscious is one with the language of the reader's unconscious. But it is proper, I believe, to give [readers] the greatest possible quantity of facts and emotions."[36] On another occasion, Levi explained:

> I initially said that I was grateful to my profession for having conferred on me a particular way of thinking and speaking. For the sake of completeness, I must express my gratitude to my profession for a second reason: it provided me with an enormous amount of raw material. The individual elements, the laws of chemistry and physics, even the terminology, seem to be to be extraordinarily useful to anyone with intentions of writing. I began writing quite by accident, as you know; it was never my intention. I succeeded in reaching the other side, to desert, so to speak, and build a bridge to the writers, because I had things to tell. But in the practice of writing, the possession of certain concepts, terms, and experiences, even in the narrower sense of laboratory experience, is a real treasure, meaning as much a walking staff as a real storehouse for someone who knows how to use it.[37]

Naturally a chemist's report on his laboratory experiments cannot be equated with his reports, in his other profession, on his experience.[38] The comparison fails at the outset because a chemist's descriptions treat the relationship between substances, instruments, apparatuses, and other material objects before, or beyond, the emotions, beliefs, attitudes, and psychological contents of the observing subject. On the other hand, the subject's relation to the world is a problem for narrative. In both cases, however, a temporal succession of events can represent the logical and/or causal connections, so that these, even if not expressed in words *lege artis,* are nonetheless intended and generally understood by the reader.

The description of facts can be simplified by the partial equivalence of temporal succession and logical-causal connection, insofar as considerations of reversibility may be excluded. Just as one can deduce from observed effects (the discharge of gas and the color of the liquid when sulfuric acid is poured on pure copper) the cause of these effects with the help of theoretical reflection, so can motives, reasons, impulses, dispositions, or other catalytic mechanisms, however theorized, be deduced from human actions. However, the restriction of description to before–after relations mostly excludes cause–effect relations: what occurred is dressed into a narrativelike description so that a narration built on this descriptive model takes up a median as well as a mediating position between the individual sentence of a report (outside of any context) and the theory-laden, discursively thorough attempt at explanation. Levi's deliberate frugality in the discursive saturation of his narratives does not keep his readers morally on a short leash, however: the author reports on himself and on others, leaving it up to the reader to judge the traces of the events according to normative (moral or legal) standards.

Narrative communication also opens up possibilities for numerous paraphrases of what occurred. Levi himself took part in such paraphrases. *Is This a Man?* was first made into a radio play in 1962 without the author's participation, and was broadcast on Canadian radio. This version was then transformed into an Italian version by Levi, for an Italian state radio production. This version then underwent a further paraphrase by Levi and Pieralberto Marchè to become a stage play, presented in 1968 by the Teatro Stabile.[39] What is communicated to the audience of Levi's experiences as an eyewitness is thus exclusively defined neither by the wording of the narration nor by the literary form. Certainly text and story are adapted to each other, but the relation between them is not static. On the other hand, a poem can be communicated in only one textual form, where paraphrase is as good as excluded, whereas a photo-narrative can be summarized, commented, narrated, and remembered, although in this case, the paraphrase suffers a loss of the iconic signs.[40] This shows that the forms and means of representation influence the processes of reception (appropriation, assimilation, understanding), so that recipients, to be true to the imperative of equality, should know *what* they are understanding.

We have already mentioned that autobiographical memory does not function as a universal analog recording device from which, every second or every nth episode can be retrieved and faithfully reproduced in a conceptual or verbal medium. In an admittedly imprecise allusion to psychoanalytic theory, recollecting an episode changes its cathexis. Such a shift in cathexis is expressed in the individual's relation to the autobiographical past, and thus also in the act of narration. If one analyzes the function of autobiographical narration in Primo Levi, one can observe a modification in the status of the eyewitness report.

Levi explains that he often had the same two dreams while in the camp: in the first, the dreamer could see a lavish meal, which he was prevented from eating, either because someone interfered, or because a screen was placed between the hungry man and the food. The second dream concerned storytelling. The dreamer wanted to tell something, but the listener acted bored, would not listen, or suddenly left.

> The symbolism of both dreams was simple. I say this to emphasize that the need for food and the need to tell are on the same basic level. The unattainable meal and the unfinished story are the apparent forms of a fear of a need that is impossible to satisfy.[41]

In the period immediately after his liberation, Levi, often with almost no purpose, satisfied his narrative urge, which had become second nature (other motives that might have made him speak are of no concern here). For this reason, the earlier narratives burst from him unmediated. In statements from his later years on the other hand, Levi integrated reflections on memory, on the function of memory, and on the valence of the narratives. His verbal intentions thus also change: if at first the eyewitness wanted to speak in his own name, he later appears as the representative of those who can no longer speak:

> I must repeat: we, the survivors, are not the true witnesses. This is an uncomfortable notion of which I have become conscious little by little, reading the memoirs of others and reading mine at a distance of years. We survivors are not only an exiguous but also an anomalous minority: we are those who by their prevarication or abilities or good luck did not touch bottom. Those who did so, those who saw the Gorgon, have not returned to tell about it, or have returned mute, but they are … the submerged, the complete witnesses, the ones whose deposition would have a general significance. They are the rule, we are the exception.… We who were favored by fate tried, with more or less wisdom, to recount not only our own fate, but also that of the others, indeed of the drowned; but this was a discourse "on behalf of third parties," the story of things seen at close hand, not experienced personally. The destruction brought to an end, the job completed, was not told by anyone, just as no one ever returned to describe his own death. Even if they had paper and pen, the drowned would not have testified because their death had begun before that of their body. Weeks and months before being snuffed out, they had already lost the ability to observe, to remember, to compare and express themselves. We speak in their stead, by proxy. I could not say whether we did or do so out of a kind of moral obligation toward those who were silenced or in order to free ourselves of their memory; certainly we do it because of a strong and durable impulse.[42]

Conclusion

The question of how representations of the Shoah from the inside are involved, transferred, and worked into the view from the outside, or how they can be (in short, How are they used?) cannot be answered comprehensively by referring to some law or by invoking a particular theory (of narration, of cultural memory, of cultural mediation, etc.).

The opposition between the view from the inside and the view from the outside does not first appear when the Shoah enters or is forced into consciousness. It becomes more acute in the case of the Shoah, however—for reporting eyewitnesses no less than for those who have to be satisfied with knowledge at second hand. Yet the opposition between the view from inside and the view from outside can be adequately articulated only insofar as one concedes the comparability of referents from the two modes of representation. Formal and other characteristics that differentiate the means of representation can only be defined in a nontrivial way when what the representations attempt to present is not simply disregarded as irrelevant. If the events, persons, actions, instruments, locations, times, the atmospheric and visual conditions (and so on) in the eyewitness reports are not also understandable or recognizable to the view from outside, the discussion of the difference between the two views would continue indefinitely, because it would have no *tertium comparationis*. In connection with this idea, our concluding remarks will consider the thematic of understanding the past in the present.

"Dog," "cat," and "canary" designate the members of certain classifications of animal, whether in letters, novels, children's books, taxonomies, guides to identification, or legal edicts. For this reason, the German order of June 1942, for example, which dictated that those who wore yellow stars, and anyone living with them, were forbidden to have pets, is easily read and understood. It requires no extraordinary insight to deduce what the pets owned by Jews and their housemates could expect from this order, nor to estimate what effect it would have on the already difficult everyday life of Jews in Berlin, Dresden, and elsewhere. How things were can readily be understood from contemporary descriptions, in whatever words these descriptions are communicated and with whatever interpretation accompanies them. In this section, I could just as well have cited my source,[43] or cited the order itself, or the testimony of other eyewitnesses, instead of summarily and perhaps all too hastily discussing it. Should interpretation and event diverge, however, the facts and extent of the divergence could hardly be identified other than by naming the referents (pets, yellow stars, housemates, edict, means of extermination) on which perspectives diverge.

That the recollection of the past into the present is determined as much by the facts as through the form and the medium of communication becomes apparent in the example of poetic texts. Abraham Sutzkefer's poem "farfrojrene jidn" [Jews frozen to death], which was written in Moscow, is dated July 10, 1944.[44] The author experienced the Shoah personally and through others, first in the Wilna ghetto, then as a partisan. As the title indicates, the poem evokes an image of dead Jews. The cascade of memories of the dead is depicted as a chill that overcomes the poet in the July heat. The first two of the twelve strophes read (in an inadequate and unpoetic translation), "Have you seen, on the snowy fields / the frozen Jews, row upon row? / They lie without breathing, marmoreal and blue / but death is not in their bodies."[45]

Since the poem is not constructed narratively, it could be annotated, explained, and analyzed in terms of its poetic qualities, but hardly paraphrased.

One has to ask what a paraphrase would even have to include: the fact that the poet was overcome by his memories on July 1944 in Moscow, or the facts that are being remembered? Even if one paraphrased both sets of facts, the alteration of the author's carefully chosen poetic language caused by the paraphrase would violate the act of recollection, even if the paraphrase specified the facts, that which the text depicts from the inside.[46] To put it differently, the paraphrase has to fail because recollection through poetry is structurally bound to the poetic form: the past communicates itself to the audience only in the act of reading or reciting.[47] That does not mean that the poetic form hopelessly estranges us from the facts. Theodor W. Adorno's statement, to write poetry after Auschwitz is barbaric,[48] is not supercilious simply because it derives from a possibly literalist aesthetic, but rather because it dismisses one of the many representational forms that are based on the reproduction of the word, that is, on the faithful actualization of the verbal traces of the events written on external memory, and thus leaves reception no more room for escape. Even the half-hearted retraction offered in *Negative Dialectics*[49] misses precisely the central point: the congruence of text and *mneme* produced by the poetic form.[50]

Primo Levi's narratives, for their part, can be considered paradigmatic because the author's choice of prose is already committed to a description of facts. This does not cancel the uniqueness of this witness's view from the very inside of the Shoah. His view from inside is also not covered over by moral or ethical lessons, from which one could already draw certainties about how to evaluate what happened. But it is not the proximity to reality of these narratives that seems to hinder our present understanding of the Shoah, but rather the involvement of description, conditioned by inert models of reception, in prefabricated interpretations, whether these have a religious, historical-metaphysical, moral, or historiographical basis. Whether one remembers the Shoah with Levi, Sutzkefer, or other poets, with platitudes from television series, with national memorials over which various religious organizations and concessionaires will disagree, with putatively sober analyses of historical material or helpless verbal flourishes, has to do first and finally with the politics of memory.

Notes

Unless otherwise noted, all translations of quotation are my own.

1. James E. Young, *Writing and Rewriting the Holocaust: Narrative and the Consequences of Interpretation* (Bloomington, Ind., 1988), 24–25.

2. The restriction of scope here to academic history is not only out of modesty, but also for reasons of methodological simplification. A comprehensive account of representing the Shoah from the outside would naturally have to include fictional, essayistic, and other genres (e.g., documentary films such as Karl Fruchtmann's 1986 polyvocal montage *Ein einfacher Mensch* [rebroadcast by *Arte* on January 26, 1995], in which a survivor's life is reconstructed by the filmmaker from auto- and heterobiographical narrative fragments).

3. This designation follows Raul Hilberg's comprehensive account, *The Destruction of the European Jews,* rev. ed., 3 vols. (New York, 1985).

4. Another example of such descriptions are paraphrased case histories from the pens of expert witnesses on both sides. See William G. Niederland, *Folgen der Verfolgung: Das Überlebenden-Syndrom Seelenmord* (Frankfurt, 1980).

5. Young, *Writing,* 24.

6. Ibid., 24.

7. Ibid., 31.

8. The pointed criticism formulated by François Dagognet against the use of the concept of nature in philosophy, as well as in metamethodological discussions, might be instructive; see François Dagognet, *Nature* (Paris, 1990).

9. Tzvetvan Todorov, *Les abus de la mémoire* (Paris, 1995), 18–19.

10. Otherwise we would forget the fact that tradition can be questioned with impunity under a republican constitution.

11. Todorov, *Les abus,* 15.

12. This meaning is also attested in the form *chorbon (status constructus: chorban);* see the glossary in Ignaz Bernstein, *Jüdische Sprichwörter und Redensarten* (Wiesbaden, 1988), xliii.

13. See, for example, Abraham Sutzkefer, *der jojresch fun regn* (Tel Aviv, 1992), 86.

14. Young, *Writing,* 143.

15. On the same subject, see Alexandre Métraux, "Über die Vergegenwärtigung der Shoah und die Politik des Gedächtnisses," *Psychoanalyse im Widerspruch* 8 (1992): 72–88.

16. According to Young, *Writing,* 200 n. 8, one of the earliest, and perhaps *the* earliest uses of the term "Holocaust" to designate the persecution of the Jews is found in a footnote in A.A. Brill's introduction to his collection of English translations of Freud. Brill writes, "Alas! Just as these pages are going to the printer we have been startled by the terrible news that the Nazi holocaust has suddenly encircled Vienna and that Dr. Freud and his family are virtual prisoners in the hands of civilization's greatest scourge." (A.A. Brill, ed., *The Basic Writings of Sigmund Freud* [New York, 1938], 32).

17. See Hans Mommsen, *Der Nationalsozialismus und die deutsche Gesellschaft* (Reinbek, 1991), 184–232.

18. Quoted in Maja Pflug, *Natalia Ginzburg: Eine Biographie* (Berlin, 1995), 164.

19. Georges-Arthur Goldschmidt, *Quand Freud voit la mer: Freud et la langue allemande* (Paris, 1988), 196.

20. On the use of historical sources in this novel, see Levi, *If Not Now, When?* trans. William Weaver (New York, 1985), 347–348 (first published in Italian as *Se non ora, quando?* [Turin, 1982]).

21. Levi, *If Not Now, When?,* 282. In the original, the passage reads, "Ho altro da dirvi, ho trovato un camion!" (see idem, *Se non ora, quando?,* 305). The German translation has, "Ich hab euch was Wichtiges zu sagen: ich habe einen Lastwagen gefunden" (see idem, *Wann, wenn nicht jetzt?* [Munich, 1986], 378–379).

22. Levi, *If Not Now,* 282.

23. See Levi, *Se non ora,* 209: "Pavel non era pratico, bisognava che l'indomani stesso qualcuno andasse sul posto con lui. Chi era pratico di camion? Chi li sapeva guidare? La banda aveva fatto a piedi piú di mille chilometri: non era forse ora di viaggiare in camion?"

24. Victor Klemperer, *The Language of the Third Reich: A Philologist's Notebook,* trans. Martin Brady (London, 2000), 227.

25. Yosef Hayim Yerushalmi, *Zakhor: Jewish History and Jewish Memory* (Seattle, 1982), 98.

26. Ibid., 99.

27. Primo Levi, "Lo scrittore non scrittore," quoted in Gabriela Poli and Georgio Calcagno, *Echi di una voce perduta: Incontri, interviste, e conversazione con Primo Levi* (Milano, 1992), 98.

28. On Levi's life and works, see Myriam Anissimov, *Primo Levi: Tragedy of an Optimist,* trans. Steve Cox (Woodstock, N.Y., 1999).

29. Primo Levi, *If This Is a Man; and, The Truce;* trans. Stuart Woolf (New York, 1959) (first published in Italian as *Se questo è un uomo; La Tregua* (Turin, 1972).

30. Primo Levi, *The Periodic Table,* trans. Raymond Rosenthal (New York, 1984) (first published in Italian as *Il sistema periodico* [Turin, 1975]).

31. Primo Levi, *The Drowned and the Saved,* trans. Raymond Rosenthal (New York, 1988) (first published in Italian as *I sommersi e I salvati* [Turin, 1986]).

32. Interview with Mario Miccinesi, "Un romanzo storico costruito secondo i modelli classici," *Uomini e Libri,* November/December 1982.

33. On autobiographical memory, see John Kotre, *White Gloves: How We Create Ourselves through Memory* (New York, 1995).

34. See Raul Hilberg, *Sonderzüge nach Auschwitz,* trans. Gisela Schleicher (Frankfurt am Main, 1987) (first published in English as *The Role of the German Railroads in the Destruction of the Jews* [1976], paper presented at the annual meeting of the American Sociological Association).

35. See Primo Levi, *La ricerca della radici: Antologia personale* (Turin, 1981), chap. 10.

36. Levi, "Lo scrittore non scrittore," 97.

37. Levi, in a talk on *The Periodic Table,* in Poli and Calcagno, *Echi,* 83.

38. On the relationship between chemistry and literature, see Giancarlo Bori, *Le divine impurità: Primo Levi tra scienza e letteratura* (Rimini, 1992).

39. On these different versions, see Ernesto Ferrero, "Cronologia," in Primo Levi, *Opere* (Turin, 1987), vol. 1, XXXIIII–LXII.

40. On citation and paraphrase, see Nelson Goodman, "Some Questions Concerning Citation," in *Ways of Worldmaking* (Indianapolis, 1978), 41–56.

41. Levi, "Lo scrittore non scrittore," 83.

42. Levi, *The Drowned and the Saved,* 83–84.

43. Victor Klemperer, *To the Bitter End: The Diaries of Victor Klemperer,* trans. Martin Chalmers (London, 1999), 56 and passim.

44. Abraham Sutzkefer, "farfrojrene jidn," in *poetische werk* (Tel Aviv, 1963) vol.1, 362–363. For biographical data, see Abraham Nowerschtern, *Abraham Sutzkefer-Bibliographie* (Tel Aviv, 1976), 52, no. 268.

45. "hoßtu gesen iber felder mit schnej / farfrojrene jidn, a rej noch a rej? // si lign on otem, farmirmlt un blo / nor tojt is in zejere kerperß nito" (*poetische werk,* 362).

46. In the eighth strophe, Sutzkefer writes that he has seen all kinds of dead, and can no longer be surprised by one: "ch'hob alerlej tojtn farsucht bis aher / un ch'ken mich schojn kejner nit wundern mer" (ibid., 362).

47. On the poetological assumption behind this claim, see Jacques Roubaud, *L'invention du fils de Leopreps: Poésie et Mémoire* (Saulxures, 1993).

48. Theodor W. Adorno, "Kulturkritik und Gesellschaft," *Gesammelte Schriften* 10.1 (Frankfurt am Main, 1977), 30.

49. "Perennial suffering has as much right to expression as a tortured man to scream; hence it may have been wrong to say that after Auschwitz you could no longer write poems" (Theodor W. Adorno, *Negative Dialectics,* trans. E.B. Ashton [New York, 1973], 362).

50. On the subject of Yiddish poetry "after Auschwitz" (*dixit* Adorno), see Rachel Ertel, *Dans la langue de personne: Poésie yiddish de l'anéantissement* (Paris, 1993).

CHAPTER 12

Albert Speer's Memories of the Future
On the Historical Consciousness of a Leading Figure in the Third Reich

HARALD WELZER

Arrived in Peking today. But when I got to the Imperial Palace, some sort of demonstration was taking place. Two, three, four thousand people—who knows! In the midst of the ebb and flow of the never-ending crowd I quickly lost all orientation; the uniformity of the people frightened me as well. I left the city as quickly as I could.
—Albert Speer, *Spandauer Tagebücher*
[Spandau: The secret diaries]

The description of this hasty departure occurs under the entry for July 13, 1959, in Albert Speer's prison diary in Spandau. The year 1959 was the thirteenth year of Speer's twenty-year prison sentence—how did he get to Peking during this period? Quite simply, by walking. And not just to Peking, but to Istanbul, to Vladivostok, to Karachi, and to other exotic regions and cities. Of the 31,816 kilometers of his journey round the earth, he had completed exactly 14,260 when he reached Peking. "If someone had told me then," reflected Speer, "at the beginning of my walk to Heidelberg, that my journey would take me to the Far East, I would have thought he was mad or that I would become so."[1]

Speer had begun his walk five years before; he meticulously recorded every kilometer traveled in one of his numerous statistics (for 1954–1955 these amounted to 2,367 kilometers; for 1955–1956, 3,326 kilometers, etc.). In reality, of course, Speer merely took a turn round the garden of Spandau prison, but he precisely worked out his imaginary itinerary in advance with the help

---

Notes for this section can be found on page 255.

of atlases, travel guides, and textbooks, and imagined himself just as precisely on the routes and in cities of his journey, including the thirst he would experience as the result of extreme drought in the desert regions, the cold in Siberia, the boredom in Vladivostok, and as mentioned, the loss of orientation in Peking. Apart from the imaginary experience of the countryside, the heroic achievement of his walk around the world was important to Speer. "Right next to the Bering Strait, still stony hill country, an endless view of a treeless rocky landscape. Sometimes I see one of those polar foxes slinking by, whose way of life I recently found out about. But I also met bear-seals and the Kamchatka beaver, called a kalan."

> The Bering Strait is 72 kilometers wide and frozen till mid March. After I heard that … I increased the number of kilometers I covered a week from fifty to sixty; by arriving at the right time, I could then still cross the Bering Strait. I am probably be the first Central European to cross over to America on foot.[2]

Reaching the Bering Strait coincided with Speer's 78,514th turn round the prison garden. That evening in his cell Speer calculated that he had gone a kilometer too far. "I found myself," he noted with concern, "already on the ice in the Bering Strait. One really has to be damned careful."[3]

If one leaves aside some of the absurdity of Speer's dreamed horizons, what his journey around the world provided him with becomes clear: with the material for statistics. Speer unceasingly calculated spatial volumes, the seconds past and remaining, the weight of earth moved in the garden, meters traveled, and so forth. His journey made him physically fit, it functioned as an alternative world to his reduced daily round in the prison, it passed the time, and it provided a confirmation, not only of Speer's unbroken productivity, but also of his unbroken heroic capacity, his gift for fulfilling every task far beyond what could be expected. Albert Speer is, of course, also the best at walking.

Let us go back in time. Albert Speer, Hitler's chief architect and later munitions minister, had always accomplished great things. Speer planned and erected Hitler's new Berlin imperial chancellery, a building of 420 rooms and 360,000 cubic meters of interior space, with a gallery twice the length of that of Versailles, within a year. Despite progressively deteriorating conditions, he increased munitions production dramatically within a year of his assumption of office (e.g., weapons by 27 percent, tanks by 25 percent, and ammunition by no less than 97 percent).[4] Although according to his own testimony he remained an artist at heart and did not like his new task, he proved himself in this domain, as in all other duties and roles with which he was entrusted, to be the top of his class. He constantly increased armaments and manufacturing production, which as late as June 1944, reached its highest level ever.[5] At the same time, with his architect friend Hitler, he pored over the plans for Germania, the new world capital; for Linz, the retirement retreat for the Führer; and for Nuremburg, the city of the imperial party cult. Yet it became ever clearer to Speer that Hitler's competence as a strategist was deeply flawed and that all the plans advanced thus far would quite possibly no longer come to fruition.

When Speer recognized, late in the day, that the radical nature of Hitler's plans quite consistently involved consigning the German people to its ruin, since it had proved itself to be the weaker, he began to distance himself from Hitler, counteracting his directions and feverishly composing memoranda, which regularly drove Hitler into a fury. Finally, Speer planned an attack on Hitler, but this, alone among his projects, failed.

At the Nuremburg trial of the main war criminals, Speer was the only one among the accused to confess to an overall responsibility for the crimes committed in the name of Germany and to distance himself from his fellow accused. This immediately won him the respect of the observers, the press, and also of the prison psychologist G.M. Gilbert, who, faced with the other accused, increasingly became a cynic.[6] As a result, Speer was not sentenced to death, but to twenty years imprisonment, which he of course considered just, even if he reported in his diary regrets of having become Hitler's munitions minister. As Hitler's chief architect, Speer would certainly have remained completely unhindered and would have been able to continue his career as an architect and city planner in bomb-damaged postwar Germany, surely in brilliant fashion.

How does a man, who had been so powerful and who was not without vanity, deal with the complete frustration, indeed the nullification of all his plans—how does he come to terms with having to consign his dreams forever to the dustbin of history and having to adjust himself to two decades of inferior existence as prisoner number 5? Initially at any rate, Speer did so by simply remaining the model pupil he had always been. When brooding in his Spandau cell, Speer catches himself repeatedly imagining that in Hitler's "worldgovernment" he would have been one of the most respected men. Yet he does the prisoner's duty in Spandau in as disciplined and upright a way as he had all his previous offices.[7] For twenty years, Speer remained the model pupil; he remained it too when he published his memoirs, his diaries, his settling of scores with the SS,[8] his rambling criticism of technology,[9] and last but not least, his architectural showcase volume, in which he accounted for—what else?—his dazzling activity as an architect during the Third Reich.[10]

Most of Speer's interpreters have overlooked precisely this point—that he was always the model architect, the model minister, the model accused, the model repenter, the model prisoner, and the model historical witness. Seen in this light, he pursued a completely unbroken line through the starkly contrasting sections of his life—admittedly always a little offended that history had not accorded him equal rank with his fellow architects Mies van der Rohe, Le Corbusier, Peter Behrens, and Bruno Taut.

Speer loved to quote what Sebastian Haffner wrote about him in the *London Observer* in 1944:

> In a certain sense, Speer is more important for Germany today than Hitler, Himmler, Göring, Goebbels, or the generals—they have all somehow become nothing more than assistants to this man, who in fact drives the mighty engine, out of which he extracts the maximum of performance. In him we see a precise realization of the revolution of the managers. Speer is not one of the striking and picturesque Nazis. It is indeed unknown whether he has any political views other than the conventional. He could have joined any other political party, as long as it gave him work and a career. He is, in a pronounced fashion, the successful average person, well-dressed, polite, not corrupt; in his lifestyle, together with his wife and six children, he is decidedly middle-class. To a far lesser extent than any other German leader does he resemble anything typically German or typically National Socialist. He symbolizes indeed a type, which in all the belligerents has become increasingly important: the pure technician, the classless, brilliant man without a background, who knows no other goal than to make his way in the world, purely on the basis of his technical and organizational capabilities.... This is his age. That of Hitler and of Himmler we may get rid of, but that of Speer, whatever may be the fate of this individual man, will be with us for a long time.[11]

Speer's ambition made him overlook the fact that Haffner not only considered him to be more important than Hitler, but in a certain sense, also more dangerous: the modern age will not be able to rid itself of Speer's type—the technocrat who performs his duty in an exemplary manner under all conditions.

Yet Speer had thought of himself as a romantic, as the last classicist, who wanted to give back to the modern age of architecture and cities capitals, marble, and human figures—admittedly, as he himself later recognized, not on a human scale, but rather with everything magnified spatially and temporally to an immoderate degree—megalomaniacal architecture for an eternal empire.

And now, with eternity, I have come to Albert Speer's historical consciousness, for which both during and after his Spandau imprisonment a curious clamping together of past and future is characteristic. In Speer's biography, as well as in his diary entries—revised diary entries no doubt—that is, in his retrospective reflections, it becomes unusually clear that, at all times, experiences refer as much to the past as to the future. As Albert Schütz has elaborated, a general principle of experience is that it carries within it unrealized future, which not only puts its stamp on the reading of the past, but also determines current interpretations and anticipations. According to Schütz, experience refers to a future and contains the consequences of anticipated actions. In Schütz's view, every experience "bears protentions of events in it, whose immediate succession is expected ... and it bears anticipations of temporally distant events in it with which current experience according to expectation is connected."[12]

The future, which is inherent to experience, is carried by the anticipation of temporally far distant events, which are perceived in a future perfect mode: it will have happened; a mode, that is, which in an anticipatory sketch already looks back on that which is imagined as having already come to pass. One example of such an "anticipated retrospection"[13] would indeed be a journey around the world, at the beginning of which the traveler who is about to set off in anticipation looks back on the various accomplished stretches of his journey.

According to this thesis, such anticipated retrospection, which I would like to illustrate below with some of Speer's writings, is, in the case of success, consummated, and then sinks, like an accomplished task, into the more or less insignificant past. However—and with regard to questions of historical consciousness and the history of experience, this is of more interest—in the case of failure, that is, in the case of the anticipated result of the action not coming to pass, the unconsummated future, which is contained in the anticipated retrospective, remains virulent and continues to have an effect, both as an interpretative element and as a motive for action. This thesis may also, incidentally, be formulated as a negative version of Bloch's theorem concerning unconsummated hope, which despite contradictory facticity, provides the impulse for revolutionary change.

Let us begin with the perhaps best-known, and at any rate, most striking example of anticipated retrospection from Speer's National Socialist past: the so-called ruin-value theory. This theory originated in 1934, at the time Speer received the commission to restyle the Nuremberg party/conference grounds according to the scale and aspirations of the Thousand Year Reich. The relatively new Nuremberg tram depot had to disappear prior to the construction of the Zeppelin field. When Speer passed by the wrecked reinforced concrete construction, out of which the iron components protruded and had already begun to rust, he shuddered at the thought that the buildings he had designed for the new Reich would at some point in history also be in such a wretched condition. As a result, Speer developed his conception of the "ruin-value," which was nothing other than an aesthetic calculation of decay: What will the structures we build today look like in a thousand years—what does this say about the ideas that we embodied in them? "The employment of particular materials as well as attention to particular structural considerations," wrote Speer, "was meant to make buildings possible, which in a state of decay, after hundreds or (so we calculated) thousands of years would resemble the Roman models."[14]

This anticipated retrospection also received a material shape: "To illustrate my ideas, I had a romantic drawing made: it showed what the grandstand of the Zeppelin field would look like after generations of neglect, covered with ivy, with collapsed pillars, the walls here and there fallen down, but in broad outline still clearly recognizable." Among Hitler's entourage this drawing was regarded as "blasphemy. The mere idea that I had calculated a period of decline for the freshly established thousand-year Reich seemed unheard of to many. But the idea struck Hitler as sensible and logical."[15] The manifestation of the greatness of a then already fallen empire designed in the future, documents in future perfect the enormous superfluity of a (negative) utopia, with which Speer, and with him, the other planners and builders of the Thousand Year Reich began their work. What becomes of this superfluity of utopia, when reality dashes any hope that the anticipated retrospection will ever materialize?

Speer had already begun to draw again when he was in prison in Nuremberg, after he had ordered paper and pencil to make notes. His diary recorded the first drawing as "view of the Zeppelin field. The old version with continuous side pillars." He commented approvingly of this drawing: "It was better, after all, than that made later. The first idea is usually the right one, if there is no fundamental error."[16] Here it is the architect who is speaking, objectively, subjecting the earlier solution to a problem to a renewed examination.

According to his diary entries, Speer's next drawings were plan sketches (for example, for the family house of an American guard[17] or for a summerhouse in Maine). After receiving some specialist magazines, he was filled, as he writes, with "the desire to draw," and he drew nothing other than a "completed ... sketch of a field of ruins with oaks." Speer does not reveal what kind of ruins were involved. In a seeming non sequitur he continued directly: "In the afternoon read Margaret Boveri's American primer with great interest. The development of the United States is impressive. A huge experiment beneath portents thoughtout on a grand scale."[18] The association between the "portents thoughtout on a grand scale" of the social development of a state that had always fascinated Speer and the "field of ruins with oaks" is in no sense accidental. The reminiscence of anticipated retrospection occurs here in a twofold manner: in a drawing analogous to those that illustrated the theory of ruin-value, and as a related effect of the "portents thoughtout on a grand scale," of which one may surmise that they referred to the technocratic imperative of postwar American society. Here, when drawing as well as reading, Speer was working on the future of his past.

Drawings of ruins continued to occupy Speer. For instance, Speer completed a sketch of a dilapidated temple, with a grieving woman sitting before it,[19] or a less abstract sketch of the fallen pillars of the portico of the great hall, which he had planned as the high point of the city design for Germania—at this stage with a modest wooden hut in the foreground.[20] But Speer's anticipated retrospection not only lived on in the form of such drawings, but also in his mania for construction, which continued unremittingly to find expression, even in Spandau prison. The former chief planner of the Third Reich, responsible not just for the rebuilding of the imperial capital, but for building in the conquered and occupied eastern territories too, built roads and cities, reduced to scale according to the measurements of the Spandau prison garden, all with his accustomed supreme exertion and to the not inconsiderable annoyance of his fellow prisoners.

> In spring I dug a pit, laid out a sunken rockery in it and in the roughly half a meter deep hollow built right-angled terraces twenty to forty centimeters high with many thousands of bricks, which, in order to get some exercise, I carted there from an unused part of the prison grounds. "What do you want to do with the stones?" asked Neurath, "I've never seen anyone bring bricks into a garden."[21]

The answer to Neurath's question is simple, even if there is no record of what Speer said to him. But he immediately adds what drove him: "If I now," he wrote, "as this morning, lie in the middle of the lawn, these brick terraces look like a little city."[22] From the view from below, lying on his back looking up, dreaming himself into a city he had built—for such a return into the anticipations of the past, hardly any effort seems too big for Speer. At the cost of a tremendous physical exertion, he grades paths through the prison garden—twenty meters long and eight meters wide. One leads from the "prison exit to my avenue flanked by flower beds, which in memory of the planned Berlin showpiece boulevard ran in a north–south direction."[23]

In all of this, Speer attached value to the same precepts for action that had characterized his planning successes in the 1930s and 1940s: a maximum of personal involvement, minute planning, a precise statistical calculation of the individual processes, including the masses of earth moved, the quantity of energy thereby expended, and the progress achieved. Hence, he reported:

> Once I had determined to build the road horizontally, I had already got to half a meter above the normal level and had thus built a kind of high road. The embankment is a welcome pretext for constructing a continuous rockery on the east side of the road. With a width of four meters I have to fetch great quantities of sand and oven-slag.
>
> These are industrious days. The success in medical figures: my blood pressure, which in recent years has been 110, has risen to 130/75, while both of my sedentary or promenading fellow prisoners only attain 100/65. Admittedly, Schirach and Heß have, of late, occupied themselves again in the garden, but only when the presence of the Russian director is looming. Their area of garden ... is, however, only a thirtieth of mine.[24]

The entries quoted are scattered over a period of fifteen years, which indicates that Speer's occupation with the anticipated retrospection was by no means confined to the first period of his imprisonment and should perhaps be interpreted as a more or less bizarre form of grieving. The opposite is the case. The objects, the means, and the range of his never-resting activity, it is true, have changed beneath the dumb pressure of circumstances, but not the modes of his activity themselves. If one takes into account that, in fact, only very few of Speer's buildings actually passed beyond the planning stage, the cities from the view from below and the boulevards in the prison garden do not, in a concrete sense, stand for the real ones, which were to put their stamp on the face of Germania; rather, they *are* them—but simply reduced in various respects to scale. Moreover, as time passed, Speer's fellow prisoners registered the deeper meaning of his activity fairly accurately. When Speer finished his second rockery, Schirach commented in passing: "Like the walls of Nineveh. Or a party conference site for garden gnomes. Magnificent!"[25]

Amidst all of this it has to be remembered that Speer's apparently manic activities unfolded within the surroundings of an uneventful, isolated, and socially extremely reduced daily routine in prison. It must necessarily remain open to speculation what form his drive to shape his surroundings would have found in other circumstances. But in this connection it is interesting to note that in the freedom of postwar German society in the 1950s, a boom in the construction of miniature worlds also occurred—to be precise, in the rapid development of what amounted to a model-building movement, in particular, of model railways. Their "world composed of landscape references, rails, bridges, signal posts and village buildings is politically neutral"[26] and creates intact miniature worlds in the middle of devastated postwar Germany. In social-psychological terms, this seems to indicate the Federal Republic's interior social world "turning Swiss" at that period. At any rate, against this background, Speer's activities seem less peculiar; at most, they once more allow his tendency toward megalomania, even in small things, to come to the fore.

In parallel with his untiring production of monumentality "en miniature," Speer followed and commented on the rebuilding of Berlin, with which he was familiar thanks to daily newspapers and architectural magazines. He jealously noted deviances from the plans originally developed under his guidance, which did not occur all that often, since some of those responsible for the reconstruction were former members of his planning staff. To be sure, the reality outside Spandau prison caught up with him in other ways, which depressed him more. As early as 1946, when he was in prison in Nuremberg, on a cold winter night when his cell was so cold that he had to put on every available item of clothing, Speer noticed that he was also wearing a winter jacket that had been developed in 1942 for the army with his advice. The hood, which he had fortunately provided for this jacket, now protected him against the worst.[27]

To Speer's consternation, he was confronted with another aspect of his creative work seven years later. His grey-haired fellow prisoner Neurath was allotted on health grounds a comfortable armchair as part of his cell furniture, which on delivery turned out to be a relic, designed by Speer, from the new chancellery. Speer's feelings at this unhoped for reunion wavered between satisfaction and melancholy. On the one hand, the design of the armchair transported him to a past that, as he said, "[was] still quite unburdened by war, persecution, foreign workers, guilt complexes. There was nothing embarrassing about the piece of furniture itself, nothing exaggerated, nothing pompous; a plain chair, good craftsmanship."[28] On the other hand, he made the sobering discovery that this chair was possibly the only thing that would remain of his tireless work of twelve years. "The chancellery has already been demolished, the Nuremberg parade ground is to be blown up, nothing else remains any more of all the grandiose plans that were to transform the architectural face of Germany. How often had Hitler said to me that the greatness of our buildings would still bear witness to the greatness of our age after thousands of years— and now this chair."[29]

Of course, Speer would not have been Speer had he remained content with this melancholy finding and gloomily contemplated the precipitate obliteration of all the gigantic plans. His way of failing is highly specific. He himself, he reflected further, had been the last classicist, the final point in a four-thousand-year architectural tradition, which had now reached its end. In addition, he added, in the future there would be no more stonemasons who could chisel a cornice out of stone, no more carpenters who could put together a staircase, no more stuccoworkers who could produce a ceiling. A Palladio or a Schinkel who had to deal with steel, concrete, and glass would simply no longer be Schinkel or Palladio—and Speer's verdict followed accordingly: "Our epoch ... was really the farewell to a long and difficult tradition. So it may not be just a coincidence that nothing remained of our plans: nothing but a chair."[30]

One notices, even without a great effort at interpretation, how Speer also reassigns failure, or rather failure in particular, to the greatness that constitutes this failure. The anticipated retrospection of the ruin-value theory reappears once more quite clearly in this construction. Further instances of fantasies about greatness in the face of its contradiction occur pervasively in Speer's notes, as in the entry in which he is infuriated to learn from the daily newspaper that the Berlin heating device and equipment plant was now working on the urgent improvement of a coal-fired geyser. "It's incredible: in plants like this not long ago the threshold to a new age was crossed. The first jet engines in the world were put to the test here; the first rockets in the world were tried out here, the first plastics developed! And now in the same place, commissions are wrestling with problems that artisans solved at the turn of the century: a coal-fired geyser with a hot and cold water regulator!"[31]

One can sum up by saying that Speer's historical consciousness was composed of apparently highly disparate elements. On the one hand, he was an artist at heart, and the last classicist among architects; on the other hand, he was a coolly planning technocrat, oriented toward the paradigms of the possible. In moments of self-infatuated overexaltation, he was a star architect on a par with "Sharun and Le Corbusier, Poelzig and Mendelssohn."[32] At other times, he was the power-hungry member of a dreamed-up world government—even if his power, though for only a relatively short time, was in no sense merely a fantasy, but was very real. The common denominator among the apparently disparate elements was the excessiveness in everything: the anticipated future, which was to be found in every facet of his activity and in every motive of his efforts, at the height of his power or, as shown, in the prison garden in Spandau.

Speer formulated the excessive aspiration itself, which not only drove him during his life, but which had every possible means of being realized available to it for a period, when he recalled what "feelings of exaltation" filled him when through his mere "signature [he] had power over billions and directed hundreds of thousands of people on the building sites." Nevertheless, he immediately went on, "I am fairly certain I would have happily given away all the power in the world, I was enough of an artist for that, if I had been allowed one perfect building, like the Pantheon, the dome of St. Peter's or one of the temple-like villas of Palladio."[33]

In this passage, someone without doubt still considers himself a genius and one could conclude the examination of a more or less interesting figure with this finding, if Speer's example did not reveal anything else: in examining him it becomes clear that the cognitive and emotional processing of the past takes place on completely different levels of consciousness. What one could call the cognitive historical consciousness operates against the background of the knowledge of how history has turned out and is capable of handling the contemporary view of things reflectively and in a revisionist way. An experiential historical consciousness, on the other hand, operates with reenactments of a past belonging directly to the individual's own life story, which is not at all susceptible to conscious reflection. Even when, as in Speer's case, on the cognitive level, the processing of and reflections on guilt and entanglement, which deserve to be taken quite seriously, are available, and from case to case provide illuminating assessments of the driving forces of National Socialist rule, something quite different asserts itself on another level of consciousness. This is the experiential-historical state, which is affected by that which was lived during a vital stage of the biography and also by what was dreamed. One should not forget that for a period of his life Speer was a socially recognized genius and that his designs for the future were embedded in a utopianism that enjoyed full social recognition. The anticipated retrospection that Speer developed in this period and that is most clearly embodied in the ruin-value theory was maintained in various forms for the rest of his life.

In experiential-historical terms, past, present, and future are, as Albert Speer's example shows, inseparable. Recollection seems here to be less a restitution than a "constitution of an area of experience of its own kind,"[34] which contains the past as a structural quality and not as a discarded story—to overstate this somewhat, as form, not quantity. Speer's experience of the present organizes itself structurally like the experience of the past, and, conversely, the remembered past exists only in agreement with the organization of current perceptions. There is a dialectical relationship between past and future, in which both become equally relevant for the purposes of interpretation and action.

I am now coming to the end, and return to the beginning—to Speer's journey to Peking and to his imaginary flight from this metropolis. Reflecting on why he decided to flee from Peking immediately, Speer concluded that in the shape of Peking "that imperial metropolis has indeed arisen, which I … had planned, but could not build. The Heavenly Palace, the giant square, the great avenue, the tremendous reception hall—for a moment, it all appeared to me like the realization of long-vanished dreams transplanted to East Asia."[35]

Notes

This Chapter was translated from the German original by a professional translation agency. Unless otherwise noted, all translations of quotations are provided by the agency.

1. Albert Speer, *Spandauer Tagebücher* (Frankfurt, 1975), 511. (Published in English as *Spandau: The Secret Diaries*, trans. Richard Winston and Clara Winston [New York, 1976]).
2. Speer, *Tagebücher*, 570.
3. Ibid.
4. Albert Speer, *Erinnerungen* (Frankfurt, 1969), 225. (Published in English as *Inside the Third Reich: Memoirs*, trans. Richard Winston and Clara Winston [New York, 1970]).
5. J. Dülffer, "Albert Speer: Management für Kultur und Wirtschaft," in *Die Braune Elite: 22 biographische Skizzen*, ed. Ronald Smelser and R. Zitelmann (Darmstadt, 1989), 258–272, here p. 265.
6. Gustav Mark Gilbert, *Nürnberger Tagebuch: Gespräche der Angeklagten mit dem Gerichtspsychologen*, trans. Margaret Carroux (Frankfurt, 1962). (First published in English as *The Psychology of Dictatorship: Based on an Examination of the Leaders of Nazi Germany*, [Westport, 1962]).
7. Speer, *Tagebücher*, 90.
8. Albert Speer, *Der Sklavenstaat* (Stuttgart, 1981) (Published in English as *Infiltration*, trans. Joachim Neugroschl [New York, 1981]).
9. Albert Speer, *Technik und Macht* (Esslingen, 1979).
10. Albert Speer, *Architektur: Arbeiten 1933–1942* (Berlin, 1978).
11. Sebastian Haffner (1944), quoted in Speer, *Erinnerungen*, 356.
12. Alfred Schütz, "Tiresias oder unser Wissen von zukünftigen Ereignissen," *Gesammelte Aufsätze vol. 2: Studien zur Soziologischen Theorie* (Den Haag, 1972). (Published in English as *Studies in Social Theory*, vol. 2 of *Collected Papers*, ed. Arvid Brodersen [New York, 1972], 268).
13. Ibid., 261.
14. Speer, *Erinnerungen*, 69.
15. Ibid.
16. Speer, *Tagebücher*, 35.
17. Ibid., 81.
18. Ibid., 81.
19. Ibid., 152.
20. Ibid., 160.
21. Ibid., 265.
22. Ibid., 265f.
23. Ibid., 513.
24. Ibid., 527.
25. Ibid., 543.
26. H. Walter, "Eins zu Eins: Ein Fotoalbum zum Wiederaufbau Deutschlands," in *Das Gedächtnis der Bilder: Ästhetik und Nationalsozialismus*, ed. Harald Welzer (Tübingen, 1995), 115–163, here p. 142.
27. Speer, *Tagebücher*, 49.
28. Ibid., 338.
29. Ibid., 339.
30. Ibid.
31. Ibid., 505.
32. Ibid., 617.
33. Ibid., 610.
34. Siegfried J. Schmidt, ed., *Gedächtnis: Probleme und Perspektiven der interdisziplinären Gedächtnisforschung* (Frankfurt, 1991), 35.
35. Speer, *Tagebücher*, 512.

Bibliography

Abraham, Hilda C., and Ernst Freud, eds. *A Psycho-Analytic Dialogue: The Letters of Sigmund Freud and Karl Abraham, 1907–1926.* New York, 1965.
Adorno, Theodor W. *Negative Dialectics,* trans. E.B. Ashton. New York, 1973.
———. "Kulturkritik und Gesellschaft." *Gesammelte Schriften* 10.1. Frankfurt am Main, 1977.
Allport, Gordon W. *Letters from Jenny.* New York, 1965.
Angehrn, Emil. *Geschichte und Identität.* Berlin, 1985.
Anissimov, Myriam. *Primo Levi: Tragedy of an Optimist,* trans. Steve Cox. Woodstock, N.Y., 1999.
Ankersmit, F.R. *Narrative Logic: A Semantic Analysis of the Historian's Language.* The Hague, 1983.
———. *History and Tropology: The Rise and Fall of Metaphor.* Berkeley, 1994.
Anzieu, Didier. *Freuds Selbstanalyse und die Entdeckung der Psychoanalyse,* vol. 1: 1895–1898. Munich, 1990.
Appleby, Joyce, Lynn Hunt, and Margaret Jacob. *Telling the Truth about History.* New York, 1994.
Ashby, Rosalyn, and Lee, Peter J. "Children's Concepts of Empathy and Understanding in History." In *The History Curriculum for Teachers,* ed. Christopher Portal, 62–88. London, 1987.
Assmann, Aleida. "Stabilisatoren der Erinnerung—Affekt, Symbol, Trauma." In *Die dunkle Spur der Vergangenheit: Psychoanalytische Zugänge zum kulturellen Gedächtnis,* ed. Jörn Rüsen and Jürgen Straub. Frankfurt, 1998.
Assmann, Jan. *Das kulturelle Gedächtnis: Schrift, Erinnerung und politische Identität in frühen Hochkulturen.* Munich, 1992.
Austin, J.L. *How to Do Things with Words.* New York, 1962.
Averill, J.R. *Anger and Aggression.* New York, 1982.
Bakhtin, M. *The Dialogic Imagination.* Austin, 1981.
Barthes, Roland. *S/Z.* London, 1975.
———. *The Responsibility of Forms: Criticial Essay on Music, Art, and Representation.* New York, 1985.
Bartlett, Fredric C. *Remembering: A Study in Experimental and Social Psychology.* Cambridge, U.K., 1932.
Bauer, Gerhard. *'Geschichtlichkeit': Wege und Irrwege eines Begriffs.* Berlin, 1963.
Baumeister, Roy F. *Identity: Cultural Change and the Struggle for Self.* New York, 1986.
Belgrad, Jürgen, Bernard Görlich, Hans-Dieter König, and Gunzelin Schmid Noerr, eds. *Zur Idee einer psychoanalytischen Sozialforschung: Dimensionen szenischen Verstehens.* Frankfurt, 1987.
Bell, Carleton J. "The Historic Sense." *Journal of Educational Psychology* 8 (1971): 317–318.
Bell, Carleton J., and D.F. McCollum. "A Study of the Attainments of Pupils in United States History." *Journal of Educational Psychology* 8 (1971): 257–274.
Berger, P., and T. Luckmann. *The Social Construction of Reality.* New York, 1966.
Bernstein, Ignaz. *Jüdische Sprichwörter und Redensarten.* Wiesbaden, 1988.
Billmann-Mahecha, Elfriede. *Egozentrismus und Perspektivenwechsel. Empirisch-psychologische Studien zu kindlichen Verstehensleistungen im Alltag.* Göttingen, 1990.

Billmann-Mahecha, Elfriede, Ulrich Gebhard, and Patricia Nevers. "Naturphilosophische Gespräche mit Kindern. Ein qualitativer Forschungsansatz." In *Mit Kindern über Natur philosophieren,* ed. Helmut Schreier, 130–153. Heinsberg, 1979.

Blum, Harold P. "The Forbidden Guest and the Analytic Ideal: The Superego and Insight." *Psychoanalytic Quarterly* 50 (1981): 535–556.

Blumenberg, Hans. *Work on Myth.* Cambridge, Mass., 1985.

Boesch, Ernst. *Symbolic Action Theory and Cultural Psychology.* Berlin, 1991.

Böhme, Gernot. "Sinn und Gegensinn—über die Dekonstruktion von Geschichten." *Psyche* 44 (1990): 577–592.

Bollas, C. *Being a Character: Psychoanalysis and Self Experience.* New York, 1992.

Bolles, Edmund Blair. *A Second Way of Knowing.* New York, 1991.

Booth, Martin. "Ages and Concepts: A Critique of the Piagetian Approach to History Teaching." In *The History Curriculum for Teachers,* ed. Christopher Portal, 22–38. London, 1987.

———. "Students' Historical Thinking and the National History Curriculum in England." *Theory and Research in Social Education* 21.2 (1993): 105–127.

———. "Cognition in History: A British Perspective." *Educational Psychologist* 29 (1994): 61–70.

Booth, W. *The Rhetoric of Fiction.* Chicago, 1983.

Boothe, Brigitte. "Die Alltagserzählung in der Psychotherapie." *Berichte aus der Abteilung Klinische Psychologie* 29.1. Zürich, 1992.

———. *Der Patient als Erzähler in der Psychotherapie.* Göttingen, 1994.

Bori, Giancarlo. *Le divine impurità: Primo Levi tra scienza e letteratura.* Rimini, 1992.

Boring, E.G. *A History of Experimental Psychology.* New York, 1929.

Boueke, Dietrich, Frieder Schülein, Hartmut Büscher, Evamaria Terhorst, and Dagmar Wolf. *Wie Kinder erzählen: Untersuchungen zur Erzähltheorie und zur Entwicklung narrativer Fähigkeiten.* Munich, 1995.

Boueke, Dietrich, Frieder Schülein, and Dagmar Wolf. "Wie lernen Kinder, eine Geschichte zu erzählen? Zur Entwicklung narrativer Strukturen." *Forschung an der Universität Bielefeld* 11 (1995): 27–33.

Braudel, Fernand. *The Mediterranean and the Mediterranean World in the Age of Philip II,* 2 vols. New York, 1972–1974.

Brazelton, Berry T., and Bertrand G. Cramer. *Earliest Relationship: Parents, Infants and the Drama of Early Attachment.* Paperback reprint, Addison-Wesley, 1991.

Bretone, Mario. *Dieci modi di vivere il passato.* Rome, 1991.

Briffault, Richard. "Our Localism." Part 1: "The Structure of Local Government Law." *Columbia Law Review* 90 (1991): 1–115.

Brill, A.A., ed. *The Basic Writings of Sigmund Freud.* New York, 1938.

Brooks, Peter. *Reading for the Plot: Design and Intention in Narrative.* New York, 1984.

Brower, Reuben, ed. *On Translation.* Cambridge, Mass., 1959.

Brown, Ann L., and Joseph C. Campione. "Communities of Learning and Thinking, Or a Context by Any Other Name." In *Developmental Perspectives on Teaching and Learning Thinking Skills: Contributions in Human Development,* ed. Denna Kuhn. Vol. 21, 108–126. Basel, 1990.

Brown, John S., Allan Collins, and P. Duguid, "Situated Cognition and the Culture of Learning." *Educational Researcher* 18 (1988): 32–42.

Bruner, Edward M. "Ethnography as Narrative." In *The Anthropology of Experience,* ed. Victor W. Turner and Edward M. Bruner, 139–155. Urbana, 1986.

Bruner, Jerome S. *The Process of Education.* Cambridge, Mass., 1960.

———. "Narrative and Paradigmatic Modes of Thought." In *Learning and Teaching the Ways of Knowing,* ed. Elliot Eisner, 97–115. Chicago, 1985.

———. *Actual Minds, Possible Worlds.* Cambridge, Mass., 1986.

———. "Life as Narrative." *Social Research* 54 (1987): 15.

———. *Acts of Meaning.* Cambridge, Mass., 1990.

———. "Autobiography and Its Genres." Paper presented at the symposium "The Construction of the Self," University of Toronto, 1994.

Bullard, T.E. *Catalogue of Cases.* Vol. 2 of *UFO Abductions: The Measurement of a Mystery.* Mount Reinier, 1987.
Bunzl, Martin. "How to Change the Unchanging Past." *Clio: A Journal of Literature, History, and the Philosophy of History* 15 (1995): 181–193.
Callahan, Raymond. *Education and the Cult of Efficiency.* Chicago, 1962.
Campell, J. *The Hero with a Thousand Faces.* New York, 1956.
Camus, Albert. *The First Man,* trans. David Hapgood. New York, 1995.
Cantril, Hadley. *The Invasion from Mars.* Princeton, 1940.
Carey, Sue. *Conceptual Change in Childhood.* Cambridge, Mass., 1985.
Carr, David. *Time, Narrative, and History,* Bloomington, Ind., 1986.
Carr, David, Charles Taylor, and Paul Ricoeur, "Discussion: Ricoeur on Narrative." In *On Paul Ricoeur: Narrative and Interpretation,* ed. David Wood, 160–187. London, 1991.
Carr, E.H. *What Is History?* New York, 1965.
Carretero, Mario, and James F. Voss, eds. *Cognitive and Instructional Processes in History and the Social Sciences.* Hillsdale, N.J., 1994.
Casey, Edward S. *Remembering: A Phenomenological Study.* Bloomington, Ind., 1987.
Chafe, Wallace. "Some Things That Narratives Tell Us about the Mind." In *Narrative Thought and Narrative Language,* ed. Bruce K. Britton and A.D. Pellegrini, 79–98. Hillsdale, N.J., 1990.
Chartier, Roger. *Die unvollendete Vergangenheit: Geschichte und die Macht der Weltauslegung,* trans. Ulrich Raulff. Frankfurt, 1992.
———. "Zeit der Zweifel: Zum Verständnis gegenwärtiger Geschichtsschreibung." In Conrad and Kessel, eds., *Geschichte,* 83–97.
Clark, Eve V. "Meanings and Concepts." In *Handbook of Child Psychology,* ed. Paul H. Mussen. 4th ed. New York, 1983.
Clark, Ronald W. *Sigmund Freud.* Frankfurt, 1990.
Collingwood, Robert G. *The Idea of History.* Oxford, 1961.
Conrad, Christoph, and Martina Kessel. "Geschichte ohne Zentrum." In *Geschichte schreiben in der Postmoderne: Beiträge zur aktuellen Diskussion,* ed. Christoph Conrad and Martina Kessel, 9–36. Stuttgart, 1994.
Cortazzi, Martin. *Narrative Analysis.* London, 1993.
Cronon, W. "A Place for Stories: Nature, History, and Narrative." *Journal of American History* 78.4 (1992): 1347–1376.
Cushman, P. "Ideology Observed: Political Uses of the Self in Daniel Sterns Infant." *American Psychologist* 46 (1991): 206–219.
Dagognet, François. *Nature.* Paris, 1990.
Danto, Arthur C. *Analytical Philosophy of History.* Cambridge, U.K., 1968.
David, Lowenthal. *The Past Is a Foreign Country.* New York, 1985.
Davies, B., and R. Harre. "Positioning: 'The Discursive Productions of Selves.'" *Journal for the Theory of Social Behavior* 20 (1990): 43–63.
Dennis, Shemilt. "Adolescent Ideas about Evidence and Methodology in History." In Christopher Portal, ed. *The History Curriculum for Teachers,* 39–61.
Derrida, Jacques. *Of Grammatology.* Baltimore, 1976.
Diamond, Stanley. "Introductory Essay: Job and the Trickster." In *The Trickster: A Study in American Indian Mythology,* ed. Paul Radin, xi–xxii. New York, 1972.
Dipple, E. *The Unresolvable Plot: Reading Contemporary Fiction.* London, 1988.
Downey, Matthew T. "Historical Thinking and Perspective Taking in a Fifth-Grade Classroom." Paper presented at the meeting of the National Council for Social Studies, Phoenix, 1994.
Dülffer, J. "Albert Speer: Management für Kultur und Wirtschaft." In *Die Braune Elite: 22 biographische Skizzen,* ed. R. Smelser and R. Zitelmann, 258–272. Darmstadt, 1989.
Dunn, Judy. *Beginnings of Social Understanding.* Cambridge, Mass., 1988.
Dworkin, Ronald M. *Law's Empire.* Cambridge, Mass., 1986.
Egan, Kieran. "Layers of Historical Understanding." *Theory and Research in Social Education* 17.4 (1989): 280–294.

Eggert, Hartmut, Ulrich Profitlich, and Klaus S. Scherpe, eds. *Geschichte als Literatur: Formen und Grenzen der Representation von Vergangenheit.* Stuttgart, 1990.
Eisenmann, Barbara. *Erzählen in der Therapie.* Opladen, 1995.
Elms, Alan. "Freud, Irma, Martha: Sex and Marriage in the 'Dream of Irma's Injection.'" *Psychoanalytic Review* 67 (1980): 83–109.
Elstein, Arthur, Lee S. Shulman, and Sarah A. Sprafka. *Medical Problem Solving: An Analysis of Clinical Reasoning.* Cambridge, Mass., 1978.
Encyclopedia of Philosophy. New York, 1967.
Epstein, Seymour. "Implications of Cognitive-Experiential Self-Theory for Personality and Development." In *Studying Lives through Time: Personality and Development,* ed. David C. Funder et al., 399–434. Washington, D.C., 1993.
Ericsson, K. Anders, and J. Smith. *Toward a General Theory of Expertise.* Cambridge, Mass., 1987.
Erikson, Erik H. "Das Traummuster in der Psychoanalyse." *Psyche* 8 (1954–1955): S.561–604.
———. *Identity and the Life Cycle.* Vol. 1. New York, 1959.
Ertel, Rachel. *Dans la langue de personne: Poésie yiddish de l'anéantissement.* Paris, 1993.
Fehrenbacher, Don E., ed. *Abraham Lincoln: Speeches and Writings.* New York, 1989.
Feldman, Carol F. *The Development of Adaptive Intelligence.* San Francisco, 1974.
———. "Genres as Mental Models." In *Psychoanalysis and Development: Representations and Narratives,* ed. Massimo Ammaniti and Daniel N. Stern, 111–121. New York, 1994.
Feldman, Carol F., and David Kalmar. "Autobiography and Fiction as Modes of Thought." In *Modes of Thought: Explorations in Culture and Cognition,* ed. David Olson and Nancy Torrance, 106–122. Cambridge, U.K., 1996.
Fell, Albert T. "Epistemological and Ontological Queries Concerning David Carr's *Time, Narrative, and History.*" *Philosophy of the Social Sciences* 22 (1992), 370–380.
Ferrero, Ernesto. "Cronologia." In Primo Levi, *Opere.* Vol. 1, XXXIII–LXII. Turin, 1987.
Feynman, Richard. *Surely You're Joking, Mr. Feynman: Adventures of a Curious Character.* New York, 1985.
Fish, Stanley. *Is There a Text in the Class? The Authority of Interpretive Communities.* Cambridge, Mass., 1980.
Fishman, Robert. *The Rise and Fall of the Suburb.* New York, 1987.
Foucault, Michel. *The Archeology of Knowledge.* London, 1972.
Fowler, Alastair. *Kinds of Literature.* Cambridge, Mass., 1982.
Frege, Gottlob. "Über Sinn und Bedeutung." *Zeitschrift für Philosophie und Kritik* 100 (1892): 25–50.
Freud, Sigmund. *Totem and Taboo.* New York, 1918.
———. "Creative Writers and Day-Dreaming" (1908). In *The Standard Edition of the Complete Works of Sigmund Freud,* ed. James Strachey. Vol. 9, 143–153. London, 1962.
———. "Vorlesungen zur Einführung in die Psychoanalyse" [Complete introductory lectures on psychoanalysis]. In *Studienausgabe.* Vol. 1. Frankfurt, 1978.
———. *The Interpretation of Dreams* (1900). In *The Basic Writings of Sigmund Freud,* ed. A.A. Brill, 149–517. New York, 1995.
Friedman, William J. *About Time: Inventing the Fourth Dimension.* Cambridge, Mass., 1990.
Frisch, Michael. "American History and the Structure of Collective Memory: A Modest Exercise in Empirical Iconography." *Journal of American History* 75 (1989): 1130–1155.
Fromm, E. *Escape from Freedom.* New York, 1941.
Frye, Northrop. *Anatomy of Criticism.* Princeton, 1957.
———. "Fictional Modes and Forms." In *Approaches to the Novel,* ed. Richard Scholes, 23–42. San Fransisco, 1966.
Gadamer, Hans-Georg. *Reason in the Age of Science.* Cambridge, Mass., 1981.
Gagné, Ellen D. *The Cognitive Psychology of School Learning.* Boston, 1985.
Gallie, W. *Philosophy and the Historical Understanding.* London, 1994.
Gardner, Howard. *The Mind's New Science.* New York, 1985.
Geertz, Clifford. *Local Knowledge: Further Essays in Interpretative Anthropology.* New York, 1983.

Gendlin, Eugene T. "Thinking beyond Patterns: Body, Language, and Situations." In *The Presence of Feeling in Thought,* ed. Bernard den Ouden and Marcia Moen, 22–151. New York, 1991.
Genette, Gérard. *Narrative Discourse: An Essay in Method,* trans. Jane E. Lewin. Ithaca, 1980.
Gergen, Kenneth J. *The Saturated Self.* New York, 1991.
———. "Mind, Text and Society: Self-Memory in Social Context." In *The Remembering Self,* ed. R. Fivush. New York, 1994.
———. *Realities and Relationships.* Cambridge, Mass., 1994.
Gergen, Kenneth J., and Mary M. Gergen. "Narrative Form and the Construction of Psychological Science." In *Narrative Psychology: The Storied Nature of Human Conduct,* ed. Theodore R. Sarbin, 22–44. New York, 1986.
Gergen, Mary M. "Life Stories: Pieces of a Dream." In *Telling Lives,* ed. G. Rosenwald and R. Ochberg. New Haven, 1992.
Gergen, Mary M., and Kenneth J. Gergen. "The Social Construction of Narrative Accounts." In *Historical Social Psychology,* ed. Mary M. Gergen and Kenneth J. Gergen. Hillsdale, N.J., 1984.
Giddens, Anthony. *Modernity and Self-Identity.* Stanford, N.J., 1991.
Gilbert, Gustav Mark. *Nürnberger Tagebuch: Gespräche der Angeklagten mit dem Gerichtspsychologen,* trans. Margaret Carroux. Frankfurt, 1962. First published in English as *The Psychology of Dictatorship: Based on an Examination of the Leaders of Nazi Germany* (Westport, 1962).
Gladwin, Thomas. *East Is a Big Bird.* Cambridge, Mass., 1970.
Glass, Arnold Lewis, Keith James Holyoak, and John Lester Santa. *Cognition.* Reading, Mass., 1979.
Glenn, Charles. "The Role of Episodic Structure and of Story Length in Children's Recall of Simple Stories." *Journal of Verbal Learning and Verbal Behavior* 17 (1978): 229–247.
Goffman, Erving. *The Presentation of Self in Everyday Life.* New York, 1959.
Goldschmidt, Georges-Arthur. *Quand Freud voit la mer: Freud et la langue allemande.* Paris, 1988.
Goodman, Nelson. "Some Questions Concerning Citation." In *Ways of Worldmaking,* 41–56. Indianapolis, 1978.
———. "Twisted Tales: Or Story, Study, or Symphony." In Mitchell, ed. *On Narrative,* 99–115.
Gordon, Scott. *The History and Philosophy of Social Science: An Introduction.* New York, 1991.
Gorman, F.R., and D.S. Morgan. "A Study of the Effect of Definite Written Exercises upon Learning in a Course in American History." *Indiana School of Education Bulletin* 6 (1930): 80–90.
Gray, Ward. *Historian's Handbook.* Boston, 1959.
Greenberg, Ramon, and Chester Pearlman. "If Freud Only Knew: A Reconsideration of Psychoanalytic Dream Theory." *International Review of Psychoanalysis* 5 (1978): 711–775.
Griffin, S. *A Chorus of Stones.* New York, 1992.
Grinstein, Alexander. *On Sigmund Freud's Dreams.* New York, 1980.
Grunert, Johannes. "Freud und Irma. Genetische Aspekte zum Initialtraum der Psychoanalyse." *Psyche* 29 (1975): 721–744.
Gülich, Elisabeth, and Wolfgang Raible, ed. *Linguistische Textmodelle.* Munich, 1977.
Habermas, Jürgen. *Handlungsrationalität und gesellschaftliche Rationalisierung.* Vol. 1 of *Theorie des kommunikativen Handelns.* Frankfurt, 1981.
Hall, G. Stanley. *Educational Problems.* Vol. 2. New York, 1911.
Hänni, Rolf, and R. Hunkeler. "Von der Entwicklung der kindlichen Erzählsprache." *Schweizerische Zeitschrift für Psychologie* 39 (1980): 16–32.
Hanson, Norwood Russell. *Patterns of Discovery.* Cambridge, U.K., 1958.
Harlan, David. "Intellectual History and the Return of the Prodigal." *American Historical Review* 94.3 (1989): 581–609.
Harris, Roy, "How Does Writing Restructure Thought." *Language and Communication* 9 (1989): 99–106.
Hartman, Frank R. "A Reappraisal of the Emma Episode and the Specimen Dream." *Journal of the American Psychoanalytic Association* 31 (1983): 555–586.

Hausen, Monika. "Zeitbewußtsein von Kindern am Beispiel einer zweiten Grundschulklasse." Diss., University of Hannover, 1998.
Hayes, John, and Linda Flower. "Identifying the Organization of the Writing Process." In *Cognitive Processes in Writing,* ed. Lee W. Gregg and Erwin R. Steinberg, 3–30. Hillsdale, N.J., 1980.
Heidegger, Martin. *Being and Time.* New York, 1962.
Hempel, Carl G. "The Function of General Laws in History." *Journal of Philosophy* 39 (1942): 35–48.
Hermans, Hubert J.M., and Els Hermans-Jansen. *Self-Narratives: The Construction of Meaning in Psychotherapy.* New York, 1995.
Heussi, Karl. *Die Krise des Historismus.* Tübingen, 1932.
Hilberg, Raul. *The Destruction of the European Jews.* Rev. ed. 3 vols. New York, 1985.
———. *Sonderzüge nach Auschwitz,* trans. Gisela Schleicher. Frankfurt am Main, 1987. First published in English as *The Role of the German Railroads in the Destruction of the Jews* (1976).
Hirsch, E.D. *Validity in Interpretation.* New Haven, 1976.
Howard, George S. "Culture Tales: A Narrative Approach to Thinking, Cross-Cultural Psychology, and Psychotherapy." *American Psychologist* 46 (1991): 187–197.
Husserl, Edmund. *The Phenomenology of Internal Time Consciousness.* Bloomington, Ind., 1964. First published in German, 1893–1917.
Ignatieff, Michael. *The Russian Album.* London, 1987.
Jakobson, Roman. "Linguistics and Poetics." In *Style in Language,* ed. T. Sebeok, 350–377. Cambridge, Mass., 1960.
James, Henry, and Bernhard Richards. *The Spoils of Poynton.* Charlottesville, 1984.
Jeismann, Karl-Ernst. "Geschichtsbewußtsein." In *Handbuch der Geschichtsdidaktik,* ed. Klaus Bergmann et al. Vol. 1, 42. Düsseldorf, 1979.
———. *Geschichte als Horizont der Gegenwart: Über den Zusammenhang von Vergangenheitsbedeutung, Gegenwartsverständnis und Zukunftsperspektive.* Paderborn, 1985.
———. "Geschichtsbewußtsein als zentrale Kategorie der Geschichtsdidaktik." In *Geschichtsbewußtsein und historisch-politisches Lernen. Jahrbuch für Geschichtsdidaktik,* ed. Gerhard Schneider. Vol. 1, 1–27. Pfaffenweiler, 1988.
Jenkins, Keith. *Rethinking History.* London, 1991.
Jenkins, Keith, and Peter Brickley, "Reflections on the Empathy Debate." *Teaching History* 55 (1989): 18–23.
Joas, Hans. *Praktische Intersubjektivität: Die Entwicklung des Werkes von G. H. Mead.* Frankfurt, 1980.
Johnson, Nancy S. "What Do You Do If You Can't Tell the Whole Story? The Development of Summarization Skills." In *Children's Language,* ed. Keith E. Nelson. Vol. 4. Hillsdale, N.J., 1983.
Judd, Charles Hubbard. *Psychology of School Subjects.* Boston, 1915.
Jurd, M.F. "Adolescent Thinking in History-Type Material." *Australian Journal of Education* 17 (1973): 2–17.
Kaplan, Stanley M. "Narcissistic Injury and the Occurrence of Creativity: Freud's Irma Dream." *The Annual of Psychoanalysis* 12 (1984/1985): 367–376.
Keller, Barbara. *Rekonstruktion von Vergangenheit: Vom Umgang der 'Kriegsgeneration' mit Lebenserinnerungen.* Opladen, 1996.
Kemper, Susan. "The Development of Narrative Skills: Explanations and Entertainments." In *Discourse Development: Progress in Cognitive Development Research,* ed. Stan A. Kuczaj II, 99–124. New York, 1984.
Kerby, Anthony Paul. *Narrative and the Self.* Bloomington, Ind., 1991.
Kermode, Frank. "Secrets and Narrative Sequence." In Mitchell, *On Narrative,* 79–97.
Kintsch, W. "Learning from Text." *Cognition and Instruction* 3 (1986): 87–108.
Klemperer, Victor. *To the Bitter End: The Diaries of Victor Klemperer,* trans. Martin Chalmers. London, 1999.
———. *The Language of the Third Reich: A Philologist's Notebook,* trans. Martin Brady. London, 2000.

König, Hans-Dieter. "Die Methode der tiefenhermeneutischen Kultursoziologie." In *'Wirklichkeit' im Deutungsprozeß*, ed. Thomas Jung and Stefan Müller-Doohm, 190–222. Frankfurt, 1993.
Koselleck, Reinhart. *Futures Past: On the Semantics of Historical Time*, trans. Keith Tribe, 116–129. Cambridge, Mass., 1989.
Kotre, John. *White Gloves: How We Create Ourselves through Memory.* New York, 1995.
Kuper, Adam, and Alan A. Stone. "The Dream of Irma's Injection: A Structural Analysis." *The American Journal of Psychiatry* 139 (1982): 1225–1234.
Kurz, Gerhard. *Metapher, Allegorie, Symbol.* Göttingen, 1982.
Labouvie-Vief, Gisela. "Modes of Knowledge and the Organization of Development." In *Models and Methods in the Study of Adolescent and Adult Thought: Adult Development*, ed. Michael L. Commons et al. Vol. 2, 42–62. New York, 1990.
Labov, William. "Speech Actions and Reactions in Personal Narrative." In *Analyzing Discourse: Text and Talk*, ed. D. Tanner. Washington, D.C., 1981. Also published in *Georgetown University Roundtable on Languages and Linguistics* (1981): 219–247.
Labov, William, and Joshua Waletzky. "Narrative Analysis." In *Essays on the Verbal and Visual Arts.* Seattle, 1967.
———. "Narrative Analysis: Oral Versions of Personal Experience." In *Language in the Inner City: Studies in the Black English Vernacular*, ed. June Helm. Philadelphia, 1972.
LaCapra, D. *Representing the Holocaust.* Ithaca, N.Y., 1994.
Langer, L. *Admitting the Holocaust.* New York, 1994.
Langer, Susanne K. *Philosophy in a New Key: A Study in the Symbolism of Reason, Rite, and Art.* Cambridge, Mass., 1942.
Langs, Robert. "Supervisory Crises and Dreams from Supervisees." *Contemporary Psychoanalysis* 18 (1982): 575–612.
———. "Freud's Irma Dream and the Origins of Psychoanalysis." *Psychoanalytic Review* 71 (1984): 591–617.
Lasch, Christopher. *The Culture of Narcissism.* New York, 1978.
———. *The True and Only Heaven: Progress and Its Critics.* New York, 1991.
Lee, Peter. "Historical Knowledge and the National Curriculum." In *History in the National Curriculum*, ed. Richard Aldrich. London, 1991.
Lehmann, Albrecht. "Rechtfertigungsgeschichten: Über eine Funktion des Erzählens eigener Erlebnisse im Alltag." *Fabula* 21 (1991): 56–69.
Leinhardt, Gaea, Isabel L. Beck, and Catherine Stainton, eds. *Teaching and Learning in History.* Hillsdale, N.J., 1994.
Leiris, Michael. *L'Age d'homme: Précédé de la littérature considérée comme une tauromachie.* Paris, 1964.
Leithäuser, Thomas, and Birgit Volmerg. *Psychoanalyse in der Sozialforschung: Eine Einführung am Beispiel einer Sozialpsychologie der Arbeit.* Opladen, 1988.
Leitner, Hartmann. "Gegenwart und Geschichte: Zur Logik des historischen Bewußtseins." Unpublished *Habilitationsschrift.* Trier, 1994.
Levi, Primo. *If This Is a Man; and, The Truce*, trans. Stuart Woolf. New York, 1959. First published in Italian as *Se questo è un uomo / La Tregua.* Turin, 1972.
———. *La ricerca della radici: Antologia personale.* Turin, 1981.
———. "Un romanzo storico costruito secondo i modelli classici." Interview by Mario Miccinesi. *Uomini e Libri*, November/December 1982.
———. *Se non ora, quando?* Turin, 1982. Published in English as *If Not Now, When?* trans. William Weaver. New York, 1985; in German as *Wann, wenn nicht jetzt?*, trans. Barbara Kleiner. Munich, 1986.
———. *The Periodic Table*, trans. Raymond Rosenthal. New York, 1984. First published in Italian as *Il sistema periodico.* Turin, 1975.
———. *The Drowned and the Saved*, trans. Raymond Rosenthal. New York, 1988. First published in Italian as *I sommersi e I salvati.* Turin, 1986.
Lévi-Strauss, Claude. *Structural Anthropology.* New York, 1963.

Liebelt, Udo, ed. *Museumspädagogik. Museum der Sinne. Bedeutung und Didaktik des originalen Objekts im Museum.* Hannover, 1990.
Liebowitz, H. *Fabricating Lives: Explorations in American Autobiography.* New York, 1989.
Lincoln, Abraham. *Speeches and Writings.* New York, 1989.
Lomas, Tim. *Teaching and Assessing Historical Understanding.* London, 1990.
Lorenzer, Alfred, ed. *Kultur-Analysen: Psychoanalytische Studien zur Kultur.* Frankfurt, 1986.
Lowenthal, David. *The Past Is a Foreign Country.* New York, 1985.
———. "The Timeless Past: Some Anglo-American Historical Preconceptions." *Journal of American History* 75 (1989): 1180–1263.
Luborsky, Lester. "Measuring a Pervasive Psychic Structure in Psychotherapy: The Core Conflictual Relationship Theme." *Communicative Structures and Psychic Structure,* ed. Norbert Freedman and Stanley Grand, 367–395. New York, 1977.
Luborsky, Lester, and Horst Kächele. *Der zentrale Beziehungskonflikt: Ein Arbeitsbuch.* Ulm, 1988.
Lucariello, Joan. "Canonicality and Consciousness in Child Narrative." In *Narrative Thought and Narrative Language,* ed. Bruce K. Britton and A.D. Pellegrini, 131–149. Hillsdale, N.J., 1990.
Luhmann, Niklas. "Generalized Media and the Problem of Contingency." In *Explorations in General Theory in Social Science: Essays in Honor of Talcott Parsons,* ed. Jan Loubser. Vol. 2, 507–532. New York, 1976.
Lukacs, John. *Historical Consciousness: The Remembered Past.* New Brunswick, N.J., 1994.
Lyons, J.O. *The Invention of the Self.* Carbondale, Ill., 1978.
MacIntyre, Alasdair. *After Virtue: A Study in Moral Theory.* Notre Dame, Ind., 1981; 2ed., 1984.
———. "Ideology, Social Science and Revolution." *Comparative Politics* 5 (1981): 321–341.
Mack, J.E. *Abduction: Human Encounters with Aliens.* New York, 1994.
Mahoney, Patrick J. "Towards a Formalist Approach to Dreams." *International Review of Psychoanalysis* 4 (1977): 83–98.
Makropoulos, Michael. *Modernität als ontologischer Ausnahmezustand? Walter Benjamins Theorie der Moderne.* Munich, 1989.
Mandler, Jean Matter. "A Code in the Node: The Use of a Story Schema in Retrieval." *Discourse Processes* 1 (1978): 14–35.
———. *Stories, Scripts and Scenes: Aspects of Scheme Theory.* Hillsdale, N.J., 1984.
Mandler, Jean M., and Nancy S. Johnson. "Remembrance of Things Passed: Story Structure and Recall." *Cognitive Psychology* 9 (1977): 111–151.
Margolis, Joseph. *The Flux of History and the Flux of Science.* Berkeley, 1993.
———. *Interpretation Radical but Not Unruly: The New Puzzle of the Arts and History.* Berkeley, 1995.
Martin, Wallace. *Recent Theories of Narrative.* Ithaca, N.Y., 1986.
Masson, Jeffrey M. *Was hat man dir, du armes Kind, getan?* Reinbek, 1984.
Matthews, Gareth B. *Dialogues with Children.* Cambridge, Mass., 1984.
Mautner, Barbara. "Freud's Irma Dream: A Psychoanalytic Interpretation." *The International Journal of Psychoanalysis* 72 (1991): 275–286.
May, Robert. "Freud and Phallic Defense." *Psychiatry* 42 (1979): 147–156.
McAdams, Dan P. *Power, Intimacy, and the Life Story.* Homewood, Ill., 1985.
———. *The Stories We Live By: Personal Myths and the Making of the Self.* New York, 1993.
———. "Personality, Modernity, and the Storied Self: A Contemporary Framework for Studying Persons." *Psychological Inquiry* 7 (1996): 295sqq.
McCabe, Alyssa. Preface to *Developing Narrative Structure,* ed. Alyssa McCabe and Carole Peterson, ix–xvii. Hillsdale, N.J., 1991.
McCloskey, Donald N. "The Problem of Audience in Historical Economics: Rhetorical Thoughts on a Text by Robert Fogel." *History and Theory* 24 (1985): 1–22.
McGuire, Michael. "The Rhetoric of Narrative: A Hermeneutic, Critical Theory." In *Narrative Thought and Narrative Language,* ed. Bruce K. Britton and A.D. Pellegrini, 219–236. Hillsdale, N.J., 1990.

McKeown, Margaret G., and Isabel L. Beck. "Making Sense of Accounts of History: Why Young Students Don't and How They Might." In *Teaching and Learning in History,* ed. Gaea Leinhardt, Isabel L. Beck, and Catherine Stainton, 1–26. Hillsdale, N.J., 1994.
McNamee, Sheila, and Kenneth J. Gergen, eds. *Therapy as Social Construction.* Newbury Park, Calif., 1992.
Mead, George Herbert. *The Philosophy of the Present,* ed. Arthur E. Murphy, with prefatory remarks by John Dewey. La Salle, 1932.
———. *The Philosophy of the Present,* ed. Arthur E. Murphy. La Salle, 1932.
Merleau-Ponty, Maurice. *Phenomenology of Perception.* New York, 1962.
———. "Everywhere and Nowhere." In *Signs,* ed. Maurice Merleau-Ponty, 126–158. Evanston, Ill., 1964.
Métraux, Alexandre. "Über die Vergegenwärtigung der Shoah und die Politik des Gedächtnisses." *Psychoanalyse im Widerspruch* 8 (1992): 72–88.
Meyer, Martina, and Jürgen Straub. *Literaturdokumentation und erste Hinweise zur Ausarbeitung einer Psychologie historischer Sinnbildung.* Bielefeld, 1995.
Miccinesi, Mario. "Un romanzo storico costruito secondo i modelli classici." *Uomini e Libri,* November/December 1982.
Michel, Gabriele. *Biographisches Erzählen—zwischen individuellem Erlebnis und kollektiver Geschichtentradition: Untersuchung typischer Erzählfiguren, ihrer sprachlichen Form und ihrer interaktiven und identitätskonstituierenden Funktion in Geschichten und Lebensgeschichten.* Tübingen, 1985.
Middleton, David, and D. Edwards, eds. *Collective Remembering.* London, 1990.
Mink, Louis O. "History and Fiction as Modes of Comprehension." *New Literary History* 1 (1970): 541–558.
———. "Narrative Form as a Cognitive Instrument." In *The Writing of History: Literary Form and Historical Understanding,* ed. Robert H. Canary and Henry Kozicki, 129–149. Madison, 1978.
Mitchell, W.J. Thomas, ed. *On Narrative.* Chicago, 1981.
Mommsen, Hans. *Der Nationalsozialismus und die deutsche Gesellschaft.* Reinbek, 1991.
Montada, Leo, et al. *Die Lernpsychologie Jean Piagets.* Stuttgart, 1970.
Müller, Herbert. *The Uses of the Past: Profiles of Former Societies.* New York, 1952.
Müller, Klaus E. *Prähistorisches Geschichtsbewußtsein,* report no. 1/94, Forschungsgruppe Historische Sinnbildung. Bielefeld, 1994.
Müller, Klaus E., and Jörn Rüsen. *Historische Sinnbildung.* Reinbek, 1997.
Murray, Henry A. *Explorations in Personality: A Clinical and Experimental Study of Fifty Men of College Age.* New York, 1938.
———. "In Nomine Diaboli." *New England Quarterly* 24 (1951): 435–452.
Nehamas, A. "The School of Eloquence." Review of "In Defense of Rhetoric" by Brian Vicker. *Times Literary Supplement* 15 (1988): 771.
Neimeyer, Robert A., and Michael J. Mahoney. *Constructivism in Psychotherapy.* Washington, D.C., 1995.
Nelson, Katherine. "The Transition from Infant to Child Memory." In *Infant Memory: Its Relation to Normal and Pathological Memory in Humans and Other Animals. Advances in the Study of Communication and Affect,* ed. Morris Moskovitch. Vol. 9, 103–130. New York, 1984.
Newman, L.S., and R.F. Baumeister. "Toward an Explanation of the UFO Abduction Phenomenon." *Psychological Inquiry* (1999): 31, 49.
Niederland, William G. *Folgen der Verfolgung: Das Überlebenden-Syndrom Seelenmord.* Frankfurt, 1980.
Nietzsche, Friedrich. *Untimely Meditations.* Cambridge, U.K., 1983.
———. "Unzeitgemäße Betrachtungen, Zweites Stück: Vom Nutzen und Nachtheil der Historie für das Leben." In *Sämtliche Werke,* ed. Giorgio Colli and Mazzino Montinari. Vol. 1. Munich, 1988.
Nisbett, R., and L. Ross. *Human Inference: Strategies and Shortcomings of Social Judgment.* Englewood Cliffs, N.J. 1980.

Nisbett, R., and Thomas Wilson. "Telling More Than We Can Know: Verbal Reports on Mental Processes." *Psychological Review* 84 (1977): 231–259.
Novick, Peter. *That "Noble Dream": The "Objectivity Question" and the American Historical Profession.* Cambridge, U.K., 1988.
Nowerschtern, Abraham. *Abraham Sutzkefer-Bibliographie.* Tel Aviv, 1976.
O'Faolai, Nuala. *The Irish Times,* September 10, 1994.
Olafson, Frederick A. *The Dialectic of Action.* Chicago, 1979.
Olson, David. "Thinking about Narrative." In *Narrative Thought and Narrative Language,* ed. Bruce K. Britton and Anthony D. Pellegrini, 99–111. Hillsdale, N.J., 1990.
Ong, Walter J. *Orality and Literacy.* London, 1982.
Oser, Fritz, and Wolfgang Althof. *Moralische Selbstbestimmung. Modelle der Entwicklung und Erziehung im Wertebereich.* 2nd ed. Stuttgart, 1994.
Pais, Abraham. *Subtle Is the Lord: The Science and the Life of Albert Einstein.* Oxford, 1982.
Pandel, Hans-Jürgen. "Dimensionen des Geschichtsbewußtseins. Ein Versuch, seine Struktur für Empirie und Pragmatik diskutierbar zu machen." *Geschichtsdidaktik: Projekte, Perspektiven* 12 (1987): 130–142.
Parry, Alan, and Robert E. Doan. *Story Re-visions: Narrative Therapy in the Postmodern World.* New York, 1994.
Pelikan, Jaroslav J. *Mary through the Centuries: Her Place in the History of Culture.* New Haven, 1996.
Perelman, Chaim. *The Realm of Rhetoric.* Notre Dame, Ind., 1982.
Perfetti, Charles A., M. Anne Britt, and Mara C. Georgi. *Text-Based Learning and Reasoning: Studies in History.* Hillsdale, N.J., 1995.
Perris, Eve M., Nancy M. Myers, and Rachel K. Clifton. "Long-term Memory for a Single Infancy Experience." *Child Development* 61 (1990): 1796–1807.
Peters, R.S. *The Philosophy of Education.* Oxford, 1971.
Petit, Maria Villela. "Thinking History: Methodology and Epistemology in Paul Ricoeur's Reflection of History from *History and Truth* to *Time and Narrative.*" In *The Narrative Path: The Later Works of Paul Ricoeur,* ed. T. Peter Demp and David Rasmussen, 33–46. Cambridge, Mass., 1989.
Pflug, Maja. *Natalia Ginzburg: Eine Biographie.* Berlin, 1995.
Piaget, Jean. *The Child's Conception of the World,* trans. Joan and Andrew Tomlinson. London, 1929. First published in French as *Représentation du monde chez l'enfant* (Paris, 1948).
———. *The Language and Thought of the Child,* with preface by E. Claparède, trans. Marjorie Gabain. 3rd ed. New York, 1959. First published in French as *Langage et la pensée chez l'enfant* (Neuchâtel-Paris, 1923).
———. *The Child's Conception of Time.* London, 1969.
———. *Genetic Epistemology,* trans. Eleanor Duckworth. New York, 1971.
———. *Introduction à l'épistémologie génétique* [Introduction to genetic epistemology]. 2nd ed. 3 vols. Paris, 1973.
Piaget, Jean, and E.Cartalis, et al. *Judgment and Reasoning in the Child,* trans. Marjorie Warden. Totowa, 1968. First published in French as *Le jugement et le raisonnement chez l'enfant* (Neuchâtel-Paris, 1924).
Pierson, M.H. "Precious Dangers." *Harpers* 290 (1995): 69–78.
Plumb, J.H. *The Death of the Past.* Boston, 1970.
Pohlen, Manfred, and Magarethe Bautz-Holzherr. "Der Fundamentalismus des psychoanalytischen Apparats und der Preis der Analyse." *Zeitschrift für Klinische Psychologie, Psychopathologie und Psychotherapie* 43 (1995): 164–174.
———. *Psychoanalyse—Das Ende einer Deutungsmacht.* Reinbek, 1995.
Poli, Gabriela, and Georgio Calcagno. *Echi di una voce perduta: Incontri, interviste, e conversazione con Primo Levi.* Milano, 1992.
Polkinghorne, Donald E. *Narrative Knowing and the Human Sciences.* Albany, N.Y., 1988.
———. "Psychology after Philosophy." In *Reconsidering Psychology: Perspectives from Continental Philosophy,* ed. R.N. Williams and J.E. Faulconer, 92–115. Pittsburgh, 1990.

———. "Narrative and Self-Concept." *Journal of Narrative and Life History* 1 (1991): 135–153.
———. "Postmodern Epistemology of Practice." In *Psychology and Postmodernism*, ed. Steinar Kvale, 146–165. London, 1992.
———. "Narrative Configuration in Qualitative Analysis." *International Journal of Qualitative Studies in Education* 8 (1995): 8–25.
———. "Explorations of Narrative Identity." *Psychological Inquiry* 7.4 (1996): 363–367.
———. "Narrative Knowing and the Study of Lives." In *Aging and Biography: Exploration in Adult Development*, ed. James Birren et al. New York, 1996.
Popper, Karl R. *The Poverty of Historicism*. London, 1957; 3rd ed., New York, 1961.
———. *The Logic of Scientific Discovery*. London, 1959.
Portal, Christopher, ed. *The History Curriculum for Teachers*. London, 1987.
Porter, Dale H. *The Emergence of the Past: A Theory of Historical Explanation*. Chicago, 1981.
Poulsen, Dorothy, Eileen Kintsch, Walter Kintsch, and David Premack. "Children's Comprehension and Memory for Stories." *Journal of Experimental Child Psychology* 28 (1979): 379–403.
Propp, V. *Morphology of the Folktale*. Austin, 1968.
Putnam, Hilary. *Mind, Language, and Reality*. Cambridge, U.K., 1975.
Quasthoff, Uta. *Erzählen in Gesprächen: Linguistische Untersuchungen zu Strukturen und Funktionen am Beispiel einer Kommunikationsform des Alltags*. Tübingen, 1980.
Quine, W.V.O. *Word and Object*. Cambridge, Mass., 1960.
Rabinov, Paul, and William M. Sullivan, eds. *Interpretative Social Science: A Reader*. Berkeley, 1979.
Randall, William Lowell. *The Stories We Are: An Essay on Self-Creation*. Toronto, 1995.
Ranke, Leopold von. *The Theory and Practice of History*. Indianapolis, 1973.
Rath, Rainer. *Kommunikationspraxis. Analysen zur Textbildung und Textgliederung im gesprochenen Deutsch*. Göttingen, 1979.
———. "Zur Legitimation und Einbettung von Erzählungen in Alltagsdialogen." In *Dialogforschung, Sprache der Gegenwart*, no. 54: *Jahrbuch des Instituts für deutsche Sprache*, ed. Peter Schröder and Hugo Steger, 265–287. Düsseldorf, 1980.
———. "Erzählfunktionen und Erzählankündigungen im Alltagsdialog." In *Erzählforschung. Ein Symposium*, ed. Eberhard Lämmert, 33–50. Stuttgart, 1982.
Rauch, J. "In the Defense of Prejudice." *Harpers* 290 (1995): 37–46.
Ricoeur, Paul, *Time and Narrative*, trans. Kathleen McLaughlin and David Pellauer. 3 vols. Chicago, 1984–1988.
———. "Contingence et Rationalité dans le Récit." In *Studien zur neueren französischen Phänomenologie: Ricoeur, Foucault, Derrida*, ed. Ernst Wolfgang Orth, 11–29. Freiburg, 1986.
———. *Zufall und Vernunft in der Geschichte*, trans. Helga Marcelli. Tübingen, 1986. This lecture was published in French as *Contingence et Rationalité dans le Récit* (Tübingen, 1986).
———. "Life in Quest of Narrative." In *On Paul Ricoeur: Narrative and interpretation*, ed. David Wood, 20–33. London, 1991.
———. "Narrative Identity." In *On Paul Ricoeur: Narrative and Interpretation*, ed. David Wood, 188–199. London, 1991.
———. *Oneself as Another*, trans. K. Blamey. Chicago, 1992.
———. "Gedächtnis—Vergessen—Geschichte." In *Historische Sinnbildung: Problemstellungen, Zeitkonzepte, Wahrnehmungshorizonte, Darstellungsstrategien*, ed. Jörn Rüsen and Klaus E. Müller. Reinbek, 1997.
Rimmon-Kenan, S. *Narrative Fiction: Contemporary Poetics*. London, 1983.
Ritter, Joachim, and Karlfried Gründer, ed. *Historisches Wörterbuch der Philosophie*. Darmstadt, 1974.
Robinson, John A. "Narrative Thinking as a Heuristic Process." In *Narrative Psychology: The Storied Nature of Human Conduct*, ed. Theodore R. Sarbin, 111–125. New York, 1986.
Rohde-Dachser, Christa. *Expedition in den dunklen Kontinent*. Berlin, 1991.
Rohlfes, Joachim. "Geschichtsbewußtsein: Leerformel oder Fundamentalkategorie?" In *Geschichte: Nutzen oder Nachteil für das Leben?* ed. Ursula A.J. Becher and Klaus Bergmann. Düsseldorf, 1986.

Rorty, Richard. *Philosophy and the Mirror of Nature.* Princeton, 1979.
Rosaldo, Renato. *Culture and Truth. The Remaking of Social Analysis.* Boston, 1989.
Rosenthal, Gabriele. *Erzählte und erlebte Lebensgeschichte: Gestalt und Struktur biographischer Selbstbeschreibungen.* Frankfurt, 1995.
Rosenzweig, L.W., and T.P. Weinland. "New Directions of the History Curriculum: A Challenge for the 1980s." *The History Teacher* 19 (1986): 263–277.
Ross, Thomas. "The Rhetoric of Poverty: Their Immorality, Our Helplessness." *Georgetown Law Review* 79 (1991): 1499–1547.
Roth, Heinrich. *Kind und Geschichte. Psychologische Voraussetzungen des Geschichtsunterrichts in der Volksschule.* 4th ed. Munich, 1965.
Roubaud, Jacques. *L'invention du fils de Leopreps: Poésie et Mémoire.* Saulxures, 1993.
Rumelhart, David E. "Notes on a Schema for Stories." In *Representation and Understanding: Studies in Cognitive Science,* ed. Daniel G. Bobrow and Allan Collins, 211–236. New York, 1975.
Runyan, William M. "A Historical and Conceptual Background to Psychohistory." In *Psychology and Historical Interpretation,* ed. William M. Runyan, 3–60. New York, 1988.
Rüsen, Jörn. *Grundzüge einer Historik.* 3 vols. Göttingen, 1983–1989.
———. "The Development of Narrative Competence in Historical Learning: An Ontogenetical Hypothesis Concerning Moral Consciousness." *History and Memory* 1 (1989): 35–59. Reprinted in Jörn Rüsen. *Studies in Metahistory,* ed. Pieter Duvenage (Pretoria, 1993), 63–85.
———. *Zeit und Sinn: Strategien historischen Denkens.* Frankfurt, 1991.
———. *Studies in Metahistory,* ed. Pieter Duvenage. Pretoria, 1993.
———. *Historische Orientierung: Über die Arbeit des Geschichtsbewußtseins, sich in der Zeit zurechtzufinden.* Cologne, 1994.
———. "Geschichte sehen. Zur ästhetischen Konstitution historischer Sinnbildung." In *Auf der Suche nach dem verlorenen Staat. Die Kunst der Parteien und Massenorganisationen der DDR,* ed. Monika Flacke, 32–33. Berlin, 1994.
———. *Historische Orientierung: über die Arbeit des Geschichtsbewußtseins, sich in der Zeit zurechtzufinden.* Cologne, 1994.
———. *Historische Sinnbildung: Interdisziplinäre Untersuchungen zur Struktur, Logik und Funktion des Geschichtsbewußtseins im interkulturellen Vergleich* (Konzept der Forschungsgruppe). Bielefeld, 1994–1995.
———. "Historische Sinnbildung durch Erzählen: Eine Argumentationsskizze zum narrativistischen Paradigma der Geschichtswissenschaft und der Geschichtsdidaktik im Blick auf nichtnarrative Faktoren." *Internationale Schulbuchforschung* 18 (1996): 501–543.
Rüsen, Jörn, Klaus Fröhlich, Hubert Horstkötter, and Hans-Günther Schmidt. "Untersuchungen zum Geschichtsbewußtsein von Abiturienten in Ruhrgebiet." In *Geschichtsbewußtsein empirisch,* ed. Bodo von Borries, Hans-Jürgen Pandel, and Jörn Rüsen. Pfaffenweiler, 1991.
Sackett, L.W. "A Scale in United States History." *Journal of Educational Psychology* 10 (1973): 345–348.
Sager, Lawrence G. "Tight Little Islands: Exclusionary Zoning, Equal Protection, and the Indigent." *Stanford Law Review* 21 (1969): 767–800.
Sarbin, Theodore R. "Emotions as Narrative Emplotments." In *Entering the Circle: Hermeneutic Investigation in Psychology,* ed. Martin J. Packer and Richard B. Addison, 185–201. Albany, N.Y., 1989.
———, ed. *Narrative Psychology: The Storied Nature of Human Conduct.* New York, 1986.
Schafer, Roy. "Narration in the Psychoanalytic Dialogue." *Critical Inquiry* 7 (1980): 29–53.
———. *Narrative Actions in Psychoanalysis.* Worcester, 1981.
———. *The Analytic Attitude.* New York, 1983.
———. *Retelling a Life: Narration and Dialogue in Psychoanalysis.* New York, 1992.
Schank, Roger C. *Tell Me a Story: A New Look at Real and Artifical Memory.* New York, 1990.
Schank, Roger C., and Robert P. Abelson. *Scripts, Plans, Goals, and Understanding.* Hillsdale, N.J., 1977.
Schapp, W. *In Geschichten verstrickt: Zum Sein von Mensch und Ding.* Hamburg, 1953.

Schelling, Walter A. "Erinnern und Erzählen." *Wege zum Menschen* 35 (1983): 416–422.
Schmidt, Hans-Günter. "Eine Geschichte zum Nachdenken. Erzähltypologie, narrative Kompetenz und Geschichtsbewußtsein: Bericht über einen Versuch der empirischen Erforschung des Geschichtsbewußtseins von Schülern der Sekundarstufe I (Unter- und Mittelstufe)." *Geschichtsdidaktik: Probleme, Projekte, Perspektiven* 12 (1987): 28–35.
Schmidt, Siegfried J., ed. *Gedächtnis: Probleme und Perspektiven der interdisziplinären Gedächtnisforschung.* Frankfurt, 1991.
Schnädelbach, Herbert. "'Etwas Verstehen heißt Verstehen, wie es geworden ist'—Variationen über eine hermeneutische Maxime." In *Vernunft und Geschichte: Vorträge und Abhandlungen.* Frankfurt, 1987.
Schnur, Max. "Some Additional 'Day Residues' of the Specimen Dream of Psychoanalysis." In *Psychoanalysis—A General Psychology,* ed. Rudolph M. Loewenstein, Lottie M. Newman, Max Schnur, and Albert J. Solnit, 45–85. New York, 1966.
Scholes, R., and R. Kellogg. *The Nature of Narratives.* New York, 1966.
Scholz Williams, Gerhild. "Geschichte und die literarische Dimension: Narrativik und Historiographie in der anglo-amerikanischen Forschung der letzten Jahrzehnte. Ein Bericht." *Deutsche Vierteljahresschrift für Literaturwissenschaft und Geistesgeschichte* 63 (1989): 315–392.
Schörken, Rolf. "Geschichtsdidaktik und Geschichtsbewußtsein." *Geschichte in Wissenschaft und Unterricht* 23 (1972): 81–89.
Schröder, Hans-Joachim. *Die gestohlenen Jahre: Erzählgeschichten und Geschichtserzählung im Interview. Der Zweite Weltkrieg aus der Sicht ehemaliger Mannschaftssoldaten.* Tübingen, 1992.
———. "Interviewliteratur zum Leben in der DDR. Das narrative Interview als biographisch-soziales Zeugnis zwischen Wissenschaft und Literatur." *Materialien und Ergebnisse aus Forschungsprojekten des Institutes für kulturwissenschaftliche Deutschlandstudien an der Universität Bremen, FB 10,* Heft 5 (1993).
Schütz, A. "Tiresias oder unser Wissen von zukünftigen Ereignissen." *Gesammelte Aufsätze vol. 2: Studien zur Soziologischen Theorie.* Den Haag, 1972. (Published in English as *Studies in Social Theory,* vol. 2 of *Collected Papers,* ed. Arvid Brodersen [New York, 1972], 268).
Segal, Judith, Susan Chipuran, and Robert Glaser. *Thinking and Learning Skills.* Hillsdale, N.J., 1985.
Seixas, Peter. "Popular Film and Young People's Understanding of the History of Native–White Relations." *The History Teacher* 26.3 (1993): 351–370.
———. "Confronting the Moral Frames of Popular Film: Young People Respond to Historical Revisionism." *American Journal of Education* 102.3 (1994): 261–285.
———. "Margins and Sidebars: Problems in Students' Understanding of Significance in World History." Paper presented at the meeting of the American Educational Research Association. New Orleans, 1994.
———. "Problems in Students' Understanding of Historical Significance." *Theory and Research in Social Education* 22.3 (1994): 281–304.
———. "Conceptualizing the Growth of Historical Understanding." In *The Handbook of Education and Human Development,* ed. David Olson and Nancy Torrance, 765–783. Cambridge, U.K., 1996.
Shemilt, Dennis J. *History 13–16: Evaluation Study.* Edinburgh, 1980.
———. "Adolescent Ideas about Evidence and Methodology in History." In *The History Curriculum for Teachers,* ed. Christopher Portal, 39–61. London, 1987.
Shiffrin, R.M., and W. Schneider. "Controlled and Automatic Human Information Processing: Detection, Search, and Attention." *Psychological Review* 84 (1977): 1–66.
Shotter, J., and K.J. Gergen, eds. *Texts of Identity.* London, 1989.
Skinner, Quentin. *Meaning and Context,* ed. James Tully. Princeton, 1988.
Sloterdijk, Peter. *Literatur und Organisation von Lebenserfahrung.* Munich, 1978.
Spacks, Patricia M. *Boredom: The Literary History of a State of Mind.* Chicago, 1995.
Spear, Norman E. "Behaviors That Indicate Memory: Levels of Expression." *Canadian Journal of Psychology* 38 (1984): 348–367.

Speer, A. *Erinnerungen*. Frankfurt, 1969. Published in English as *Inside the Third Reich: Memoirs*, trans. Richard Winston and Clara Winston (New York, 1970).
———. *Spandauer Tagebücher*. Frankfurt, 1975. Published in English as *Spandau: The Secret Diaries*, trans. Richard Winston and Clara Winston (New York, 1976).
———. *Architektur: Arbeiten 1933–1942*. Berlin, 1978.
———. *Technik und Macht*. Esslingen, 1979.
———. *Der Sklavenstaat*. Stuttgart, 1981. Published in English as *Infiltration*, trans. Joachim Neugroschl (New York, 1981).
Spence, Donald P. *Narrative Truth and Historical Truth: Meaning and Interpretation in Psychoanalysis*. New York, 1982.
Spotnitz, Hyman, and Phyllis W. Meadow. *Treatment of the Narcissistic Neuroses*. New York, 1976.
Staudinger, Ursula, and Paul Baltes. "Weisheit: Gegenstand psychologischer Forschung." *Psychologische Rundschau* 47 (1996): 57–77.
Stein, Nancy L., and Tom Trabasso. "What's in a Story: An Approach to Comprehension and Instruction." In *Advances in Instructional Psychology*, ed. Robert Glaser. Vol. 2., 213–267. Hillsdale, N.J., 1982.
Stern, Daniel. *The Interpersonal World of the Infant: A View from Psychoanalysis and Developmental Psychology*. New York, 1985.
Stierle, Karlheinz. "Geschehen, Geschichte und Text der Geschichte." In *Geschichte—Ereignis und Erzählung*, ed. Reinhart Koselleck and Wolf-Dieter Stempel, 530–534. Munich, 1973.
Stone, Lawrence. *The Causes of the English Revolution, 1529–1642*. London, 1972.
Straub, Jürgen. "Biographische Sozialisation und narrative Kompetenz: Implikationen und Voraussetzungen lebensgeschichtlichen Denkens in der Sicht einer narrativen Psychologie." In *Biographische Sozialisation*, ed. Erika Hoerning. Stuttgart, 1977.
———. *Die Prinzipien der historischen Forschung*. Vol. 2 of *Rekonstruktion der Vergangenheit: Grundzüge einer Historik*. Göttingen, 1986.
———. *Historisch-Psychologische Biographienforschung: Theoretische, methodologische, und methodische Argumentationen in systematischer Absicht*. Heidelberg, 1989.
———. "Identitätstheorie im Übergang? Über Identitätsforschung, den Begriff der Identität, und die zunehmende Beachtung des Nicht-Identischen in subjekttheoretischen Diskursen." *Sozialwissenschaftliche Literatur-Rundschau* 14 (1991): 49–71.
———. "Kultureller Wandel als konstruktive Transformation des kollektiven Gedächtnisses: Zur Theorie der Kulturpsychologie." In *Psychologische Aspekte des kulturellen Wandels*, ed. Christian Allesch, Elfriede Billman-Mahecha, and Alfred Lang, 42–54. Vienna, 1993.
———. "Identität und Sinnbildung: Ein Beitrag aus der Sicht einer handlungs- und erzähltheoretisch orientierten Sozialpsychologie." *Jahresbericht ZiF* 94/95, 42–90. Bielefeld, 1996.
———. "Zur narrativen Konstruktion von Vergangenheit: Erzähltheoretische Überlegungen und eine exemplarische Analyse eines Gruppengesprächs über die 'NS-Zeit.'" *Bios: Zeitschrift für Biographieforschung und Oral History* 9 (1996): 30–58.
———. "Geschichte, Identität und Lebensglück: Eine psychologische Lektüre *unzeitgemäßer Betrachtungen*." In *Historische Sinnbildung*, ed. Klaus E. Müller and Jörn Rüsen, 165–194. Reinbek, 1997.
———. "Personale und kollektive Identität: Zur Analyse eines theoretischen Begriffs." In *Identitäten*, ed. Aleida Assmann and Heidrun Friese. Frankfurt, 1998.
———. *Handlung, Interpretation, Kritik: Grundzüge einer textwissenschaftlichen Handlungs- und Kulturpsychologie*. Berlin, 1999.
———. *Verstehen, Kritik, Anerkennung: Das Eigene und das Fremde in der Erkenntnisbildung interpretativer Wissenschaften*. Göttingen, 1999.
———. "Handlungsbegriffe und Handlungserklärungen: Typologische Unterscheidungen unter besonderer Berücksichtigung des narrativen Modells." In *Handlungstheorie: Begriff und Erklärung des Handelns im interdisziplinären Diskurs*, ed. Jürgen Straub and Hans Werbig. Frankfurt, 1999.
Strieber, W. *Communion: Encounters with the Unknown—A True Story*. New York, 1987.

Stückrath, Jörn. "Die 'Wendung' wider das Chaos: Zur Rekonstruktion und Kritik von Hayden Whites tropologischer Theorie der Geschichtsschreibung." Paper presented at the conference "Narrativität und Fiktionalität," Bielefeld, June 1995.

Sutter, Tilmann. "Entwicklung durch Handeln in Sinnstrukturen: Die sozial-kognitive Entwicklung aus der Perspektive eines interaktionistischen Konstruktivismus." In *Soziale Kognition und Sinnstruktur*, ed. Tilmann Sutter and Michael Charlton. Oldenburg, 1994.

Sutton-Smith, B. "Presentation and Representation in Fictional Narrative." *New Directions for Child Development* 6 (1979): 37–60.

Sutzkefer, Abraham. "farfrojrene jidn." *poetische werk*. Vol. 1, 362–363. Tel Aviv, 1963.

———. *der jojresch fun regn*. Tel Aviv, 1992.

Swearingen, C. Jan. "The Narrative Dialogue and Narration within Dialogue: The Transition from Story to Logic." In *Narrative Thought and Narrative Language*, ed. Bruce K. Britton and A.D. Pellegrini, 173–197. Hillsdale, N.J., 1990.

Taylor, Charles. "Interpretation and the Sciences of Man." In *Interpretive Social Science: A Reader*, ed. Paul Rabinow and William M. Sullivan, 25–72. Berkeley, 1979.

———. *Philosophy and the Human Sciences*. Cambridge, U.K., 1985.

———. *Sources of the Self: The Making of the Modern Identity*. Cambridge, Mass., 1989.

Tennyson, Alfred. "The Passing of Arthur." In *The Norton Anthology of English Literature*, ed. Meyer H. Abrams. 4th ed. Vol. 2. New York, 1979.

Thorndike, Edward L. *Education: A First Book*. New York, 1912.

———. *Educational Psychology*. New York, 1923.

Todorov, Tzvetan. *The Poetics of Prose*. Ithaca, N.Y. 1977.

———. *Les abus de la mémoire*. Paris, 1995.

Toulmin, Steven, and David Leary. "The Cult of Empiricism in Psychology, and Beyond." In *A Century of Psychology as Science*, ed. David Leary and S. Koch, 594–617. New York, 1985.

Tourtellot, A.B., *Lexington and Concord: The Beginning of the War of the American Revolution*. New York, 1959.

Trilling, L. *Sincerity and Athenticity*. Cambridge, Mass., 1971.

Ulrich, Laural Thatcher. *A Midwife's Tale: The Diary of Martha Ballard*, New York, 1990.

van Dijk, T.A., and W. Kintsch. *Strategies of Discourse Comprehension*. New York, 1983.

von Borries, Bodo. "Geschichtsbewußtsein, Lebenslauf und Charakterstruktur: Auswertung von Intensivinterviews." In *Geschichtsbewußtsein und historisch-politisches Lernen*, ed. Gerhard Schneider, 163–183. Pfaffenweiler, 1988.

———. "Geschichtliches Bewußtsein und politische Orientierung von Jugendlichen in Ost- und Westdeutschland 1992." *Neue Sammlung* 34 (1994): 363–382.

———. *Das Geschichtsbewußtsein Jugendlicher. Eine repräsentative Untersuchung über Vergangenheitsdeutungen, Gegenwartswahrnehmungen und Zukunftserwartungen von Schülerinnen und Schülern in Ost- und Westdeutschland*. Weinheim, 1995.

von Borries, Bodo, Hans-Jürgen Pandel, and Jörn Rüsen, eds. *Geschichtsbewußtsein empirisch*. Pfaffenweiler, 1991.

von Ranke, Leopold. *The Theory and Practice of History*. Indianapolis, 1973.

Vygotsky, Lev S. *Mind in Society: The Development of Higher Psychological Processes*. Cambridge, Mass., 1978.

Walter, H. "Eins zu Eins: Ein Fotoalbum zum Wiederaufbau Deutschlands." In *Das Gedächtnis der Bilder: Ästhetik und Nationalsozialismus*, ed. H. Welzer, 115–163. Tübingen, 1995.

Watson, James D. *The Double Helix: A Personal Account of the Structure of DNA*. New York, 1969.

Weaver, R.B., and A.E. Traxler. "Essay Examination and Objective Tests in United States History in the Junior High School." *School Review* 39 (1931): 689–695.

Weir, Ruth. *Language in the Crib*. The Hague, 1962.

White, Hayden. *Metahistory: The Historical Imagination in Nineteenth-Century Europe*. Baltimore, 1973.

———. *Tropics of Discourse: Essays in Cultural Criticism*. Baltimore, 1978.

———. "The Value of Narrativity in the Representation of Reality." In Mitchell, *On Narrative*, 5–27.

———. *The Content of the Form: Narrative Discourse and Historical Representation.* Baltimore, 1987.
White, Michael, and David Epston. *Narrative Means to Therapeutic Ends.* New York, 1990.
Whitman, Roy M., Milton Kramer, and Bill J. Baldridge. "Dreams about the Patient: An Approach to the Problem of Countertransference." *Journal of the American Psychoanalytic Association* 17 (1969): 702–727.
Wiedemann, Peter M. *Erzählte Wirklichkeit.* Weinheim, 1986.
Wineburg, Samuel S. "Historical Problem Solving: A Study of the Cognitive Processes Used in the Evaluation of Documentary and Pictorial Evidence." *Journal of Educational Psychology* 83 (1991): 73–87.
———. "On the Reading of Historical Texts: Notes on the Breach between School and Academy." *American Educational Research Journal* 28.3 (1991): 495–519.
———. "Reading Abraham Lincoln: An Expert/Expert Study in the Interpretation of Historical Texts." *Cognitive Science* 22 (1998): 319–346.
———. "Historical Thinking and Other Unnatural Acts." *Phi Delta Kappa* 80 (1999): 488–499.
Wineburg, Samuel S., and J. Fournier. "Thinking in Time." *History News* 3 (1993): 26–27.
———. "Contextualized Thinking in History." In *Cognitive and Instructional Processes in History and the Social Sciences,* ed. Mario Carretero and James Voss, 285–308. Hillsdale, N.J., 1994.
Yerushalmi, Yosef Hayim. *Zakhor: Jewish History and Jewish Memory.* Seattle, 1982.
Young, James E. *Writing and Rewriting the Holocaust: Narrative and the Consequences of Interpretation.* Bloomington, Ind., 1988.
Young, K. "Edgework: Frame and Boundary in the Phenomenology of Narrative." *Semiotics* 4 (1982): 277–315.

Notes on Contributors

Elfriede Billmann-Mahecha, is a professor of psychology in the Department of Educational Science, University of Hanover, Germany. Billmann-Mahecha's general research topics are historical consciousness, moral development, cultural studies, and methods of qualitative research. Her publications include *Egozentrismus und Perspektivenwechsel. Empirisch-psychologische Studien zu kindlichen Verstehensleistungen im Alltag* (1990), *Psychologische Aspekte des kulturellen Wandels* (1992, co-edited with Christian G. Allesch and Alfred Lang), *Kulturwissenschaft. Felder einer prozeßorientierten wissenschaftlichen Praxis* (2001, co-edited with Heide Appelsmeyer).

Brigitte Boothe, is a professor of clinical psychology at the University of Zurich, Switzerland. Boothe's general research topics are the Psychoanalysis of femininity, communication and understanding in psychoanalytical treatment, and narrative theory. Her publications include *Der Patient als Erzähler in der Psychotherapie* (1994), *Psychoanalyse der frühen weiblichen Entwicklung* (1996, with Annelise Heigl-Evers), *Der Körper als Bedeutungslandschaft* (1997, with Annelise Heigl-Evers), and *Erzählen als Konfliktdarstellung—Psychoanalyse im Dialog* (1999, co-edited with A. Wyl).

Micha Brumlik, is a professor of education at the Johann Wolfgang Goethe University, Frankfurt/Main, Germany. Since October 2000, he is research director of the Study- and Documentation Centre on the History and Impact of the Holocaust (Fritz Bauer Institut), Frankfurt/Main. Brumlik's general research topics are the theory of socialization, philosophy of education, and the intellectual history of Jewish-Christian cultural relations. His publications include *Kein Weg als Deutscher und Jude* (2000), *Die Gnostiker. Der Traum von der Selbsterlösung des Menschen* (2000 [1992]), *Deutscher Geist und Judenhass. Das Verhältnis des philosophischen Idealismus zum Judentum* (2000), *Vernunft und Offenbarung. Religionsphilosophische Versuche* (2001), and *Bildung und Glück. Versuch einer Theorie der Tugenden* (2002).

Jerome S. Bruner, is professor emeritus of psychology, formerly at the New School for Social Research, and since 1991, Research Fellow in Law School at New York University. Bruner's general research topics are the psychology of development, pedagogical psychology, narrative psychology, the psychology of language, cognitive psychology, and the psychology of cultural practices. His publications include *Actual Minds, Possible Worlds* (1986), *Acts of Meaning* (1990), and *The Culture of Education* (1996).

Kenneth J. Gergen, is Mustin Professor of Psychology at Swarthmore College. Gergen's general research topics are the social construction of knowledge, relational theory of action, therapy research, technology and society, and psychology and its historical context. Gergen's publications include *The Saturated Self. Dilemmas of Identity in Contemporary Life* (1991), *Realities and Relationships* (1996), *Relational Responsibility* (1999), *Social construction in context* (2001), and *Social construction, a Reader* (2003).

Monika Hausen has studied educational science at the University of Hanover, Germany. In her thesis, she investigated the time concepts of eight-year-old-children. The topic of her dissertation is the development of historical consciousness in children from the first to the fourth grade.

Alexandre Métreaux, is Fellow at the Otto Selz Institute of the University of Mannheim. Métreaux's general research topics are history and the theory of science. His publications include *Leibhaftige Vernunft: Spuren von Merleau-Pontys Denken* (1986, with Bernhard Waldenfels), *Geschichte der höheren psychischen Funktionen* (1992, co-edited with Lev Semënovic Vygotskij), and *"The Emergent Materialism in French Clinical Brain Research", in:* Graduate Faculty Philosophy Journal, 22 (2000).

Donald E. Polkinghorne, is professor of psychology at the University of Southern California, Los Angeles. Polkinghorne's general research topics are narrative psychology, qualitative research, and theoretical psychology in an interdisciplinary perspective. His publications include *Narrative knowing and the human sciences* (1988), *"Reporting Qualitative Research as Practice,"* in: Representation and the Text: Reframing the Narrative Voice (1997); and *"Narrative and Personal Identity,"* in: Phenomenology and Narrative Psychology (1997).

Peter Seixas, is a professor in the Department of Curriculum Studies at the University of British Columbia, Vancouver. Seixas's general research topics are historical consciousness and didactics of history. His publications include *Knowing, Learning, and Teaching History* (2000, co-edited with Peter N. Stearns), *History, Memory and Learning to Teach. Encounters on Education* (2003, co-edited with Daniel Fromowitz and Petra Hill), and *"Social Studies"* in: Handbook of Research on Teaching (2001, fourth edition).

Donald P. Spence, is professor emeritus of psychiatry at the Robert Wood Johnson Medical School, Piscataway, N.J. Spence's general research topics are psychoanalysis, therapy research and narrative psychology. His publications include *Narrative Truth and Historical Truth* (1982), *The Freudian Metaphor* (1987), and *The Rhetorical Voice of Psychoanalysis* (1994).

Jürgen Straub, is professor of Psychology at the University of Chemnitz. He was research director and member of the management committee at the Institute for Advanced Studies in the Humanities Essen (Kulturwissenschaftliches Institut Essen, KWI) from October 1999 to September 2001. Since April 2004, he leads the Graduate School on Intercultural Communication—Intercultural Competence, at the KWI. Straub's general research topics are the psychology of cultural practices, methodology of qualitative research, identity theory, biography research, and historical consciousness. His recent book publications include *Übersetzung als Medium des Kulturverstehens und der sozialen Integration* (2002, co-edited with Joachim Renn and Shingo Shimada); *Transitorische Identität. Der Prozesscharakter des modernen Selbst* (2002, co-edited with Joachim Renn), *Lebensformen im Widerstreit* (2003, co-edited with Burkhard Liebsch), *Handbuch der Kulturwissenschaften, Bd. 2: Paradigmen und Disziplinen* (2004, co-edited with Friedrich Jäger), and *Pursuit of Meaning. Advances in Cultural and Cross-Cultural Psychology* (2005, co-edited with Carlos Kölbl, Doris Weidemann and Barbara Zielke).

Harald Welzer, is the head of the research group on Interdisciplinary Memory Research at the Institute for the Advanced Study of the Humanities Essen (Kulturwissenschaftliches Institut Essen). He teaches social psychology at the Universities of Hanover and Witten-Herdecke, Germany. Welzer's general research topics are political psychology, theory of socialization and methodology. His publications include *Transitionen: Zur Sozialpsychologie biographischer Wandlungsprozesse* (1993), *Das Gedächtnis der Bilder: Ästhetik und Nationalsozialismus* (ed., 1995); *Verweilen beim Grauen: Essays zum wissenschaftlichen Umgang mit dem Holocaust* (1997), *Das kommunikative Gedächtnis: Eine Theorie der Erinnerung* (2002), and *Opa war kein Nazi. Nationalsozialismus und Holocaust im Familiengedächtnis* (2002).

Samuel S. Wineburg, is a professor of educational psychology and history at the University of Washington, Seattle. Wineburg's general research topics are historical consciousness and historical understanding, pedagogical psychology and didactics. His publications include *Mr. Stinson's Vietnam: Moral Ambiguity in the History Classroom* (1993, co-edited with Judith Kleinfeld), *Knowing, Teaching, and Learning History: National and International Perspectives* (2000, co-edited with Peter N. Stearns and Peter Seixas), *Interdisciplinary Curriculum: Challenges to Implementation* (2000, co-edited with Pam Grossman), and *Historical Thinking and Other Unnatural Acts: Charting the Future of Teaching the Past* (2001).

Index of Names

A

Adorno, Theodor W., 242
Aesop, 26, 34
Allport, Gordon W., 4
Angehrn, Emil, 60, 62
Aristotle, 26, 73
Assman, Aleida, 51
Astren, 199ff.
Austin, John L., 110
Averill, James R., 112

B

Bakhtin, Michail, 102
Ball-Kaduri, -, 230
Barnes, Julian, 35
Barthes, Roland, 29
Bauer, Gerhard, 47
Baumeister, Roy F., 13, 125, 127
Beaudelaire, 28
Beckett, Samuel B., 28, 30
Beethoven, 39
Bell, J. Carleton, 189f.
Berger, —, 99
Blumenberg, Hans, 11, 12
Booth, Wayne, 129
Boothe, Brigitte, 58, 67, 69, 70, 84
Bollas, Christopher, 120, 124
Borries, Boris von, 171
Boueke, Dietrich, 56, 59, 167
Bremond, —, 57
Bradbury, Malcolm, 30
Bruner, Jerome S., xiii, 5, 6, 7, 13, 19, 45f., 54, 75, 83, 192, 200
Burke, Kenneth, 35f.

C

Calvino, Italo, 30, 35
Campbell, Joseph, 104
Carr, E. H., 143, 157
Chartier, Roger, 85
Cicero, 187
Clifton, Rachel K., 165
Clark, Ronald W., 223
Chomsky, Noam, 6
Coleridge, 36
Collins, —, 25
Columbus, Christoph, 172
Cournot, 72

D

Danto, Herbert C., 51
DeLillo, Don, 30
Dewey, —, 61
Dijk, T. van, 197
Douglas, Stephan, 196
Downey, Matthew T., 144
Droysen, 80
Dunn, Judy, 36
Dworkin, Ronald, 37

E

Elstein, Arthur, 194
Englehardt, Tom, 150
Epstein, Seymor, 6
Epston, David, 15

F

Feynman, Richard, 25

Flavell, 83
Flower, Linda, 196
Foucault, Michel, 35
Fowler, Alastair, 33
Francesco, della, 35
Frege, Gottlob, 32
Freud, Siegmund, 4, 68, 138, 212, 214, 215, 216
Friedman, William J., 179, 180
Fromm, Erich, 126
Frye, Northrop, 33, 103

G

Gadamer, Hans-Georg, 8
Gagné, Ellen, 194
Garnes, Roger, 30
Geertz, Clifford, 34
Gergen, Kenneth J., 54, 58, 65, 122, 126
Gergen, Mary, 107
Gilbert, G. M., 247
Goldschmidt, Georges-Arthur, 233
Goodman, Nelson, 26
Gorman, F. R., 191
Gray, Ward, 195
Guare, John, 30, 35

H

Haffner, Sebastian, 247, 248
Hall, G. Stanley, 188
Hänni, Rolf, 168
Hanson, Norwood R., 17
Hawthorne, 31
Hayes, John, 196
Hegel, Georg W. F., 19, 39
Heider, Fritz, 83
Herodotus, 47
Hesiod, 30
Heussi, Karl, 47
Hobsbawm, Eric, 35
Homer, 30
Hunkeler, R., 168

I

Ignatieff, Michael, 145

J

Jakobson, Roman, 31, 201
James, Henry, 128, 129

Jeismann, Karl-Ernst, 50, 52, 77, 164, 183
Jody, 199f.
Jenkins, Keith, 148
Joyce, James, 30f.
Judd, Charles Hubbard, 189, 190

K

Kant, Immanuel, xv, 49
Kennedy-Onassis, Jacqueline, 35
Kintsch, W., 197
Klemperer, Viktor, 234
Kohlberg, Lawrence, 48, 83
Koselleck, Reinhard, 72

L

Labov, William, 38, 57
Langlois, 194
Lasch, Christopher, 120
Lee, Peter, 142, 144
Leiris, Michel, 27
Leitner, 71
Leo III, 37, 39
Levi, Primo, 234, 236, 237, 238, 239
Lévi-Strauss, Claude, 12
Lévy-Bruhl, Lucien, 136
Lincoln, Abraham, 196
Lodge, David, 30
Lorenz, Konrad, 136
Lowenthal, David, 145
Luckmann, Thomas, 99
Lukacs, John, 18
Luther, Martin, 172

M

MacIntyre, Alasdaire, 101, 114
Mandler, Jean M., 7, 12, 83
Marx, Karl, 39
Mauss, Marcel, 136
McAdams, Dan P., 14
McCaby, Alyssa, 7
McCloskey, Donald N., 195
McCollum, D. F., 190
Mead, George Herbert, 51, 83, 137, 173
Melville, Herman, 32
Merleau-Ponty, Maurice, 8, 19
Meyer, Martina, 164
Mink, Louis O., 115

Morgan, D. S., 191
Murray, 4
Myers, Nancy M., 165

N

Napoleon I, 39
Nelson, Katherine, 166
Newman, L.S., 125, 127
Nietzsche, Friedrich, 44, 50
Nisbett, R., 195, 196
Nixon, Richard, 35
Novick, Peter, 146, 191

O

O'Brien, Edna, 33f.
O'Neil, 198
Ong, Walter, 102

P

Pais, Abram, 25
Pandel, Hans-Jürgen, 51
Peel, E. A., 192
Perris, Eve M., 165
Peters, R. S., 192
Piaget, Jean, xiiiff., 24, 48, 83, 136, 137, 138, 139, 173
Pippin, 38f.
Plumb, J. H., 146, 157
Polkinghorne, Donald E., 16, 54
Popper, Karl, 107
Putnam, Hilary, 29

Q

Quine, Williard v. O., 107, 108

R

Rath, Rainer, 66
Ricoeur, Paul, 12, 14f., 18f., 26, 47, 60, 62, 71-73, 75, 78, 102
Robbe-Grillet, Alain, 26
Romain, Jules, 28
Rosenthal, Gabriele, 69
Rosomovsky, 39
Rumelhart, David E., 58
Rüsen, Jörn, xv, 52, 53, 62, 76, 77, 142, 144, 145, 149, 157, 164, 167, 169, 180

S

Sackett, L. W., 191
Sarbin, Theodore R., 4, 16
Schafer, Roy, 15
Schank, Roger C., 16
Schapp, Wilhelm, 115
Schülein, Frieder, 56, 167
Schütz, Albert, 248
Seely-Brown, 25
Seignobos, Charles, 193
Shemilt, Dennis, 145, 193
Shulman, Lee S., 194
Skinner, Quentin, 207
Šklovskij, Viktor, 30
Speer, Albert, 245-254
Spence, Donald P., 15, 54
Sprafka, Sarah A., 194
Stace, W. T., 39f.
Stein, Nancy L., 55
Sterne, Laurence, 30
Stierle, Karl-Heinz, 47
Straub, Jürgen, 164, 179
Sutzkefer, Abraham, 241
Swearingen, C. Jan, 12

T

Taylor, Charles, 28, 65
Tennyson, Alfred, 38
Thorndike, Edward L., 188
Todorov, Tzvetvan, 31, 231
Trabasso, Tom, 55
Trilling, Lionel, 128

U

Ulrich, Laural T., 144
Updike, John, 30

V

Vygotsky, Lev S., 12

W

Waletzky, Joshua, 57
Watson, James, 25
Welles, Orson, 29
White, Hayden, vii, 30, 38, 63, 65, 73, 107, 115, 148
White, Michael, 15

Wilson, Thomas, 195, 196
Wolf, Dagmar, 167
Woolf, Virginia, 31
Wundt, Wilhelm, 208

Y

Yeats, W. B., 26
Yershalmi, Yosef Hayim, 236
Young, James, 65, 228, 229, 232
Young, Katherine, 103

www.ingramcontent.com/pod-product-compliance
Lightning Source LLC
Chambersburg PA
CBHW071222080526
44587CB00013BA/1470